# Understanding Third World Poli

**Also by B.C. Smith**

*Field Administration: An Aspect of Decentralization*
*Decentralization: The Territorial Dimension of the State*
*Bureaucracy and Political Power*
*British Aid and International Trade* (with O. Morrissey and E. Horesh)
*Good Governance and Development*

# Understanding Third World Politics

## Theories of Political Change and Development

**Fourth Edition**

B. C. Smith

palgrave
macmillan

First edition 1996
Second edition 2003
Third edition 2009
Fourth edition 2013

Published by
PALGRAVE MACMILLAN

Palgrave Macmillan in the UK is an imprint of Macmillan Publishers Limited, registered in England, company number 785998, of Houndmills, Basingstoke, Hampshire
RG21 6XS.

Palgrave Macmillan in the US is a division of St Martin's Press LLC,
175 Fifth Avenue, New York, NY 10010.

Palgrave Macmillan is the global academic imprint of the above companies
and has companies and representatives throughout the world.

Palgrave® and Macmillan® are registered trademarks in the United States,
the United Kingdom, Europe and other countries

ISBN 978-1-137-00323-2   hardback
ISBN 978-1-137-00325-6   paperback

This book is printed on paper suitable for recycling and made from fully
managed and sustained forest sources. Logging, pulping and manufacturing
processes are expected to conform to the environmental regulations of the country
of origin.

A catalogue record for this book is available from the British Library.

A catalog record for this book is available from the Library of Congress.

10  9  8  7  6  5  4  3  2  1
22  21  20  19  18  17  16  15  14  13

Printed in China

*For Liam and Laura, again*

# Contents

# List of Illustrative Material

**Tables**

**Figure**

**Boxes**

# Preface

The main purpose of this new edition remains that of providing a critical introduction to the attempts of political science to explain political change in less-developed countries. The central focus will be on the issues and controversies that have dominated the analysis of Third World politics since the first wave of post-Second World War independence, and the evaluation of the main theories that have been formulated in order to provide explanations of political development in poor, post-colonial countries.

Three aims have guided the preparation of this edition: to update the content where necessary, especially the statistical data in Chapter 1; to consider new conceptual and analytical developments; and to change the illustrations and case material where appropriate to reflect key political changes in underdeveloped countries since the third edition – notably: foreign interventions in the Middle East (Chapter 3); state repression in North Africa (Chapter 4); the emergence of new parties in North Africa, India, and South Africa (Chapter 5); the political significance of public sector management reforms, especially in Africa (Chapter 6); military coups in Guinea, Mauritania and Honduras, and Egypt's new military leadership (Chapter 7); secession in the southern Sudan (Chapter 8); the so-called 'Arab Spring' of 2011 (Chapter 9); and the continuing worsening in the condition of political rights and civil liberties (Chapter 10). Each chapter will contain a short case-study illustrating the factors relevant to a particular type of political change.

Chapter 1, 'The Idea of a Third World', begins with a discussion of how well the concept of a 'Third World' reflects social and economic developments in low- and middle-income countries. Of particular note is the extent to which the expression still resonates among those concerned about world poverty; inequalities both material and socio-political (such as human rights); and environmental issues, as evidenced by bodies such as Third World Solidarity, Third World Network Africa, and the Third World Centre for Water Management. Alternative labels are considered, including the notion of a 'Global South', reflecting the incorporation of post-colonial economies into the global economy by the exploitation of cheap labour and resources, privatization, trade liberalization, economic deregulation, and the power of international organizations, capitalist corporations, and economic blocs. The aim of this examination will be to show how far indicators of underdevelopment are changing (thereby calling into question the concept of a 'Third World'), and to link such changes to the theories about political change which are the subjects of later chapters.

The chapter has been updated with economic, social, and political data from the World Bank's World Development Indicators; the UNDP's annual Human Development Reports; the ILO's World Employment Reports; and the annual reviews of democratization carried out by Freedom House, under the headings 'Political independence', 'National incomes', Industrialization', 'Integration into the world economy', and 'Human development'. These are the areas of change and progress most relevant to the theories of political change that are assessed in the book. Progress in economic terms raises fundamental questions about the relationship between social and economic modernization and the emergence of Western political institutions. Disparities between the developing and developed worlds have led to controversies about development, underdevelopment, and the consequences of contacts between rich and poor countries. Rates of change in economic status are seen as relevant to political stability and the challenges to regimes that are prompted by material and social inequality. Subsequent chapters also consider the political importance of such characteristics as poverty and inequality, dependence on foreign investment, industrialization and urbanization. Given the growing economic strength of the so-called 'BRIC' economies, especially Brazil, India and China, it remains important to point out the lack of correspondence between economic indicators on the one hand, and social and political developments on the other.

Chapter 2 is the first of two chapters dealing with the main macro-theoretical perspectives on the overall quality of political change in the Third World. It provides contemporary illustrations of how political functions are performed in contemporary Third World countries to show how far contemporary Third World politics deviate from the model of a modern political system formulated by functionalism and its key concepts of continuity, progress, complexity, and specialization. Contrasts are drawn between how civil society, political parties, legislatures, bureaucracies, judiciaries, and the media function in Third World states, and the functionalists' predictions about interest articulation, interest aggregation, rulemaking, rule application, rule adjudication, political communication, political socialization, and political recruitment. Further examples illustrate how poverty, ethnic conflict, the persistence of cultural attributes, religion, and the distribution of rewards in developing countries reveal problems with functionalism's concepts of tradition, secularization, change, and integration.

The subject of Chapter 3 is the concept of neo-colonialism and the facilitation of non-territorial imperialism by the internationalization of capital after 1945. The chapter examines the significance of formal independence for post-colonial societies and the assumption that constitutional independence would mean that indigenous governments would have sovereign state power at their disposal. Of particular significance for political science is that the *political* manifestations of neo-colonialism prove difficult to describe in concrete terms. The nature of the economic linkages is more easily described than political consequences. The *political* content of neo-colonialism is identified as the local power of external economic interests, comprador elites, and aid dependency. A contrasting perspective arguing that formal independence fundamentally changed political life in new states is also examined.

Dependency theory, with roots in the crisis of US liberalism in the late 1960s and a major critique of development theory, adds the idea of 'peripherality', or satellite status, to the concept of neo-colonialism. The main constituents of this approach are described: the 'hierarchy' of states, the concept of 'underdevelopment', the nature of capitalism, 'disarticulation', and the effect of economic dependency on the structure of political power. The relationships between dependency and economic performance, social class, and democratization are also explained. The effects of neo-liberalism, 'humanitarian military intervention', and conflict between global capitalist forces and national political interest (such as those represented by the new left in Latin America) are examined.

Chapters 4 to 7 deal with institutional aspects of political development, and attempt to produce valid theoretical statements about the most significant political institutions in Third World societies: the state, political parties, the bureaucracy, and the military. Chapter 4 is structured around three central controversies in the analysis of the state: the legacy of colonialism, society versus state-centred approaches, and the effects of globalization. In the section on the pluralist state as the destination of political evolution, the chapter contrasts pluralistic assumptions with evidence from the repressive regimes of North Africa, among others, which have been exposed in responses to pro-democracy pressures and confrontations. Pluralism, embodying freedom of speech and association, continues to stand in contrast to the flawed electoral processes, corruption, concentrations of executive power, and authoritarian capitalism that characterize Third World states.

The pluralist model of the political system is contrasted with Marxist theorizing about the state. Different Marxist conceptions of the state are illustrated, and the Bonapartist model is applied to Pakistan and Tanzania. Two models which place the bureaucracy at the centre of the post-colonial state are examined, followed by a comparative framework which shows how state action and structure are not only influenced by the political environment, but actually influence political culture and collective action. Claims made by political scientists about the implications of globalization for the state are critically reviewed.

Chapter 5 explains the role of political parties in Third World political systems. Ideological foundations in class, European political ideas, religion, ethnicity, and populism are examined. Political parties as machines built around clientelistic networks are compared with those based on policy programmes to show that learning and adaptation through fundamental policy innovations are the main ways in which politicians build programmatic parties. Explanations of party systems, especially the single-party system, are assessed and illustrated, and the relationship between party systems and democratization in the Third World is examined utilizing the concepts of institutionalization, partisan dealignment, and multi-party-ism.

The survival of parties as institutions is also of concern as the movement for democracy gathers momentum in the Third World. Therefore the chapter examines the sustainability of new political parties, and shows how factionalism and patronage have often been critical for the survival of parties. Other conditions required for organizational survival are illustrated by evidence from a number of countries.

Chapter 6 considers the political significance of bureaucracies in Third World states, and distinguishes between different concepts of bureaucracy and different sources of bureaucratic power. Claims that the bureaucracy has formed a new kind of ruling class in Third World countries are examined. The theory of 'access' and the kind of rationality implied by bureaucratic allocations of scarce resources are also explained. Attempts to reduce the political significance of bureaucracy, through economic liberalization, and new principles of public management are described. These entail contracting public services out not only to the private sector, but also to the 'third sector' of non-governmental organizations, creating problems of accountability. Recent public sector reform initiatives are examined with particular reference to the distributional impact of privatization, attempts to create expert and politically neutral civil services, and the politics of the new public management discourse.

The aims of Chapter 7 are, first, to identify the methodological problems encountered when explaining military intervention in politics, especially those associated with quantitative analysis. Next, different types of intervention are identified. The *coup d'état* has taken different forms, including the *autogolpe* or self-*coup* such as that by Peruvian President Fujimori. Explanations of *coups d'état* are assessed: social mobility, the demands of the middle class, level of economic development, the political culture, the military's organizational strength and culture, and foreign influences. The chapter concludes by discussing a major concern in newly democratizing countries emerging from military dictatorship: how to ensure that the military 'remain in barracks' throughout the transition to, and consolidation of, democracy.

Chapter 8 deals with *secession* and the demand for independence on the part of ethnic or national minorities. Examples show that the response to secessionist demands from national governments is usually severe. The primordialist, situationist, and constructivist theories of nationalism are contrasted and compared. Four theories of separatism are then examined: political integration, internal colonialism, 'balance of advantage', and class structure. Explanations of nationalism and secession need a class dimension. This is because of the social stratification found within cultural minorities; the predominantly petty-bourgeois leadership of ethnic secessionist movements; and the significance for the outcome of nationalism of the reaction of the dominant class in the 'core' community to nationalist political mobilization.

Chapter 9, on instability and revolution, begins by identifying the conceptual problems associated with the analysis of political instability – its normative content, the type of regime involved, and the lack of a satisfactory operational definition of 'instability'. It then examines possible causes of instability: levels of poverty, rates of economic growth, the revolution of rising expectations, foreign influences, ethnicity, the political culture, inequality, crises of authority, and political institutionalization. Political, social, economic, and cultural inequalities are important catalysts of political instability, and context – the nature of the state, cultural demography, and economic conditions – affects the likelihood of conflict at all levels of horizontal inequality.

The chapter ends by identifying the theoretical and empirical weaknesses of some explanations: that correlation does not necessarily prove causality; that poor and underdeveloped countries can be stable, especially if authoritarian; that political stability might *cause* affluence and economic growth; and that high rates of growth and stability have gone together in some countries.

Chapter 10 first discusses the contested concept of democracy, and the proposal that much democracy in the Third World is of 'low intensity' – that is, it creates democratic procedures without deepening democratic participation. It then examines theories of democratic transition which identify the main causes of authoritarian breakdown. The variability of democratic transitions has generated controversies about the relative significance of elite and mass pressure for change, the frequency of democratic regression, and the persistence of authoritarianism.

The chapter explores what have been shown to be prerequisites of democratic consolidation: national affluence, with its implications for equality and class development; the 'autonomy of political factors'; the political culture (and the problem of the direction of causality); civil society as a counter-balance to the power of the state; the balance of power within democracies; the importance of institutional development to democratic consolidation; and pressure from foreign sources seeking to promote democracy and good governance. Attention is paid to the change in US foreign policy from supporting dictatorships to the promotion of democratic regimes.

Political institutionalization is one aspect of the 'new institutionalism' that has provided another framework for the comparative analysis of democratization. A controversy over the relative merits of presidentialism and alternative types of political executive for democratic governance and stability are assessed. Also important for understanding the significance of the institutionalization of political power is the analysis of the major forces working for and against democracy, including presidentialism, the establishment of independent legislatures and the rule of law, and the roles of informal as well as formal institutions.

The conclusion of the final chapter, Chapter 11, is that a democratic developmental state should be able to secure economic progress, as well as providing political benefits in terms of political rights, freedoms, and participation. However, in view of the success which some authoritarian states have had in developing their societies economically and socially, the chapter considers the argument that development and democracy might not be compatible. While authoritarianism has often failed to provide economic and social progress, the study of developmental states reveals that a particular type of state intervention is required, together with a unified and competent bureaucracy, nationalistic political and bureaucratic elites, and 'embedded autonomy' in relationships between state and society. These are by no means widely found among conditions in the Third World, so the chapter considers the grounds for pessimism regarding future democratic development.

I should like to thank Helen Caunce at Palgrave Macmillan, and a number of anonymous referees, whose generous supply of constructive criticisms helped the process of revision enormously. Responsibility for remaining defects is mine alone.

B. C. SMITH

# List of Abbreviations

| | |
|---|---|
| APEC | Asia–Pacific Economic Cooperation |
| BJP | Bharatiya Janata Part |
| ECLA | United Nations Economic Commission for Latin America and the Caribbean |
| FAO | Food and Agriculture Organization |
| FARC | Revolutionary Armed Forces of Colombia |
| FDI | foreign direct investment |
| GDP | gross domestic product |
| GNP | gross national product |
| GNI | gross national income |
| IMF | International Monetary Fund |
| KMT | Kuomintang |
| LDC | least developed country |
| MB | Muslim Brotherhood |
| MDC | Movement for Democratic Change |
| MNC | multinational corporation |
| NGO | non-governmental organization |
| NIC | newly industrialized country |
| NLD | National League for Democracy |
| NPM | new public management |
| NRM | National Resistance Movement |
| OAS | Organization of American States |
| PAP | People's Action Party |
| UN | United Nations |
| UNDP | United Nations Development Programme |
| UNESCO | United Nations Educational, Scientific and Cultural Organization |
| WHO | World Health Organization |
| ZANU-PF | Zimbabwe African National Union – Patriotic Front |

# 1

# The Idea of a 'Third World'

## The concept of a 'Third World'

Gunnar Myrdal, winner of the Nobel Prize for economics in 1974, once said that in the relationship between rich and poor countries there has been diplomacy by language, meaning that in the developed, and to a lesser extent the underdeveloped, countries there has been a constant search for an acceptable name for this latter group. Consequently, no one has come up with a label that claims universal acceptance. The search is fraught with difficulties, not least ideological ones. The terminology of comparative politics, particularly as far as post-colonial countries are concerned, is largely expressive of attitudes rather than precise analytical concepts (Goulbourne, 1979). Given this, and the fact that economic changes throughout the world since 1945 have called into question any simple categorization, it seems appropriate to begin by explaining why continuing with the label 'Third World' remains defensible.

It is not enough to say that the alternatives all have their drawbacks and so any one is as good as another. But it is useful to ask what the alternatives are. Some analysts prefer 'developing countries', but cannot all countries be described as 'developing' in some direction or another? If we reserve 'development' for movement in a particular direction, then it has to be made explicit what path should be regarded as development and what should not. 'Developing' risks all the dangers of ethnocentric evolutionism though, as a conceptualization of social and political change, it has had an enormous impact on development studies and comparative politics, as will be seen in Chapter 2.

'Modernizing' is equally value-laden, being generally associated with Westernization (Hulme and Turner, 1990). 'Less-developed' faces similar risks by avoiding the key questions: less-developed than what, and according to which parameters?

The concept of the 'South' reflects some of the frustrations felt when trying to compare and contrast regions of the world. But this label is not only geographically dubious, in its implication that all southern hemisphere countries are less-developed, and that no poor countries are found in the

North; it also fails to recognize important economic and political differentials, as well as implying a non-existent solidarity. The concept of 'the South' is further called into question by the fact that poverty has embedded a 'South' in most countries of the North, that the South's economic elites are fully integrated into Northern economies, and that competing paradigms within the international community have undermined the North–South divide as an explanation of global poverty. Consequently, 'the image of a polarisation between a Northern developed hemisphere and a Southern developing hemisphere no longer offers a perfectly clear representation of reality' (Thérien, 1999, p. 724). However, the notion of a 'global South' draws attention to the incorporation of post-colonial economies into the global economy by the exploitation of cheap labour and resources, privatization, trade liberalization, economic deregulation, and the power of international organizations (the World Trade Organization, International Monetary Fund, and the World Bank), capitalist corporations (e.g. United Fruit, ITT, Bechtel, Occidental Petroleum, Talisman Oil, Halliburton), and economic blocs (e.g. North American Free Trade Agreement and Free Trade Agreement of the Americas).

Some analysts prefer the label 'underdeveloped', a concept that has taken on a very specific meaning and which, as will be shown in Chapter 3, denotes a particular kind of interrelationship between countries and a particular process of change. It is easy to understand the appeal of 'underdevelop' as a transitive verb in distinguishing those countries whose exploitation made possible the development of their exploiters. The idea that advanced societies secured their own advancement by underdeveloping poor countries is at the heart of dependency theory.

This leaves the concept of a 'Third World'. To be able to evaluate the different positions adopted by those who have entered into dispute about whether 'Third World' is a meaningful concept, it is necessary to separate out the different perceptions that people have about the countries which they think deserving of the label.

## Third World solidarity

Originally, 'Third World' referred to a group of *non-aligned* countries outside the great power blocs based on the United States and the Soviet Union. The French demographer and economic historian, Alfred Sauvy, coined the term in the early 1950s. It was meant to convey the idea of a 'Third Force' separate from the Western and Eastern blocs of the Cold War period. 'Non-alignment' in the military and diplomatic spheres is one of the earliest qualities associated with Third World status. This stance was most strikingly represented by the Bandung Conference attended by the representatives of 29 African and Asian countries in 1955 (Berger, 2004).

During the Cold War, 'Third World' also conveyed *solidarity* among developing countries which had in common their primary producing economic status, their relative poverty, their dependence on agriculture, and their distinctive forms of economic regime neither modelled on the Eastern bloc of planned economies nor the Western, free market system. The Third World fell outside the first world of advanced capitalist democracies and the second world of industrially advanced communist countries. But it was not merely a residual category of states that were neither liberal-democratic nor communist-totalitarian. It was a significant grouping in that its members were mainly agrarian, were much poorer than northern states, and had been subjected either to colonialism or to other forms of economic and political intervention by Western imperialism.

An interesting deviation from this model of the global economy was Mao Tse-tung's grouping in which the USA and the USSR constituted the first world, Japan, Europe and Canada made up the second world, while Africa, Latin America and most of Asia formed the third world. The claim being made here was that *both* the USA and the USSR were imperialistic, with their developed satellites as the second world and the primary producing former colonial possessions of the first and second worlds forming the third world. So, the OPEC countries would, despite their wealth, fall into this third group (Dirlik, 2004). Mao was clearly influenced by relationships between China and the USSR, worse at that time than between China and some capitalist states.

The Third World has also represented an *anti-imperialist* alliance against colonialism, neo-colonialism and racialism. Third World countries sought solidarity against the continuing intervention and involvement of the powerful economies in the developing economies and polities of the world, in an attempt to strengthen economic sovereignty at a time when it was obvious that political and economic autonomy did not necessarily go together, and that the achievement of constitutional independence did not guarantee freedom internally from external constraints. This idea will be revisited when we come to look at the concept of 'neo-colonialism' in Chapter 3. The idea of a Third World thus tries to capture a common experience of exploitation by richer and more powerful societies.

Since the early 1970s, this economic solidarity has evolved into a campaign for a *new international economic order* under which developing countries would secure greater national control of their natural resources, and protect their economies by collectively agreeing to the prices of raw materials upon which so many of their economies were dependent. The objective was to strengthen through collective action the position of individual Third World countries *vis-à-vis* their main trading partners and sources of foreign investment. In addition, Third World countries wanted to gain greater access to markets in industrialized countries for their own manufactured goods by persuading governments to lower the trade barriers that protect domestic industries from Third World competition. This call was taken up by the United Nations and the World Bank, both arguing for the liberalization of global markets and a reduction in the level of protectionism in OECD countries. The costs of protectionism in the rich countries of the world extend beyond blocking imports from the Third World to include negative capital transfers, higher real interest rates, unequal competition in international services, and closed markets for technology. A more rapid transfer of technologies to give Third World countries access to the advanced technologies required by the industrialization process also forms part of this aspect of Third Worldism.

Related proposals have included a World Development Fund to which all countries would contribute on a sliding scale related to their national income; the development of the sea bed to provide new sources of food; and the international development of alternative energy sources. Through the United Nations Educational, Scientific and Cultural Organization (UNESCO), Third World countries try to act collectively to resist the pressures from the Westernized mass media, and the cultural, educational, and scientific imperialism which introduces inappropriate technology and educational values into their societies. Solidarity was also shown at the World Trade Organization meeting in Doha, Quatar, in 2001 when developing countries formed effective alliances on intellectual property rights, drug patents, and the agenda of future negotiations, shifting the balance of power away from the rich industrialized nations. However, subsequent meetings forming the Doha round of talks concerning the development of poor countries have failed to obtain agreement on trade rules which would benefit poor countries as trading partners. If anything, divisions between rich and poor countries deepened between 2001 and 2011.

Finally, Third Worldism has also been associated with the idea of *regional coherence* through pan-nationalist movements. The Third World might not represent a grouping of countries all with identical interests, but within the Third World there could be groups of states that shared interests cutting across national boundaries – for example, the pan-Arab world or the pan-African world. Such concepts were important to political leaders in developing countries in the 1960s. Here was an attempt to prove that national boundaries were not going to be as important as they were in other parts of the world. National boundaries were seen as the creation of European colonialism, especially in Africa. Thus, they were to some extent alien, reflecting a colonial past and causing lasting problems. Regional institutions were set up to reflect this internationalism and some still exist, though without the significance that they were originally intended to have.

**Changing worlds**

The Third World has changed much since the earliest visions of solidarity, and continues to do so. Consequently, a label that conveys a message of homogeneity of socio-economic conditions and political purpose is increasingly unacceptable to commentators from both North and South (Hulme and Turner, 1990).

The first form of heterogeneity that needs to be recognized is cultural. The term 'Third World' has been considered by some as demeaning to the diverse range of polities, cultures, histories, and ideologies found within it. The Third World is not a 'uniform stagnant mass devoid of distinctive character'. The peoples of the Third World should not be denied identity, character, personality, and responsibility. Treating the Third World as an undifferentiated mass also risks seeing it as 'an association of countries dedicated to the moral blackmail of a guilt-afflicted West' (Toye, 1987, p 6). The idea that responsibility for Third World poverty lies wholly with the developed world might also be regarded as patronizing.

A growing heterogeneity is in economic strength. As will be seen, there are disparities of wealth within the Third World, whether measured by per capita GNP, annual growth rates, or rates of industrialization. Expert observers and international organizations such as the World Bank now distinguish between the rich poor countries, the middle poor and the poorest countries, even to the extent of referring to the last group as the Fourth World – the poorest of the poor, or the least developed of the developing countries. World Bank statistics are presented in such categories, and other organizations such as the United Nations (UN) also differentiate in their policy-making. Some of the cut-off points between these categories are pretty arbitrary (Worsley, 1984) but, nevertheless, there are real differences when one compares Bangladesh with, say, Malaysia. Some aid donors distinguish between the poor and the poorest with the aim of directing their development assistance at the latter countries.

Neither has the Third World's experience of globalization been uniform. It has been argued that the 'globalization' of market economics and pluralistic democracy, apparently heralded by the end of the Cold War, further challenges the validity of the concept of a Third World (Berger, 1994). The process of globalization integrates economies, cultures, and technology. The end of the Cold War and the demise of communist regimes in Russia and Europe, it has been argued, meant that all countries were converging politically on liberal democracy and economically on capitalism. Democratization seemed to be on the advance. The main sources of international conflict seemed to be irreversibly weakening. The world had reached, according to Francis Fukuyama (1992), the 'end of history' beyond which there could be no further evolution.

Whether such convergence ever occurs remains to be seen but, as Fukuyama himself recognized, it remains a distant prospect for most of the Third World. The 'end of history' concept is also of little help in understanding conflicts between Third World countries, such as Venezuela and Colombia, or the tensions between the so-called Democratic Republic of Congo and its neighbours in central Africa. There is still strong resistance to convergence on liberal democracy in many Third World countries, including Zimbabwe, China, and Burma. Indeed, it has been suggested that what distinguishes membership of the Third World is the lack of consensus over the rules of the 'game' of politics (Kamrava, 1995).

A consensus about liberal democracy is certainly not shared by much of the Islamic world. In fact, Islamic regimes are diametrically opposed to the basic tenets of democracy, especially freedom of speech, freedom of belief, political equality, the rule of law, and the separation of state and religion. Other Third World regimes call themselves democratic but find it difficult to operate democracy's formal procedures, such as free and fair elections, and virtually impossible to provide the material and social foundations for the enjoyment of full political rights and participation. Within the Third World, there are also those who regard the claim that history is ending in liberal democracy and capitalism as yet another form of Western neo-colonialism.

An alternative view of the post-Cold War era is that, far from reaching a consensus on economic and political values, ideological conflict has been replaced by a clash of cultures and religions, or 'civilizations' as Samuel Huntington would have it (1996). The dominant post-Cold War conflict from this perspective is between Islam and the West.

Such categorization again offers an excessively uniform and inclusive image of the two contestants. It also falsely equates culture with religion. The Third World in the post-Cold War era consists of far more societies and cultures than allowed for by a duality of civilizations. Large regions of the Third World can be subsumed under neither category. Political and diplomatic relations between the West and other countries include tensions which are hard to fit within this view of the world order, such as the United States' relations with Venezuela, China, and Cuba, or the UK's relations with Zimbabwe. America's relations with China and India are high on the State Department's list of priorities, and the UK's diplomacy is as much concerned with illegal immigration, drug trafficking, relations with Europe, and the country's economic interests, as with counter-terrorism. When the West is involved in societies that are predominantly Islamic, it is always in alliance with one or more Moslem-based factions or elites, rather than hostile to Islam as such. Iraq, Afghanistan, Saudi Arabia, and Pakistan are obvious examples.

Many significant changes within the Third World itself also cannot be fitted into this model of 'civilizations', most notably between Asia and sub-Saharan Africa. Africa's exports to Asia have grown to make Asia the third most important destination for African exports after the EU and USA. Africa's imports from Asia have also grown faster than from other regions. African development is especially dependent on trade, investment, and aid from China. Bilateral trade between China and Africa was worth US$115 billion in 2010.

The Third World's relations with China are becoming as important as its relations with some Western states. Chinese investment in the Third World reached US$49.5 billion in 2010, mainly by state-owned enterprises involved in extracting natural resources. Chinese investment in Africa, for example, includes offshore oilfields (Nigeria), petrochemicals (Sudan), mobile phones (Zimbabwe), roads (Rwanda and Kenya), railways (Angola), and forestry (Mozambique). China has also significantly increased aid to Africa, raising concerns that the absence of political conditionalities with Chinese aid could put human rights in Africa even further at risk (Naidu and Jansson, 2011).

China has also become a major source of aid to the Third World, providing more interest-free and concessionary loans between 2008 and 2010 (US$110 billion) than the World Bank. Chinese aid expanded by nearly 30 per cent per year on average between 2004 and 2009, totalling US$39.3 billion by 2010. The emergence of rapidly growing Third World economies such as India and China as donors and trading partners not only offers new economic policy options to recipient governments, it also provides an opportunity for ideas about 'development' to be revised under the influence of non-Western economic and political interests (Six, 2009).

Another feature of Third World diversity relates to the benefits of globalization – increased trade, foreign investment, and the dissemination of technology – which are by no means spread equally across the Third World. Some regions, such as East Asia, have taken advantage of globalization to generate growth in manufactured exports. Others remain marginalized because of their continuing dependence on primary commodities. The spread of information and communications technologies is very uneven. The poorest countries of the Third World have dangerously small shares of world trade and access to foreign investment.

Consequently, economically, many developing countries are falling further and further behind developed countries, while a few have economies growing faster than those of developed countries. Notable here are India and China, the former doubling its growth rate between 1980 and 2000, the latter averaging almost 8 per cent per annum per capita since the late 1970s. Since these two countries account for over half the world's poor, their achievements have brought about a reduction in global poverty.

However, the majority of poor countries have not only seen poverty increase. They also lack the governmental capacity to cope with the threats of globalization, especially financial instability, bio-invasion, international crime and terrorism, the power of international institutions (such as transnational corporations, the World Trade Organization and IMF, and over 26,000 international non-governmental organizations (NGOs)), and the growing gap between rich and poor.

As some less-developed countries have welcomed, or at least accepted, the inevitability of foreign investment and the dependency that it brings, including subordination in the international division of labour, non-alignment has been further undermined. So, even by the end of the 1960s, Third World countries were by no means behaving in unity towards East–West relations. A stridently anti-communist group of Asian states emerged – Indonesia, Malaysia, Singapore, Thailand, and the Philippines. This brought an end to the Third World as a coherent voting block in the United Nations, splitting it along ideological lines. Similarly, in 1979, at the United Nations Conference on Trade and Development (UNCTAD V), the more industrialized of the Third World countries vetoed a code of conduct for multinational corporations (MNCs) that the less-industrialized Third World states wanted to bring in, demonstrating their need to avoid antagonizing MNCs on whose presence even the rich Third World countries so heavily depend for their development. Thus, the economic basis of non-alignment had become very weak by 1980, and the majority of Third World countries were soon very 'aligned' (Worsley, 1984, p. 324).

Other developments have further undermined Third World solidarity. Many organizations expressing regional common interests have been weak or have disappeared. Those organizations that have survived have been geared to the economic interests of particular regions – for example, the Central American Common Market, the Latin American Free Trade Association, and OPEC. Some organizations cut across the North–South divide, for example APEC. Others have radical agendas, such as the Bolivarian Alternative for the Americas (ALBA), which offers an alternative development strategy to the neo-liberalism imposed by the IMF and World Bank, and opposes US hegemony in Latin America.

Domestic economic problems in Third World countries can also erode solidarity. Policy failures, mismanagement and debt have forced some Third World countries to become inward-looking, leading to the conclusion that 'Third World solidarity has become a thing of the past' (Westlake, 1991, p. 16). However, it should be noted that the original Group of 77 developing countries – established in 1964 to promote their collective economic interests and enhance their negotiating power on international economic issues – now has 130 members. Such international groupings expose the problems and concerns of Third World countries: the persistence of poverty, unequal land distribution, food insecurity, trade barriers, the decline in the terms of trade for primary commodities, and environmental threats from climate change.

The demise of communist regimes in eastern and central Europe and the former USSR has produced a degree of homogeneity between the first and second worlds, at least in terms of economic systems, which makes references to developing countries as a 'Third' group or force less and less meaningful. It has been argued that the globalization of market economics and pluralistic democracy, apparently heralded by the end of the Cold War, further challenges the validity of the concept of a Third World (Berger and Weber, 2009), although markets may dominate economies in societies where government is far from democratic, and global capitalism is constantly associated with crises, conflicts, and violence which cause the most suffering in poor countries.

Finally, solidarity has been seriously undermined by warfare between Third World states, notably the Iran–Iraq conflict, the Gulf War, conflict between India and Pakistan, war in Southeast Asia in the late 1970s, and war in the centre and Horn of Africa. The consequent human suffering and economic loss cannot be underestimated when considering Third World 'solidarity'.

## Third World poverty

A different type of objection to the concept of a Third World derives from its association with poverty. Defining a group of countries as 'poor' might obscure the fact that there are classes that enjoy immense wealth. To talk about poverty-ridden peoples in less-developed countries can act as a form of mystification, deflecting attention away from internal stratification. Poor countries do not consist entirely of poor people. Great internal inequalities persist – and sometimes increase – regardless of a country's overall economic performance. At the same time, elites in Third World societies often appear to have more in common with Western elites than with their own dispossessed masses (Toye, 1987; Berger, 1994).

This is not to say that poverty is solely the result of the domestic maldistribution of power and has nothing to do with dependence on the more powerful economies in the world. But it does alert us to the possibility that those two things are related – that dependency within the world economic system actually benefits some classes in the Third World. The term 'comprador bourgeoisie' was coined to convey the idea of an alliance between an indigenous middle class and foreign investors, MNCs, bankers, and military interests. There is, thus, a need to relate global stratification to relations between internal social strata. Insofar as it obscures the heterogeneity of social classes, each with its own political objective, the concept of a Third World constitutes mystification designed to conceal dependency and exploitation, as well as a device allowing rulers of Third World countries to present a common interest between themselves and the masses in order to disguise their own alliance with metropolitan interests.

## Third world values

Though there are powerful arguments for concluding that 'the age of the Third World has passed irrevocably into history' (Berger, 2004, p. 30), it is still important to preserve the term in order to convey key values associated with it. It could be dangerous to stop talking about the Third World and so further fragment that group of countries. A degree of solidarity must somehow be preserved simply because, as individual states, they are bound to be weak in their relationships with the developed world. It is notable how the expression still resonates among those concerned about world poverty, inequalities both material and socio-political (such as human rights), and environmental issues, as evidenced by bodies such as Third World Solidarity, Third World Network Africa, and the Third World Centre for Water Management. Attempts to question its validity may be mischievous and misleading. It implies neither inferior values nor some lower numerical order but, rather, a set of specific characteristics that are unique in more than one way to the countries of Asia, Africa, and Latin America. It represents the broadly similar, though not exactly identical, nature of these countries' experiences in the processes of development – including, in particular, inequalities, injustice, and domination by external forces, economic and military (Berger and Weber, 2009).

The term thus serves the important function of reinstating the significance of global economic relationships, and the disastrous social and political consequences for countries with such a small share of the world's income. It also provides a 'vital corrective' to the idea that international politics can only be seen in terms of a 'clash of civilisations' or religious traditions (Randall, 2004).

## A definition

In order to identify the subject matter of this book, to convey the diversity of the social and economic conditions within the Third World, and to provide an outline of the major changes taking place there, an indication of the key characteristics of Third World status must be given. For the purpose of this survey, the Third World will be defined as a group of countries which have colonial histories and which are in the process of developing economically and socially from a status characterized by low incomes, dependence on agriculture, weakness in trading relations, social deprivation for large segments of society, and restricted political and civil liberties. This definition recognizes the changes which are most relevant to understanding political development.

The following sketch of Third World status and trends will follow the components of the definition: the achievement of political independence, average income levels, industrialization, integration into the world economy, and human development. By this definition, the Third World comprises approximately 100 states in Africa, Asia, the Middle East, Latin America, and the Caribbean. Their combined population of over 5 billion accounts for 77.5 per cent of the world total, and their territories cover over half the world's land area (World Bank, 2011c).

## Political independence

A minority of countries that would be regarded as part of the Third World by other criteria have not experienced colonialism at some stage in their histories. For the majority, a significant variation is the length of time that they have been independent, with most Latin American countries gaining political independence in the early nineteenth century and most African countries only after the Second World War. Experience of imperial political control and economic penetration varied considerably, as did the routes taken to independence (roughly divided between constitutional negotiations and armed struggle). However, the legacy of imperialism and colonialism was everywhere profound, transforming political institutions and processes. New geo-political boundaries were drawn. Reactions against alien rule mobilized new political forces and alliances. Indigenous social structures and political systems were altered by European economic interventions and settlement.

In fact, the imperialist impulse produced a complex pattern of colonial intervention in the world's pre-industrial societies. In addition to the varying balance of economic, strategic, and diplomatic interests, and cultural expansionism prompted by a confidence in the superiority of Western civilization, there were highly variable local factors that conditioned the impact of European intervention. These included material conditions and the different political organizations encountered when the decision was taken to move from a purely commercial relationship with pre-industrial societies to their political incorporation into an imperial structure.

Neither did the European powers promote their cultures in the same way and to the same degree. Britain's approach to the dissemination of its culture was far more pragmatic than some of its continental neighbours, in that it sought to preserve indigenous cultures, values, and social structures where it suited the colonial power politically to do so. It was possible for British imperialists to talk at one and the same time about the great benefits to their colonial dependencies of the liberties that followed the flag, while at the same time respecting and reinforcing caste and feudalism. Britain's need for political control and the maintenance of stability was consistent with the preservation of indigenous practices. In many parts of West Africa, for example, with the exception of inhuman punishments for criminal offences defined according to local customary law, existing customs and laws were left intact. It was far easier to keep a population quiescent when it was partly governed by its own institutions, laws, and customs, although ultimately subject to the local representatives of the British Crown. A hierarchy of colonial officials extended from the Secretary of State for the Colonies at the apex down to district commissioners in charge of large populations and supervising the exercise of customary law by indigenous judges and law-makers regarded as legitimate by the local population.

The French and Portuguese, by contrast, attempted assimilation. This meant that native peoples were to be turned into Europeans, particularly through Western education. This had significant implications for the development of areas in which local political elites identified closely with Europe and European culture. There was a much more vigorous policy, albeit in reality aimed at a select minority and with limited effect (Berman, 1984), in French than in British territories of turning local people into local versions of the populations of the imperial power. The assumption was that local culture was an obstacle to the spread of European civilization.

The availability of fertile land and the possibility of utilizing it for peasant cash cropping or plantations for tea, coffee, sugar, and cotton also varied. Sometimes, the land could only be exploited for produce that was already indigenous to the area. The introduction of cash crops from abroad (such as rubber into Malaya from Brazil) was not always feasible. The availability of deep-water harbours which could be linked to the interior by railways and roads also affected the pattern of colonial intervention. The whole structure of communications and transportation was a highly variable factor. Initially, rivers were the key to expansion, allowing penetration into the interior without any significant capital outlay. Traditional communication routes tended to determine the spatial pattern of colonial investment. The presence of minerals was another factor – copper in East Africa, gold and diamonds in Southern Africa, and tin in Bolivia, for example. Climatic conditions also differed, making East Africa far more conducive to European settlement than West Africa.

A further variable was the indigenous social structures of the colonized territories. Some local communities were extremely simple in their economic activities, being based on hunting and gathering. Some were nomadic pastoral communities, surviving on the basis of livestock which was grazed over regular transhumance routes. Other societies had complex agrarian systems with highly elaborate organizations for production, distribution, and exchange. Levels of urbanization varied considerably, too, with some societies based on towns that performed the roles of administrative and commercial centres. Some areas were feudalistic in terms of relations between landowners and their tenant cultivators, whereas elsewhere more egalitarian systems were found, with land held in common and individual plots cultivated by families without rights to alienate or accumulate. Concepts of rent and tenancy were absent from such cultures, as were the political relationships that accompany them.

Different forms of political organization were encountered. There were centralized state structures immediately recognizable as such by Europeans: ancient kingdoms with clearly articulated forms of political authority and state functionaries recruited according to explicit rules; traditional leaders were surrounded by civil and military officialdom; territorial divisions were created for purposes of administration, taxation, and the enforcement of laws. Such structures of government were highly suitable for the purposes of colonial administration, especially in the context of the pragmatic approach to managing dependent territories mentioned earlier. Indirect rule meant using the indigenous political structures for imperial objectives. There were obvious political advantages in using the legitimacy conferred upon traditional leaders who were at the same time loyal to, and dependent on, the colonial administration. Exploiting military and commercial superiority was thus made easier.

The colonial powers found it relatively easy to persuade indigenous rulers to accept this integration of their own traditional systems of decision-making and adjudication into the colonial state hierarchy. Claimants to the throne received the support of the colonial authorities in return for their loyalty and cooperation. Corrupt, incompetent, or insubordinate rulers were easily deposed and there were always more cooperative princes, chiefs, and emirs to replace them (Berman, 1984). Colonial officials became the real power behind the thrones of indigenous rulers, intervening according to the precise needs of the European presence. Such interventions had to be greater if there were a need to remove local people from their land through legislation and other instruments of colonial policy. Elsewhere, there was simply a need to preserve conditions under which cash crops could be produced by peasant cultivators according to traditional methods of cultivation. Here, indirect rule was a most appropriate form of colonial administration.

Not all indigenous political structures were so familiar and useful to colonial government. In the acephalous societies, without formal positions of permanent leadership, government was organized without separate institutions for making laws, adjudicating in disputes and performing other civil and military functions on behalf of the community. Far less familiar forms of authority were used to manage society's communal affairs, such as age groups, lineages, clans, or elders. An interpretation of the wisdom of ancestors might be needed to solve disputes over land, family affairs or economic activities, make decisions concerning the welfare of the community, or deal with conflicts with neighbouring communities. In societies without obvious structures of chieftaincy or other political offices, it was much more difficult to integrate indigenous political authority into an imperial system. Offices had to be artificially created for the purposes of colonial government, a source of great discontent and alienation in the communities affected, sometimes leading to political and social disorder.

A consequence of such local economic, social and political variety, combined with the varying motivations of the imperialists, was that different forms of colonial intervention developed. In some areas, plantations were set up in which industrialized forms of agricultural production were created, requiring large numbers of waged labourers and European managers. Elsewhere, mining activities required the creation of an industrial labour force. In other areas, imperialism benefited from peasant cash cropping without changing the relations of production by the introduction of waged labour or new technology. Another variation on the colonial theme was European settlement on the best land available, leading to permanent commitments on the part of white minorities. It was common to find more than one form of colonial intervention in a single colony – as in Kenya and Tanganyika, where peasant production was combined with plantation and settler agriculture. Economically, one form was usually dominant, as in the Gold Coast, where peasant commodity production dominated a colonial economy that included European-owned mining operations (Berman, 1984).

**National incomes**

The majority of countries in the Third World are found in the low-income or lower-middle-income categories used by the World Bank and defined in terms of gross national income per capita. Differences in per capita incomes vary greatly between regions of the world and, as Table 1.1 shows, the Third World continues to lag behind the developed economies. However, the gap in real incomes between some Third World countries, especially those in East Asia, and the industrialized countries has narrowed considerably since 1945. Per capita incomes throughout the Third World rose relatively quickly

**Table 1.1**   *Per capita national incomes and growth in GDP, 1980–2010*

| Region | GNI per capita (US$) | | | Growth GNI per capita (%) | | | Growth in GDP (%) | | | |
|---|---|---|---|---|---|---|---|---|---|---|
| | 1980 | 2000 | 2010 | 1980 | 2000 | 2009 | 1980 | 2000 | 2010 | 2013f |
| Low income | ... | 256 | 510 | ... | 1.3 | 2.2 | 2.2 | 3.5 | 7.3 | 6.3 |
| East Asia and Pacific | 263 | 930 | 3,691 | 5.5 | 6.0 | 6.3 | 7.1 | 7.5 | 9.6 | 8.2 |
| Latin America and Caribbean | 3,610 | 3,899 | 7,802 | 4.1 | 2.4 | –3.0 | 6.1 | 4.0 | 6.0 | 4.0 |
| Middle East and North Africa | 1,392 | 1,652 | 3,839 | –4.3 | 2.1 | ... | –1.1 | 3.4 | 3.1 | 4.0 |
| South Asia | 232 | 432 | 1,213 | 3.7 | 2.7 | 6.6 | 6.4 | 4.3 | 9.3 | 7.9 |
| Sub-Saharan Africa | 556 | 488 | 1,165 | 1.8 | 1.1 | –2.8 | 4.0 | 3.6 | 4.8 | 5.7 |
| High income | 16,499 | 25,244 | 38,658 | 0.3 | 3.1 | –4.0 | 1.3 | 4.1 | 2.7 | 2.6 |

NOTE:   f = forecast.
SOURCES:   World Bank (2007), table 1, p. 289; World Bank (2010), table 1, p. 378; World Bank (2011a), table 1, p. 2.

in the 1960s and 1970s, levelled out in the 1980s, and grew by 2.1 per cent per year until the end of the century.

Economic growth in the Third World has accelerated since 1995 and, during the first five years of the twenty-first century, Third World incomes grew faster than in rich countries for the first time in post colonial history (UNDP 2001; World Bank 2007b). However, this did not cancel out the longer-term divergence of incomes between rich and poor countries: between 1970 and 2010, incomes in developed countries grew by 2.3 per cent on average, while in developing countries per capita incomes grew by only 1.5 per cent. In some regions of the Third World, incomes have stagnated or fallen. The divergence between regions mainly occurred in the 1970s so that, whereas by 1980 per capita gross domestic product (GDP) was growing at 6.7 per cent in East Asia and 3.2 per cent in South Asia, it was falling in Latin America and sub-Saharan Africa. Per capita incomes in sub-Saharan Africa continued to fall in real terms until 2009 and were given a further boost in 2010, when GDP grew by 4.8 per cent. Latin America also recorded strong growth in 2010 compared with the 2.1 per cent fall in GDP in 2009 (World Bank, 2011a and 2011b).

Although per capita growth in low-income countries remained positive during the height of the economic crisis in 2009, a decline in the rate of economic growth is forecast for the Third World between 2010 and 2012, due mainly to an anticipated slowing of Chinese economic expansion, political turmoil in the Middle East and North Africa, and inflationary pressures in Latin America and South Asia. If China is taken out of the equation, growth in the Third World, as a whole, slips to 4.5 per cent from 7.3 per cent between 2010 and 2011. Oil exports and Chinese investments are expected to make sub-Saharan Africa the only Third World region likely to see accelerated economic growth between 2010 and 2011.

Per capita income is a useful measure for comparing national wealth, but it is an average which reveals nothing about levels of poverty or inequality, both of which have been related to Third World political developments, particularly instability.

There are 1.4 billion people in the Third World living in poverty as measured by the number surviving on less than US$1.25 a day. Poverty has declined from 1.8 billion in 1990. The proportion of people living in poverty fell from 46 per cent to 27 per cent. This is mainly due to achievements in East Asia, especially China and India (Poku and Whitman, 2011). Yet, nearly half the population in low- and middle-income countries live on less than US$2 a day (see Table 1.2). About one third of the world's poor live in India. The economic crisis of 2008–09 led to 40 million more people living in poverty than was expected from pre-crisis trends.

**Table 1.2**   *Third World poverty, 1990–2015*

| Region | Population living on less than $1.25 a day (%) | | | Population living on less than $2 a day (%) | | |
|---|---|---|---|---|---|---|
| | *1990* | *2005* | *2015* | *1990* | *2005* | *2015* |
| East Asia and Pacific | 56.2 | 16.8 | 5.9 | 81.0 | 38.7 | 19.7 |
| Latin America and Caribbean | 12.2 | 8.2 | 4.7 | 22.4 | 16.6 | 10.7 |
| Middle East and North Africa | 5.8 | 3.6 | 1.3 | 23.5 | 16.9 | 7.2 |
| South Asia | 53.8 | 40.3 | 22.4 | 83.6 | 73.9 | 57.1 |
| Sub-Saharan Africa | 56.5 | 50.9 | 35.8 | 76.0 | 72.9 | 57.7 |

SOURCE:   World Bank (2011b), box 1.1, p. 14.

The World Bank estimates that there will still be 1 billion people in developing countries living on less than US$1.25 in 2015. Many Third World countries, especially in Africa, will not achieve the UN's Millennium Development Goal of halving the proportion of people in poverty by 2015. Sub-Saharan Africa is expected to have almost 36 per cent of people still living in extreme poverty (UN, 2011).

High growth rates may help reduce absolute levels of poverty, but they are frequently accompanied by rising income inequality (Renwick, 2011). Other developments contributing to income inequality include technological advances and financial globalization. While trends in inequality in the Third World do not follow any regional pattern, overall inequality has increased over the last 20 years, particularly because of increases in countries with large populations, such as China. Africa and Latin America have the world's highest levels of inequality.

Inequality in developing countries is illustrated by a comparison of the percentage shares of income of the poorest 20 per cent of the population. The picture is varied, with some countries showing slight improvement. The data is only illustrative, since household surveys differ in method and type of data collected, especially whether income or consumption expenditure is used as the indicator of living standards (see Table 1.3). The progress achieved by some countries still leaves substantial inequality. Indeed, inequality is the reason that the Millennium Development Goals will not be reached (Vandermoortele, 2011). Table 1.3 compares the shares in national income or consumption of the poorest and richest quintiles in developing countries that have managed to maintain or increase the poor's share since the early 1990s.

**Table 1.3**    *Inequality: poorest and richest quintiles' share of national income or consumption, selected countries*

| Country | Percentage share of | | | |
| | Poorest quintile | | Richest quintile | |
| | 1990 | 2009 | 1990 | 2009 |
| --- | --- | --- | --- | --- |
| Brazil | 2.2 | 3.3 | 65.0 | 58.1 |
| Chile | 3.6 | 8.6 | 60.5 | 57.0 |
| Costa Rica | 3.8 | 4.2 | 49.6 | 55.4 |
| Indonesia | 9.4 | 7.6 | 38.9 | 44.9 |
| Thailand | 5.9 | 6.7 | 52.2 | 47.2 |
| Malaysia | 4.7[c] | 4.5 | 53.1 [c] | 51.5 |
| Morocco | 6.6[b] | 6.5[f] | 46.3 [b] | 47.9[f] |
| Tunisia | 5.9 | 5.9[d] | 46.3 | 47.9[d] |
| Ghana | 7.0[a] | 5.2[e] | 42.7[a] | 48.6[e] |
| Nigeria | 4.0 [c] | 4.4[g] | 49.9 [c] | 54.0[g] |
| Tanzania | 7.4 [c] | 6.8[f] | 41.6 [c] | 44.8[f] |
| Uganda | 6.0 [c] | 5.8 | 49.1 [c] | 50.7 |

NOTES:    [a] = 1989, [b] = 1991, [c] = 1992, [d] = 2005, [e] = 2006, [f] = 2007, [g] = 2010.
SOURCES:    UN (2011); World Bank databank.worldbank.org.

## Industrialization

Low per capita incomes have been related historically to the Third World's economic dependence on agriculture. Incomes tend to rise as countries industrialize and the size of the manufacturing sector increases. These are important goals for developing countries, though the social disruption caused by industrialization has been related to political instability in a number of post-colonial economies.

All regions of the Third World have shown a decline in the contribution of agriculture to GDP since 1990 (see Table 1.4) though, where there is subsistence farming, much agricultural production is not exchanged, making it difficult to assess changes in production accurately. The general trend in the structure of Third World output has been from agriculture to manufacturing and services.

Expansion of the service sector has been particularly pronounced, both in terms of growth in output and value added as a proportion of GDP. Average annual growth in the service sector remained constant from 1980 to 1998, followed by a rise in the contribution of the service sector to GDP from 46 to over 55 per cent by 2009. Third World manufacturing, generally the most dynamic part of the industrial sector, has actually declined since 1990.

**Table 1.4** *Value added as a percentage of GDP, 1990–2009*

| Economy | Agriculture | | Industry | | Manufacturing | | Services | |
|---|---|---|---|---|---|---|---|---|
| | *1990* | *2009* | *1990* | *2009* | *1990* | *2009* | *1990* | *2009* |
| Low income | 29 | 25.7 | 31 | 24.4 | 18 | 12.9 | 41 | 49.9 |
| East Asia and Pacific | 20 | 11.3 | 40 | 45.0 | 29 | 31.7 | 40 | 43.4 |
| Latin America and Caribbean | 9 | 6.1 | 36 | 30.6 | 23 | 16.8 | 56 | 63.4 |
| Middle East and North Africa | 15 | 8.1 | 38 | 5.4[a] | 13 | 3.7 | 47 | 45.8[a] |
| South Asia | 30 | 18.2 | 26 | 26.8 | 17 | 15.3 | 44 | 55.0 |
| Sub-Saharan Africa | 18 | 13.1 | 34 | 29.6 | 17 | 12.7 | 48 | 57.2 |
| High income | 3 | 1.4 | 33 | 26.2 | 22 | 16.6 | 64 | 72.4 |

NOTE:  [a] = 2006.
SOURCES:  World Bank (2001), table 12, p. 297; World Bank, *Databank*, http://databank.worldbank.org.

**Table 1.5**    *Employment shares by sectors and regions (%)*

| Economy | Agriculture | | Industry | | Services | |
|---|---|---|---|---|---|---|
| | *1999* | *2009* | *1999* | *2009* | *1999* | *2009* |
| Developed | 5.6 | 3.7 | 27.6 | 23.4 | 66.9 | 72.8 |
| East Asia | 47.9 | 36.9 | 23.8 | 27.8 | 28.3 | 35.3 |
| South-East Asia and Pacific | 49.3 | 44.3 | 15.9 | 17.8 | 34.8 | 38.0 |
| South Asia | 59.5 | 53.5 | 15.4 | 18.9 | 25.1 | 27.6 |
| Latin America and Caribbean | 21.5 | 16.3 | 21.4 | 22.1 | 57.1 | 61.6 |
| Middle East | 22.1 | 19.1 | 25.9 | 26.1 | 52.1 | 54.8 |
| North Africa | 29.2 | 27.8 | 20.5 | 22.5 | 50.3 | 49.7 |
| Sub-Saharan Africa | 62.4 | 59.0 | 8.8 | 10.6 | 28.8 | 30.4 |

SOURCE:    ILO (2011), table A10, p. 67.

Employment in agriculture has also declined, though the sector still employs 40 per cent of developing countries' workers, compared to 3.7 per cent in developed economies. The agricultural share of employment is highest in sub-Saharan Africa and Asia, accounting for 59 and 53.5 per cent of total employment, respectively. In most regions, employment in services has grown faster than employment in industry, throwing doubt on the theory that economic development produces a shift from agriculture to industry. In East Asia, the sector's share of total employment was 38 per cent in 2009, while industry's share fell to 17.8 per cent – see Table 1.5 (ILO, 2011).

**Integration into the global economy**

The growing involvement of Third World economies in trade is bringing about closer integration into the global economy. Foreign trade has increased as a percentage of GDP in all regions of the Third World (see Table 1.6). The annual growth rate in the export of goods and services from low-income countries reached 10.1 per cent in 2008, before the recession reduced this to 2.1 per cent the following year. Average rates of annual growth in the export of goods and services from low- and middle-income economies have almost equalled those by high income economies since the mid-1960s. Merchandise trade by low-income countries increased from 28.6 per cent of GDP in 1990 to 51 per cent in 2008, before falling to 47.9 per cent in 2009. Trade in services increased from

**Table 1.6**  *Third World trade, 1990–2009*

| Economy | Trade (% of GDP) | | Exports (annual % growth) | | Merchandise trade (% of GDP) | | Trade in services (% of GDP) | | FDI (% of GDP) | |
|---|---|---|---|---|---|---|---|---|---|---|
| | *1990* | *2009* | *1990* | *2009* | *1990* | *2009* | *1990* | *2009* | *1990* | *2009* |
| Low income | 32.6 | 57.5 | 6.4 | 2.1 | 28.6 | 47.9 | 9.5 | 12.9 | 0.5 | 2.3 |
| Lower-middle income | 39.9 | 56.1 | 5.8 | –7.1 | 31.2 | 44.6 | 8.4 | 12.6 | 0.6 | 2.6 |
| East Asia and Pacific | 43.4 | 64.7 | 7.8 | –9.9 | 47.0 | 51.3 | 7.3 | 7.8 | 1.6 | 1.6 |
| Latin America and Caribbean | 31.9 | 42.0 | 6.8 | –10.5 | 23.3 | 33.7 | 5.6 | 5.9 | 0.7 | 1.9 |
| Middle East and North Africa | 57.3 | 71.4[a] | 12.1 | 8.4 | 42.5 | 53.2 | 9.3 | … | 0.2 | 2.6 |
| South Asia | 20.3 | 43.1 | 8.9 | –6.0 | 16.4 | 31.0 | 4.2 | 11.5 | 0.1 | 2.3 |
| Sub-Saharan Africa | 51.8 | 63.4 | … | … | 41.9 | 52.9 | 10.8 | 13.5 | 0.4 | 3.1 |
| High income | 38.0 | 47.5 | 18.9 | 23.6 | 32.3 | 42.1 | 7.9 | 12.6 | 1.1 | 2.0 |

NOTE:   <sup>a</sup> = 2007.

SOURCE:   World Bank, *Databank*, http://databank.worldbank.org.

9.5 per cent to 14.8 per cent in 2008, declining to 12.9 per cent in 2009. Exports from low-income countries reached 22.2 per cent of GDP in 2009 and 26.1 per cent from lower-middle-income countries, compared with 23.6 per cent of the GDP of high-income countries. However, though the Third World's share has increased, it still only accounts for less than one third of global trade.

A major economic problem of the early post-colonial years was the Third World's dependence on the export of small numbers of primary commodities whose prices were subject to severe fluctuations. Even as late as 1990, only in South and East Asia did the value of manufactured exports exceed that of primary commodities. Manufactured exports from Third World countries have grown and the export of primary commodities has declined as a percentage of merchandise exports. Low- and middle-income economies accounted for 16 per cent of world merchandise exports in 1990. By 2005, this had risen to almost 30 per cent. But the value of manufactured goods in total exports varies considerably from one Third World region to another. And globalization has not shifted economic power towards poor countries. Most international trade is still between a small number of rich, developed countries. Trade liberalization benefits these rather than poor countries (Scott and Wilkinson, 2011).

Foreign direct investment (FDI) is another route by which developing countries have become increasingly integrated into the global economy. FDI increased by nearly six times between 1985 and 1995, and tenfold over the following 10 years. However, the US$24 billion of FDI into the 48 least developed economies in 2010 amounted to only 2 per cent of global FDI. Growth in FDI has been accompanied by increased intervention by the largest MNCs, such as BP, British American Tobacco, Rio Tinto and Siemens. The economic and financial crisis which began in 2009 reduced the flow of FDI, especially to Asia.

A striking trend since 2000 has been the growing importance of other developing countries as sources of FDI, especially China, India, and Brazil. China's investment in the least developed countries (LCDs) increased from over US$45 million in 2003 to over US$980 million in 2008, or 3 per cent of total FDI to LDCs (UNCTAD, 2011). Brazil invested a total of US$11.5 billion abroad in 2010 (ECLAC, 2011, p. 12).

## Human development

The measurement of human development provides another dimension of Third World status. The UN regularly monitors human development and since 1990 has presented its conclusions in the form of a Human Development Index (HDI). Despite progress in human development over

**Table 1.7**   *Human Development Index trends, 1980–2010*

| Region | HDI | | Average annual HDI growth (%) |
| --- | --- | --- | --- |
| | *1980* | *2010* | *1980–2010* |
| Developed | 0.727 | 0.862 | 0.57 |
| Developing | 0.411 | 0.590 | 1.24 |
| Arab States | 0.396 | 0.588 | 1.32 |
| East Asia and Pacific | 0.383 | 0.643 | 1.73 |
| Latin America and Caribbean | 0.573 | 0.704 | 0.68 |
| South Asia | 0.315 | 0.516 | 1.65 |
| Sub-Saharan Africa | 0.293 | 0.389 | 0.94 |
| Least developed countries | 0.251 | 0.386 | 1.44 |

NOTE:   The United Nations Development Programme's Human Development Index (HDI) is derived from scores given for life expectancy at birth, adult literacy levels, average years of schooling, and real GDP per capita (to indicate purchasing power). The two educational variables are combined but with different weightings, and growth in the human development value of increases in income is assumed to fall after a certain level is reached. The three indicators are averaged to provide each country with a score from 0 to 1.
SOURCE:   UNDP (2010b), table 2, p. 151.

the past 30 years, measured by life expectancy, educational attainment and the purchasing power of incomes, there are still substantial contrasts between the developed and developing worlds, as well as between groups of poorer countries (see Table 1.7).

The annual average growth in human development was 1.44 per cent for the LDCs between 1980 and 2010, with developing countries as a whole recording growth of 1.24 per cent. This has helped reduce the gap between social conditions in the developed and developing worlds. Only three of the 135 countries surveyed have failed to record a higher level of human development since 1970: the Democratic Republic of Congo, Zambia, and Zimbabwe. Convergence between rich and poor countries is mainly due to achievements in health and education, since the gap has widened when measured by incomes.

Health status is measured by infant mortality, maternal mortality, life expectancy, and malnutrition. Progress has been made in all areas since 1970, though this has not been distributed evenly across the Third World. Infant mortality has declined by 59 per thousand live births in developing countries, though the rate of decline has been slower than in developed countries. Infant mortality is eight times higher than in developed countries.

The rate of maternal mortality has improved slightly, but not enough to reach the UN's Millennium Development Goal of reducing the number of deaths in childbirth by three quarters between 1990 and 2015. Between 1990 and 2008, the maternal mortality ratio in developing countries fell from 440 deaths in childbirth per 100,000 to 290. Maternal mortality remains high, mainly as a result of malnutrition, inadequate health care, and frequent pregnancies. Sub-Saharan Africa and South Asia account for 87 per cent of global maternal deaths (UNDP, 2011).

Malnutrition has also improved, though 99 per cent of the world's 1 billion malnourished people live in the Third World, with 63 per cent in Asia and 26 per cent in sub-Saharan Africa. The proportion of people in developing countries who are undernourished has remained at 16 per cent since 2000, but the number has increased from 818 million to 837 million. However, the proportion of under-fives who are underweight declined between 1990 and 2009 from 30 per cent to 23 per cent. The situation is worst in South Asia, where 43 per cent of children under five are underweight.

Good health is undermined by unsafe water and bad sanitation. A lack of access to safe drinking water causes loss of life on a large scale in the Third World, including the lives of some 4,000 children each day. Despite some progress in recent decades, there are still over 884 million people in developing countries, over one third of them in sub-Saharan Africa, using unsafe sources of drinking water. In addition, while almost all who live in developed countries enjoy good sanitation, 2.6 billion people in developing countries are subjected to unhealthy and undignified sanitary conditions (WHO/UNICEF, 2010).

As a consequence of improved health and nutrition, life expectancy in the Third World has increased from 45.5 years for low-income countries in 1970 to 57.4 in 2009 (see Table 1.8). This compares with 80 for high-income countries. In sub-Saharan Africa, life expectancy is under 53 years. Furthermore, it is feared that decades of improvement in mortality rates will be wiped out by the AIDS epidemic, causing 1.8 million deaths annually. Malaria is proving resistant to treatment, and tobacco-related deaths are likely to increase to more than 12 million per year by 2025 (World Bank, 1993).

Consequently, the rate of progress in key areas of health has slowed since 1990. Progress in average life expectancy slipped from the additional 6 years achieved between 1970 and 1990 to 4 years between 1990 and 2010. The rate at which infant mortality has improved also slowed during this period. These developments have been caused mainly by the HIV epidemic, especially in parts of sub-Saharan Africa, but also by civil war and the introduction of fees for health care.

Progress in education has been marked, at least in terms of the proportion of children of primary school age enrolled in school. It reached 89 per cent in 2009. But the quality of education in developing countries falls far

**Table 1.8**   *Human development 2009: health and education*

| | Life expectancy at birth (years) | Infant mortality (under 5 per thousand live births) | Educational enrolment (primary, %) | Adult literacy (%) | Access to improved water (% of population, 2008) |
|---|---|---|---|---|---|
| High income | 80 | 7 | 95.7 | 98.4 | 99.6 |
| Low income | 57 | 118 | 80.9 | 61.4 | 63.8 |
| Middle East and North Africa | 71 | 33 | 91.4 | 74.4 | 87.3 |
| East Asia and Pacific | 72 | 26 | 94.4[a] | 93.5 | 87.9 |
| Latin America and Caribbean | 74 | 23 | 95.1 | 91.1 | 93.4 |
| South Asia | 64 | 71 | 90.7 | 61.1 | 86.7 |
| Sub-Saharan Africa | 53 | 130 | 76.3 | 62.3 | 59.7 |

NOTE:   [a] = 2007.

SOURCE:   World Bank *Databank*, http://databank.worldbank.org.

short of that available in developed countries. East Asia has made the most progress in expanding education, while South Asia and sub-Saharan Africa still lag behind, with adult literacy rates well below the average for developing countries. Progress in education includes an increase in the average primary school completion rate in low- and middle-income countries from 62 per cent in 1994 to 87 per cent in 2004, and a reduction in gender disparities. However, the rate at which enrolment in primary education was increasing slowed down between 2004 and 2009, recording an increase of only 2 percentage points.

Inequalities are found in social well-being as well as incomes. Inequalities in health and education are found between urban and rural areas, between men and women, and between income groups. There is generally greater poverty in rural areas and more severe problems of malnutrition, lack of education, life expectancy and substandard housing. Infant mortality rates are above average for rural populations and among the poor, since access to health care is dependent upon income. The disabled are found disproportionately among the poor (World Bank, 2006).

In all regions of the Third World, women do worse than men in terms of health, nutrition, and education. The proportion of girls enrolled in primary and secondary education has increased in recent years, but large inequalities remain in sub-Saharan Africa and South Asia. Women can also be expected to work longer hours for lower wages than men. They face more cultural, legal, economic, and social discrimination than men – even poor men (World Bank, 1990). When a country's Human Development Index is adjusted for gender disparity, every country's value declines, showing that '[G]ender inequality remains a major barrier to human development' (UNDP, 2010b, p. 89). Rankings change too, showing that some countries do better than others. Other significant disparities for women lie in employment opportunities and earnings.

Human development is increasingly being thought of as encompassing political factors, such as the level of democratization and the protection afforded to human rights. In 1987, roughly three fifths of the developing world's governments were not democratic. However, in the late 1980s pressures towards democratization and the rule of law built up from a number of factors acting in unison: the economic failure of authoritarianism; structural adjustment programmes demanded by multilateral and unilateral aid donors; the rise of Western neo-liberal ideology in the late 1970s; the spread of pro-democracy movements in all regions of the Third World, as well as Eastern Europe; and the collapse of communism.

Despite some advances towards less authoritarian forms of government – in Zambia, South Korea, and Taiwan, for example – the experience of the Third World with democratization has been mixed. By the end of the twentieth century, democracy and freedom were the dominant trends in Latin America and the Asia Pacific region. In Africa, by contrast, a minority of countries had free societies and electoral democracy. No countries in the Arab world were rated 'free'. Furthermore, all the downward trends were found in developing countries. Democratic gains in Guinea, Tanzania, India, Nepal, the Philippines, and Indonesia have been offset by regressive developments in Mexico, Côte d'Ivoire, Zambia, Pakistan, Fiji, Sri Lanka, and Malaysia. The Arab Middle East still has a huge 'democratic deficit', with no states rated 'free' in 2011 (respecting a broad array of basic human rights and political freedoms). All but 7 of the 47 countries rated 'not free' by Freedom House in 2011 were in the Third World. Most Third World states fall into the 'partly free' and 'not free' categories. Democratization has stagnated in recent years, with governments in all regions guilty of suppressing political opposition, civil society, and freedom of assembly. The deterioration in political rights and civil liberties since 2005 threatens the gains made since the post-Cold War era in Africa, Latin America, and Asia (Freedom House, 2011).

## Conclusion

Many of the problems which characterized the group of countries originally labelled the Third World by Western analysts, and which prompted solidaristic action by Third World leaders, persist. The countries conventionally categorized as part of the Third World do not all rank the same in terms of the indicators of Third World status used here. But all confront some of the problems associated with Third World status, and most of the 50 low-income countries experience them all. So, while Brazil, an upper-middle-income country, has a gross national product (GNP) per capita of US$4,420, life expectancy is lower than Vietnam's with a GNP per capita of US$370. Tanzania, a low-income economy, has a higher ratio of trade to GNP than upper-middle-income Mexico. Manufactured goods account for only 10 per cent of middle-income Ecuador's exports of merchandise, compared with 84 per cent of low-income Pakistan's. Diamonds may contribute 80 per cent of Botswana's foreign exchange earnings, 50 per cent of government income, and 33 per cent of GDP, yet dependence on this single commodity has transformed the country from one of the poorest in the world to one of the richest in Africa. However, life expectancy is 40 years, mainly due to a high incidence of HIV infection, and attempts to diversify industry have faltered. Infant mortality is high in most low-income countries, but this is also the case in upper-middle-income Gabon. Almost as large a proportion of Bangladesh's population has access to safe water as Uruguay, though the latter has a per capita GNP 16 times greater.

Subsequent chapters will consider the political importance of such characteristics as poverty and inequality, dependence on foreign investment for economic development, industrialization and urbanization as aspects of modernization, and progress in the protection of human rights and freedoms. The dependency which has featured in much of the discussion about the nature of the Third World has also been central to interpretations of the changes which are taking place there. In one sense, the expression 'Third World' represents a challenge to 'development' as autonomous growth and progress. The controversies within the social sciences about development, underdevelopment, and the consequences of contacts between rich and poor countries will form the substance of later chapters. Chapter 2 examines an approach to understanding political change in terms of the relationship between social and economic modernization, and the emergence of Western political institutions.

# 2

# The Developing Political System

## New states and comparative politics

The independence won by former colonies in the 1950s and 1960s meant that a large number of new states appeared in the international political arena. It was felt by some political scientists that existing tools of political analysis were inadequate for the task of including these new states within a single comparative framework. Western political science up to this point had been based on the comparison of institutions and, even more restrictedly, institutions found in Western industrialized societies. The need for a theoretical framework that could cope with a variety of exotic political systems led a group of mainly American political scientists to formulate a functionalist theory of political change, drawing on structural-functionalist social anthropology. Structural-functionalism appeared to provide a comparative framework of concepts that could be used to explain how, in non-Western and pre-industrial societies, unfamiliar social structures could perform the functions needed in all political systems (Almond and Coleman, 1960; Almond, 1965).

This chapter explains a major theoretical perspective on the nature of political change occurring in Third World states. It seeks to provide an understanding of the main arguments of the functionalist perspective on comparative politics by providing contemporary illustrations of how political functions are performed in Third World countries. The aim is to show how far contemporary Third World politics deviate from the model of a modern political system formulated by functionalism. Functionalist predictions concerning interest articulation, interest aggregation, rule-making, rule application, rule adjudication, political communication, political socialization, and political recruitment will be contrasted with how civil society, political parties, legislatures, bureaucracies, judiciaries, and the media function in Third World states. Poverty, ethnic conflict, the persistence of tradition, religion, and the distribution of

28

rewards in developing countries are shown to expose problems with functionalism's concepts of tradition, secularization, change, and political integration.

## Social structures and political functions

Functionalism was a way of addressing societies that were rapidly achieving the status of nation states with apparently modern political institutions such as legislatures, parties, constitutions, and executives, but grafted onto structures that were totally unfamiliar to most Western observers other than anthropologists. The functionalists therefore abandoned comparative methods based on structures in favour of one based on functions. If structures were persisted with, the resultant analytical tools would be inappropriate. The search for constitutions, parties, pressure groups, legislatures, and bureaucracies would be fruitless in societies whose government did not depend on such structures.

A set of functions has to be performed in all societies no matter how complex or simple, industrialized or agrarian. The task is to establish what these are and then seek out the structures that perform them in different societies. Functions have to be performed by social structures, or sets of roles performed by individual members of the set. Roles are thus distinguished from persons. When roles are performed in a particular set, they constitute a social structure. Individuals thus make up numerous different structures. A member of the role set of the family contributes to that structure as well as to the other structures to which they contribute roles – at work, in religious ceremonies, in the interpretation and enforcement of law and custom, in community associations, in political organizations, and so on. In pre-modern societies, age may determine to which set an individual contributes. Age-grades then become an important structure for the performance of political functions.

Comparative politics could no longer prejudge the question of structures. If communities are found to enforce their rules not by courts, police forces, prisons, and the other institutions of the state but, rather, by contests between the injured parties, tempered by public opinion within lineages, as in the Nuer of the southern Sudan, it should not be assumed that such societies were disorganized, chaotic, or without the means of governing themselves. They might be societies without governments but they were not without government, or regular ways of performing necessary political functions. Structures existed to perform those functions. Familiar legislative structures might not exist to make legally binding rules, but other social structures would exist to perform this function of articulating rules, perhaps by age-groups.

Another major contrast drawn by the functionalists between developed and developing societies was in the existence of boundaries between social, political, and economic systems. In traditional societies these often appeared to be lacking, whereas in a modern society, according to the functionalists, it was possible to separate structures that were primarily economic from those that were primarily social or political.

## The organic metaphor

The concept of 'function' suggests, among other things, an analogy between a society and a biological organism. In biology, 'function' refers to the contribution which different parts of an organism make to its maintenance. So, organizations such as political parties or administrative agencies can be explained by reference to the purposes they serve for the functioning of the organism as a whole.

Political development theory borrowed two other key ideas from biology: *interdependence* and *equilibrium*. Interdependence means that when one component of an organism changes, the organism as a whole is affected. For example, the emergence of mass political parties or the mass media 'changes the performance of all the other structures of the political system, and affects the general capabilities of the system in its domestic and foreign environments'. If the change is dysfunctional to the system, 'the dysfunctional component is disciplined by regulatory mechanisms, and the equilibrium of the system is re-established' (Almond, 1965, p. 185). Political systems tend towards equilibrium. Institutions preserve their character or, at most, change slowly.

The functionalists needed both a theory of the political system – a more appropriate label than 'state', given the existence of stateless societies – and a theory of change or development. Change is progressive. Societies change from being traditional to being modern and developed, implying improvement and progress in the way that societies are governed.

## The political system

The functionalist theory of the political system rests on five key concepts: politics, system, structure, culture, and function.

*Politics* are social relationships involving the legitimate monopoly of physical coercion, following the Weberian definition of the state (Weber, 1919). Political activities are directed at control of or influence over the use of coercive power. Whatever the values prompting demands for action by the authorities, and whatever the nature of the action called for, ultimately these relate to the coercive power of the political system.

The concept of *system* conveys the interrelationships between the parts of a polity so that when there is change in one part of the system, other parts will be affected. A political system is made up of particular roles involving the monopoly of physical force and the establishment and maintenance of a process by which inputs are converted into outputs. The political process generates both demands for policies and a number of supports for governmental outputs. Those demands and supports on the input side are converted into outputs through political processes. All societies have ways of converting inputs into outputs. They constitute its political system. In all societies, there are interactions which produce political outputs by means of the employment or threat of employment of legitimate physical compulsion.

The political system is, thus, a set of interrelated structures for maintaining order and responding to the changing pressures of the environment. These structures would, in part, be regulative and coercive, concerned with the suppression of dissent. They would also be distributive, shifting resources between sectors of society. Extractive structures would draw resources from society through such means as taxation.

The idea of *structures* as sets of interrelated roles that make up the political process enables functions to be described without preconceived ideas associating particular functions with corresponding structures. So, for example, a legislature is a set of interrelated roles performing the function of making legally binding rules.

The concept of *culture* brings into the framework of political analysis the idea that all societies contain discernible attitudes and dispositions towards politics. A society in crisis is often a society in which the dominant political culture is being undermined by competing sets of beliefs. It can no longer sustain the level of support needed by the political system for it to survive. The political culture thus consists of values about how politics should actually be conducted, and how the processes of government should be carried on. The legitimacy adhering to the structures and processes of government is expressed through a society's political culture. The obligations that are the consequence of that legitimacy relate to the rules of the political system.

In any given society, there may well be different political cultures that give rise to conflict. One of the problems of becoming modern was seen in cultural terms as a problem of persuading people in post-colonial societies to accept the boundaries of the nation-state as legitimate when those boundaries had their origins in alien rule. The processes of government might also lack legitimacy if they are based on unacceptable forms of authority again derived from an alien source. Thus, adaptation to forms of democracy inherited from foreigners may also be difficult. This is frequently referred to as the problem of political integration, a major source of political instability in Third World societies. Political integration will be returned to in Chapter 8, when different explanations for nationalism and secession are considered.

Finally, there is the concept of *function*, central to the needs of the comparative analyst. The universal attributes of political systems can only be conceptualized in terms of functions. The functionalists claimed that every society, however organized politically, at whatever level of development, and whatever the political structures through which government is carried on, will have social structures to perform eight political functions.

Demands are formulated and brought into the political arena through *interest articulation*, so that the conversion process can transform demands into outputs. What in developed societies might be the most typical structure performing that function (pressure groups and similar forms of association) will not necessarily be found in pre-industrial or transitional societies. The development of civil society varies from one country to another, and full freedom of association, the mark of a developed political system, is rarely found. For example, the Philippines has a strong civil society, with many organizations incorporated into decision-making. Such groups are capable of concerted action to remove corrupt and authoritarian leaders, as in the case of Ferdinand Marcos in 1986 and Joseph Estrada in 2001. Nevertheless, left-wing pressure groups and church activists are vulnerable to military intimidation, undermining political dialogue, damaging democracy, and departing from the model of a developed political system.

Political interests and their demands have to be combined so that coalitions can be formed that are powerful enough to overcome other combinations of interests. This is the function of *interest aggregation*. In an absolute monarchy or an African chiefdom, interests of different sections of the community would be 'aggregated' by rulers enjoying the right to interpret the wishes of their people. In a modern society, the classic structure for interest aggregation is the political party. In some Third World political systems, such as Ethiopia, it has been necessary to aggregate many different political movements, all based on ethnicity, into blocs that could form governments capable of holding a multi-ethnic society together. Unfortunately, for legitimate and stable political development, political parties have too often aggregated too few interests in an exclusive way – for example, by defining 'interests' in terms of ethnic identity. In Kenya, the reflection of ethnic divisions in party competition has been a major source of instability. Even parties that have attempted to appeal to interests that cut across tribe, such as the Forum for the Restoration of Democracy, have split into ethnically based groups (Carey, 2002). Some political parties – for example, in Thailand – resemble pressure groups representing the interests of powerful political bosses, rather than organizations for aggregating interests behind ideologies or policy platforms.

All political systems have to make authoritative and legitimate rules that can be supported by legitimate sanctions. This is the function of *rule-making*. Modern societies have developed specialized structures for this known as 'legislatures'. In traditional societies, such structures may be absent but the function will be performed somewhere in the political system. Most Third World countries have functioning legislatures – one exception being Saudi Arabia, where rule-making is in the hands of an absolutist monarchy. Other departures from the model of a developed political system are found. Not all legislatures have sovereign law-making powers. In Iran, for example, a Council of Guardians consisting of Muslim scholars and lawyers can veto legislation passed by parliament (*Majlis*) that does not conform to its interpretation of Islamic law. Rule-making powers may also be shared between legislatures and executives, especially in presidential systems – for example, South Korea.

Once made, legal rules have to be enforced and applied. The modern structure for the function of *rule application* is bureaucracy. Countries vary in the extent to which their public bodies display the positive characteristics of bureaucracy. Too often, bureaucrats are inefficient, recruited by patronage rather than on merit, and corrupt. The abuse of official powers for personal gain is a major problem of governance in developing countries. In Libya, for example, the tax system under the Gadaffi regime was especially vulnerable to corruption, with arbitrary decisions made about tax liabilities. In Laos, corruption is particularly evident in administrative agencies concerned with forestry, land ownership, and environmental protection. In Bangladesh, corruption is particularly intense in the police, customs, and National Board of Revenue. In 2009, over half the adult population of Cambodia, Nigeria, India, and Uganda paid a bribe to officials in one or more public services (Transparency International, 2010).

Conflicts arising from the application of rules to specific cases and circumstances require structures for adjudication. *Rule adjudication* is, thus, another universal political function. In modern societies, the judiciary would be the specialized structure performing this function. However, most political systems draw the judiciary into rule-making as well as arbitration, especially when courts are empowered to rule on constitutional matters.

The importance for political development of specialized judicial structures lies in their separation from the other branches of government and, thus, their ability to adjudicate free from political interference. This independence is too often compromised by political interference from the executive. For example, lack of security of tenure and a politicized appointment process in Côte d'Ivoire means that the administration of justice is highly vulnerable to executive and even military interference, despite constitutional guarantees of judicial independence. In many Third World countries, the rule of law has deteriorated significantly due to the erosion of judicial independence. Judicial impartiality is also frequently undermined by corruption.

All political systems equally require means for the communication of demands and rules between the authorities and the people. In modern society, the mass media constitute the social structures responsible for the function of *political communication*. In traditional society, structures would reflect the technology available as well as the type of social organization that had developed. For political development to occur, the social structure of the mass media should ideally be independent of the state. Private ownership and dependence on advertising revenue will introduce biases in the information provided, which only a diverse range of outlets in each type of media can guard against. But freedom from state control (if not ownership) should prevent governments from using the mass media to ensure only its interpretation of events reaches the public. In the Third World, such independence is all too often lacking. In all regions, the majority of countries have media which are restricted by the state in some way.

Incursions into the freedom of the press have been particularly noticeable in Venezuela, Thailand, the Philippines, Ethiopia, Eritrea, Uganda, Argentina, Peru, and Bolivia. The main methods used by the state to suppress political opposition are the takeover of media outlets (Côte d'Ivoire), the withholding of licenses (Zimbabwe), libel actions and violence against journalists (including state sponsored murder in the Philippines, Pakistan, and Sri Lanka), control of the internet (China and Iran), and restrictions on media coverage (Malaysia).

All societies have to transmit their dominant political values from generation to generation. All have ways of conveying to the younger generation what they ought to believe about political obligation, authority, and the rightful exercise of power. How the function of *political socialization* is performed varies considerably from one society to another. The relative prevalence of the family, educational institutions, or other associations will differ from society to society. The role of different social structures in processes of socialization will depend upon the development of the educational system and access to it, the opportunities offered by civil society for political experiences, and the status of the mass media. In the Third World, political socialization too often occurs in divisive contexts which emphasize exclusive identities such as ethnicity or religion. Parochial loyalties then prevent the development of consensus about the basic principles of government. Such divisions may be further exacerbated by experience of political instability or civil war which leaves groups permanently hostile to fellow citizens, whether divided by class, ethnicity, or religion. The danger, then, is that the current holders of state power will attempt to impose an ideological consensus by restrictions on freedom of association (as in the single party state), or through government agencies charged with indoctrination, such as Iran's Ministry of Islamic Guidance (Kamrava, 1995).

Finally, individuals have to be recruited into roles and offices. The function of *political recruitment* requires the following of some kind of routine in both traditional and modern societies. Processes of political succession have to be devised – election, inheritance, merit, physical might, and other principles by which people are recruited into political roles and perhaps permanent offices. The roles that perform the universal political functions have to be filled by acceptable methods. These clearly change over time.

Many Third World states depart from modern principles of political recruitment into both political and administrative offices. Rather than filled on the basis of merit, recruitment into public offices is often based on nepotism or patrimonialism. Formally, and in constitutional documents, there may be a structure of rational-legal authority, but informally political and administrative authority operates according to different rules, those of patrimonialism (Brinkerhoff and Goldsmith, 2002). In Bangladesh, for example, this results in the occupation of public office for personal gain rather than public service, representation based on personalized favours and obligations rather than the interests of constituents, 'non-compliance with the formal rules of democratic politics' rather than political and administrative accountability, and distrust of politicians and bureaucrats rather than a sense of legitimacy (Wood, 2000).

## Political change

Functionalism seeks to do more than just provide a new language for identifying the universal features of political systems. It provides a framework for understanding change. In practice, the functionalists were more concerned with the characteristics of societies in some process of transition, rather than with the elaboration of political models for 'traditional' or 'modern' societies. Their major areas of interest were the new nation states emerging on the international scene into which virtually all traditional societies had been more or less fully incorporated, usually through the operation of colonialism. Comparative politics was redesigned to explain the effects of the interactions between the traditional structures and cultures of communities incorporated into the new states that had been produced by colonialism and nationalistic reactions to it.

The most important change for the political functionalists was the association of increasingly specialized structures with single political functions in modern societies. Change also takes place in the political culture during modernization, or while the political system is in the process of transition.

Political structures become more specialized and differentiated as societies become more modern. This process is part of the growing social differentiation, specialization, and complexity found within modernizing societies. Specialization of political roles is part of becoming a modern polity. Whereas in a traditional absolute monarchical polity there would be found, bound up in a single structure – that of the royal court – a multiplicity of functions such as rule-making and rule adjudication, in a modern society with its pluralist democracy there would be found specialized structures performing single functions. Traditional political structures were described as typically 'multi-functional'. As societies develop, structures become less multi-functional.

Change in political culture means secularization, a process by which societies become more rationalized. It occurs when people perceive that the circumstances around them are changeable by human intervention. If religious belief, such as fatalism, prevents society from seeing the environment in that way, then religion may become an obstacle to modernization. A rational or secular basis of social values does not accept the facts of life as unalterable or sacred. Secularization means enabling people to differentiate between the sacred and the profane, the religious world and the world of material objects. It does not interpret everything in terms of a set of beliefs about what is sacred and what has been handed down since time immemorial. Those beliefs may remain, but people begin to separate them from secular concerns, the latter then being exposed to rational scrutiny. Becoming modern means not only developing the administrative capability to change society, but also developing ways of thinking that permit phenomena to be confronted and changed by human agency, by setting goals and working out the means of achieving them. As societies develop, they acquire systems of government that are problem-oriented and designed to perceive, analyse and meet the needs of society as articulated through political demands.

Bureaucracy epitomizes rational government and the idea of linking means to ends, of defining an objective and calculating what needed to be done to achieve it. Bureaucracy – based on rules, expertise, plans and calculations – is the ideal form of authority for the rationalization of politics. Rational-legal authority combines the idea of means being related to ends with the idea that rules, offices, and public action would no longer reflect heredity, tradition, custom, or charisma. Rules reflect an understanding of cause and effect in the political sphere. Rather than respect rules simply because they are endorsed by custom, religion, or traditional values, rules are respected because they are instrumental.

Greater rationality is supported by the growth of scientific and techno-logical knowledge in particular, and socio-economic development in general, as has been born out by cross-national surveys of social and polit-ical values comparing developed and developing societies. Development shifts people's attitudes 'from an emphasis on traditional values to an emphasis on secular-rational values' (Inglehart and Welzel, 2005, p. 6).

The secularization of politics is also important for nation-building. It enables the political system to supersede sub-national loyalties such as tribe or religion, seen as parochial and pre-modern. It involves creating a consensus to support the new order by mobilizing the community to regard the nation-state, not some primordial grouping, as the legitimate political unit. Communities are mobilized to articulate demands and supports. This is all part of not just becoming modern, but of producing an integrated soci-ety, a major achievement of a developed political system.

Secularization also allows the development of a political system's 'capability' to formulate policies, enforce decisions throughout the terri-tory, and develop a problem-solving capacity, especially through bureau-cracy, so that public policies can be executed effectively and efficiently. Such capabilities are extractive, regulative, distributive, symbolic, and responsive (Almond, 1965), and are dependent on the system's resources. The more developed the political system, the more able it would be to build up its resources and, in turn, that would be dependent on the existence of differentiated and specialized political structures, especially bureaucra-cies. Only with a highly efficient bureaucracy, based on the principle of merit recruitment and organized rationally as a specialized institution, can a political system develop its full capabilities to provide itself with resources and the power to implement decisions.

Survey evidence comparing attitudes and behaviour in developed and developing countries supports the theory that secularization increases with modernization. More prosperous societies have become more secular, while a particular feature of poor societies – insecurity – accounts for the persistence and growth of 'religiosity' in the Third World. As societies become more modern, the threat of poverty, disease, malnutrition, and premature death recedes, and good governance, human rights, equality, and political stability become more secure. Modernization means that 'the need for religious reassurance becomes less pressing under conditions of greater security' (Norris and Inglehart, 2004, p. 18).

Political development is thus part of the cultural change experienced during economic and social modernization. Secularization and rationaliza-tion require changes in cultural patterns. These changes were conceptual-ized as 'pattern variables', or patterns of related values with which people make judgements about other members of their society, or the way people orient themselves within social relationships (Parsons, 1966). Social change is essentially a matter of how we perceive people with whom we come into contact, whether in the family, wider social organizations, territorial communities, occupations, or politics.

Traditional society is characterized by *particularism* whereas modern society is characterized by *universalism*. A particularistic judgement of, or response to, a fellow member of society applies special values because of a unique relationship between the people involved. Members of a kinship group or family will judge each other according to criteria applicable to that group relationship alone. When one only has values that can be utilized in the context of unique social relations, a society is at the traditional end of the continuum. When judgements can be made on universal criteria, regardless of other dimensions of social relationships, society is at the modern end. When there are standards which can be applied to any individual, regardless of their position in society, universalism is said to exist. Criteria of performance that are defined independently of the status of those being evaluated constitute a pure form of universalism.

Political development also entails progress from *ascribed status* to *achieved status*. The former implies the existence of inherent qualities associated with the specific individuals concerned. For example, in a society which respects the wisdom of its older members that wisdom is assumed to exist by definition as soon as one becomes an elder. It is not appropriate to apply independent tests of competence. Achieved status depends upon a capacity to satisfy independent and abstract criteria that are defined independently of the other qualities of the individual concerned. When status is inherent in the person, society is traditional. Where status is acquired by the achievement of abstract qualities defined in terms of objective criteria, such as educational qualifications, society is modern. Ascriptive political office would be represented by an inherited position, whereas achievement would be exemplified by a bureaucrat recruited on the basis of acquired characteristics defined as necessary for particular tasks to be performed.

A third pair of cultural patterns contrasts *affectivity* with *neutrality*. 'Affectivity' refers to emotional attachments between people. Neutral attachments are based on instrumentality and objectives external to personal relationships.

Finally, traditional *diffuseness* is contrasted with modern *specificity*. Diffuse relations refer to the complex web of interconnections that link people together, involving many roles and aspects of their lives. Here, judgements can only be made about a total person. Their different roles cannot be separated for purposes of evaluation and the definition of social relationships. When society is formed on the basis on specificity, it is possible to distinguish the different roles performed by individuals and to be concerned with just one of them – as employer or employee, landlord or tenant, for example. Individuals in modern societies are seen as involved in a multiplicity of single-stranded relationships. Specificity signifies the separateness of social relations and their relative independence from each other. Diffuse relations combine all aspects of the individual's role in society and it is not possible to exclude consideration of some of these different aspects when individuals interrelate. Relationships are multi-stranded. No individual can abstract one of those relationships and give it an independent existence.

Such variables enable us to see how far a society has changed along different dimensions. The assertion of the individual's value in universalistic terms supports political equality and mass participation on an individual basis. Individuals would not see political roles as being ascribed by tradition and custom to predetermined groups. Political power could be enjoyed by all on an equal basis.

Political development is thus made possible by profound social change. Secularization has important political consequences both for the role of the individual in the political system and for recruitment into political office. The emergence of rational-legal authority has profound implications for the nature of the state, not least in the opportunity which it opens up for bureaucratization. Clusters of pattern variables provide models of social organization in which the political significance of universalism, achieved status, neutrality, and specificity is plain. Of particular importance to the study of political development is the effect of structural differentiation on the specialization of political roles in developing societies.

Much of what is expressed by this approach to political development has become almost commonplace. As a way of organizing information about political phenomena, it has become an integral part of political science. It is debatable whether students of comparative politics have developed superior theories. Functionalism drew attention to the importance of seeing societies as consisting of interdependent parts so that one could adopt a dynamic, rather than static, approach to the analysis of systems of government. The study of politics had hitherto adopted a rather insular, normative and legalistic format which functionalism completely changed.

Political development theory inspired the production of a large number of monographs – over 200 by 1975 – yet, many shared Eckstein's assessment that the result of all this effort was 'mostly muddle' (Eckstein, 1982, p. 451). However, the many criticisms to which functionalism has been subjected have themselves formed an important part of the process of acquiring a clearer understanding of political change in the Third World. A debt is owed to functionalists for stimulating so much debate about political change and for forcing critical assessment of their ideas, even though theoretical and conceptual weaknesses leave functionalism unable to provide a comprehensive theory of political change.

## The problem of 'tradition'

The concept of 'tradition' poses numerous problems. First, there is the tendency to see it as an obstacle to development. Resistance to change on the part of social groups may be seen as the 'burden' of tradition and an inability to break with outmoded ways of perceiving the world when, in fact, rational calculations are being made about the economic and political risks that are inevitably associated with disturbances to the *status quo*. Resistance to change may reflect a system of incentives operating under conditions that include poverty and dependency. A reluctance to abandon tradition may result less from modernity's inappropriate values, and more from the uncertainties associated with incomplete transitions to modern economic and political relations and their promise of protected property rights, honest bureaucracy, freedom of association, and democratic party systems (Brett, 2009, p. 243). Furthermore, the secular and the rational may benefit some groups in society much more than others.

Second, tradition is associated with ethnic identity, when the primordial values of tribe and race come into conflict with the modern individualistic values of people who think of themselves as members of a nation state, rather than members of some sub-national collectivity such as a linguistic group. Again, 'modern' factors, such as economic exploitation or political discrimination, may lead people to identify with an ethnic group, rather than a nation dominated by a rival minority.

Traditional cultures and social structures also consist of diverse norms and values. Old traditions are not necessarily displaced by new norms and social structures. They can and do exist side by side. In politics, traditions persist in pre-modern forms of authority based on patriarchy, theocracy, feudalism, patrimonialism, heredity, and the social hierarchies of tribe and caste (Brett, 2009). For example, in Asia political elites have drawn upon traditional values and perceptions, as well as modern cultural traits, in order to legitimize policies for economic development. In Thailand and Korea, 'traditional and indigenous cultural symbols complemented modernity, which elites imported from abroad', with traditions present in varying degrees depending on whether 'traditional culture supplied appropriate tools for economic modernization', as Confucian respect for education and authority evidently did in South Korea (Compton, 2000, pp. 183–4). If 'tradition' is used as a residual concept, defined by reference to the logical opposites of modern, the variability found both within and between traditional societies is obscured (Tipps, 1973).

## Secularization and religion

The resurgence of religion in parts of the Third World, especially as a foundation for political mobilization, indicates that modernization does not necessarily bring about secularization (Razavi and Jenichen, 2010). The growth of 'political religions' in the Middle East, Africa, the Caribbean, Asia, and Latin America not only undermines the secularist assumptions of evolutionary political development, it also raises the question of whether religious politics is a reversion to tradition. Whether Christian or Moslem, Hindu or Buddhist, progressive or conservative, religious politics has been in part a response to the failure of governments to secure economic prosperity and social well-being that is equitably distributed. It is also a reaction to the failure of secular ideologies to deliver socio-economic development, as well as a response to the undesirable consequences of modernity, including political repression, economic and political corruption, loss of cultural identity, and community dislocation. While there may be continuity from pre-modern forms of politics in which religious and political authority and processes were undifferentiated, contemporary forms of political religion are formed by the impact of political and economic modernization (Haynes, 1993). Haynes claims that political religiosity 'is not a "return" to religion, but the latest example of a periodic utilization – stimulated by perceived crisis – of religion to help pursue secular goals' (Haynes, 1999, p. 245). However, there seems sufficient evidence of political religion being a reversion to and revival of pre-modern traditions, values, and practices, and a rejection of modernity, for the issue to at least remain unresolved.

It is difficult to see religion as a less rational alternative to secular politics when, in the otherwise contrasting cultures of Latin America, the Middle East, Central and Southern Africa, and Southeast Asia, religion remains a source of popular mobilization, alternative notions of legitimacy, resistance, and even insurrection. It has come to fill an ideological vacuum. It can be revolutionary or reactionary (or evolve from one to the other). Where religion is identified with the state, it tends to be a conservative force (as in Saudi Arabia) but, where it is distanced from politics, it tends to be anti-establishment, as in Central and South America (Haynes, 2009; Deneulin and Rakodi, 2011). In parts of Asia, religious mobilization has decidedly modern political objectives: to marginalize ethno-religious minorities, as with Indonesia's education law of 2003; to assert class interests – for example, of the urban poor; to create clientelist networks through which employment and other economic advantages can be obtained; to construct transnational identities in the face of globalization; and to reinforce the power of governments providing facilities for religious practices, Islamizing the educational, legal, and economic systems, and co-opting influential religious leaders (Ufen, 2009).

In many parts of the Third World, political choices and actions are increasingly the result of religious judgements. In India, for example, the last 25 years have seen 'a much more explicit expression of religion in public life', typified by Sikh extremism and Hindu nationalism (see Box 2.1). In Pakistan, the influence of Islam now 'makes it very difficult for there to be open debate on such questions as women's rights, the position of minorities, and the rigid law on blasphemy' (Taylor, 2005, pp. 219 and 225). In South Africa, liberation theology has challenged oppressive social structures, mobilized the masses, and endorsed revolution (Hilliard and Wissink, 1999). In Burma, the Buddhist monastic community played a major role in mobilizing opposition to the military junta when secular pro-democracy groups were virtually crushed.

In Latin America, liberation theology's fusion of religion, social analysis (drawing inspiration from Marxism), and political activism has implications for the secular presuppositions of development theory, in that religious values are not secondary to social and political reform. Religion is not merely being used as a convenient instrument of political mobilization and solidarity. It represents a new awareness of class conflict and exploitation (Levine, 1988).

Secularization of the state by technocratic elites in some Middle Eastern countries has magnified the ideological significance of Islam, especially for the poor and other excluded classes. As well as spiritual guidance, it has provided a political framework and an alternative to the materialism and immorality associated with modernization and secularism (Kedourie, 1992; Omid, 1992). But, in so doing, it shows how politics based on religion combines traditional and modern elements. For example, millenarianism and commitment to an Islamic order (as in Iran) is accompanied by nationalism on the part of the clergy (Ram, 1997). Fundamentalist opposition in Saudi Arabia combines Islamic and modern Western concepts such as human rights and administrative probity (Kostiner, 1997). The appeal of religious movements such as the Iranian Shi'ites is related to secular concerns such as growing social inequality, political repression, corruption, foreign exploitation, and cultural division (Banuazizi, 1987). Some interpretations of Islam find no difficulty in incorporating capitalism with the idea of the state as the realization of divine sovereignty, and the source of law as transcendental (Judy, 1998). The notion that state and religion cannot be separated is a modern one in Islamic thought and, according to some Islamic scholars, not sanctioned by sacred prescriptions. Indeed, 'no Muslim society is governed solely with reference to religious law' (Filali-Ansary, 2003, p. 235).

However, while some interpretations of Islam accommodate political pluralism, and some Islamic reformers are 'laying the foundations for an Islamic Reformation' (Wright, 1996, p. 66), the practical consequences

**Box 2.1** *Democracy in India*

India's post-colonial history of democracy has defied expectations based on a theory of political development derived from understandings of social and economic modernization. Democracy has been sustained despite an initially low level of economic development, high levels of poverty, low levels of literacy and urbanization, and profound ethnic, religious, linguistic, and social divisions and discord. Yet, since 1949, with the exception of a brief period of 'emergency' from 1975–77, political life has been conducted within the framework of a democratic federal constitution requiring a universal franchise exercised during regular fair and free elections contested by a multiplicity of political parties at Union and State levels, and leading to orderly transitions of power from government to opposition. Unlike in neighbouring states, Indian democracy has been underpinned by a politically neutral military and professional (though inefficient) bureaucracy. Despite the initial legislative domination of the Indian National Congress, new parties have emerged based on the incorporation and accommodation of interests from social backgrounds of varying levels of diversity – some regional, such as the Janata Dal; some caste-based, such as the Bahujan Samaj Party; and some class-based, such as the communist Left Front in West Bengal, Kerala, and Tripura.

Yet, the peace of democratic politics has frequently been shattered by the prominence attached to primordial identities, leading to communal violence. Traditional political identities and behaviour are derived from caste, religion, and ethnicity. While caste-based parties have secured enough power at state level to implement policies guaranteeing quotas for different castes in higher education, employment in public services, and legislative seats, such particularism allows the economic subordination and deprivation which give lower castes a common class interest to go unremedied, and inhibits the formation of national citizenry. Such traditional identities have nevertheless to function within distinctly modern processes of political negotiation, cooperation, and compromise – that is, of interest aggregation. Thus, attempts to unite Hindus solely on the basis of religion failed. Muslims have sought alliances with parties representing Hindu castes in order to thwart Hindu extremism. The mobilization since the 1970s of lower castes into political parties forced the Bharatiya Janata Party (BJP) to form coalitions with other sectional interests and social groups. In Uttar Pradesh, the Bahujan Samaj Party secured power in 2007 by attracting not only Dalits and other lower-caste groups, but also voters from among upper-caste Brahmins. Competitive elections force caste-based parties to seek wider support and move from particularistic to more universalist identities. Indeed, the representation of traditional cultural identities within Indian democracy may actually have strengthened this modern form of government 'by allowing its poorer citizens to vernacularize important norms, institutions and practices' (Bhatt 2004; McMillan 2008; Ruparelia, 2008, p. 41).

of political Islam are rarely liberationist. With the partial exception of Turkey, Islamic societies are ruled by traditional or modernizing autocracies, or radical Islamic regimes – namely Iran and Sudan. Political Islam seeks to establish states governed by Islamic laws intolerant of alternative beliefs, and lacking the civil rights and political equality characteristic of liberal democracy. Political Islam may be motivated by a sense of injustice, social frustration, poverty, and political exclusion, but it favours the Islamization of law and, ultimately, the rejection of democracy. The radicals want the Sharia to take precedence over laws promulgated by elected assemblies, and discrimination against minorities, women, and other faiths to be legalized. Political Islam may not be a monolithic movement, and some moderates endorse consultation, consensus, majoritarianism, pluralism, and respect for human rights. But both moderates and radicals seek to establish an Islamic state based on Sharia, in which there will be little room for tolerations of dissent, equality of civil liberties, or political pluralism: 'when one focuses on their fundamental convictions, their most cherished values, and the kind of social and political order they aspire to create, moderates have far more in common with radicals than they do with Western-style democrats' (Denoeux, 2002, p. 73).

## Dichotomous models

Functionalist models of traditional and modern society tell very little about the dynamics of transition from one to another. For example, in terms of Parsons' pattern variables, developed countries can be shown to be particularistic in the behaviour of their social classes and private interests, as well as ascriptive, especially at the higher levels of business management and among the poor. Recruitment may be achievement based, but reward is often based on age and family obligations (e.g. in Japan). Roles are frequently 'diffuse' rather than functionally specific within such power structures as the military-industrial complex of the United States (Kiely, 1995).

Conversely, underdeveloped countries frequently demonstrate universalism in their educational systems and mass media, in labour unions and in liberation movements. The economic and political leadership thrown up by military coups and emerging bourgeoisies throughout the Third World cannot be described as normatively ascriptive. Role assignment by achievement is also widely found among the poorer classes of poor societies. In the distribution of rewards, achievement accounts for more than ascription in underdeveloped countries. Roles may be found to be functionally diffuse in underdeveloped countries, especially among the poorest and richest strata, though the middle-class military officers, police officers, bureaucrats, junior executives, and administrators are functionally specific in their roles. Such people 'serve specific functions of making the whole exploitative system function in the diffuse but particular interests of those who have achieved control' (Frank, 1972b, p. 335).

Neither 'tradition' nor 'modernity' should be seen as packages of attributes. Modernization may be selective, with rapid social change in one area obstructing change in others, rather than tradition being the sole obstacle to development. Hence, the eventual realization among political scientists of the modernization persuasion that modernization and political stability do not always go together: modernization in one sphere does not necessarily produce compatible ('eurhythmic') change in another. Once it is recognized that traditional values and practices may persist in otherwise modern societies, further doubt is thrown on the idea that tradition impedes change. Furthermore, if the destruction of tradition proves not to be necessary for 'modernization', except in purely tautological terms, then traditional societies must be seen as being able to develop in directions other than towards 'modernity' (Tipps, 1973).

### The concept of 'integration'

The functionalist model of a politically developed society exaggerates harmony and integration. It has difficulty accommodating conflicting interests and the differential power of social and economic groups. The idea that different parts of the political system are mutually supportive is a distortion. The functionalists directed their attention mainly towards the factors in society which maintain consensus and stability. This is understandable, given the areas of natural science which they and their social anthropological precursors chose as analogous to social science.

Functionalism's systemic theorizing sees society in organic terms, with specialized and interdependent parts functioning to satisfy the requirements of the whole for survival. The structures of the political system are presented in a neutral light as a mere arena for the resolution of conflict, one that is impartial as regards the contestants. But this conception of society as a functional unity is a mystification of social reality. What is functional for one group may be dysfunctional for another, perhaps to the extent of undermining the vitality of the whole.

Functionalism is more concerned with the integration of interests into a single normative pattern than with instability or conflict as sources of social change. Conflict over the allocation of scarce resources is seen as resolved within a framework of common values. Functionalism cannot explain the very changes that were its *raison d'être* because it concentrates on the prerequisites of the maintenance of the *status quo*. The tendency to regard everything that exists, including the characteristics of the political system, as functional and therefore desirable becomes normatively supportive of existing social arrangements. Social inequality and stratification, for example, are functional because society has motivated people to seek higher rewards and induced people to perform the duties attached to their station in life. This fails to show how choices can be made between the values which, though functional to an existing system, would be dysfunctional to an alternative one. When utility is found in all patterns of behaviour, conflict becomes regarded as pathological or abnormal. Such a view of society will be favoured by some 'parts' (or interests), but will work to the disadvantage of others. Thus, political realities present a challenge to the functionalist paradigm.

This encourages a conservative bias in functionalism (Abrahamson, 1978). Some functionalists, such as Merton, argued that functionalism is radical. Institutions and practices are given no inherent value, only their consequences matter. They are only preserved until they cease to be of utility to society. That allows for as much change as a society feels it needs to achieve its goals. However, the main thrust of functionalism is towards a conservation of what already is in place. It encourages a search for the benefits of surviving institutions. New generations have to be socialized into the existing mores of society. Structures are expected to have positive, functional consequences, and so contribute to the persistence of a society. Functionalism guides enquiry towards explanations of how societies maintain themselves and survive under their present arrangements. Institutions are assumed to contribute to the health of the whole social and political fabric. Approaching institutions by seeing them as supportive of society implies some normative consensus which is then endorsed by the investigator who credits those institutions with positive values by deeming them to be functional.

The conservative bias of functionalism became increasingly visible when the focus of attention moved to explanations of crisis, instability, and disorder. Crisis is seen to be a problem for elites to identify and to which to respond. Order is made the highest political good. Opponents of regimes are described as 'system wreckers': 'the interest in order of those at the top is given logical precedence over the interest in social justice of those below' (Sandbrook, 1976, pp. 180–1). Authoritarianism is then seen as a legitimate way for elites to manage crisis. Supposedly value-free, scientific models of political development end up leaving a strong ideological message (Cammack, 1997; Brett, 2009).

### Unilinear development

The fallacy of placing societies on a continuum between traditional and modern, along which all societies progress during their histories, led to the proposition that new states were replicating the European experience from the sixteenth to the nineteenth centuries. This formulation under-states a very fundamental difference: that the history of the advanced societies does not include colonization by more powerful countries. This makes it impossible to think of a unilinear developmental process. The new states of the world were structured by the old in a way which does not apply to the histories of countries whose own development was made possible by their exploitation of pre-industrial and pre-capitalist societies (Pratt, 1973). The West's development was built, some would say, on the active *underdevelopment* of weaker societies and economies (see Chapter 3).

Unilinear models of change are teleological, yet there is no preordained path to development for all societies. Cultures and traditions vary too much from one society to another, and the process of modernization varies from one time period to another. Furthermore, defining development in terms of direction, rather than content, means that anything that happens must be seen as part of the process of development. The concept loses util-ity as it loses precision and specific content (Kothari, 1968; Huntington, 1971).

Thus, modernization theory can be accused of denying underdeveloped countries their own histories, ignoring the connections between these histories and the histories of developed countries, overlooking the fact that penetration by foreign influences had not produced development or led to 'take off', and misrepresenting the histories of today's developed countries as not having benefited from the exploitation of the underdeveloped soci-eties (Frank, 1972b).

Underestimating the significance of such historical factors was compounded by a lack of consideration of continuing relationships with the powerful economies of the West. Continuities from colonialism that call the significance of political independence into question were ignored, especially economic and military aid programmes, interventions by inter-national financial organizations such as the World Bank, and investments by multi-national corporations (Pratt, 1973).

In 1987, Almond attempted to rebut the charge that developmentalism's theory of change was unilinear, arguing that developmentalists had always recognized that new states might develop authoritarian (rather than demo-cratic, pluralist) tendencies. He also claimed that the school never neglected international influences on domestic politics. However, it is noticeable that he restricted his refutation of the unilinearity charge to an awareness of authoritarianism. He did not attempt to answer the criticism that modernization theorists ignored the implications of colonialism and continuing economic dependency for the current autonomy of Third World countries. His lively critique of dependency theory did not dispel doubts that modernization theory can provide a framework for understanding the unique relationships between rich and poor countries. In 1970, he argued explicitly 'against the simple diffusionist notion of unilinearity in the early 1960s'. However, the interaction of economics and politics which Almond insists was always a feature of comparative studies of political development – such as the political consequences of industrialization, or the distributional effects of economic growth – does not encompass the factors which critics regarded as significant and distinctive of Third World status (Almond, 1987, p. 449).

**Ethnocentric analysis**

Consequently, political development theory appears ethnocentric, judging progress by reference to Western, and largely Anglo-American, values and institutions. It is difficult to avoid the conclusion that the perspective on change was determined as much by ideological leanings as by rigorous scientific investigation, leading critics to complain of 'widespread complacency towards American society, and the expansion of American political, military and economic interests throughout the world', which constitutes a form of cultural imperialism (Tipps, 1973, pp. 207–10). The end-state appears to be the system of government in the country producing the major exponents of the theory (Holt and Turner, 1966). There is nothing wrong *per se* in advocating a functionalist view of politics, such as the separation of powers, to which output functions clearly correspond. A distinction between the input side of the political equation, conceptualized in terms of socialization, recruitment, interest articulation and aggregation, and communication; and the output functions of rule-making, application, and adjudication, is useful (Varma, 1980). It asserts the relationship between the mechanisms for public participation and those for liberal government. The input functions imply mass participation on the basis of political equality in a modern society.

Indeed, while it is untenable to predict progress along a single path towards a universal, Western destination, there is nevertheless normative justification in advocating the convergence of less developed countries (LDCs) on a model which reflects the values underpinning democracy. It may be 'highly unlikely that LDCs will be able to make a shift to fully developed liberal institutions in a single giant stride, but this does not mean that they should be willing to accept anything less as their long-term goal'

(Brett, 2009, p. 4). It must be 'progressive' for a political system to respect freedom of association, rather than intimidate opposition groups, as in the Philippines; for parties to attract support across a wide range of interests, rather than appeal to exclusive ethnic identities, as in much of Africa; for elected representatives to make the laws, rather than a Council of Guardians, as in Iran; for bureaucracies to administer the law impartially, rather than in response to bribes; for judges to resolve disputes free from political interference by the President, which undermines the rule of law in Zimbabwe; for the mass media to communicate freely, rather than for journalists to fear harassment, intimidation, and murder, as in Sri Lanka; for people to be socialized into politics by free institutions, rather than be subjected to a state-imposed ideology; and for political and administrative positions to be filled on merit by election or appointment, rather than by nepotism and patrimonialism, as in Tunisia before the popular uprising in 2011.

However, such advocacy is a far cry from a scientific explanation of political change.

## Change and causality

In biology, the analysis of function is related to the analysis of causality. In political development theory, the move from description to causality was never really achieved. So, the claim of functionalism to be a *theory* has been seriously questioned. It has been acknowledged as an elaborate description and classification, able to describe social practices which are strange and difficult to comprehend. But, as an explanation of causality, functionalism suffers from the fact that it is tautological – no explanation can be disproved because things are defined in relation to themselves. A practice is said to persist because it contributes to the maintenance of society. Its persistence is taken to prove that the society is motivated to maintain itself. If the practice ceases, this has to be taken as indicative that it was no longer functional to society's maintenance. Statements about the causes and consequences of social and political practices are merely true by definition, not proved by explanation (Dowse, 1966).

Originally functionalists offered no theory of change. They devised concepts to compare systems presumed to be at different stages of development. But there is no explanation of a dynamic process. Later, key changes that occur as a society becomes more developed politically were identified. Even then, however, 'the stress was on the elaboration of models of different types of political system, not different types of change from one system to another' (Huntington, 1971, p. 307).

The problem was that political development was taken as a given. Meanings had to be attached to the concept, leading to a proliferation of definitions and conceptual entropy. No adequate account was given of the forces that drive societies along the development path. The lack of agreement on what political development actually meant made it impossible to posit a *theory* of change (Cammack, 1997).

When the shortcomings of political development theory in solving the problem of explaining political change were eventually acknowledged, theorists abandoned the attempt to predict the direction of change, concentrating instead on relationships between specific significant variables indicative of development – for example, the causes of political stability, or the destabilizing effects of changes within the political system. The central question became: what type of change in one component of a political system (culture, structures, groups, leadership, policies and so on) can be related to change, or its absence, in other components?

## Biological analogies

The analogy with biological organisms proved insufficiently close to provide valid explanations of social and political phenomena. It is very difficult to talk about the normal or pathological functioning of society, in the way that we can about organisms, without making massive value judgements. Societies can change their structures. Organisms do not. It is not possible to examine the numerous instances of the same social function as it is with biological organisms. The analogy thus leads social explanation up a cul-de-sac. It does not provide the opportunity for theoretical explanation that the assumed parallel between natural and social science appears to offer.

## Definitions

Some of the definitions used by functionalism are controversial. 'System' is defined in terms of what a system does. So, a political system which does not perform the functions which such systems are defined as performing ceases, by definition, to be a political system. Again, the explanatory power is reduced to a tautology. Any statement about the political system is either true by definition because that particular system is doing what all political systems do, or is not about political systems at all. The same is true of 'structure'. When structures are perceived and qualified by their salient functions – when the question is not what a structure is but, rather, what it is for – it is not possible to distinguish between structure and function and thus provide accurate descriptions of the former (Sartori, 1970).

The term 'function' is equally problematic. The word is used in different ways without the differences being fully acknowledged. 'Function' can mean maintaining something: for example, the function of the political system is to integrate society and allow it to adapt. Function can also mean merely a task, such as when the 'function' of a political organization is to articulate an interest. The functionalist literature tends to switch from the more mundane meaning to the almost mathematical meaning of function as the result or consequence of some other factor in the social equation.

The concept of 'boundary' is also controversial. If political systems could not be clearly differentiated from the economic and the social as, say, in China or the Soviet Union, it was heavily value-laden to say that they were, as a consequence, less developed than a society where state and economy operate in their own self-contained spheres. It may or may not be justifiable to prefer such separation, or *laissez-faire*, but it is not a scientific stance to say that a more modern society creates clear boundaries between polity and economy. That begins to look like a subterfuge for saying that societies where there is heavy state involvement in the economy are backward. This leaves aside the fallacy of assuming capitalist societies themselves demarcate between politics and economics. In fact, in all societies people move from one system to the other by virtue of the different roles which they perform. The boundaries are blurred, even if we wish to distinguish between societies where polity and economy are closely integrated because of public ownership, state planning, or collectivization, and societies where that is less so. To insist on an analytical boundary being drawn between the processes of politics and those of social integration and adaptation, or between the political system on the one hand, and churches, economies, schools, kinship, lineages, and age sets on the other, either leaves non-boundary systems or non-political systems; or makes statements about political systems true by definition and untestable empirically (Holt and Turner, 1966).

## Changes of emphasis

The pessimism about Third World politics that set in after what was perceived to be the failures of the United Nation's first Development Decade, together with American support for authoritarianism abroad (especially in Latin America) when directed towards the containment of revolutionary forces and the preservation of order (Higgott, 1983), led to subtle changes of emphasis in modernization theory. Three such changes can be distinguished.

First, the possibility of regression as well as progression was recognized. For example, it should not be inferred from developmental concepts such as 'structural differentiation' and 'cultural secularization' that trends in such directions are inevitable. Development theory had to accommodate the possibility that political systems might 'decay' (Huntington, 1965).

The second significant reorientation was towards an emphasis on political stability and social order. Political development theory had always been concerned to some extent with threats to stability, such as mass participation. It became increasingly concerned with factors associated with the maintenance of regimes, elites, and political order, as well as with restrictions on the capability of systems of government to produce decisions, policies, and interventions that can be enforced successfully. This change of emphasis was particularly damaging for some of the evolutionary assumptions of functionalist political theory (O'Brien, 1972; Cammack, 1997).

Finally, a stronger emphasis was placed on political integration, another dimension of political stability and social order, and the problem of producing a political consensus in the midst of cultural diversity. New states encounter many obstacles to the creation of a sufficiently widespread sense of loyalty and obligation to the nation and its government: parochial loyalties, incomplete governmental control of its territory, conflicting values of elites and masses, and a lack of organizational ability for collective purposes. This was seen as the problem of nation-building (Weiner, 1965).

## Conclusion

Functionalist development theory raised the questions and identified the issues which remain central to an understanding of Third World politics, many of which remain unresolved: What effect does the lack of effective political institutions have? Which types of political change are consistent with stability and 'integration'? What are the relationships between political norms, structures, and behaviour? How do new patterns of political authority emerge from old ones? How do governmental processes select and transform political demands into public policies? (Apter and Rosberg, 1994).

However, the attempt to establish a unifying theory of political development was eventually abandoned. Dependency theory, derived substantially from a critique of ideas about social and political development, gained in popularity. Definitions of 'development' proliferated, reflecting a fragmentation of interests into specialized studies of institutions, areas, and processes. Disillusionment with the lack of political development in many parts of the Third World made earlier theorizing appear 'naively optimistic'. Eventually, as new states turned increasingly to authoritarianism, the hopes of political science for a grand theory of political development faded, 'and interest, productivity and creativity abated' (Almond, 1987, p. 444).

# 3
# The Politics of Neo-Colonialism and Dependency

## Constitutional independence

The two decades following the Second World War saw the final and most dramatic wave of independence sweep across the European empires in Asia, the Middle East and Africa – either as a result of more or less peaceful negotiations between the leaders of the nationalist movements and the European powers, or as the outcome of wars of liberation. There followed 'one of the great transformations in modern history', when all but a few million of the 780 million people living in the colonial possessions of the imperial powers 'freed themselves from subject status' (Barratt Brown, 1963, pp. 189–90).

Politically, it was assumed that indigenous governments, representing the interests of local people rather than alien groups, would have sovereign state power at their disposal. Their relationships with the governments of other sovereign states would be those of independent nation states entering into treaties and agreements within the framework of international law. Economically, it was assumed that, following independence, the process of 'diffusion' would continue as capital, technology, and expertise spread. Foreign aid and investment would increase the productive capacity of the less developed economy (Mack and Leaver, 1979; Rosen and Jones, 1979).

However, a very different perception of the relationship between sovereign states is conveyed by the term 'neo-colonialism', originally coined by mainly Third World leaders who found that the achievement of constitutional independence and sovereignty did not give total freedom to the governments of the newly formed nation-states. Political autonomy was found to be something of a facade behind which lurked the continuing presence of powerful Western financial and economic interests. The end of colonial government was not seen by leaders such as Nkwame Nkruma, the First Prime Minister of Ghana and author of a book entitled *Neo-colonialism: the Last Stage of Imperialism*, and Julius Nyerere, the first President of

Tanzania and author of *Freedom and Development*, as ending economic colonialism.

The core of the neo-colonialist argument is that political and economic freedom cannot be separated. Economic power and the political power that flows from it reside elsewhere, even when 'independence' has been achieved (O'Connor, 1970). The new rulers of the former colonies found that major economic resources were controlled from metropolitan centres that hitherto had ruled their countries directly. Independence appeared largely symbolic.

Subtle and indirect forms of domination were made possible by the structure of the economies bequeathed by the colonial powers at the time of constitutional independence. Colonialism had failed to develop the economies of the colonized territories beyond the small but important sectors needed by the European economies, and for which colonial rule was imposed. The post-colonial economy was characterized by a high level of dependence on foreign loans, technology, foreign investment, and foreign aid which, together, often 'decapitalized' the host economy through a net outflow of capital, with more being extracted in excess profits than being invested locally (Rosen and Jones, 1979). For example, Latin America was a net exporter of capital in the form of profits and interest throughout the 1980s, contributing to economic stagnation and declining living standards, with average per capita income shrinking by 11 per cent, and the number in poverty increasing by 60 million to 196 million, or 46 per cent of the total population (Robinson, 1999).

## Dependency theory

The neo-colonialist model reflected the real, rather than symbolic, significance of independence from a colonial power. However, continuing economic relationships between poor and rich countries were not placed in a broad theoretical framework to produce an interpretation of the continuity between imperialism and independence. This was not achieved until the idea of neo-colonialism was incorporated into a theory about an international system of economic subordination.

Dependency theory originated in the analysis of Latin American countries where independence had been achieved in the early or mid-nineteenth century, but where problems of foreign economic exploitation persisted, similar to those found in countries that were still colonies, or had only recently achieved independence. It adds the idea of 'peripherality' or 'satellite status' to the concept of neo-colonialism (Philip, 1990). It was designed to explain why the political benefits of industrialization through import substitution had failed to materialize. Industrialization was expected to strengthen economic sovereignty and weaken traditional society. In Latin America, for example, the power of the traditional landed oligarchy would be undermined, paving the way for democracy. Industrialization should also redress the extreme inequalities found in post-colonial societies, and contribute to the integration of the rural masses who, formerly isolated on plantations and traditional farms, would become closely incorporated into society through new economic opportunities and improved standards of living. This would then contribute to the reinforcement of political stability. When the rural masses were marginalized by semi-feudal forces dominating the rural areas, political stability was always at risk.

Such economic integration would produce not only political stability, but also democracy. The state would gain legitimacy by its association with the industrialization process, and by contributing to social and political equality, as well as economic efficiency. National sentiment would be strengthened, especially for rural people hitherto allied economically and politically with rural oligarchies – economic and religious – rather than the state. The goal of import substitution and industrialization strategies was political integration into a liberal democratic state (Dos Santos, 1973).

Dependency theory sought to explain the failure of these strategies to solve the problem of dependency, or produce the intended political outcomes. By the end of the 1960s, dependency had increased, but now upon foreign capital goods such as machine tools, plant, and technology. Income distribution had become more, not less, unequal. Inequality developed a new dimension – that between the rural and urban areas. People displaced from the land were not absorbed into new industrial activities and thereby integrated into the social fabric, largely because the new industries were capital rather than labour intensive. New forms of marginalization were created in the slum populations gathered on the fringes of the major urban and industrial centres. Instead of integration into a modern economy, disparities in social and spatial terms, together with new forms of marginalization, were brought into being as a growing proportion of the population found themselves without jobs, education, political influence, security, or proper shelter. Such people were politically highly volatile and therefore not committed to political stability. Their exclusion from politics did not engender consensus towards the state.

The state had become subservient to the multinational companies that controlled the industrialization process. Politics became more authoritarian and repressive, rather than liberal democratic and pluralist, as governments tried to cope with the social strains brought about by the industrializing process. Managing the industrial labour-force as well as the marginalized masses seemed to require military dictatorship, rather than pluralist democracy.

## The elements of dependency theory

There are five main strands in dependency theory: the idea of a hierarchy of states, the concept of 'underdevelopment', a view about the nature of capitalism, propositions concerning 'disarticulation', and the effect of economic dependency of the structure of political power.

*Hierarchy* finds its expression in 'centre-periphery' or 'metropolitan-satellite' models of relations between the great world centres of capital and the economies that are dependent upon them. A hierarchy of centres and peripheries connects all levels of exploitation between one country and another, and within the countries of the periphery. There is a steady extraction of surplus through the different levels in the hierarchy: from peasant to landlord; from landlord to local merchant; merchant to subsidiary of a multinational corporation (MNC); subsidiary to headquarters of the MNC; headquarters to the major financial institutions of the West. Mining, commercial, agricultural, and even military centres within the peripheral satellites constitute 'micro-metropolises' in relation to their hinterlands of small towns, mines, and *latifundia* which themselves relate in the same way to isolated workers. Similar relations of exploitation link industrial firms to the suppliers of components; large merchants and financiers to small traders and moneylenders; and city merchants and landowners to small rural producers and consumers (Frank, 1966 and 1969a).

A satellite within this hierarchical structure will only experience development when its ties to the metropolis are weak: 'no country which has been firmly tied to the metropolis as a satellite through incorporation into the world capitalist system has achieved the rank of an economically developed country' (Frank, 1969a, p. 11). In Latin America, the periods of autonomous industrialization have occurred historically during periods when trade and investment ties with Europe were loosened by European wars and economic recessions. The same applies to relatively isolated regions within peripheral societies: the less integrated into the world mercantilist and then capitalist systems, the greater the growth of manufacturing and exports. The least developed and most 'feudal-seeming' regions are those which had the closest ties to the metropolis in the past. The incorporation of a satellite into the metropolitan-led hierarchy chokes off development, making it more difficult for industrialization and sustained development to take place.

Underdevelopment refers to a continuing relationship of exploitation where, at any one level in the chain, the full economic surplus is not available for reinvestment. It is removed, ultimately accumulating in the metropolitan centres (Frank, 1969a; Dos Santos, 1973). Far from experiencing development as a result of ties with metropolitan centres (which is what

modernization theory tells us occurs), such ties hold the peripheral economy and society back.

Consequently, backwardness arises from the subordination of poor
countries to the development of rich countries. Underdevelopment could
not be explained in terms of an earlier stage on the path to modernity. The
circumstances under which advanced countries progressed cannot be
repeated: 'The now developed countries were never *under*developed,
though they may have been *un*developed' (Frank, 1966, p. 18).
Dependency is a continuing relationship, not confined to an imperialist
past but, rather, continuing in the neo-imperialist present. Formal political control is not necessary for a relationship of dependency and exploitation to be maintained through structures of foreign capital intervention.

Most peripheral countries retained pre-capitalist economic and political
relationship in a 'dual' society of progressive and traditional economies,
including feudal forms of political authority and economic structure.
Capitalist relations of production – private property, free wage labour, and
freedom of contract – were absent in many of the societies on the periphery. Goods were produced under pre-capitalist relations of production,
often feudalistic and involving peasant production on tenancies closely
controlled by landlords, controls that extended far beyond what is bought
by the payment of a wage. Dependency often sustained the production of
goods through feudalistic tenancies, bonded labour, controls over the
movement of the population, and other non-capitalist controls exercised at
the point of production.

Consequently, many Third World societies included the remnants of pre-
capitalist political authority, particularly in the rural areas. Landed
oligarchies dominated the local peasantries in ways that are inconsistent
with capitalist forms of political authority. The remnants of feudalism were
among those factors that made it difficult for democratic government to
survive. Political equality and the political freedoms that are the necessary
corollary of economic freedom are incompatible with the power of such
landed oligarchies.

The concept of *disarticulation* attempts to distinguish between forms of
international dependency. Since a developed capitalist economy can be
dependent upon another, it might be argued that dependency is not peculiar
to the poor countries of the Third World. For example, the UK economy is
dependent on other economies, including America and Japan, for foreign
investment, through foreign ownership of economic resources, and as a
result of interventions by MNCs.

Dependency theorists, however, argued that there is an important difference between that kind of dependency and the dependency experienced in
the Third World. When there are two developed economies with a degree
of inter-penetration of capital between them, the advanced nation remains

an independent centre of capital accumulation. This has consequences for the structure of political forces in that society. When, however, a peripheral society experiences dependency, a distinctive form of capitalism is produced. The poor society's economy is conditioned by the expansion of the stronger economies in ways which are quite different to the relationships between two developed economies. In particular, the conditioning or 'disarticulation' of the poor economy discourages internal growth by transferring the benefits of growth abroad (Frank, 1972a; Roxborough, 1979; Amin, 1982).

## The politics of neo-colonialism and dependency

The political manifestations of foreign economic involvement were difficult to describe in concrete terms, except for those for whom politics is merely an epiphenomenon of the economic. One reason for this was that much contemporary political science accepted the constitutional formalities as accurate representations of reality. Another was that the economy was seen as a completely separate sphere or system of action. The economic power of the decolonizing state and the political influence this conferred were not considered. Political science had largely concerned itself with institution-building during the decolonization process and the 'preparations' for independence in those colonies where the relationships between nationalists and the imperial powers could be described as such, involving more or less peaceful diplomacy and negotiation, rather than wars of liberation. Thereafter, politics was seen as the concern of an internally and externally sovereign state. Conflicts with other sovereign states, including the former colonial powers, were interpreted as matters of international law and diplomacy, and left to the specialists in those fields. The political aspects of international economic relations were neglected.

Even the political scientists and political economists who focused on the continuing economic dependency of post-colonial states rarely demonstrated how the mechanisms of the internal political consequences operated. The nature of the economic linkages could easily be described and debated, but the domestic political effects were largely left to be inferred from them. For example, the uneven distribution of primary resources among new states was said to have a greater effect on governmental orientations than internal interests. The power of foreign interests could even be measured by 'the ratio of export–import trade to overall GDP of the host country'. Mining concerns were said to constitute 'rival governments' (Bretton, 1973, pp. 25–6 and 205). General policy constraints on post-colonial governments were noted, such as limitations on monetary policy by the high propensity to import (Hymer, 1982). Integration into colonial economic blocks strengthened external influences on national governments' room to manoeuvre and national economic interests.

Despite such difficulties, an attempt can be made to distinguish between the different consequences of neo-colonialism and dependency for national politics in Third World states. Dependency means that domestic politics is dominated by foreign organized interests, comparador elites, multilateral and bilateral aid donors, the forces of globalization, and new class formations.


### The political power of external interests

The neo-colonialists can first be identified as organized interests, wielding political power internally, though externally oriented economically and carrying more political weight than economically marginal local groups. Foreign corporations, banks, and trading houses were well-positioned within the post-colonial economy to exert influence over national governments and counter nationalistic economic pressures. In the immediate post-independence years, indigenous small-scale capital entrepreneurs had nothing like the same influence as the multinationals which, in many cases, controlled the commanding heights of the economy. Companies such as Unilever, the Firestone Corporation or United Fruit dominated the economies of new states.

Organizations representing external interests were able successfully to contain the range of policy and ideological choices open to governments within limits acceptable to themselves (Berman, 1974). MNCs could inhibit development planning by limiting the government's tax raising capacity through transfer pricing and the movement of production from one country to another (Hymer, 1982). Foreign owners and managers of foreign capital received special advantages. In francophone Africa, for example, '*la presence française*' meant the complete penetration of public life by such interests and their pressure groups. In Kenya, European organizations representing the agriculture-based industries exerted great influence on policy-making because of dependence for competitiveness on European involvement. In the 1960s, the foreign owners of the greater part of non-agricultural capital were also represented locally by 'a substantial bureaucracy employed by the branches of foreign firms ... mainly themselves foreigners', although increasingly including Kenyan Africans. As this ownership spread, so the political power of foreign capital increased (though, in the interest of nationalist economic ideology and rhetoric, it had to be ritually humiliated: Leys, 1975, p. 174).

In Senegal and the Côte d'Ivoire, the influence of French interests on government boards, chambers of commerce, and informal meetings of businessmen exceeded the power of parliaments, cabinets, and political parties (Bretton, 1973). After independence in the Côte d'Ivoire, French private interests were dominant in the commodities which formed the basis of the economy (coffee, cocoa, and cotton). Manufacturing and processing were mainly in foreign hands, and governments had to obtain the approval of big foreign firms with the equipment, trade outlets, capital, and skills for groundnut shelling, cotton ginning, and cocoa cleaning, before formulating any policies towards indigenous producers.

'Rights' and privileges were demanded by foreign interests as a result of their economic power: land concessions, prospecting rights, exemptions from customs duties and taxes, and privileges in the cultural sphere. The economic cooperation offered by the USA often included the demand that the United States Information Agency ('a top intelligence arm of the US imperialists') be granted preferential rights to disseminate information (Nkrumah, 1965, p. 246). Cultural neo-colonialism also rested on the dependence of newly independent states on Western ideas and methods in education, administration, and the professions (Berman, 1974). The top executives of the subsidiaries of MNCs, the largest corporations in the country of operations, were influential in the social and cultural life of the host country, as well as in its politics. Governments dependent on the information coming from such sources were unable to work out their own solutions to the problems, such as poverty, which are of no particular interest to foreigners (Hymer, 1982).

The nationalists of the post-independence era found neo-colonialism to be operating in diverse ways other than legitimate pressure group activity. Nkrumah described how neo-colonialists 'slip past our guard' through military bases, advisers, media propaganda, evangelism, and CIA subversion. Military dependence on the former colonial powers for arms, training, advisers, and basic military doctrine has been seen as one of the most visible aspects of neo-colonialism. The success or failure of a *coup d'état* was often dependent on the level of external encouragement. In Africa, the 'metropolitan centres, especially France, have assumed the role of arbiters of the survival of particular regimes' (Berman, 1974, p. 6). France's neo-colonial role continued into the 1990s in Rwanda, Zaire, Gabon, and Togo.

## Comprador elites

Neo-colonialism and dependency led to the development of mutual interests between local elites and external organizations, including foreign governments and MNCs. Merchants, 'expanding and thriving within the orbit of foreign capital', formed a 'comprador element' of the native bourgeoisie which, together with 'native industrial monopolists', acted as 'stalwart defenders of the established order'. Large landowners not only benefited from foreign capital, but also found outlets for their produce, employment opportunities for members of their families, and rising land values in the neo-imperial connection (Baran, 1957, pp. 194–5).

Indigenous elites, the most important being the bureaucracy and indigenous management cadres employed by foreign companies, have an interest in maintaining economic arrangements in which foreigners hold a major stake. The close contacts between members of the national politico-administrative elite and external organizations then 'makes the distinction between domestic and international affairs meaningless' (Berman, 1974, p. 9). The 'mutuality of interest' across national boundaries between national economic elites and the senior management of transnational corporations and banks produced a 'transnational class formation' of an international oligarchy or 'corporate international bourgeoisie' with local and international 'wings' which ensured that public policy supported the interests of international capital (Becker and Sklar, 1987).

The foreigners are usually the dominant partners because of their superior resources, information, and negotiating skills compared with national governments. Governments, labour organizations, and most non-business institutions and associations are 'far behind' MNCs in terms of financial, technological, and administrative strength (Hymer, 1982). While foreign interests are thus included in the policy process, indigenous interests not represented by the elite are excluded. Institutions for representation and participation (parties, local governments, trade unions, and youth organizations) have been left powerless relative to the bureaucracy.

Dependent economic development also requires the demobilization by repressive governments of the popular forces which had formed movements for independence. Non-popular, pro-Western regimes, often resting on alliances between the military and indigenous propertied classes, were the political prerequisites of economic growth (McMichael *et al.*, 1974).

### Aid dependency

Another source of external influence on public policy in dependent states is official aid, which increasingly has been linked to 'conditionalities'. Aid is used as a lever to determine domestic government policy. Donors can withdraw vital aid if the neo-colonial governments fail to adopt policies favouring the interests of the donor government or firms based in the donor economy. In this way, the donor government secures strategic and diplomatic advantages, as in 1983 when the United States Congress made economic assistance to developing countries conditional upon support for

American foreign policy. Economic interests that the donor represents secure a profitable policy environment. Special loans from a multilateral agency such as the International Monetary Fund (IMF) or the World Bank come with conditions attached, such as a requirement to cut public expenditure programmes, particularly food subsidies and social services. Implementing them can lead to political unrest.

Other conditions on which bilateral aid is given have included the award of contracts to firms in the donor country and the purchase of arms. The 'war on terror' launched by the USA in 2001 has increased the amount of military aid available to countries identified as fighting terrorism, including the Philippines, Pakistan, Indonesia, Saudi Arabia, and Egypt, regardless of human rights concerns. Thus, donors continue to allocate substantial amounts of aid for strategic and commercial reasons, despite the ending of the Cold War.

Aid also affects the power structure of neo-colonial society. It increases the power of those in command of the state apparatus relative to any opposition. The power of the bureaucracy is enhanced by aid, this being the channel through which aid flows. Technical assistance programmes to national defence and police forces strengthen these sections of the political elite. Much of the aid from developed countries is in the form of military assistance, which has affected the distribution of political power in neo-colonial society. Food aid distorts the neo-colonial economy and society by enabling recipient governments to avoid land reforms and changes in methods of agricultural production which would reduce external dependency and the power of the landed classes. Aid has also biased development towards urban rather than rural society (Bauer, 1971; Lipton, 1977; Mack and Leaver, 1979).

Most donors now require public services to be privatized, despite the threat of increased poverty that this brings. Privatization has meant massive price increases unrestrained by regulatory bodies, forcing poor families to reduce spending on food and put school-aged children out to work. The increased cost of services has driven people into poverty in Vietnam, Bangladesh, China, and Cambodia. Services are often not supplied to poor communities which are not profitable. Allowing the private sector to supply profitable areas undermines the revenues of the public services left to cope with unprofitable communities. Privatization also drains staff from public services, especially in health care, again benefiting affluent members of society (Hilary, 2004).

Debt relief, which since 1996 has become a major objective of international aid for the most heavily indebted poor countries, also comes with strings attached. For example, the IMF and World Bank's Heavily Indebted Poor Countries Initiative requires 'sound' economic policies, the adoption of a poverty reduction strategy, and economic adjustment and reform

**Table 3.1**    *Aid as a percentage of GNI, 1990–2009*

| Economy | 1990 | 2000 | 2009 |
|---|---|---|---|
| Low and middle income | 1.5 | 0.9 | 0.8 |
| East Asia and Pacific | 1.2 | 0.5 | 0.2 |
| South Asia | 1.5 | 0.7 | 0.9 |
| Latin America and Caribbean | 0.5 | 0.2 | 0.2 |
| Middle East and North Africa | 3.7 | 1.0 | 1.1 |
| Sub-Saharan Africa | 6.2 | 4.0 | 4.9 |

SOURCE:    www.databank.worldbank.org.

programmes to maintain macro-economic stability. These requirements are not always compatible.

Even when aid policy requires recipient countries to feel 'ownership' of projects and programmes, and responsibility for their success, aid still comes with conditions attached. These may recognize the threats posed by economic reforms and restructuring, and aim for laudable objectives such as poverty relief and good governance. But developing countries still need to demonstrate that they provide an environment of policy and institutions that is conducive to reform. The latest doctrine on aid is that it should support reforms that originate from domestic political pressures. In the past, aid has not been very successful in stimulating donor-specified reforms. Recognition that aid is likely to be more effective and sustainable if a recipient country's government feels committed to the project now informs aid policy, but governments still know what donors expect and require.

Budgetary restraints, coupled with public scepticism about the effectiveness of aid in donor countries, led to a 25 per cent fall in the volume of aid in the 1990s. Aid to countries judged to have poor policy environments fell particularly sharply. As a percentage of developing countries' Gross National Income (GNI) (see Table 3.1), aid fell from 1.5 per cent in 1990 to 0.8 per cent in 2009. Despite conditionalities, more aid is required is some regions, notably Africa, where the economic growth needed to reduce poverty cannot be achieved by domestic savings and private investment.

**Dependency and globalization**

Since 1980, the integration of poor countries in the global economy has taken a new turn. The spread of formal, or procedural, democracy has freed an often vibrant civil society to mobilize disadvantaged and marginalized sections of society into different forms of political activism, including electoral politics. Yet, inequality and poverty have grown in most regions of the Third World, and especially Latin America. The opportunities created by democratization for lower class mobilization and political pressure have been negated by the economic forces of global capitalism, to such an extent that developing (and, indeed, developed) societies have become even more dominated by the interests of capital.

Globalization has strengthened the political power of international capital and its local representatives. Neo-liberal policies have been designed to integrate national economies into the global by enabling international capital to be fully mobile. Deregulation and privatization have removed the state from key areas of economic decision-making: 'the state defers to the market as the sole organizing power in the economic and social sphere'. However, the state retains its power over labour, through laws ensuring labour 'flexibility', reductions in real wages, the withdrawal of the social wage through the privatization of health care and education, the neglect of human rights, controls over political activism, and 'a transfer of income from labour to capital' (Robinson, 1999, pp. 44, 49). While the more strident forms of authoritarianism which characterized earlier forms of economic dependency may have largely disappeared, economic globalization having forced the dismantling of dictatorships, market forces have effectively countered the formal political rights of the non-propertied classes.

International capital also limits the policy choices of Third World governments. 'Free trade imperialism' under the hegemony of the USA deprives developing countries of the right to use protectionism to promote industrialization, denying them a policy option enjoyed by developed countries in their early stages of development.

Consequently, even the centre-left regimes in Brazil, Argentina, Uruguay, and Bolivia, elected with the expectation that their anti-poverty rhetoric would be put into operation, have benefited capital over labour. The power of employers over workers has been increased, wage controls have been imposed, and social programmes have been cut. Privatization has been extended and agribusinesses subsidized. Land redistribution policies have been abandoned, while MNCs have been encouraged to exploit natural resources (especially in Bolivia). The state regularly resorts to violence against political protest: 'the great majority of Latin Americans – workers, peasants, the unemployed and the poor – have suffered grave consequences as a result of the support given to "centre-left" parties and coalitions by movements to which they belong' (Petras, 2006, p. 290).

Structures of socio-economic power remain intact and reflected in the class nature of public policy. Government ministers have strong ties with international and domestic capital, and financial institutions – banks, the

World Bank, and IMF. These currently dominant capitalist interests are confronted by trade unions, mass movements in urban areas, landless agricultural workers, poor peasants, and Indian militants. In Colombia, the Revolutionary Armed Forces have yet to be defeated. Yet, it is often easy to co-opt the leaders of popular movements and economic organizations with lucrative government posts (Petras, 2006). The populism of ostensibly left-leaning politicians has proved to be a veneer covering the inevitable disparities in political power under global capitalism.

States that incur the displeasure of the USA and its allies may also have to face the threat of 'humanitarian intervention', including military invasion, to promote democracy, enforce capitalism, and secure elites and governments committed to protecting the national interests of the USA as represented by neo-conservative values, through 'authoritarian social engineering'. Contemporary imperialism thus brings about a kind of cultural revolution in 'liberated' states by creating a vacuum in which there is no consensus about the shape of post-intervention society. Political space is created for conflict between irreconcilable interests such as Iraq's Shiites and Sunnis, or between capitalism's newly impoverished and its new economic beneficiaries (Kiely, 2010, pp. 194–203). 'Humanitarian' intervention can too easily become an excuse for using military force to depose a ruler with acts of dubious legality which escalate beyond original intentions, and where the real objectives of the interventionists is to secure economic benefits for their own country. Libya in 2011 is an obvious case in point. When the West's economic and political interests are best served by the incumbent government, as with oil supplies and military bases in Bahrain in 2012, less concern is shown about the repressive nature of the regime.

The humanitarian argument is also invoked when other justifications for military interventions are exposed as fraudulent. When the official reasons for the invasion of Iraq in 2002 were shown to be untrue, and it became necessary to distract attention from the direct access to Iraq's oil reserves gained by Western oil companies, the US government claimed that it was humanitarian to overthrow a tyrant. The US-led invasion of Afghanistan in 2001 was initially justified as self-defence against terrorists sheltered by the Taliban regime. Subsequently, it was portrayed as a humanitarian and pro-democracy deposition of a repressive regime.

## Dependency and class structure

Finally, class structure is also affected by economic dependency. The powerful indigenous groups in Third World societies (merchants, landowners, financiers, industrial capitalists, privileged sections of the labour force, and state bureaucrats) are junior partners within the structure of international capital or 'satellite classes whose interests are tied to the *dependencia* syndrome' (Rosen and Jones, 1979, p. 254; Schuurman, 1993). These 'clientele classes' have a vested interest in the existing international system and perform domestic political and economic functions on behalf of foreign interests. They enjoy a privileged, dominant and 'hegemonic' position within society 'based largely on economic, political or military support from abroad' (Bodenheimer, 1971, p. 163). The policies of governments reflect the vested interests of the ruling class in the continuation of dependency.

The following clientelist elements can be identified:

> Large-scale industrialists involved in production for the local market and with a powerful presence in the state are more likely to be *associate power-sharers* with imperial interests. Import-exporters tied to foreign markets, shipping and credits are likely to be *dependent power-sharers*. Joint ventures, in which industrialists produce for foreign markets, drawing on foreign technology, capital and management, and with little direct representation in the state, are likely to be *subordinate collaborators*. (Petras, 1981, p. 18)

Dependency thus produces a locally powerful indigenous class of merchants not engaged in production, which is primarily in the hands of foreign enterprises, while the emergence of an industrial bourgeoisie is blocked. So, the development of the political institutions upon which a domestic bourgeoisie thrives – those of the liberal democratic state – is blocked, too. The nature of dependency has a profound impact on the development of the state and the political forces within it. The capitalist state in its democratic form requires a certain kind of ruling class, one whose interests will be protected by such a state. If it does not have such a unified ruling class because of external dependency, the political consequences will be some kind of authoritarian regime (see Box 3.1).

The class structure of peripheral society is determined by the position of that society in the international division of labour – whether the country has been predominantly an agricultural export economy with a rural-based oligarchy, an enclave economy based on the extraction of natural resources, or an import substitution economy with an industrial and financial bourgeoisie. None of these ruling classes has a vested interest in the reproduction of a working class through better health, housing, and education because there is a surplus of labour in excess of industry's needs created by a combination of stagnating agriculture, population growth, and capital intensive industrialization (Hein and Stenzel, 1979).

**Box 3.1   *Class in Brazil***

In Brazil, groups 'expressing the interests and modes of organization of international capitalism' gained disproportionate influence over policy-makers during industrialization. An ideological as well as economic affinity between the holders of economic power and the 'anti-populist' sectors of the military and technocracy enabled the latter to gain in influence not only in modernizing the administration, but also in the repressive functions of the state, culminating in the *coup d'état* of 1964. Other sections of the ruling class declined in power – including agrarian, merchant, and some industrial interests, the traditional bureaucratic component of the middle class, and career politicians – while organized sections of the working class were successfully marginalized.

Changes in the relative power position of different elites and classes were expressed through the accumulation process, requiring that 'the instruments of pressure and defense available to the popular classes be dismantled' so that wage levels could be kept low. This included unions and political organizations through which wage earners had defended their interests during the populist period. In allowing the military to repress the working class, parts of the bourgeoisie lost control of the political process, especially the party system, elections, press freedom, and liberal education.

Different 'patterns of dependence' accounted for shifts in the relative power of different classes. Moving beyond import substitution in an attempt to reduce dependency meant moving away from a stage of development that was 'significantly controlled by the local bourgeoisie'. The role of international monopolies became comprehensive, including the remaining areas of primary exports, the private manufacturing sector, and even public enterprises such as the state oil monopoly PETROBRAS. The political consequence of this economic realignment was an autocratic, developmentalist, military-bureaucratic regime (Cardoso, 1973).

## The independent state and class power

The conclusions reached by dependency theorists have not gone unchallenged. Critiques have focused in particular on the significance of independence for indigenous class structures, the economic performance of some post-colonial states, dependency theory's level of generality, and the problematic concept of 'hierarchical' relations between states.

The view that formal political independence had not substantially modified the relations of domination and exploitation between the capitalist imperialist powers and the new states of the Third World was refuted by the British Marxist Bill Warren (1973 and 1980). While not denying that imperialism persisted 'as a system of inequality, domination and exploitation'

(1973, p. 4), Warren argued that the term 'neo-colonialism' obscured the role played by the achievement of formal sovereignty and its consequences. Independence, together with other socio-political and economic trends, had created the conditions for significant capitalist industrialization. These trends included collaboration between imperialist and Third World governments to suppress anti-capitalist movements.

Political independence, far from being a sham, represented a significant change in the internal politics of former colonies, mainly because it provided a focus for the domestic state management of economic processes. The newly independent state became the focal point of the economy. Formal independence gave Third World states 'institutional control'. The powers to establish central banks and para-statals, enforce export and import currency controls, and implement taxation and public spending 'stem directly from independence' and affect far more than industrialization, especially the reinforcement of capitalist social relations of production, commodity production in agriculture, and economic restructuring 'along lines more suitable to a successful indigenous capitalism' (Warren, 1973, p. 13). The state exercised powers to direct investment and channel external capital whether from aid, MNCs or foreign countries. This led to it becoming a significant actor in the national political system and not totally subject to external political forces.

Third World states, and the elites which controlled them, proved able to negotiate successfully with foreign investors over profit levels, wages, rents, pricing policies, volumes of output, transportation needs, sources of supply, taxes on MNCs, export policies, and other interventions in the domestic economy. They had shown themselves capable of taking controlling action against foreign firms located in their territories, including nationalization, the acquisition of majority shareholdings, joint ventures and service contracts. Independence provided opportunities for the national bourgeoisie, liberal reformers, democratic socialists, communists, or military populists to alter relationships with rich countries. Independent governments could enter into alliances and trade agreements that were not open to them before, strengthening their bargaining positions in international economic relations. The bargaining power of newly independent countries was further increased by collective organizations such as OPEC and the Andean Pact.

Neo-colonialism meant only that newly independent governments could not *immediately* exert their bargaining power, because of skills shortages and delays in establishing effective state institutions and representation on international bodies. It also provided ideological support for, and international acceptance of, 'Third World bourgeois nationalism' – 'a fundamental ideological condition for the creation of modern nation-states out of states previously characterized by feudal particularism, religious and communal division, and all varieties of patriarchal backwardness' (Warren, 1980, p. 185).

Post-colonial growth and development were thus based on increasingly autonomous, nationalistic, political leadership, and produced conditions for the development of capitalism *significantly* different from those preceding formal independence. Capitalist forces might have been exploitative (as they always are), but at least they were national. National classes and their political representatives acted autonomously towards subordinate classes and foreign interests. National independence meant that the fundamental political conflicts were between classes, not nations (Brewer, 1980).

New ruling groups, often petty bourgeois in nature, could mobilize themselves. The absence of a fully formed national bourgeoisie has been compensated for by a state apparatus which has assumed the role of a bourgeois ruling class. So, Third World societies had acquired their own indigenous ruling class, not in the form of a private property-owning bourgeoisie but in the form of a public property-directing state apparatus, particularly the bureaucracy. Conditions increasingly existed for the formation of a national bourgeoisie and, therefore, the forms of control, management, and politics that such a class requires. The state became a focal point of political pressure of an urban petty bourgeoisie demanding higher standards of living and consumption, all of which encouraged manufacturing and industrialization.

Kenya provides an example of the emergence of an independent, indigenous, capital-accumulating bourgeoisie under conditions where, according to dependency theory, it could not happen. A class of agrarian capitalists was able to use its strong representation in the state apparatus to increase the rate of indigenous capital accumulation through policies on trade licensing, monopolies, state finance capital, private credit, and state capitalist enterprise (Leys, 1978). Independence also encouraged the development of social movements which gave added momentum to economic development. Popular, diffuse indigenous pressures for higher living standards were stimulated, a major internal influence sustaining industrialization policies. Therefore, it should not be assumed *a priori* that an independent local capitalist class cannot develop. Rather, the factors that stimulate or inhibit its development should be analysed. Among the former are the scope for rural capitalism, the significance of the informal sector, and global capitalism. Among the latter are ethnic conflict, state administrative capacity, and parasitic political leadership (Leys, 1996).

Other problems arise from dependency theory's treatment of class. First, the theory's revolutionary socialist solution to the problem of dependence does not carry conviction in the absence of a structural analysis that demonstrates there are classes or movements on which a revolution could be based. There is very little analysis of oppression, exploitation, or class-based organizations. The failure to explain underdevelopment by reference to the interplay of political, social, and economic forces thus exposes dependency theory to the charge that it is ahistorical (Leys, 1977).

Second, spatial entities and social classes are conflated. Relations between classes, such as landlords and peasants, are presented as comparable to relations between geographical tiers in the metropolitan satellite hierarchy. Relations of exploitation among classes are identified with transfers of value between spatial regions. The implication is that an exploiting class at one stage in the centre-periphery hierarchy is exploited by the class at the next higher stage. Such an assumption provides no basis for an analysis of the political behaviour of different socio-economic groups when 'the real relation of exploitation is a direct wage relations between the workers and the corporation as a unit of capital' (Brewer, 1980: 173).

Third, the problem of why capitalist societies find it so difficult to sustain the institutions and forms of state that are associated with the development of capitalism is not fully explored. The concept of 'disarticulation' takes us a little further than saying that propertied classes that do not like what is happening under parliamentary government do not hesitate to support military intervention, or that there is a contradiction between the material inequalities of capitalism and the political equality of democracy. But that contradiction is an inadequate explanation in many Third World countries where there is no fully developed working class.

Finally, dependency theory over-generalized its treatment of social classes. Its weak analysis of the class content of the metropolitan-satellite 'chain' means that the qualities of the different social relations within it are left unspecified. The analysis of class in dependency theory is thus insufficiently dynamic. Dependency theorists failed to examine changes in class relationships within the periphery which could alter relationships with external interests. For example, the emergence of new classes can cause 'shifts in peripheral economic activity and relations with the metropolis', as when metropolitan interests are 'displaced' from the agro-mineral sector by national social forces such as peasant and industrial labour movements or the petty bourgeoisie (Petras, 1975: 305).

## Dependency and economic performance

It is difficult to reconcile the impressive growth in per capita incomes achieved by a number of dependent economies with dependency theory. Some newly industrialized countries (NICs) confirmed the significance of the state in autonomous national economic development and of the national bourgeoisie in using that state apparatus in order to promote high rates of growth along capitalist lines. The NICs have been classified among the most *dirigiste* regimes, with state intervention at all levels in support of private capital. They are among the most planned, and some would say corporatist, economies. In supporting private capital, the state has inter- fered with the free operation of market forces by the suppression of organ- ized labour, the lowering of wages, and the weakening of political opposition to government policies. Foreign investment has been welcomed. Protected enclaves have been provided, such as free trade zones for high growth activities in which enterprises qualify for tax relief and enjoy a docile labour force, and where import tariffs and export licences are easily available. All this has been provided on behalf of what appears to be a dominant property-owning class.

So, the NICs require us to think again about neo-colonialism. Their histories strongly suggest that not everything is determined by the interna- tional division of labour, and that political leaders can exploit, within limits, commercial links (to diversify trade), domestic assets (or even liabilities, such as debt), and a range of external sources of aid and loans (Seers, 1981). Elsewhere – for example, Zambia, Saudi-Arabia, and Sri Lanka – the capitalist sectors have developed when foreign investment has been used to produce goods for world capitalist markets. In some African countries, too, capitalism 'has accomplished more than dependency theory allows' (Leys, 1996, p. 121). What has held development back is lack of know-how, enterprise, capital, and pre-capitalist social and political tradi- tions (Nove, 1974). Relations between centre and periphery are non-zero- sum games, so 'economic relations with the metropolitan centre may act as an enormously powerful engine of growth in the periphery' (Cohen, 1973, p. 217). Foreign capital, even with a net outflow, can add to the total of domestic capital by the multiplier effect of investment-generated local payments such as wages, taxes, and purchases of local supplies. Developing countries can also reduce their dependency by using bargain- ing strength derived from the developed economies' dependence on them (Philip, 1990). It is also reasonable to argue that, in some regions, develop- ment requires more, not less, foreign intervention in the form of capital investment (Emmanuel, 1974 and 1976).

Such criticisms have received some support from comparative statisti- cal analysis. An analysis of data on 30 tropical African countries in the middle and late 1960s found measures of dependency unrelated to economic performance variables. In the mid-1960s, African countries with high ratios of exports and imports to GNP, and high levels of foreign capital, had the best economic records. However, when this research made a distinction between 'market dependency' (a generalized feature of the international capitalist system) and 'economic power dependency' (meaning an economy conditioned by the decisions of individuals, firms, and agencies in metropolitan centres), it found the latter negatively related to economic performance, lending support to dependency theory (McGowan, 1976; McGowan and Smith, 1978).

## Levels of generality

Dependency theory operates at too high a level of generality and conceptual imprecision for it to be refutable at the macro-level, or applicable at the micro-level (Higgott, 1983; Leys, 1996). It is too static and unhistorical to explain successfully the distinctive elements of economic and political development in backward countries, and the mechanisms of social reproduction, modes of social transformation, and modes of politics. Operating at such a high level of generality makes it difficult to focus on the specifics of a particular country at a particular moment in history and how important they have been to development prospects (Philip, 1990). Past politics, and policy instruments in particular, receive only cursory treatment (O'Brien, 1975). The size of a developing country's population, its ethnic or linguistic composition, its degree of self-sufficiency in natural resources (particularly energy), its physical location in relation to countries better endowed in terms of population, technology, or military threats – such factors make a great deal of difference to the prospects for development but tend to be overlooked by dependency theory. They cannot be described merely as features of world capitalism, or the chain or hierarchy of metropolitan-periphery relationships. As factors affecting the room for manoeuvre which governments have, they would not disappear if the international capitalist system did not exist. So, any explanation which overlooks such details must be deficient (Seers, 1981).

The function of the state in Third World societies cannot be reduced to external, international economic influences. Legacies of authoritarian government, ideologies of corporatism and populist nationalism, patterns of patron–client relations, the aggregation of local interests, the internal evolution of social and political forces – all produce variable styles of state action that are not wholly externally induced (Long, 1977; Smith, A. D., 1979). Hence, the importance of considering the evidence supporting different theories of the Third World state (in Chapter 4).

## Hierarchy

Restricting the idea of a hierarchy of domination or influence to relations between rich and poor countries is also questionable. Critics have denied that there are qualitative as well as quantitative differences between rich and poor countries which make their dependency distinctive in international terms. Dominance, dependence, influence, and the inter-penetration and internationalization of capital apply just as much at the core or centre of the world capitalist system as at the periphery (Kay, 1975; Lall, 1975; Bernstein, 1979). 'Interdependence' and 'dominance' better express relations between states, because 'dependence' implies that some countries are economically independent, which is never the case (Brewer, 1980, p. 178).

Dependency theory's argument is that in the core economies cultural, legal, and political institutions are the product of indigenous development in the way that they are not in peripheral, and particularly ex-colonial, societies. Here, institutions have developed from those originally imposed from outside. The class structure of dependent societies is also more a reflection of external economic interests than of the distribution of material resources and interests within the country (Larrain, 1989). What is significant in Third World dependency is the representation in some general sense of external foreign interests, rather than a class structure – and political configurations representing it – which are purely contained within the borders of that country.

But does this provide a firm analytic base for distinguishing dependent from non-dependent politics? Class relations in poor countries, where the rich benefit from mutual interests with the rich in rich countries, seem comparable to class relations in developed countries. So, perhaps all societies are in the pyramid of social, political, and economic dominance, with the apex occupied by the most powerful capitalist country and the bottom by the poorest countries. It is difficult to find some special horizontal dividing line which separates dependent from independent economies and societies.

## The political significance of independence

It is easier to judge the economic analysis underpinning theories of neo-colonialism and dependency than to evaluate their contributions to an understanding of Third World politics. The main problem is that dependency theory does not make a systematic attempt to demonstrate the political consequences of dependency. It was predominantly an explanation of economic relations, leaving political relationships to be derived from them. It has a distinct tendency to see the state as epiphenomenal – that there is nothing to be explained in terms of the state, social classes and movements, politics, and ideology other than as derivatives of the economy and without an independent role of their own. The state is merely a consequence of relationships and power structures that lie elsewhere – namely, in the economy (Leys, 1977; Goulbourne, 1979; Hoogvelt, 1982).

Empirical tests of dependency theory have produced conflicting results as regards political consequences. Analysis of cross-sectional aggregate socio-economic and political variables for 20 Latin American states in the 1960s found the *greater* the dependency, the higher the level of political participation, the better the government's democratic performance, and the less chance of military intervention, though the greater the level of civil strife. But a study of Africa in the 1960s found that dependence and inequality were related – in line with hypotheses derived from dependency theory (McGowan, 1976; Vengroff, 1977; McGowan and Smith, 1978). A difficulty with this type of test is the operationalization of concepts. The serious limitations of aggregate data techniques are shown by some of the indicators used to measure aspects of a 'dependent' economy and society – the level of unionization and voting turnout as measures of class structure, for example (Kaufman *et al.*, 1974).

## Conclusion

The critique of neo-colonialist explanations and dependency theory can be summarized as a doubt that dependence can be causally related to underdevelopment. Dependence is either so general that it fails to have any explanatory value in the context of poor societies, or it arbitrarily selects certain features of international capitalism to produce a definition of dependence. Those features similarly do not allow the important distinctions between rich and poor, developed and underdeveloped, independent and dependent to be made in the way that dependency theory wants to.

Nevertheless, dependency theory served an important function in the analysis of development, especially in Latin America (Larrain, 1989). Its emphasis on the weak and relatively dependent position of the less advanced economies of the world was timely and a necessary corrective of much development theorizing at the time, especially ideas about unilinear economic development and 'dual economies' (Luton, 1976). It called attention to the ideological implications of pluralistic and structural-functional development theorizing, challenging the conventional wisdom that economic development in Latin America is inevitably consistent with US interests (Ray, 1973, p.6). Its 'militant critique' of a highly ideological developmentalism that ignored social classes and treated the state as an instrument of popular will or the public interest, showed that underdevelopment was not a 'primal' or 'original' condition. Dependency theory 'stimulated the empirical study of institutional and structural mechanisms of underdevelopment' such as MNCs, fiscal policies, capital expenditures, and aid programmes (Leys, 1977, p. 93). It showed that capital does not necessarily break down non-capitalist modes of production, but can bolster 'archaic political and economic forms' through alliances with pre-capitalist social forces.

Neo-colonialism and dependency arise in large part from the need felt by developing countries for investment capital that cannot be sourced locally. Foreign exchange crises caused by the fluctuating value of primary products and insufficient domestic savings can only be averted by borrowing, foreign investment, and aid. The modern and dynamic sector of the economy consequently falls increasingly under the control of MNCs, giving them a growing role in the economic development of poor countries.

The political consequences of this growing economic presence affects the state in the Third World which, as will be shown in Chapter 4, facilitates globalization by creating the conditions which enable international capital to remain a major force in domestic politics. Consequently, Western states continue to exploit their advantages and power over Third World economies, mainly through 'global' corporations with national roots.

# 4
# The State and Politics in the Third World

## Analysing the state

The different attempts to explain the nature of Third World politics in terms of encounters with richer countries make reference to the form of the state and the configuration of political interests sometimes articulated by the state and sometimes suppressed by it. There are contrasting theoretical perspectives to assist understanding of the state in the Third World. The nature of the state – the institutions through which legitimate power (political authority) is exercised and enforced – is central to the study of politics in any country. Third World conditions produce additional reasons why the analysis of the state is necessary for an understanding of politics in developing countries.

First, there is the legacy of colonialism which social scientists of very different ideological points of departure have recognized to be a formative influence on the contemporary state in developing countries. The key question posed here is whether the post-colonial state can develop the attributes of a pluralist political system or a distinctive relationship to new class formations. The next two sections of this chapter present these contrasting interpretations of the state in post-colonial society.

Second, there is a controversy between the proponents of society-centred and state-centred approaches to the state, the former presenting the state as an arena for the resolution of conflicts between private interests, the latter regarding the state as an independent force with its own policy agenda (Nordlinger, 1987). The conviction that the state must be 'brought back in' to politics will be assessed in this chapter, together with the claim that, in so doing, the socio-economic context of politics is in danger of neglect.

Third, there is a controversy about whether the forces of globalization have rendered the state obsolete, or at least transformed state power. This forms the latest stage in a long debate about whether states in the Third World are capable of governing, why some have been so much more successful than others in bringing about development, and why seemingly strong state structures frequently fail to implement policies and programmes.

## The pluralist political system

We saw earlier that political developmentalists preferred the language of the political system to that of the state, encouraging us to think of the institutions and processes at the centre of government in politically neutral terms (Coleman, 1960). Following the ideas of the German sociologist Max Weber, the functionalists saw the political system as a set of social relationships for converting, through the use of legitimate physical compulsion, demands and supports into outputs – decisions, statutes, laws, regulations, investments, and so on. Government then becomes a neutral set of arrangements consisting of political institutions and recognized procedures for interpreting political demands, resolving political conflicts, and producing outputs that satisfy those demands.

From this perspective, the state is perceived as an arena in which conflicting interests compete for scarce resources. It is a means of managing competition, so that the state is recognized as a legitimate way to settle such conflicts. The pluralist view of the political system sees its governmental functions as neutral in relation to the interests of different groups in society. It may be likened to an umpire, administering impartially the rules of the game without bias in favour of any particular player. The pluralist view of the state sees modern society as divided into competing elements which nevertheless find a kind of equilibrium. None is persistently more dominant than any other. None gets its way to the exclusion of others to a disproportionate extent. In this respect, pluralists are building upon traditional ideas of liberal democracy and the role of the state – though, rather than focus on the individual as the unit of analysis, they are focusing on groups. They see society as consisting not of atomized individuals – the egotistical rational person seeking their own interests in a society which the state has a duty to preserve – but of groups and associations. Only by cooperating with similarly placed and like-minded people can individual interests be protected. Complex modern societies produce such associations for the articulation of political interests.

Pluralism finds equilibrium in the power of different groups, partly because of cross-cutting loyalties. No group will have an interest in pushing its demands excessively to the exclusion of other groups in society because individuals are members of a multiplicity of groups and associations. As producers, our demands for higher incomes from wages will not be pushed to an excessive degree because we are also consumers who have to pay the price of those increased costs of production. Attachments and loyalties cut across other groups as well. There is not only a balance of competing forces, but also multiple memberships of different and sometimes overlapping groups. This serves to reduce extremist demands.

In the context of poor and developing societies, the pluralist view of the state assumes that, as pre-capitalist social structures and economic arrangements are replaced by capitalism and industrialization, so the authoritarian political institutions associated with the pre-capitalist era, especially feudalism, will also be swept aside. They will be replaced by the institutions of the liberal democratic state, perhaps in the form of a parliamentary democracy in which interests are protected by freely formed associations, freely competing electoral alliances, and freely articulated ideas about public policy preserved and protected by civil and political rights such as freedom of speech and association, universal suffrage, and freedom of the press (Carnoy, 1984).

Such an approach to the state is also likely to see a sharp distinction between society and polity. It does not reveal how much state intervention there will be. Those on the neo-liberal end of the liberal democratic spectrum of ideas will reduce the role of the state to the minimum. Those at the social democratic end will allow a considerable role for the state. But the extent of intervention will be an outcome of the interaction between competing groups. It will be the result of the success that some groups have in protecting their interests via publicly funded state interventions, as opposed to the success that other groups have in protecting their interests by maintaining levels of state activity, public expenditure, and taxation to a minimum, thereby maximizing the level of private incomes. But even though there might be considerable state intervention, even including elements of public ownership, polity and economy are seen as separate and independent spheres of social action.

Another feature of the pluralist state is to play down the significance of class divisions in society. Liberal democratic and pluralist assumptions about society are that it may be disaggregated along occupational, gender, ethnic, or regious lines, but not into classes. Class may be used as a summation of some of those other more significant factors indicating occupation, income, and lifestyle. But class is not seen as an identity around which people form alliances in order to compete for scarce resources politically. If a concentration of power is found, as in some undeveloped political systems, it is assigned to particular groups or elites, such as the executive and bureaucracy in a tutelary democracy, the military in a modernizing oligarchy, or a dynasty in a traditional oligarchy (Almond, 1960). But a notion of class that involves mutual antagonism, and irreconcilable economic and political interests is rejected. So, there is no sense in the pluralist model of the state of diametrically opposed interests, one gaining only if another suffers.

This view of the state, though not particularly well-articulated, was adopted by some of the imperial powers in their attempts – often hesitant, partial, and delayed – to prepare colonies for independence. These were the assumptions of the constitution-builders when independence seemed inevitable, and even desirable. They were also the assumptions of many within colonial society who collaborated with the processes of constitutional design. The leaders of some nationalist movements had similar views about the nature of the state. Many had, after all, been educated in the prisons and universities of the British Empire. Where they departed from it was less in the direction of Marxism than in the direction of some indigenous modification such as African socialism or the traditions of Indian village communities. Nationalist leaders such as Nyerere and Gandhi harkened back to what they regarded as a golden era preceding European intervention and, while not being so romantic as to think that the clock could be turned back, nevertheless advocated values which had been lost and which could be retrieved to the advantage of a society that would henceforth be developing according to its own prescription.

Historically, however, the post-colonial state has been far from neutral in its dealing with society, and socio-economic groups have been far from equally empowered in their dealing with the state. The state in the Third World has rarely, if ever, developed as a politically neutral institution. Under some circumstances, it has been able to maintain a degree of autonomy from social classes and other social divisions. But, usually, the state has been discriminatory, on either ethnic or class grounds.

The Third World state has frequently fallen under the control of elites from dominant ethnic groups. State power has then been used to promote the political and economic interests of those groups at the expense of others. For example, in Sudan the Islamic government has favoured the Arab people of the north against the African communities of the south. In Kenya, the post-colonial government has been dominated by the Kikuyu people, leading to communal violence whenever elections in an otherwise stable democracy are suspected of having been rigged. Since 1971, the government of Malaysia has implemented policies amounting to positive discrimination in favour of Malays, and against the ethnic Chinese, in business, education, and the civil service. The Malays, who constitute 60 per cent of the population, are dominant politically, while much economic power is held by members of the Chinese community.

Even where the post-colonial state has been weak, as throughout most of sub-Saharan Africa, it has not acted impartially. Rather, political elites have used state resources and patronage to benefit themselves and the communities they represent. Governance is dominated by prebendalism, under which state offices are exploited as 'benefices' of the office-holders. Legitimacy is bought by sharing the spoils with designated communities.

The state 'lacks the autonomy from society that makes it an instrument of collective action. Instead it tends to respond to community pressures and demands that undermine its authority as a public institution' (Hyden, 2006: 65).

Neither is the Third World state neutral in class terms. Capitalism in all its forms, including its current global stage, requires the exploitation of labour. For example, in Latin America's capitalist states the law operates in favour of the economically powerful, mainly by allowing them to break it with impunity. Powerful economic interests are able to flout the laws on taxation, money-laundering, child labour, slave labour, and drug-trafficking. Law enforcement agencies combine violations of the rule of law with actions to protect the rich from 'dangerous elements' amongst the poor and underprivileged. As a consequence, 'Political democracy, which now prevails across the continent, has not created a truly civil democracy where the rights of the citizen are scrupulously observed' (Munck, 2003, p. 69). Material, as distinct from legal, inequality results from the state's enforcement of neo-liberal economic restructuring, which everywhere adversely affects the poor and increases the share of national income taken by the rich.

Consequently, social movements, trade unions, and other organizations representing the poor and underprivileged find themselves engaged in struggles against the state, rather than other organized economic interests with the state as neutral arbiter. The neo-liberal agenda requires the state to protect and promote property rights, deregulate labour markets in favour of employers, and weaken trade unions: 'Historic rights and victories won by labour are being replaced and eliminated from the world of production' (Antunes, 2003, p. 235).

In the Third World (as elsewhere), the power to influence governments is never equally distributed. So, another precondition of democratic pluralism is missing. This inequality may result from restrictions on freedom of association imposed by the regime, or from a maldistribution of resources needed if social and economic interests are to be empowered.

In the first category are found countries where constitutional guarantees are absent or routinely violated in practice. In Burma, freedom of association is not protected by the Constitution. Only pro-junta organizations, into which the government has mobilized people, are permitted to be active in politics. Independent trade unions are illegal. In Iran, the Constitution permits the formation of political associations provided they do not violate 'the criteria of Islam or the basis of the Islamic republic' (Article 26). This enables the government to turn a blind eye to attacks by paramilitary groups on dissidents. There are no free and independent trade unions, and workers are denied the right to strike. Freedom of expression is compromised by censorship and the prosecution of journalists for comments critical of the regime. In Algeria, the government has withheld formal authorization from NGOs that have been critical of government policies. Human rights groups have faced harassment from the authorities. A number of Third World governments have used the post- September 11, 2001 'war on terror' as an excuse to criminalize the opposition and clamp down on civil society, including ethnic-based associations in Nigeria and community groups demonized as Western agents in Namibia, South Africa, and Uganda (Howell *et al.*, 2006, p. 15).

In addition, civil society has not developed in a way which gives all interests an equal opportunity to influence governments. In an era of global capitalism, the interests represented by business and industrial associations are dominant, forming as they do part of the ideological consensus on neo-liberal economic restructuring, which gives them greater access to government than other groups. They also have greater financial resources and greater sanctions to bring to bear on governments than workers, peasants, and the poor (Kamat, 2004).

## The post-colonial state

The pluralist view of the state has consequently been challenged by approaches which focus on the state as a potentially autonomous and dominant actor in the political process. A need was seen to 'bring the state back in' to political analysis. This was not only a reaction against modernization theory, which replaced the state with a concept of the political system in which governments mechanically converted demands into policy 'outputs'. There was also dissatisfaction with economistic interpretations of the state as epiphenomenon, giving economic and property relations such a determining significance that other institutions – political, legal, cultural, and ideological – become merely a reflection of them. Such economic reductionism was found in dependency theory, with its implication that the dominant class in a peripheral society could only play a comprador role.

Marxism provides a framework for the analysis of the Third World state, but offers not one but five concepts of the state (Jessop, 1977). First, there is the idea of the state as a kind of *parasite*, particularly through a privileged, bureaucratic caste. The state extracts resources from society not for purposes of social reproduction, but to sustain an elite. Governments become parasitical when officials and politicians use their powers to accumulate wealth for themselves or members of their families. This has been an all-too-familiar feature of post-colonial politics, especially in Africa. Political leaders have granted themselves permits, licenses, and loans which give them access to capital, foreign exchange, land, contracts, and business opportunities. Simple embezzlement of state revenues is another method.

Second, there is the idea of the state as *epiphenomenon*, when economic and property relations are given such a determining significance that other institutions – political, legal, cultural, and ideological – are merely a reflection of them and are entirely explained by their dependence on prevailing economic relations. An epiphenomenal view of the state finds evidence for the power of different classes in the structure of economic relations and the policies pursued by governments. The state is 'a moment of class power relations', as well as a set of political institutions. Under globalization, the nation state functions as 'a particular constellation of class forces and relations bound up with capitalist globalization and the rise of a transnational capitalist class'. Nation states 'advance the agenda' of global capital. Power shifts from national classes to those 'whose interests lie in global circuits of accumulation'. Government programmes to restructure economies in favour of exports, private markets, and the free movement of capital are 'an essential requisite for the activity of transnational capital'. A 'political restructuring' follows, redistributing power in society and state towards the interests of transnational capital and its local allies (Robinson, 2001, p. 165–85). In Central America, for example, 'the tremendous structural power that accrues under the global economy to the transnational elite and their local counterparts has shifted the terms of struggle between dominant and subordinate groups', exacerbating the concentration of economic resources in the elite and the pauperization of the masses (Robinson, 1998, p. 493).

Third, there is the idea of the state as an instrument of class domination, an executive committee for managing the affairs of the whole bourgeoisie. This comes close to being a view of the state as a neutral instrument which can be controlled equally effectively by any class which achieves a position of economic dominance. The state is not pluralistic in the sense of being a neutral arbiter, but is a set of institutions existing independently of social forces and which, at different stages in history, will be controlled in the interest of a dominant economic class, whether it be the landed aristocracy in a feudal economy or the industrial bourgeoisie of early capitalism.

The class structure of post-colonial society has not always lent itself to analysis in terms of capitalist class domination through the institutions of the state. Most societies emerging from colonialism did not have an industrial working class or indigenous bourgeoisie. The dominant class was likely to be bureaucratic rather than capitalist. The landed classes tended to be feudal rather than capitalist. The rural masses were divided between landless labourers and peasants, with frequent movements between the two groups. Foreign capital had also to be accommodated in the class structure.

However, as economic development has taken place, class conflict has formed a more familiar pattern. As post-colonial elites have accepted, or been forced to accept, a neo-liberal approach to the state, the state's role under capitalism of preserving the dominance of the middle classes has emerged in a purer form. Following the 1997–98 financial crisis in East Asia, the powers of the state have been rolled back, and class conflict under democratic political arrangements has had to be managed. Foremost here has been the coalition of business elites and the state in the control of labour. For example, in Thailand trade unions have been repressed, minimum wage legislation has been left un-enforced, and food staples in the urban areas have been subsidized. Education expenditure has been biased in favour of primary and tertiary education and against secondary, a pattern which is 'understandable from a political standpoint: mass education at the primary level extends government control and helps to instil a national identity, and good university education is necessary for the children of the elite' (Jansen, 2001, p. 361). The private sector has been released from government regulation, and the state has limited itself to investment in physical infrastructure, especially roads and irrigation, though over-concentrated in the Bangkok region. While poverty has declined, gains from economic growth have not been evenly distributed, leaving Thailand with the highest level of inequality in East Asia.

Fourth, there is the notion of the state as a factor of *cohesion*, where the state is involved in regulating struggles between antagonistic classes, and using both repression and concession to moderate and manage those conflicts while sustaining the economic and political dominance of the most powerful economic class, and preserving the social relationships which a capitalist economy requires. Here, the state operates through a combination of repression and concession. Zimbabwe under the Zimbabwe African National Union – Patriotic Front (ZANU-PF) government of Robert Mugabe provides examples of most forms of repression at the disposal of the state: the elimination of tribal enemies and political rivals, the intimidation of voters and leaders of civil society, and physical attacks on critical journalists and lawyers representing opposition activists. Opponents of a government or regime can be imprisoned or placed under house arrest, as in the case of Aung San Suu Kyi, the leader of Burma's democratic opposition who spent almost 18 years under house arrest. Harassment through the courts can also be effective in limiting opposition – as in Singapore, where opposition leaders are frequently sued for libel, sometimes facing bankruptcy as a result. Governments may give tacit support, or turn a blind eye, to the use of private paramilitary groups against the opposition. In Colombia, the military has been accused of supporting paramilitary groups in a 'dirty war' against human rights activists and civilians sympathetic to leftist rebels. In Syria, the response in 2011 of the Baathist regime of

President Assad to political demands for change included arbitrary arrest and detention, torture, imprisonment following rigged trials, close control of the media, and the use of tanks and artillery against protestors.

The alternative to repression when managing crisis in the capitalist state is the award of concessions to those most adversely affected by the economic system. These include subsidies to food, education, and health care. The poverty reduction strategies required of Third World governments as a condition attached to aid from the World Bank and IMF can be seen as safety nets to accompany the neo-liberal economic restructuring required by international capital, and a means of pre-empting political protest and dissent. For example, the Bolivian Emergency Social Fund was created to counter resistance to the economic 'shock therapy' of the New Economic Programme (Weber, 2004).

## The Bonapartist state

The idea of the state being a factor of cohesion, managing and manipulating class struggles without fundamentally damaging the economic system that preserves the dominance of a particular economic class, is close to the idea of the state as something that can stand aloof from the immediate interests of even the dominant economic class in society for a longer-term aim – that of moderating class conflict and preserving the social and economic system. Bonapartism is a model of the state that is not merely the product of a dominant class and an instrument to be wielded by whichever socio-economic group is dominant. It is not simply an executive committee of the bourgeoisie. The state is, rather, almost autonomous and able to free itself to a degree from civil society, not to manage conflict neutrally, but to protect the long-term interests of a bourgeois class against the irreconcilable interests of other classes.

To some social scientists examining the post-colonial state this interpretation seemed to be enormously perceptive and resonant. Post-colonial society appeared to have a number of competing bourgeois factions whose conflicts needed to be managed in the long-term interest of capitalist growth and the social institutions upon which such development depended – in particular, private property and the right of accumulation.

This model of state autonomy was inspired by a particular country, Pakistan, at a particular period in its history (see Box 4.1). It did not always fit the post-colonial situation in other countries. Imperialism and the penetration of foreign capital had been less intrusive in some regions than in South Asia. The internal social structure was consequently very different at the time of independence. In Tanzania, for example, the ethnic composition of society was relatively untouched by European intervention. It consisted

> **Box 4.1   *Relative autonomy in Pakistan***
>
> When Pakistan first succumbed to military rule in 1958, the relationship between class and state in post-colonial society gave the state *relative autonomy* from class control. The state in Pakistan in the 1950s was not merely a set of institutions controlled by a dominant class. Its autonomy was not complete because it was not totally neutral, or independent of all class forces. The state was neither autonomous in the pluralist sense, nor was it the prisoner of a single dominant class.
>
>     The specific circumstances of the propertied classes in Pakistan meant that three could be identified: a national bourgeoisie, whose interests centred on the ownership and control of industrial capital; an indigenous landed class dominant in the agricultural sector, and consisting of a relatively small number of wealthy and powerful rural families owning large tracts of arable land; and a metropolitan bourgeoisie. While the significance of a national bourgeoisie can be readily appreciated because they are actively present in the economy and polity, the metropolitan bourgeoisie is much less visible or tangible. The interests of these three propertied classes were found to be competing, but not contradictory. They were in competition with each other for the resources which were under the control of the state.
>
>     The state essentially performed a function of mediation between conflicting propertied classes. Their interests were not contradictory, since they all had in common one essential value – the preservation of private property in the social relations of production. But they had clearly competing interests. A particular kind of state was most appropriate for this mediating role, one that could free itself to a degree from the direct control of a faction of the bourgeoisie. Such a state needed a 'bureaucratic-military oligarchy', a regime that would be sufficiently removed from the immediate interests of any one of those three classes to be able to exercise independent power and manage conflict, provided it did not challenge their common interest in private ownership of the means of production. So, whereas the national bourgeoisie in a developed capitalist society, or the metropolitan bourgeoisie in a colony, could establish their dominance, this was not possible in post-colonial conditions where 'none of the three propertied classes exclusively dominates the state apparatus or subordinates the other two. This specific historical situation confers on the bureaucratic-military oligarchy in a post-colonial society a *relatively autonomous* role' (Alavi, 1972 and 1990).

of a large number of small groups with no pattern of inter-ethnic dominance. A class of relatively rich peasant cultivators developed, but not a class of large landowners receiving part of their wealth in rents. Some of the richer peasant producers became petty-capitalist, investing in other activities such as local trade, but the extent to which this constituted any kind of new socio-economic class was very limited.

The relations of production within the different societies that made up Tanzania were communal, based on settlements consisting of kin-groups, and lacking landlords or employers of landless labour. The relationships between producers were those of kinship and ethnicity. Some ethnic groups, notably the Masai, were pasturalist. By the time of independence, a class structure, brought about by the combination of indigenous economy and foreign intervention, hardly existed. Rural people produced goods on the basis of small-scale communities with land held in common. Land could not be alienated and accumulated. Rights to occupancy and cultivation alone attached to individuals and families. There was a relatively small basis for a landed oligarchy, or an industrial or commercial middle class, the last being mainly Asian in origin. An embryonic working class was also beginning to emerge at the time of independence based on textiles, motor transport, and tobacco processing.

The most powerful African class in the process of formation was as a petty bourgeoisie of teachers, civil servants, prosperous traders, and farmers. The East African colonial state had subordinated pre-capitalist, though non-feudal, social formations to the needs of colonial capitalism. Pre-capitalist agriculture had moved towards commercialization without 'quasi-feudal stopovers' and the indigenous bourgeoisie was confined to mainly Asian traders (Shivji, 1973 and 1976; Saul, 1974).

Thus, class conditions in Tanzania differed considerably from those in Pakistan. It is correspondingly more difficult to think of the state as having to mediate between well-articulated class interests, including those owning capital and those with only their own labour, as well as divisions within the capital-owning classes, including capital located outside the country. The metropolitan bourgeoisie, most notably represented by MNCs, was much more powerful than indigenous classes.

The post-colonial East African state had nevertheless not become international capital's 'executive committee'. It retained a measure of autonomy because of its role in the production process and strategic position within the economy. The growing level of state intervention in the economy, with the state as the country's major employer and the main vehicle for social mobility for those able to obtain educational qualifications, again appeared to parallel the Pakistan situation. The state was a means to economic power, rather than an instrument of an already dominant economic class. Class formation takes time, and African experience confirms that in the interim the state can independently act in a mediatory role and affect the process of class formation by the success or failure of its policies – for example, in protecting local firms from foreign competition (Kasfir, 1983, p. 8).

State autonomy was sometimes a temporary feature of the immediate post-independence period, quickly giving way to control by a dominant class. In Kenya, for example, the dominant class following independence was the metropolitan bourgeoisie. This was the interest that the post-colonial state articulated. The state in such a peripheral economy supported metropolitan capital against its main rival, a newly emerging property-owning middle class. The struggle did not have to be mediated. It had been won by metropolitan capital. The state performed municipal functions on its behalf. Domination of the mass of the population by foreign capital required the existence of domestic class interests, in this case the petty bourgeoisie, allied to foreign capital through joint interests. State power was not relatively autonomous but, rather, protected the dominant classes through policies to subsidize the petty bourgeoisie and subdue organized workers by means of clientelism, ideological domination, and official repression (Leys, 1975).

In India, too, the over-developed state was a temporary phenomenon. As society became more complex and the private sector grew stronger and more diversified, so the political institutions representing classes in society became stronger and the bureaucracy took on a more subservient role. A significant bourgeoisie emerged which, despite the presence of foreign capital, captured control of the state (Wood, 1977).

## An overdeveloped bureaucratic state

Another distinctively post-colonial feature of this theory of state structure is the idea of an overdeveloped bureaucratic state apparatus. Two factors in particular contributed to this phenomenon. First, colonialism produces a distorted state structure. Certain institutions which had been particularly significant for colonial government, and which had a relatively long history, had been highly developed – namely, the bureaucracy, the military, and the police. A central feature of colonial government was a heavy reliance on these institutions. Colonialism required a state structure which would enable control to be exercised over all indigenous classes. This state apparatus had to be bureaucratic. The bureaucratic-military nature of the colonial state constituted an 'overdeveloped' state.

The Indian subcontinent had probably had the longest history of democratic development of any part of the empire but, even here, the bureaucratic state apparatus was overdeveloped. This would be the case to an even greater degree in countries where there had been virtually no experience of parliamentary and representative government before independence. In territories where nothing had been done to prepare for democratic self-government, the distortion was even greater. Experience of parliamentary government prior to independence varied enormously. Even where it was considerable, the bureaucracy still emerged with prestige, power, and status, monopolizing the knowledge and expertise required for running a government and developing a society. Government was the main source of employment for professional people and the highly educated. It absorbed the supply of technical expertise. For example, long practice in the mobilization and organization of people for political ends through the Congress movement in India still did not produce a capacity to control a highly developed administrative system in the years immediately following independence.

Colonialism in Tanganyika had also left a relatively highly developed bureaucracy, although one that had not been extensively penetrated by Africans. Africans were only recruited into positions of influence in meaningful numbers on the eve of independence, when it was essential to replace expatriate officialdom with local people. The colonial state was paternalistic rather than mediatory. The state apparatus, particularly in its bureaucratic form, was more overdeveloped in relation to civil society and the private sector where capitalism, either in agriculture or industry, had hardly begun to emerge.

Second, this bureaucratization was intensified by the disproportionate involvement of the state in managing the post-colonial economy. Where the private sector is small, where the market as a basis for the arrangement of production and distribution is weak, and where the economic activity of the state is significant, the state becomes the key economic actor. It is the major employer. It plays a prominent role in managing the flow of international finance from aid, loans, and foreign investment. The state becomes the source of capital. It controls its use. An extensive state apparatus supports economic development, even when it is in the form of an emerging capitalist system. Public sector management, state marketing and rationing of scarce foreign exchange and consumer goods, state ownership, the provision of an infrastructure of communications, energy supply and transportation, the creation of a legal structure for commercial transactions, maintaining political stability to create confidence among investors – all are the responsibility of the state and contributed to bureaucratic overdevelopment.

Bureaucratic control over economy and civil society was extensive everywhere, following independence. Some countries, such as Tanzania, had single-party regimes. In addition to the state bureaucracy there was a party bureaucracy, adding to the overdevelopment of the state apparatus. The party's own hierarchy of officials corresponded to the hierarchies of state officials in the structure of administration. However, this system was somewhat paradoxical. Appointed state officials were powerful. But a party bureaucracy could constitute a counter-balance to the state bureaucracy and its colonial inheritance in terms of structures, processes of decision-making, status, and prestige. Party bureaucracies, arguably representing a democratic check on state bureaucracy, complicate the picture of the relationship between bureaucracy and other political institutions. To the extent that the two bureaucracies are highly integrated, however, especially when civil servants are appointed on the basis of partisan criteria, the distinction between the two organizations can become completely blurred. If a provincial commissioner (a civil servant) only occupies that office because the correct partisan credentials are held, to what extent are such officials a different species of bureaucrat as far as the ordinary citizen is concerned?

The bureaucracy could also be central to the interests of competing socio-economic groups – as in Mali, where it became the focus of political competition. In the absence of other fully developed institutions, political pressure and lobbying was directed towards the bureaucracy, which became the arena in which political conflict was fought out (Meillasoux, 1970).

The high-performing Asian economies have also managed economic development to varying degrees through bureaucratic and technocratic means, rather than through liberal democratic politics, with the state's technocratic elite operating autonomously from civil society and seeking 'bureaucratically determined goals' (Jones, 1997, p.199). The bureaucracy was insulated from 'growth-compromising pressures' from agricultural interests, and weak commercial and industrial classes. A meritocratic bureaucracy provided stability, a capacity for strategic planning, and competent, coherent administration. There was, however, successful 'collaborative linkaging' with economic interests, allowing the bureaucracy to mobilize resources for developmental aims (Weiss and Hobson, 1995, pp. 162–8).

## The bureaucratic-authoritarian state

In Latin America, the persistence of military regimes in relatively advanced societies with long experience of independence led to a different kind of bureaucratic dominance. The historical sequence typified by Brazil, Argentina, Chile, Uruguay, and Mexico through the 1960s and 1970s moved from rule by oligarchies of powerful families, through populist politics and on to bureaucratic-authoritarianism.

Contrary to the theory that economic development encourages more pluralistic and democratic politics, Latin America became more authoritarian. Higher levels of industrialization and growing GNP per capita were linked to retreats from democratic competitive politics. It is useful to compare the bureaucratic-authoritarian model with that of the relatively autonomous post-colonial state, because of the claim that, as societies develop economically and socially, the latter model becomes less viable. Latin America seems to present evidence of bureaucratic-authoritarianism accompanying, and even growing, as societies become more economically advanced.

In dependent economies, the process of modernization did not lead to the gradual enrichment of mass politics but, rather, to the collapse of political systems in which the working classes and lower-middle classes were important participants in, and beneficiaries of, the dominant coalitions. Populist politics, notably in Argentina under Peron, produced movements that sought mass support – but to maintain an elite, rather than to promote an ideological position. This is a form of politics from which the masses can acquire influence and benefits. The important question is why populism so often degenerated into repressive authoritarianism, often of a military character, together with a regressive redistribution of wealth in favour of the economically privileged.

Three factors in 'constellation' account for the movement to bureaucratic authoritarianism: regime, coalition, and policies. By *regime*, is meant the existence of civil rights, freedoms, electoral competition, and organized interests – compared with repression, intimidation, gerrymandering, ballot-rigging, and the other practices which undermine and destroy the democratic process. *Coalition* refers to the class and sectoral composition of the dominant political group. *Policies* refer to the distribution of resources among different classes and sectors of the economy. Each constellation is seen as the result of relationships between three key aspects of socio-economic modernization: levels of industrialization, levels of political activism among the lower classes (or 'popular sector'), and the growth of technocratic occupations in both the public and private sectors. Constellations of regime, coalition, and policies reflect constellations of levels of industrialization, activism, and technocracy.

Bureaucratic-authoritarianism is characterized by a *regime* in which electoral competition is eliminated and other forms of political participation are closely controlled by the authorities, a *coalition* of high level military and civil technocrats working with representatives of foreign capital, and a *policy* of promoting advanced industrialization.

One particular development identified here as more significant than others is the greatly increased role of technocrats in society. Technocrats do not have a great deal of time for democracy. Participation, consensus-building, negotiation, and compromise all run counter to the values of the technocrat. Democracy is seen as an obstacle to economic growth. The bureaucracy and the military are identified as being the main repositories of such technocracy on the state side, and forming a natural coalition with the technocrats leading the private sector. Managers and engineers, rather than shareholders, are the dominant influences in industry. A new professionalism within the military supports technocratic views of the economy and society generally. Problems are seen as needing solutions that can only be provided by those with the training and qualifications. Democracy gives way to the power of those with knowledge. This line of analysis touches upon other interpretations of military intervention in Third World politics. A coalition between civil and military officials seems natural – not simply because they have the same paymaster, but also because they espouse the same technocratic approaches to politics.

The origins of bureaucratic-authoritarianism lie in the need for governments to satisfy the demands of national entrepreneurs and the indigenous middle class, while at the same time enacting policies in support of foreign capital. Different countries have had different degrees of success in handling this contradiction. Brazil was better than Argentina at integrating the national bourgeoisie after establishing political and economic stability to ensure large injections of foreign capital. The case of Chile shows that the pre-*coup* crisis and post-*coup* repression in the 1970s were so extreme that there was great difficulty in attracting foreign investment.

Bureaucratic-authoritarianism is not exclusively associated with later phases of industrial modernization in Latin America. There are other regimes where it seems equally likely that the phenomenon has appeared at different phases of industrial development. Certainly, the 'regime' and 'coalition' features of bureaucratic-authoritarianism have been experienced in other regions of the Third World. What may be distinctive about the Latin American case is the association with a particular policy – that of promoting advanced industrialization. Further refinement of the concepts would make it possible to identify whether one type of policy is a necessary condition for a bureaucratic-authoritarian state, or whether certain kinds of regime and coalition are consistent with other policies for the distribution of resources within a society. In the case of Latin America, interaction between regimes and policy changes seems to cut across the bureaucratic-authoritarian/non-bureaucratic-authoritarian distinction (Collier, 1979). The possible explanations of the rise of authoritarianism are many and varied. Not all confirm the 'deepening of industrialization' hypothesis, or the preceding strength of the 'popular' sector.

## State–society dialectics

Inquiry into the Third World state encounters an ambitious attempt to produce a comparative framework designed to encompass states in all regions of the world, whatever their level of wealth, industrialization, or economic development. Here, the state was to be 'brought back in' as part of a dialectical relationship with a political environment that shapes state action and structure as well as being affected by them (Evans *et al.*, 1985).

The scope for autonomous state action varies according to the type of state structures available to support such interventions. Some states are better placed than others constitutionally, politically, and culturally. Bureaucracies vary in levels of centralization and integration. Constitutional powers vary in their degree of dispersal among sub-national governments. Administrative agencies differ in the degree of penetration by organized interests. State executives vary in their level of power over representative legislatures. Organizational structures are themselves the consequence of past state policies, which vary from country to country.

States will also vary in the extent of their capacity to implement their policies. Capacity is affected by such factors as the ability to control the state's territory, the availability of human and financial resources, and the organizational instruments available for the achievement of the state's objectives. The quality of such factors will not necessarily be spread evenly across all policy areas. The fact that, historically and comparatively, states are found to have different capacities in different policy areas warns against the categorization of states as either 'strong' or 'weak'.

The capacity of a state to intervene internationally or domestically also depends on the state's relationships with the social, economic, and political environment. Capacity is affected by relationships between state authorities and domestic socio-economic groups. For example, military success depends upon effective fiscal capacity which, in turn, requires a willingness on the part of key sections of the population to be taxed. In the domestic arena, successful state interventions, such as in pursuit of economic objectives, equally depend on relationships with economic interests. The successful pursuit of industrialization in a developing country, for example, may depend upon the state achieving autonomy from agrarian interests, as in Taiwan.

The capacity of states is more or less balanced by the capacities of organized sections of civil society and the international economy. Analysis of the state thus requires a method of inquiry that is *relational*. Effective policy implementation may be as dependent on networks of support as much as on the state's own instruments of intervention. State and society consist of actors in complementary, as well as conflicting, relationships.

Hence the importance of recognizing that states affect the development of the political process. States are powerful and autonomous organizational actors, capable of shaping society, as well as being shaped by it. Such recognition must extend to modern and emerging democracies, and not just totalitarian and authoritarian states, where the primacy of the state as an actor in control of social and economic development is more obvious.

Through its administrative, legal, and coercive systems, the state structures its relationships with civil society, as well as relations within civil society. First, state structures affect the political culture – on society's perceptions and judgements of political rules, roles, and processes – rather than it just being the product of cultural differences in political life.

Second, state structures affect the way collective action is mobilized for political ends, and the formation of political groups and movements. The configuration of interests and interest groups in a society reflects the composition of state interventions in society and economy. The state's organization, patterns of intervention in economic and social life, and public policies determine which group interests are activated, which social cleavages are politicized, and which political demands are pressed. Political identities and attempts to capture control of parts of the state apparatus are responses to state intervention. For example, working-class political orientations have historically been affected by the timing of democratization in relation to industrialization; by the administrative structure of the state; and by legal conditions bearing on working class organizations, such as trade unions. States may induce different forms and levels of corporatism which influence the way sectional interests are defended. Social movements reflect in part variations in constitutional, legal, and coercive state apparatuses. Economic intervention by bureaucratic authoritarian regimes in Latin America affected social resistance by reducing the state's capacity to dominate civil society. Shrinking the public sector can undermine social forces behind political opposition.

Third, the structure of the state is related to the way in which political interests are mediated by political parties. For example, the extent to which the state bureaucracy is free from partisan control determines how far it can be used as a source of political patronage and, therefore, how far political parties need to secure electoral support by promising the spoils of office, or by offering ideologically coherent programmes capable of securing majority support within the electorate. State administrative structures also influence party organization and styles. Variations in relationships between the state administration and party organization also affect the kinds of issues that regularly appear on the political agenda – collective versus divisible benefits, for example.

Fourth, the political expression of class interests is never wholly economically determined. This is because the ability of classes to achieve consciousness, mobilization, and representation is affected by the structures and activities of states. For example, working-class activism has historically been conditioned by the nature of the state – and, in particular, the extent to which state and society are sharply differentiated, and the extent to which workers are incorporated into a political system based on locally rooted political parties wielding patronage. The political capacity of dominant socio-economic classes is also a function of state structures – such as decentralized forms of administration, or parliamentary forms of political decision-making – and not simply an extension of class interest.

An autonomous state does not automatically mean a reduction in the power of all social groups. The game is not zero-sum. State autonomy and the power of socio-economic groups and interests can increase or decrease together. For example, transnational corporations have stimulated a capacity for autonomous state action on economic issues. Similarly, a reduced state capacity to intervene in the economy may be deliberately selected by state elites in order to protect other state capacities, such as in the area of control and repression, and thus manage the expression of grievances by economically disadvantaged groups.

However, strong state interventions are likely to encourage interest groups to mobilize to exert pressure on policy-makers, or even colonize parts of the state apparatus. State autonomy and group power may increase simultaneously, but only temporarily, as newly mobilized and empowered groups exert influence, and reduce the scope – and possibly capacity – for further state interventions, at least in that particular policy area. We are thus presented with the intriguing conclusion that state intervention in the economy provides an environment supportive of working class mobilization and participation in policy-making.

The thrust of this theory is that political analysis needs to recognize a dialectical relationship between state and society. In activating group identities, politicizing some social conflicts and not others, and selecting social identities on which political conflict is based, the state influences the meanings and methods of politics for different groups and classes. The state is not solely the product of social cleavages and interests. Sectional interests and classes seek to influence the state. But the way they do so, and their capacity to do so, depends on the state structures with which they interact.

## Globalization and the nation state

It has been argued that the forces of globalization are increasingly rendering the state obsolete. Thus, debates about the nature of the state become redundant. How convincing is this stance?

There is by no means consensus on what 'globalization' means, but the term tries to capture aspects of international relations which must be delineated if the argument about the contemporary relevance of the state is to be assessed.

Economically, globalization refers to an accelerating process of international transactions in the form of trade, investment, and capital flows. Globalization also has social and cultural dimensions. Cultural uniformity is encouraged by increased travel and migration, and the media networks of rich Western countries. Global communications networks have far-reaching consequences for businesses, governments, educational institutions, voluntary bodies, and community groups. Social globalization is reflected in the illicit trade in drugs, laundered money, weapons, and women. Civil conflicts threatening political stability are fuelled by the global traffic in weapons and mercenaries. Global markets put huge pressure on the environment.

The nation state is said to be undermined by these forces. National policies for economic development, employment, social protection, and fiscal objectives are made redundant by mobile capital, global markets, and transnational industrial production. Nation states are rapidly being reduced to a 'municipal' role in the global system, providing the required infrastructure, physical and legal, for international capital (Hirst and Thompson, 1999). Transnational networks of production, trade, and finance relegate national governments to 'transmission belts' for global capital. World market forces are more powerful than state actions, both domestically and in the international arena, so that while state *intervention* may have increased, the state's *effectiveness* in providing what markets do not – security, financial stability, law and order, and public goods such as infrastructure – has declined (Strange, 1996).

Global capital also imposes a discipline on states, leaving governments only with policy choices that are consistent with a free market. The welfare state is ruled out. National sovereignty has been displaced by global and regional institutions (e.g. free markets and free trade) and organizations such as the IMF, the World Trade Organization, the Association of Southeast Asian Nations, Asia-Pacific Economic Co-operation, and the Southern Cone Common Market. Forms of international cooperation between states have proliferated (to deal with crime, terrorism, migration, and capital flows) and the number of international agreements (treaties, charters, and covenants) has grown enormously. Global governance and politics is not only conducted through international organizations, but also through international NGOs, social movements and pressure groups – such as Greenpeace, the International Confederation of Free Trade Unions, the World Muslim Congress, the International Red Cross, and the Catholic Fund for International Development (Held *et al.*, 1999).

Such conclusions for the nation state are only convincing if the significance of globalization is exaggerated and the need for the state underestimated.

The picture of globalization as a completely supranational economy is false. The economic world is still made up of national economies in which most companies are embedded, subject to national regulations and benefiting from state power which provides stability and security in financial markets, free trade, and the protection of commercial rights, albeit within the context of growing international trade and investment (Hirst and Thompson, 1999, 270–4). Indeed, the state is a key facilitator of globalization by creating the conditions under which international capital is a major force in the domestic politics of contemporary states. The fact that policies change under the influence of domestic and international pressures found within the global economy does not distinguish the state from earlier incarnations (Bisley, 2007).

Support for the international order, then, has to be managed at the national level through the institutions of the state. Powerful nation states are required if international regulatory regimes, trading blocs, agencies, economic policies, and treaties are to be effective. Nation states represent societies on international agencies and regulatory bodies, supporting international decisions with national laws and policies. Only through nation states will such agencies be endowed with legitimacy by, and accountability to, those societies (Hirst and Thompson, 1999). National governments are becoming *more* important in promoting and regulating international trade and investment. National institutions, government strategies, and position in the international system allow states to mediate and resist the effects of globalization. The fact that pressure for the establishment of international treaties and conventions may come from international, non-governmental sources – such as human rights activists (most of which are nationally based), or the 'will of the international community' does not mean that states no longer have to consent to international law (Held *et al.*, 1999, pp. 6–14, 63).

A growth in the scale of international relationships in which states are engaged does not necessarily diminish the power of states to decide when it is in their interests to participate in activities which have formed part of the context of sovereign statehood for centuries (Krasner, 1995). It is wrong to confuse a changing world with which states have to cope with a diminution of state power. States have always had to respond to changing economic, military, technological, ecological, and cultural developments. It is also debatable how far it is anything new for states to be subjected to the threats which 'mobile capital' is able to pose. Has it really required globalization to generate 'powerful pressures on states to develop market-friendly policies, including low public deficits and expenditure, especially on social goods … [threatening] welfare budgets, taxation levels and other government policies' (Held and McGrew, 2000, p. 13)? This has always been the experience of states that have to accommodate capitalism.

Neither is economic interdependence new, and is arguably less significant for national governments than it was in the nineteenth century. Western states are as involved in the exploitation of their advantages and power over Third World economies as at any time in the past, mainly through 'global' corporations with national roots. 'Global governance' is a euphemism for an international system in which national governments, especially Western, are the main actors. The international economy may restrict policy choices by national governments in some policy sectors, but it expands them in others. The demise of the state from globalization only becomes a convincing idea if one accepts a false conception of statehood as 'an absolute, indivisible, territorially exclusive and zero-sum form of public power' (Held *et al.*, 1999, pp. 6–9).

A continuing need for the state also arises from the threats to livelihoods from globalization, especially in developing countries. While trade increases incomes on average, it does not guarantee that inequalities will not increase and poverty remain. Trade liberalization also produces 'adjustment' costs as labour and capital shift to export industries. Global competition has led to a growth in 'flexible' (i.e. precarious) employment conditions. Only states can provide safety nets to protect vulnerable people, or manage the political conflict and crime caused by poverty (Hirst and Thompson, 1999). The costs of economic adjustments also need to be moderated by retraining, health care, and macroeconomic policies that produce economic stability. Social policies are needed to protect people not only in the context of changing labour markets, but also from declining cultural diversity and the damage done to public services by deliberate reductions in state resources. This calls for policies that invest in skills, promote job-creation, strengthen workers' rights, generate tax revenues, improve the efficiency of tax administration, reduce military spending, and support culture and the arts. The state is also needed to remove barriers in developing countries excluding people from the benefits of information technology, through policies for group access, training, and adapting technology to local skills (UNDP, 1999).

Globalization may have produced a 'transnational capitalist class' which promotes the interests of national capital through international business networks and organizations, but they nevertheless focus their attention on securing state power by backing neo-liberal presidential candidates in national elections – such as Felipe Calderon of Mexico in 2006, or mobilizing their supporters in the military, should an anti-capitalist movement capture state power, as in Venezuela in 2002. Electoral victories for reformist leaders and parties in Brazil and Chile also show how the redistribution of wealth and power can only be pursued through organs and agencies of the nation state implementing social welfare measures, anti-poverty programmes, social investments, and agrarian reforms. Social movements and pressure groups campaigning on behalf of workers' rights, the rights of women, environmental protection, ethnic minorities, the rights of indigenous people, and the homeless focus their demands on national governments with the power to implement reforms or even restructure the state in the direction of participatory and egalitarian democracy. Globalization has not reduced the relevance of the state, though it has made it more difficult for political movements representing the interests and rights of workers, the unemployed, the pauperized, and the economically marginalized to capture state power and to protect the vulnerable against the ravages of capitalism. Clear evidence of this is found in the failure of leftist governments to reduce levels of inequality, exploitation, and the costs of market failure (Robinson, 2010).

The state also has the leading role to play in environmental protection. Environmental degradation and pollution are consequences of economic growth, whether or not generated by globalization. However, insofar as globalization stimulates economic growth, whether this entails pollution depends on environmental policies pursued by national governments, such as the removal of subsidies from environmentally harmful activities, transparent environmental regulation, and information and education about environmental problems (e.g. the public disclosure of factory pollution, as in Indonesia and the Philippines).

The state is also needed to provide a legal and fiscal context that encourages economic development. The rule of law is necessary to provide social and economic security and the enforcement of economic obligations (Hirst and Thompson, 1999). Government policies protecting property rights are needed to attract capital investment, a problem for the poorest developing countries being their *exclusion* from a global order which denies them investment and a reasonable share of world trade. Capital market flows are very volatile and can create financial crises, as in East Asia in 1997–98. Reducing the risks of such crises and their consequences for incomes, social unrest, and crime requires national institutions and policies, such as strong legal and regulatory regimes for the financial sector.

Consequently, economic globalization gives rise to a need for a strong state. Weak states, such as those throughout much of Africa, lacking the rule of law, honest and accountable government, policy-making capacity, and efficient public services, can neither absorb the benefits of globalization nor manage its negative consequences: 'African economic growth and development in the era of globalization are hamstrung by weak states' (Lawson, 2003, p. 39). The costs of globalization – lost livelihoods, depressed wages, and unemployment – need to be managed by policies that are of some benefit to the losers: redistribution, social safety nets, and progressive taxation. The developmental states of Asia also demonstrate that while global economic structures were important for their success, state capabilities were more important. It is also widely recognized, even among the advocates of neo-liberal economic policies, such as the World Bank, that effective states are needed if markets are to function properly and democracy is to amount to more than a procedural formality (Batley, 2002).

Even if the assertions about overwhelming globalization are accepted, it does not follow that the state is powerless to moderate the effects of international economic forces. What is significant is that states vary hugely in their *capacity* to do so. And capacity is not a function of globalization. Such capacity – to respond to economic change by mobilizing investment, increasing manufactured exports, and coordinating technological innovation – is the key variable in the analysis of the state in a global economy (Weiss, 1998).

## Conclusion

The literature on the post-colonial state aids understanding of the factors identified by dependency theorists as being central to the nature of the state in the Third World – in particular, the role of the bourgeoisie and its level of development. Foreign capital is part of the class structure of the peripheral state. However, it does more than compete with the national bourgeoisie. It affects the rate and direction of its development. Indigenous classes do not develop autonomously. They are distorted by the presence of foreign capital, which is not merely another class in competition with indigenous classes but actually affects the formation and coherence of indigenous classes, and strengthens the mediatory role of the state.

However, a single model of the post-colonial, relatively autonomous, and bureaucratically oligarchic state cannot be applied everywhere. The range of historical conditions in the Third World is too great.

There is also scope for confusion regarding the concept of 'overdevelopment'. This concept is applied to the state in relation to civil society and its class structure, overdevelopment arising from the state's original need to protect the interests of imperial capital against indigenous economic interests or classes. But it is also applied to internal state structures, with the bureaucracy being overdeveloped in relation to other political institutions. The connection between the two seemingly separate propositions lies in the argument that the power of the bureaucracy *within* the state enables the state to maintain a degree of autonomy from any class in civil society, even after independence from the imperial power. The institutions that would allow classes in society to control or even colonize the state apparatus, and to dominate the bureaucracy, are insufficiently powerful.

It might also be asked why, particularly when there were no strong indigenous classes to be subdued, an *overdeveloped* state should be needed. The colonial state at the time of independence in East Africa did not appear to be particularly strong in terms of civil and military personnel, or percentage of national income taken by government revenues and expenditure, let alone overdeveloped. The post-colonial state was typically smaller, relative to population and size of the economy, than advanced capitalist countries and less involved in the ownership of productive forces or interventions in social life (Leys, 1976; Ziemann and Lanzendorfer, 1977; Crow, 1990).

'Bureaucratic authoritarianism' is a fair description of Latin America's militarized regimes, provided that the differences in the regimes and their economic policies are also recognized. Further conceptual refinement is needed within each part of a 'constellation' – regime, coalition, and policy – in order to appreciate the degree and nature of differences between bureaucratic authoritarianism and other types of state (Collier, 1979). As an analytical model, it declined in significance in the 1980s as civilian politics was restored, competitive party systems established, and economic liberalism enforced (Cammack *et al.*, 1993).

The dialectical approach brings to the fore important interrelationships between state and civil society. But it does not distinguish itself sufficiently from other approaches to politics which also accept that the state is structured by its environment; that states are actors in the international arena; that strategically placed elites are capable, under some circumstances, of taking control by military force; that state elites, especially professional bureaucrats, make contributions to foreign and domestic public policy that are more influential than those made by political parties and pressure groups; and that autonomous state action is motivated, in part, by the desire of state elites to reinforce their power and prerogatives.

There is also a danger that the state will be reified when construed as an autonomous actor influencing, and being influenced by, international and domestic contexts. However, the theory does suggest some potentially fruitful lines of further inquiry in its interpretation of the impact of state intervention on the mobilization of political interests and the form that such mobilization might take. Critiques which attempt to restore socio-economic factors as the determinants of politics (such as Migdal *et al.*, 1994) not only need to show how their approach differs. They also have to avoid confusing state powerlessness with state incompetence. The damaging consequences of economic mismanagement do not indicate a loss of power on the part of state authorities so much as demonstrate the dreadful influence of powerful but venal and incompetent state leadership.

While it is debatable how far nation states have not ever had to share power or contend with forces cutting across national boundaries, there is no doubt that the international economic and governmental system is more complex, 'influencing institutional agendas' and changing the balance between national, regional, and international legal frameworks (Held *et al.*, 1999: p. 81). However, the nation state remains at the centre of these complexities and takes the lead in managing their domestic and international consequences.

The concept of globalization may also provide states and governments with a convenient myth with which to discipline society to meet what is presented as the inevitable, impersonal, and unalterable requirements of the global marketplace (Held and McGrew, 2000). If governments cave in under pressure from MNCs over investment rights, environmental regulation, or food production, it is because they choose to favour corporate interests, not because they are subject to the natural laws of some global order. And if international governance is needed to deal with the international costs of globalization, such as the growing inequality between countries, the international threats from civil conflicts occasioned by financial volatility, or global crime, hopefully it can move towards more representative, democratic and transparent bodies than the currently dominant agencies – the IMF, World Bank and World Trade Organization.

# 5

# Political Parties and Party Systems

## Parties and mass mobilization

Political parties are the most important institutions of political mobilization in the context of mass politics. Whatever the nature of a civilian regime – whether based on the principles and institutions of liberal parliamentary politics, monopolistic forms of political leadership, or on some interpretation of Marxism-Leninism – political parties reflect the fact that government is no longer the prerogative of an hereditary elite or alien oligarchy, but rests to some degree on the support or mobilization of the masses. Parties emerge whenever the notion of political power comes to include the idea that 'the mass public must participate or be controlled' (LaPalombara and Weiner, 1966: 3).

A party may mobilize and control support through ideological devices or even repression, but it has to be managed so that power can be captured and the legitimacy of constitutional office secured. The objectives of parties are many and varied, seeking revolutionary change or maintaining the *status quo*, but they all require the mobilization of mass support. Parties accommodate demands for greater political participation and, in various ways including repression and patronage, help manage the conflict that such mass participation in politics inevitably produces. Political parties are both a consequence of a process of political change and a cause of further change by increasing a society's capacity to cope with crises of integration, participation, and distribution (LaPalombara and Weiner, 1966).

Defining a political party is difficult, especially in the Third World, because of the immense variety to be found. However, a satisfactory definition is that parties are:

> associations formally organized with the explicit and declared purpose of acquiring and/or maintaining legal control, either singly or in coalition or electoral competition with other similar associations, over the

103

personnel and the policy of the government of an actual or prospective sovereign state. (Coleman and Rosberg, 1964: 2)

It is easier to classify what Third World parties do than provide a definition that will encompass all manifestations of them. Classification is also easier than explanation of change in party system and organization: two issues to be explored later. The main classifications to be used by political science have been based on functions, ideology, and party system. Typologies have also been formed from a combination of these factors.

## The functions of political parties

Political parties in developing countries perform a number of roles (Coleman and Rosberg, 1964; LaPalombara and Weiner, 1966; Randall, 1988; Cammack *et al.*, 1993). First, they can, in some circumstances, *endow regimes with legitimacy* by providing ideologies, leadership, or opportunities for political participation, or a combination of all three. By providing a means of peaceful political succession within a competitive party system, they legitimize the authority of government based on mass participation and representation (Yanai, 1999). In competitive situations, parties permit a degree of rotation of power among the different elites which they sustain.

Second, they can act as a *medium for political recruitment*, perhaps simultaneously creating opportunities for upward social mobility. In developing countries, political parties provide the most important civilian route into a political career. Within certain ideological perspectives, parties perform a different kind of recruitment role. They mobilize people into self-help projects at the local level in an attempt to supplement government interventions under conditions of extreme scarcity of resources. Such mobilization is often associated with the socialization function referred to below (p. 105), as local party organs attempt to spread the party's doctrine among the masses.

Third, parties provide opportunities for *the formation of coalitions* of powerful political interests to sustain a government. This is the function of interest aggregation, which is most important in competitive systems when electoral and legislative majorities have to be formed by the broadening of political support. Such aggregation can assist in the process of political integration if parties are successful in drawing support from across identities, such as tribe or language group, to which people feel an attachment greater than that to the nation state. Not all parties seek to secure legislative majorities, however. In the Arab world, Islamist parties – such as Egypt's Muslim Brotherhood, or Morocco's Justice and Development Party – have frequently chosen not to contest enough seats to win a majority. This is partly because of fear of government repression and partly because their main objective – the Islamization of society – can be achieved through the movement's religious, educational, charitable, and social service activities (Hamid, 2011).

Parties also act as the *conduits of upward pressure* from the rank and file membership, affiliated organizations representing special interests such as women, youth, or trade unions, and, when required to compete for office through the ballot box, the electorate. Some parties have represented traditional oligarchies as in parts of West Africa, for example, where oligarchs adapted the modern institution of the party to their own political ends. In a constitutional arrangement that assigns one person one vote, even an aristocracy has to obtain mass support. It has the advantage of being able to trade on the traditional allegiances of naturally deferential societies within the wider context of more egalitarian principles. Other parties have been based on the demands of the professional classes such as teachers, lawyers, and low ranking officialdom. Ethnicity is often a parallel defining factor limiting membership and cutting across occupational and economic interests. Often, rather than act as conduits of influence from below, parties give political elites the machinery through which to manipulate ethnic, religious, linguistic, and regional identities in order to secure power (Manning, 2005).

Parties also contribute to *political socialization*, affecting the attitudes of party members and the wider public on such matters as the management of the economy, national identity, and the legitimacy of government. By giving participants a vested interest in the continuation of party politics, parties can contribute to the consolidation of democracy (Gunther and Diamond, 2001). However, socialization can include attitudes and beliefs that are inimical to democracy, such as hatred for supporters of the opposition, as in Kenya, following multi-party elections in 1992 and 1996, and Zimbabwe in 2008. In India, the RSS (Rashtriya Swayamsevak Sangh) which gave birth to the Hindu Nationalist Bharatiya Janata Party (BJP) has much in common with fascist parties. Such socialization can lead to violence, which then becomes part of the party's heritage into which subsequent cohorts are socialized.

Political parties should also be major *influences on public policy* by devising programmes to attract a workable aggregation of interests or through the application of official ideology to current problems. In the past, however, parties usually have had a minimal impact on public policy in Third World countries, and even more rarely exercised any effective supervision of policy implementation (Randall, 1988). Policy options are, after all, often restricted by dependence upon foreign aid which comes with conditions attached, especially neo-liberal economic restructuring.

However, there is growing evidence, especially from newly democratiz-ing polities, that parties can be relevant to policy outcomes. For example, parties are crucial to strategies designed to reduce poverty by the empow-erment of the poor. Experience in some of the states in India and parts of Latin America suggests strongly that the opportunity to elect pro-poor parties to office makes a significance difference to the strength of public policies designed to alleviate poverty, especially if the parties are unified rather than fragmented, and with a coherent ideology and programme (Moore and Putzel, 1999).

Finally, political parties have been seen as necessary for *political stabil-ity*. Stability depends on a society being able to absorb the increasing level of political participation by the new social forces generated by economic modernization. Parties offer the principal institutional means of organizing that participation in constructive and legitimate ways, especially if the parties are created before the level of participation gets too high. A combi-nation of high levels of participation and strong party organization provides a defence against anomic politics and violence, and reduces the risk of military intervention.

## Party ideology

Inevitably, given their appeal to certain class interests, the ideological posi-tions of Third World parties have often resembled those of their First and Second World counterparts. Western ideologies have been adapted to provide a common framework of values for very heterogeneous societies and to strengthen national integration. Both socialism and communism have been deployed in the Third World for such aims. But they have been adapted to the particular context in which they are to be a guide to action. Special versions have been developed – such as Tanzania's African social-ism, which purports to draw on traditional communal values, as well as European ideas about equality. Chinese Marxism-Leninism has also devel-oped its own distinctive qualities.

Where capitalism has developed over a prolonged period, as in the rela-tively lengthy post-independence histories of Latin American countries, parties most clearly reflect class interests in their ideological stances. Conservative parties are supported in Argentina, Colombia, and Equador by coalitions of landlords and the Catholic Church. Liberal parties are supported by coalitions of urban business interests. They compete for the support of workers and peasants with socialist and communist parties (where these are not proscribed). Some parties have been nationalistic and, to a limited extent, ethnically based. Bolivia's Movement Toward Socialism is an ethnic party that deploys elements of a European ideology to protect the interests of indigenous people. Most European ideologies have been represented in Latin American politics, at one time or another.

In most parts of the Third World, however, ideological developments and the political organizations based on them have been distinctive in a number of important respects. First, the ideologies of Third World political parties have often been derived more from religion than from the materialistic ideologies of the West which were expected to take a hold in many post-colonial societies. Examples are the Hindu communal parties in India, and the Moslem party in Indonesia. The development of Islamic political ideologies is increasingly significant in many regions of the Third World.

Second, some parties have developed to defend the distinct way of life of different ethnic communities, for example Malays, Chinese, and Indians in Malaysia. Ideologies reflect the culture of these distinctive communities, rather than class interests (Chandra, 2011). In India, caste provides the foundation for some parties, as in the case of the Bahujan Samaj Party representing Untouchables. Elsewhere, and especially in Africa, the tendency of political parties to reflect ethnicity and regional consciousness, rather than identities that cut across such cleavages and unite people on a national scale, has been a cause of their weakness and the weakness of governments built on such party competition (Diamond, 1988). Concerns about the divisive effects of parties based on tribe, language, clan, race, or religion, have even led to them being banned in some countries, including Kenya, Sierra Leone, and Nigeria, despite recent transitions to democratic pluralism. Such bans have so far had little effect on political stability (Randall, 2008; Bogaards *et al.*, 2010).

Ethnicity as a basis for party organization and support in countries such as Zambia, Kenya, and the Democratic Republic of Congo (formerly Zaire) was encouraged by part of the colonial heritage – namely, the absence of any other significant identity by which to mobilize people into electoral politics. This type of mobilization was then consolidated by political leaders who used ethnic discrimination and patronage to secure support. Where ethnicity has been less significant as a focus of political identity, the party system has been more genuinely competitive and therefore democratic (Carey, 2002).

Third, political parties in the Third World are frequently populist. This is a style of leadership, rather than an ideology. It seeks to mobilize people regardless of class by denying the significance of class and of any class-based ideology. Populism tries to mobilize all interests under a single conception of the national interest. It rejects the idea that groups have irreconcilable interests. All share a common interest represented by a particular party and its leadership. Society is presented as 'cellularized' into factions whose common interests outweigh their particular, and possibly conflicting, interests as illiterates or intellectuals, young or old, producers or consumers, men or women, peasants or urbanites, bureaucrats or clients. Social diversity is not regarded as a barrier to the identification of a more important common interest.

Populism is, thus, a way of presenting a view of society that stresses homogeneity, rather than diversity. In order to appeal to all interests in society, populist parties and leaders define special interests in ways that make them ultimately reconcilable. Issues associated with particular interests, or which are divisive, are, where possible, avoided. Leaders specifically aim to prevent the development of a consciousness of conflicting interests. The methods used include building support on the basis of rewards, rather than ideological conviction, and expressing contradictory policy objectives incoherently. Populism is inevitably conservative since it seeks to prevent alternative perspectives to the *status quo* developing. Populism has often been used to justify a single-party regime, as in Syria, where the Constitution endorses the Baa'th Party as the sole instrument for consolidating 'unity for our popular masses', meeting 'our people's needs and interests', and unifying 'the resources of the people's masses'. This has produced 'Populist Authoritarianism' under which different sections of society are mobilized through the single party and corporatists institutions. This authoritarianism has been particularly concerned with the preservation of a secular state threatened by radical Islamic groups (Hinnebusch, 2008).

In some countries, the structure of post-colonial society lent some support to this way of viewing the political world, particularly those that appeared to be devoid of significant class distinctions simply because economic underdevelopment had prevented classes from emerging fully. Congress in India must rank as one of the most successful populist parties. It attracts support from very different sections of society whose interests might appear to be incompatible. It has proved able to manage an alliance between different kinds of class structure, those of the rural and urban areas, even when such stratification has been overlaid with linguistic, ethnic, communal, and religious differences.

There have been two dominant preoccupations in the analysis of Third World political parties. One concerns the development and survival of party systems, including single-party systems, and their significance for democracy. The other concerns the survival of parties as organizations.

## Party systems

Observations of the tendency in the early 1960s for single-party systems to emerge in Africa led Coleman and Rosberg to produce a typology of parties based on a combination of ideological, participative, and organizational variables. This enabled them to contrast a 'pragmatic pluralist' pattern with a 'revolutionary-centralizing' pattern. Pragmatic pluralist parties were those that generally tolerated the persistence of traditional politics, only partially and intermittently tried to mobilize support, and assimilated group interests to a limited extent. In contrast, revolutionary-centralizing parties espoused a modernizing ideology, were highly committed to mass political participation, and developed monolithic and centralized organizations.

This classification was used to explain the level of success achieved by African countries in solving the problem of national integration, both in the sense of 'transcending the elite-mass gap' and in the sense of territorial integration. However, it proved difficult to develop a theory of successful political integration as distinct from identifying integration as a function that parties can perform, especially in the single-party system of government. Coleman and Rosberg were able to go little further than stating that 'In all but a few of Africa's new states the primary structure ... for coping with the myriad parochial and ethnic pressures is the national political party, the single or dominant party currently governing the state' (Coleman and Rosberg, 1964, p. 691).

A similar combination of regime and ideology is employed by LaPalombara and Weiner (1966) in their classification of parties in developing countries. First, they distinguish between competitive and non-competitive systems, and then two dimensions along which parties differ within each system. *Competitive systems* are associated with large and/or ethnically fragmented countries such as India, Nigeria, Malaysia, and Sri Lanka. One dimension of such a system ranges from 'hegemonic', where one party dominates for a long period, to 'turnover', where change in the party of government is frequent. Single-party hegemony within competitive politics is represented by Malaysia which, at national level, has been governed since 1974 by a permanent coalition, the Barisan Nasional, which uses electoral manipulation and discrimination against opponents in a system of electoral authoritarianism to perpetuate its dominance, thus creating an 'electoral one-party state' (Wong *et al.*, 2010).

The second dimension distinguishes between ideological and pragmatic parties. This typology has theoretical value insofar as 'the particular combination of hegemony or turnover, ideology or pragmatism that a party pattern manifests may tell us something about how the parties relate to social, economic and political development' (LaPalombara and Weiner, 1966, p. 37). The typology was also useful if one was interested in the ability of parties to manage conflict effectively: 'in competitive systems the ideological-hegemonic and the ideological-turnover systems are less able to cope (short of repressive measures) with conflicts than either pragmatic-turnover or pragmatic-hegemonic systems' (LaPalombara and Weiner,

1966, p. 418). Another hypothesis offered is that any drive for hegemonic control is likely to be made by parties with a strong ideological position.

Party control in a *non-competitive system* is, by definition, likely to be hegemonic, rather than 'turnover'. Combinations of hegemonic party systems and the ideological variable produce three main types of single-party system. The one-party authoritarian system (such as in Mali, Ghana, and South Vietnam in the 1960s) treats opposition as a threat to revolutionary or nationalistic objectives. The one-party pluralist system is characterized by a pluralistic party organization and a pragmatic ideology, as in Mexico's Institutional Revolutionary Party. The one-party totalitarian system has the state itself as an instrument of the party whose objective is social and economic transformation, as in China, Vietnam, and North Korea.

### Single-party systems

In some cases, party systems in the Third World have resembled their Western counterparts, offering a degree of electoral choice, legitimate political opposition, and accountability to the interests ranged in support of them electorally. Others have resembled the democratic centralism of the former Soviet Union and Eastern bloc. In some countries, multi-party politics has survived more or less intact since independence, as in India. Elsewhere, it has appeared intermittently, as in Nigeria. But the Third World has produced important variants of its own, most notably the single-party system in the context of parliamentary government and capitalist economy, as in Kenya until 1991. Single-party regimes prove that capitalism often requires the negation of liberal democracy, rather than guaranteeing it.

What features of post-colonial politics explain the emergence of single-party regimes? First, an 'aura of nationalist *legitimacy*' was conferred on a single nationalist movement at independence, seen as the victor over imperialism and securing overwhelming electoral support (Kilson, 1963, p. 266). Such an achievement was taken as evidence that the organization could continue to reflect the common interests of all sections of society. Popular support then enabled the dominant party to make it unlawful for other parties to exist, so that a single-party state is established *de jure* as well as *de facto*. Not all single-party regimes outlaw other parties but, when they do not, it has been very common for them to put obstacles other than the law in the way of effectively organized opposition.

Second, the single-party tendency was said to reflect the *autocratic* form of government which was the new state's inheritance both from colonialism and traditional government. Pluralism and multi-party democracy are not inherited from the past. Rather, autocracy is the dominant aspect of political history. The situation that party leaders confronted at independence had been formed by the autocratic power of the departing colonialists, a culture supported by, in the case of African societies at least, elements that were predisposed towards more authoritarian forms of government (Coleman and Rosberg, 1964). Multi-party democracy was too alien an importation for it to survive in the local political culture, traditions, and history. Perceptions of tradition and what was appropriate for a particular society combined with the colonial legacy – such as a centralized administrative apparatus, paternalism, and electoral systems – to give unfettered control to a party that has not necessarily gained a plurality of the votes. Where the legacy was different, a plurality of parties stood a better chance of survival (Randall, 1988).

Third, the political culture of the new indigenous leadership was *elitist* – governments were believed to possess a monopoly of wisdom and legitimacy. Since there were few, if any, other social or political organizations that could compete with the concentration of professional knowledge that existed within government, it was difficult to dispute this claim.

Fourth, the leadership culture was also *statist*. The state was regarded as the modernizer and agent of development. Multi-party democracy was often perceived as a luxury that could not be afforded. The immense problems confronting the governments of new states meant that discontinuities in the pursuit of public goals were an indulgence. However, there is little evidence that the absence of party competition has everywhere been better for policy outcomes, such as economic development and social equality (Sirowy and Inkeles, 1991).

The leadership was also *nationalist*, emphasizing national unity as the paramount goal, condemning any sub-national sentiment to tribe, religion, region, or other centres of political attachment and loyalty as destructive of national integration. Political leaders in new states undoubtedly encountered many separatist tendencies. The need for political order made the single-party system attractive. A strong party could assimilate the social forces generated by modernization that would otherwise threaten political stability.

Another factor is that political office is not readily relinquished, least of all in the Third World context. The *rewards of political office* in the context of underdevelopment are so great that there must always be a temptation to manipulate politics to exclude the organized opposition. This goes further than mere corruption, serious though this problem is. The problem is rather that the state, being the main engine of economic development, is something that those whose aspire to benefit socially and economically from such development need to control. An emerging bourgeoisie cannot look to other sources of capital. Production, trade, and commerce all depend upon capital channelled through the state which also controls licences, the law governing labour relations, and access to foreign exchange, import licenses, and export permits. The state is thus an organization which has to be captured by any group that wishes to accumulate economic resources. Political power and political careers bring huge rewards that are not lightly conceded to opponents.

It was also believed that the *classless* nature of some Third World societies removed the need for more than one party. Tanzanian society, for example, was composed of a number of more or less equally balanced ethnic groups without any major forms of social and economic stratification. So, it was thought too homogenous to need more than one party to represent interests effectively.

Not all new states came into existence on the basis of a *preparation for independence* in a Western European constitutional mould. The build-up to independence in Algeria, Indo-China, Angola, and Mozambique was rather different, involving armed conflict. Sometimes, Marxist-Leninist ideology played a part. Such an ideology, perhaps having its origin in mobilization for a war of liberation, identifies party with state and nation. Anything outside the party, and certainly anything that opposes it, is almost treasonable by definition. An organization founded to wage war under such ideological motivation would have an automatic propensity to form the sole leadership in the context of post-war civilian politics.

Acceptance of single-party government was made easier by apparently *democratic tendencies* within some sole parties. It appeared as though some parties could sustain democratic decision-making within the party sufficient to compensate for the lack of choice between parties. In Tanzania, for example, intra-party democracy allowed for just as much (or as little) discussion of alternatives as inter-party democracy. Consequently, some political leaders in the Third World claimed, not without some justification, that the policy choices offered by, say, Democrats and Republicans in the USA were no greater than the choices being made within the mass organizations of sole parties and between the candidates which those parties sponsored in parliamentary elections. Different factions within a single party could also compete for political office.

Finally, following independence in many new states, the political leadership argued that *traditional society* had its own forms of democratic decision-making that could be adapted to contemporary conditions without needing more than one political party. Leaders such as Julius Nyerere of Tanzania and Leopold Senghor of Senegal claimed that traditional African decision-making was based on consensus, unity, and egalitarianism, claims on which historical research has thrown some doubt (Riley, 1991). A more convincing explanation for the appeal to a pre-colonial Golden Age might be that it was necessary for political leaders to distance themselves from the institutions and values associated with the colonizers.

   Political leaders have also found it advantageous to distance themselves from the ethnic conflict and discrimination associated with many multi-party systems in the Third World. For example, between 1986 and 2006, when the first multi-party elections in 25 years were held, Uganda was governed by a National Resistance Movement (NRM). This was known as a 'no-party system', under which other parties were allowed to exist but not to contest elections. The NRM leadership associated multi-party politics with ethnic exclusion and political instability. By making all citizens members of the Movement, it was hoped to generate ideas about policies that would be judged on their merits. A combination of intra-organizational democracy, and restrictions on alternative political organizations, made the Ugandan system a 'hegemonic party-state', with leaders of the Movement occupying all important political offices, rather than a dominant party system such as characterized much of the post-colonial history of Mexico and Taiwan (Carbone, 2003).

   The development of an alternative form of democracy to that of Western liberalism appears more natural still when it is recognized that, for much of the post-independence period, Third World countries lacked the two vital conditions, one economic and one political, which preceded liberal revolutions in the seventeenth and eighteenth centuries in the West: the availability of capitalist enterprise, finance, and skills; and a loyalty to the nation, rather than an ethnic community. All this put 'a premium on the mass movement with strong ideological leadership' (Macpherson, 1966, p. 27).

## The demise of party government

A more alarming tendency has been for parliamentary and party politics to collapse altogether under the impact of political crises. Party systems have often given way to military rule. Both single- and multi-party regimes seem to have fared equally badly in terms of the political stability which they were able to secure. It is difficult to find any pattern in the decay of party systems. Single-party systems sometimes survived, as in Kenya or Tanzania, when others succumbed to military *coups*, as in Ghana. Multi-party systems have sometimes survived, notably in India, but elsewhere they have not (for example, in Pakistan or Nigeria). Between 1960 and 1969, 10 of the 15 multi-party states in Africa had experienced military intervention. Of the 20 single-party states, 11 had had *coups*.

   It is not surprising that some commentators started to write off party-systems generally as a total failure. This is reflected in the general down-playing of the political significance of Third World parties (Randall, 1988). Yet, in some countries party government has survived for a very long time. The continuity of some Third World party systems is now greater than in

Eastern Europe. There is no shortage of examples of countries with long histories of party government. There are also examples of the military being instrumental in the reinstatement of parties, albeit to legitimize the military's role in politics.

There are no obvious explanations for the survival of party government. Economic growth, which might be expected to increase prosperity and therefore a sense of satisfaction with the regime, has not guaranteed the survival of party systems. Social structure might offer an explanation in that stratification based on class seems to provide a better basis for competitive politics than vertical cleavages based on race, language, or religion. However, social factors such as class, and related indicators of stratification such as urbanization and literacy, do not appear to be systematically related to patterns of party survival (Randall, 1988).

It is more difficult to account for the stability of a party system than to explain variations between systems. Explanations of the latter include the legacy of colonialism, the time that parties have to take root and become established (India and Jamaica are examples of countries in which political parties have long histories), and whether independence was won by war or negotiation, the former method leading to the creation of the 'party-army' of national liberation such as the FLN in Algeria, which had great difficulty in transforming itself into a civilian political movement after the French withdrew.

## Party systems and democratization

In the past two decades or so, international influences and democratization movements have encouraged an acceptance of multi-party politics. Aid donors have added political pluralism, 'good governance', democracy, and respect for human rights to their list of conditions attached to international development assistance. For example, in 1990 President Mitterrand of France warned African leaders at the 16th Franco-African Congress that 'France will link its contribution to efforts designed to lead to greater liberty and democracy'. In 1991, the British Minister for Overseas Development announced that British aid policy would require recipient governments to move towards pluralism, the rule of law, democracy, and respect for human rights. Multilateral aid agencies such as the World Bank have added to the pressures demanding 'good government' in return for aid (Williams and Young, 1994, p. 84).

Such pressure combined in the early 1990s with the influence of the momentous events in Eastern Europe and the Soviet Union on domestic political groups demanding political reforms and, especially, an end to the single-party regime. Competitive party politics have emerged in a number of countries as a consequence, most notably Nepal, Angola, Ghana, the Côte d'Ivoire, and Zambia.

It is clear from the role played by political parties that their significance for the process of democratization is immense. The success of democratization is, in part, dependent on the existence of institutionalized parties and party systems of government. The consolidation of democracy is widely regarded as conditional upon the institutionalization of regular electoral competition between parties which can adapt to new constitutional rules. Parties have been crucial to opposition to authoritarian rule, when they mainly had the characteristics of social movements (for example, the African National Congress before majority rule in South Africa). Such political movements need to 'institutionalize' themselves in readiness for the establishment of electoral competition (Ware, 1996). However, it should not be forgotten that not all political parties are committed to democracy. There are many in Islamic societies that seek to establish regimes that are more theocratic than democratic, and multi-party democracy is not yet on the political agenda in China or North Korea.

The concept of party system 'institutionalization' (developed by Mainwaring and Scully, using Latin American data) helps us to compare prospects for democratic consolidation in different countries. 'Institutionalization' was deemed to be found when:

- the rules governing party competition are commonly observed, widely understood, and confidently anticipated;
- there is stability in the number of parties competing for office;
- parties are strongly rooted in society, affecting political preferences, attracting stable electoral support, and demonstrating continuity in ideological terms;
- political elites recognize the legitimacy of electoral competition as the route to office;
- party organizations exist independently of powerful leaders, with well-resourced nationwide organizations, and well-established internal procedures for recruitment to party offices.

The more party systems are characterized by these qualities, the more institutionalized they are; the fewer the qualities, the more 'inchoate' the system.

Latin American democratization supports the hypothesis that an institutionalized system encourages moderation, coalition building, and compromise; 'inchoate' systems pose risks for democracy of unpredictability, complexity, weak legislatures, personalism, and fragile legitimacy. Institutionalized party systems mean party organizers have a vested interest in party competition, and party discipline makes government effective.

Citizens support parties rather than demagogues. Interests are pursued through elections as policies and programmes are compared and assessed. Conflicts are more easily mediated and managed. Political competition is restricted to democratic processes and political accountability is effective. Participation can be channelled and consent expressed (Mainwaring and Scully, 1995; Arce, 2010).

While an institutionalized party system may not be a sufficient condition for the consolidation of democracy, it would seem to be a necessary one. However, in the 'third wave' of democracy the party systems in poorer countries tend to be inchoate. Consequently, their democracies are characterized by personalism, weak accountability, electoral volatility, uncertainty and, most significant for democratic consolidation, low legitimacy conferred both on parties and on party systems. In some countries, including Guatemala and Peru, electoral volatility is such that parties are so unstable, short-lived, electorally insignificant, and lacking in identity that they constitute 'party non-systems'. When the analysis of the effects of party system institutionalization was extended to Africa, wide variations in the level of institutionalization were found, but with the majority of countries falling into the 'inchoate' category. There is also evidence of a virtuous circle: an institutionalized party system is a 'requisite for democratic government' but, the more experience a country has of democracy, the higher the level of party system institutionalization (Mainwaring, 1998; Kuenzi and Lambright, 2001, p. 463; Sanchez, 2009).

Partisan loyalty is necessary for party institutionalization and stability. But such attachments are being weakened in new democracies (as well as established ones) by the mass media and organized interests. In new democracies, party attachments are of declining importance to political elites who can mobilize electoral support through the mass media. There are fewer incentives now for political elites to build strong partisan loyalties and organizations than were present in the early democracies, when elites were dependent on parties to win elections. In the older democracies, parties created new citizens by extending the franchise and affiliating organized interests such as trade unions, whereas in newer democracies 'parties have been less central in the struggle to expand citizenship, and they never had the far-reaching social functions or fostered the strong identities that they did in the early democracies' (Mainwaring and Zoco, 2007, p. 166). Electoral volatility ensues (measured by the turnover of support from one party to others from one election to the next), which has worrying implications for democratic stability if party attachment is necessary for party institutionalization. This 'dealignment' was confirmed by a comparative study of electoral systems conducted in 2003. Only six Third World countries were included among the countries examined, so the results have to be treated with caution by those interested in the institutionalization of parties in developing countries. But the most significant finding was that, as opportunities for participation in democratic elections increase, partisan attachments are likely to become stronger (Dalton and Weldon, 2007). It is important to add that partisanship must be associated with parties that accept free and fair competitive elections as a means of forming governments.

Another factor in the relationship between party systems and democratization is the number of parties in the system, and the stability of two-party competition compared with a multi-party system. A multi-party system should be less stable because two-party and dominant-party systems are more likely to assimilate new groups into the political system. In the multi-party system, the assimilation of new social forces into politics can only be done by increasing the number of parties. However, a preference for a two-party system may simply reflect Eurocentric and Anglo-American biases, a confusion of governmental with regime instability, and an assumption that party politics is dominated by a single Left–Right dimension when, in Third World countries, other dimensions of conflict, such as ethnicity and religion, are superimposed. A multiplicity of parties provides for the representation of all interests, encouraging lawful political participation and reducing incentives to engage in political violence.

This controversy remains unresolved, though one comparative study of Third World democratization found only 'weak and fragmentary' support for the hypothesis that democratic consolidation was more likely under a multi than a two-party system (Power and Gasiorowski, 1997; see also Lijphart, 1984). This is relevant to the propensity for countries emerging from authoritarianism to spawn a multiplicity of political parties. For example, in Tunisia 81 parties emerged following the uprising in the spring of 2011 to contest the 217 seats in the new constituent assembly.

Type of party system also helps explain whether or not governments will target social spending on the poor. Party systems that allow leaders to secure office despite narrow electoral support are unlikely to initiate poverty alleviation programmes. In democracies with a small number of parties and stable party systems, such as Costa Rica and Sri Lanka, politicians seek broad electoral alliances, including links with pro-poor non-governmental organizations. In democracies with fragmented systems, such as Thailand, with unstable support for a large number of parties that are based on individual leadership rather than programmes, parties respond to narrow interests, a lack of incentives to provide poverty alleviation programmes, and the vetoes of coalition partners. Even elected authoritarian regimes, as in Mexico until 2000, where elections are held regularly, but where one party dominates in a virtual one-party system, have incentives to respond to the needs of the rural poor if confronted by a pro-poor opposition movement, a loss of urban support, a loss of credibility as a developmental regime, or demands for democratization. However, such programmes are also more likely to be instruments of social control than empowerment (Niles, 1999).

## The survival of parties as organizations

We have seen that one element in the institutionalization of party systems of government is the strength of parties as organizations. Strong parties are adaptable (e.g. in shifting from opposition to government), complex, autonomous (e.g. from narrow socio-economic interests), and coherent (Dix, 1992). A comparison of Korea, Taiwan, and 12 Latin American countries showed that democracy requires strong parties, as well as institutionalized party systems (Stockton, 2001). Consequently, the sustaining organizational characteristics of parties have become a topic of analytical interest, setting the very difficult task of discovering whether something that happens to a party's internal organization is crucial to its long-term existence.

Analysis of parties in French-speaking West Africa in the early 1960s led to a distinction between 'mass' and 'patron' parties. This was based on differences in organizational structure (particularly at the local level), size of membership (including its social composition), finances, functions, methods, and patterns of authority. All such organizational factors reflected the way in which party leaders related to the rest of the population. Mass parties – such as the Democratic Parties of the Côte d'Ivoire and Guinea, or the Union Soudanaise – sought the adherence of all individuals, whereas patron parties – such as Niger's Union Nigerienne – 'usually terminated their structure simply with the adherence of influential notables or patrons'. Patron parties were weakly organized, undisciplined, and with little direct membership participation. Local patrons were relied upon to reach the local community. The individual was of interest to patron parties 'only insofar as he happened to be included in the franchise, provided candidates for election and the minimum machinery for bringing the voter to the polls' (Morgenthau, 1964, pp. 336–41).

Mass parties, in contrast, had extensive organizations, performed the function of 'social integration' through their mass membership, and were interested in all aspects of their members' lives, not just their voting choices. Organizational strength thus requires a mass membership. Parties become stronger the more they can institutionalize mass support and develop a complex organization linked to socio-economic bodies such as trade unions (see Box 5.1). For example, the current weakness of Renamo in Mozambique lies in its reliance on a centralized and personalized leadership, with minimal party organization or institutionalization. In contrast,

---

**Box 5.1   *The Egyptian Muslim Brotherhood***

Before the change of regime in 2011, the Muslim Brotherhood (MB) was technically banned in Egypt but allowed to function, albeit under constant surveillance by the authorities, and to take part in elections through independent candidates, or in alliance with one or more of the legal parties. Though the Brotherhood is part of political life in a number of Arab countries, it is not an international organization. The national movements are autonomous, though members from different states meet occasionally to discuss ideology and world events.

The Brotherhood created a base in civil society in the 1980s through the colonization of student bodies and the professional unions which regulate doctors, lawyers, engineers, pharmacists, and other occupations. It has a mass membership of some 600,000, of whom about 100,000 are activists. At the lowest level of the organization, members are grouped into small 'families' or *usra*. Above this, there is a territorial hierarchy of 'subsidiary populaces', 'subsidiary areas', and 'regional sectors'. At the apex stands the 100-strong Consultative Council, which meets annually to elect a 'Guidance Office' or 15-member executive bureau; discuss the executive bureau's plans for the coming year, including the budget; and approve the previous year's accounts. The head of the Guidance Office is the movement's leader or 'Supreme Guide'. This organizational structure has proved to be an effective channel of communication, mobilization, and liaison not only within the Brotherhood, but also with whatever party is fronting for the movement (currently the Freedom and Justice Party). It also has to manage divisions within the movement, mainly around whether it should concentrate on religious evangelism or engage in national politics.

The Brotherhood is well-funded by donations and tithes from individuals and unions, as well as some mosques, banks, and businesses. A major source of funds is foreign governments and charities, especially in Kuwait and Saudi Arabia. The movement's financial strength enables it to run schools, clinics, hospitals, and a range of welfare services benefiting the poor, including support for widows and orphans, and relief in emergencies such as the 1992 earthquake (Soage and Franganillo, 2010; Trager, 2011).

---

Bolivia's governing party, the Movement Toward Socialism, has succeeded in the difficult task of mobilizing indigenous people by investing in a party organization and exploiting its support base in the country's strongest civil society group (Manning, 2010; Rice, 2011).

Party survival requires an elaborate internal apparatus to mobilize society, and to penetrate it through a mass membership involved in a local as well as a central organization. Parties then create a sense of national legitimacy and become successful instruments of political recruitment. Parties survive because they have firm grass roots. Where parties fail to create machinery for transmitting interests, opinions, and needs upwards to the policy-making elite, and only create channels of communication and coercion downwards from the leadership to the masses, they experience difficulty surviving. A local organization has significance beyond organizational structure, and embraces a whole approach to the management of society and economy, as well as political education, indoctrination, and control.

While developing an ideology and communicating are crucial to creating a sense of legitimacy, recent trends indicate a significant shift in the relationship between party leaderships and their mass memberships. In Latin America, party organization has changed in respect of relations with affiliated bodies. These have become less important for mobilization and financial support than the mass media and external funding. In India, too, Congress has an elaborate organizational structure not only at the grass roots, but also at state, provincial and district levels, with a high level of internal democracy. However, as in Latin America, party organization and grass-roots political activity have been neglected in favour of 'increasing reliance on the electronic media, advertising and whirlwind campaigning' (Sridharan and Varshney, 2001, p. 221). This is not to imply that grass-roots organization can safely be abandoned. Latin American experience shows that 'virtually all electorally successful parties ... have learned to cultivate clientelistic ties at the grass roots' (Coppedge, 2001, p. 176).

Organizational survival also depends on making the party leadership representative of a broad range of interests (Randall, 1988). For example, the United National Independence Party in Zambia was successful in making the leadership representative of a wide range of social elites. There also has to be a balanced membership. Activists who sustain the organization through membership drives, fund raising, candidate selection, voter mobilization, and party debate have to be balanced with professional experts in different policy fields. There must also be a balance between nominal members and party activists, and between collegial leadership and a willingness to remove leaders who are out of touch with members and the electorate. A balance has also to be struck between the principle of open membership to whoever supports the party's ideals and objectives, and a rule of restricted access, either to avoid capture by interests that would narrow the party's electoral appeal, or to ensure effective action in government or opposition (Graham, 1993). Leaders that devote themselves to the party, rather than using it a stepping-stone to jobs elsewhere, such as in the government bureaucracy, are also required (Huntington, 1968).

The strength of party organization is also dependent upon consistency – in ideological position, discipline (among members and elected representatives), patterns of internal organization, rules of leadership succession, and methods of mass mobilization. A weakness of the Kuomintang (KMT) in Taiwan was its lack of a routine method for organizing succession, making the cohesion of the party vulnerable during any change in the leadership. Organizational reform became unavoidable when the party was defeated in 2000 by the Democratic Progressive Party, especially new procedures for the election of party chairman and central committee, leaving the party strong despite its loss of office (and access to patronage) and the transition to multi-party democracy (Chu, 2001).

The volatile party systems of Latin America, in which fewer than 20 per cent of the 1,200 parties competing in twentieth-century elections survived more than one election, suggest another explanation for party survival: adaptation to the political environment. Party survival may be a function of 'political Darwinism' when adaptability to changes in the environment (urbanization, rising crime, regime change, inflation, growing inequality, economic decline, economic liberalization, and so on) proves impossible for all but the fittest. The survivors are those that cope with economic stresses, and provide organizational alternatives to those that have failed – for example, the strong party discipline of Brazil's Workers' Party in contrast to the anarchy within the Partido de Movimento Democratico Brasiliero. Strength of party identification among voters is another crucial variable in this explanation of party survival (Coppedge, 2001).

Autonomy from 'founding personalities' is also needed, as well as significant financial and human resources, including professional staff (Mainwaring, 1998; Stockton, 2001). Funding and institutional autonomy, including freeing the party from domination from the civil bureaucracy or military, are also important organizational features (Randall, 1988). It has to be noted that India's Congress Party, with considerable bureaucratic infiltration, seems to be the exception to this.

In poor countries, there are few resources to sustain political parties, other than such as can be obtained from public office. Thus, foreign support may be necessary for a new party to survive, especially if its natural constituency is among the poor. For example, the Ugandan Democratic Party depends for its survival on overseas support which it receives via an NGO – the Foundation for African Development, which is funded by the German Konrad Adenauer Foundation. Overseas support, especially if channelled through government agencies, can end up disproportionately benefiting the ruling party, and contributing to the emergence of one-party dominant systems, as in El Salvador and Cambodia (Carbone, 2003; de Zeeuw, 2010).

## Factionalism and clientelism

The strength of party organization in the Third World has frequently been dependent upon the distribution of patronage and the allocation of state resources and positions within the military and bureaucracy. The distribution of rewards to supporters and clients on a personalized basis can be crucial for the survival of a political party.

Clientelism represents a rational form of behaviour for people under conditions of inequality and when parties need the support of regional, ethnic, and personal factions (Clapham, 1982). The following 'core analytical characteristics' of the social interactions and exchanges involved in patron–client relations can be identified:

- they are particularistic and diffuse;
- resources are exchanged, both economic and political (support, votes, protection, solidarity);
- resources are exchanged as a 'package', not separately;
- the relationship is strongly unconditional and long-term;
- there is a varying amount of solidarity in the relationship;
- it is based on informal, and not necessarily legal, understandings;
- patron–client relations are entered into voluntarily;
- the vertical nature of patron–client relations undermines horizontal solidarities, especially among clients;
- and the relationship is based on strong inequality and power difference. (Eisenstadt and Roniger, 1981)

Political and economic changes, particularly the development of the state and the spread of capitalism, have fundamentally altered the nature of patronage. Patron–client relations increasingly take the form of brokerage and mediation between clients in their dealings with government and the market. Such relationships are likely to decline as government revenues increase, allowing voters to be offered universal benefits. The voters' interests can then be indicated directly through choice of party, obviating the need for mediation through patrons (Elliot, 2011). Analysis of 'programmatic' parties, or parties offering policy packages to voters, rather than services to clients, in 12 Latin American countries in the late 1990s confirmed that socio-economic development reduces voters' preferences for clientelist rewards, and increases the attractiveness of collective goods such as redistributive social policies. Changes in the relationship between voters and parties in favour of 'programmatic linkages' occur when increased levels of income, education, and skills make voters more socially, economically, and physically mobile and less dependent on patrons. Conversely, a period of economic decline is likely to produce a reversion to clientelist politics (Kitschelt *et al.*, 2010).

Clientelism is thus likely to decline in significance when parties form along ideological lines, mobilizing political support on the basis of horizontal, rather than vertical, linkages (e.g. class, rather than kinship). The significance of clientelism in politics is further reduced by the bureaucratic allocation of public services on the basis of legal entitlements. The development of a universalistic political culture, and institutions of civil society through which citizens can pursue their individual rights and entitlements, also provide alternatives to clientelism (Roniger, 1994).

Nevertheless, clientelism remains a significant component of the electoral process in many Third World countries. Political parties are compelled to recruit from among local patrons and brokers in order to secure the political support of their clients. The links between leaders and followers in party factions are therefore highly personalized. Special interests pursue their objectives through such links with the political authorities. Party leaders offer support and protection to those who accept and support their leadership. Identity with a leader will cut across conflicting interests, so that the leaders of factions have to mediate between the groups who support them. In India, for example, political parties, notably Congress, have had to incorporate many different kinds of loyalty – those based on caste, landlord–tenant relations, language, tribe, and religion. However, when elections are dominated by voters' concerns about which candidate will secure rewards in the form of public services, as in most Middle Eastern and North African states, they cease to be an effective mechanism for a democratic change of government. Opposition candidates are simply denied access to state resources, and consequently fail to secure electoral support (Lust, 2009).

While people's livelihoods and economic opportunities are dependent upon the rewards for political loyalty which successful patrons can distribute in the form of jobs, contracts, loans, and welfare benefits, all aspects of life become politicized. Competition for votes to secure a patron's success becomes so intense that it can lead to violence, as has increasingly become the case in Sri Lanka (Hoglund and Piyarathne, 2009).

Within parties, different interests are often expressed through factionalism, which can have highly variable consequences for the durability of political parties. Factions are an informal aspect of party organization. They are the inevitable consequence of alliances and coalitions between leaders and followers that have no ideological foundation but which are designed to secure electoral support. Relationships between leaders of factions and their followers are based on a range of social and economic conditions, such as feudalistic tenure systems (when a landowner can guarantee electoral support from tenants because of their economic dependency), cultural loyalties, and other traditional obligations. Alternatively, the factional linkage may be tribal, linguistic, or caste-based.

Factionalism leads to a segmentary form of party politics. The internal structures of factions are very much alike and political relations within them are always transactional, instrumental, and dependent. Factionalism is stimulated by the rewards which are accessible to those in political office. Class interests and conflicts are overlaid by the common interest of patron and client. Factional conflict is about obtaining a broader basis of followers, so the outcome of conflict does not change the social structure. The conflicts between factions are not ideological. They are conflicts over resources, over influence at key points in the decision-making structure of party and government, and over the ability to gain enough followers to win office so that patronage can be extended and the size and power of the faction can be increased. Success breeds success in a system of patronage. Leaders who win office can be expected to use their powers of patronage to enlarge their faction, drawing others into their sphere of influence. Leaders can then seek higher office, greater patronage, and an enlarged following. Factional politics within parties and patron–client relationships produce a distinctive image for Third World parties.

If a leader fails to mediate successfully between different interests, his faction may split. If the split runs the length of the party, factional conflict may lead to a new party being formed. A successful party thus has to contain centrifugal forces, and contend with factors that encourage factionalism and undermine party unity, such as caste or communalism in India. India's Janata Party has failed to develop a cohesive organization because of caste conflict, and the geographical and cultural divisions between people of the same caste (ironically, for a party whose aim is an egalitarian reform of the caste system) (Bjorkman and Mathur, 1996; Sridharan and Varshney, 2001).

## Conclusion

Political parties have proved indispensable to most types of regime in the context of mass politics. They enable the masses to be mobilized, managed, co-opted, and coerced. They have been used to prohibit opposition to the regime. In deeply divided societies, they have represented exclusive identities and so inhibited national integration through the aggregation of interests. They have socialized people into divisive beliefs and attitudes, derived from religion, race, and ethnicity.

Yet parties have also proved indispensable to the process of democratization. They have led opposition to authoritarianism. They constitute a foundation for pluralist democracy by providing electorates with the choices between leaders and policies which are essential for representative and accountable government. They mobilize support so that power can be secured and transferred peacefully. They provide a medium for political recruitment. They act as channels through which rank and file members and affiliated bodies influence the leadership in its choice of policies. They can empower the poor and other politically marginalized groups. They contribute to political stability by endowing regimes with legitimacy. Democratic consolidation requires the institutionalization of party competition.

The survival of parties and multi-party systems is thus relevant to political stability, especially in newly democratizing states. The 'problem' of political instability is primarily seen in terms of the demise of party politics, especially of the competitive type. Not surprisingly, the attention that has been paid to political instability in the Third World has focused particularly on the supplantment, usually by the military, of a civilian form of government based on a system of parties. Military intervention, political stability, and the process of democratization are the subjects of later chapters. But, first, the political role of bureaucracy must be examined, including its capacity to provide public services equitably.

# 6

# Bureaucracy and Political Power

## The challenge of bureaucracy

Bureaucracies are powerful institutions in all political systems. Public officials cannot be thought of as merely the neutral implementers of the political decisions of others. In the Third World, the bureaucracy has come to be regarded in some circumstances as the most powerful political institution. We have already touched upon ways in which the bureaucracy is so regarded. Theories of the post-colonial state have employed the concept of a bureaucratic oligarchy, clearly implying that government is in the hands of the paid officials of the state.

This chapter distinguishes between different concepts of bureaucracy and shows that all are contained in the analyses that have been carried out of the role of the bureaucracy in Third World societies and states. Sources of bureaucratic power are categorized, as well as bureaucratic features which have been taken to be signs of the emergence of a new kind of ruling class. Bureaucracy also implies a certain kind of rationality in the context of the official allocation of scarce resources, requiring consideration of the concept of 'access'.

## Concepts of bureaucracy

One of the problems when studying bureaucracy is that the term carries different connotations for different people. A number of different definitions have been attached to the term. This conceptual ambiguity can, however, be put to good use. If we remind ourselves of the different meanings of bureaucracy, we can explore its full significance as a political force, a significance which extends well beyond the implementation of public policy.

'Bureaucracy' can simply refer to a government's *administrative agencies* staffed by public servants. It is synonymous with public administration, consisting of organizations set up as part of the modern state to carry out the policies of decision-makers. The state needs specialized institutions for implementing public policy and employs large numbers of people who make it their career to serve the state in a professional capacity. The bureaucracy thus refers to the public services and the organizations into which they are structured. It is a category of governmental personnel and offices that are filled in a particular way. It tells us no more about the way those organizations function, or about the political power that the bureaucracy might exercise – either over the formulation of public policies, or their mode, and even degree of implementation.

Part of the importance of public bureaucracies in developing countries arises from the demands that have been made on governments to stimulate development by providing a social and economic infrastructure, and engaging directly in production. After independence, state bureaucracies were seen as promoters of social and economic change through planned development programmes (Jain, 1992). Even when the ideology has been predominantly capitalist and free-market, the state has intervened to support private capital. In the newly industrialized countries (NICs) of Southeast Asia and Latin America, the state and the bureaucracy have been highly interventionist. In the Philippines, the civil service continues to expand, despite efforts to trim the bureaucracy. A combination of presidential patronage and a wide range of policy objectives – in health, education, housing, security, environment, law and order, and support to economic sectors – is responsible. In Tanzania, instead of reducing the size of the bureaucracy, the public service reform programme started in 2000 has accompanied an increase in the numbers of government agencies and personnel (Mamuya, 2008; Robles, 2008; UNDP, 2010a).

Within democratic theory, it is assumed that the bureaucracy will be both accountable to those who have been elected to govern, and politically neutral and independent in the advice they give members of the executive. This enables them to serve whichever set of party leaders forms a government following competitive elections. But accountability is difficult under the political conditions typically found throughout the Third World. Whether the aim is to curb unacceptable personal behaviour (such as corruption, or nepotism), or improve performance (by checking on probity and efficiency), accountability requires legislative oversight, transparency, and judicial review. How effective such mechanisms will be depends on the historical legacies of colonialism, the effectiveness of political opposition, and the level of judicial development, as the experiences of Southeast Asian countries demonstrates (Fritzen, 2007).

Bureaucratic neutrality is undermined by patronage and the political leadership's demand for partisan loyalty and affiliation. Single-party regimes have required bureaucrats to be card-carrying party members.

Military juntas have encouraged and rewarded political bias. Civil service jobs are used as rewards for services rendered. For example, in Cambodia the bureaucracy has been highly politicized by a combination of political appointments and pressure on officials to identify themselves with the ruling party. In Latin America and the Caribbean, most government jobs 'are assigned on the basis of political party affiliation, social class, ethnic group, nepotism or family connections' (Meacham, 1999, p. 282). Patronage, rather than merit, fills civil service posts, either to reward party activists or bring loyal experts into government, despite the presence of statutes establishing merit-based and politically neutral career structures. Consequently, a change of government can lead to large-scale changes in personnel – as many as 30,000 officials in Mexico and 25,000 in Panama, for example. In South Africa, partisan control of appointments, promotions, transfers, and performance assessment includes requiring candidates to be card-carrying ANC members. Such departures from the democratic model of public administration, under which staff should be recruited solely on merit, can – and, in Africa, have – produced administrative systems that are inflated, inefficient, ineffective, dishonest and, of course, politically biased (Adamolekun, 2002; Fritzen, 2007; Cameron, 2010; Grindle, 2010).

The concept of bureaucracy also identifies a particular kind of *organizational structure* in which people are recruited into positions of authority in a special way. Bureaucracy is a rational means for the performance of collective tasks, especially those requiring large-scale organization. This clearly implies that some organizations may be more bureaucratic than others. Insofar as they are, they have clearly distinguishable features. They have clear lines of command from one level of a hierarchy to another. Recruitment to positions or offices within a bureaucracy is on the basis of merit demonstrated by the acquisition of relevant qualifications, or success in a competitive entry test. Officials are dependent on a salary. They do not own the means of administration. They cannot take personal possession of a share of any revenues that they might be empowered to collect. Officials are merely paid a salary in return for their services to the state.

This reinforces the demarcation of official jurisdictions. There is a clear division of labour within a bureaucratic organization. It is divided into different offices to which attach certain clear-cut powers – regular, stable, and precisely defined authority. This is sometimes represented graphically in an organogram (or organizational chart) set out as a pyramid of offices. The officials occupying such offices have clearly defined powers laid down in abstract rules. Their authority will be closely prescribed by those rules. They will be engaged in applying general rules to specific cases. This is a particular feature of government bureaucracies and, especially, those bureaucrats who encounter members of the public on a face-to-face level. They deal with citizens as claimants, people who feel they are entitled to some benefit that the state has to allocate, and who fall within the category of need that the state has defined and to which they are entitled. The task of the bureaucrat is to make the allocation in a fair, impersonal, and impartial way, treating like cases alike and having regard for nothing other than the factors that the regulations deem to be relevant. The bureaucrat is interested in nothing about a claimant other than such matters as the regulations define as significant for arriving at a decision. If, for example, the official works for a small farmers development programme which defines entitlement in terms of size of land-holding, all the official needs to know is how much land the applicant occupies. All other aspects of the claimant's life – age, gender, race, tribe, caste, language, family size, place of origin – are irrelevant, unless the law brings one or more of them into the calculation.

In the Third World, cultural values have inflicted numerous departures from a model of bureaucracy which should, in theory, provide efficient policy implementation and fairness for the individual citizen. Third World bureaucracies have been marred by 'bureaupathologies', especially goal displacement (when following routine procedures is given precedence over the aims of the policy), disdain for the needs of clients, powerful opposition to change, and preoccupation with official status. Many such defects can be explained by cultural norms. In East and Southeast Asia, for example, these norms include family obligations, superstition, fear of losing 'face', exaggerated respect for authority, rank and qualifications, discrimination against women, and the need to avoid conflict in decision-making (Turner and Halligan, 1999).

This brings us to another meaning of bureaucracy, and one which most readily occurs to the citizen: *inaccessible administration* – rigid decision-making bound up in 'red tape', and insensitivity to personal circumstances and needs as defined by the citizen, rather than the official. These are the 'dysfunctional' or 'pathological' traits of bureaucracy. Rational organization and procedures deteriorate into inefficiency. In particular, 'strict adherence to regulations' induces 'timidity, conservatism and technicism', as well as conflict with clients (Merton, 1952, p. 367). Bureaucracy becomes an end in itself and, thus, self-defeating. It becomes characterized by buck-passing, inflexibility, excessive impersonality, over-secretiveness, unwillingness to delegate, and reluctance to exercise discretion (Heady, 1959). Such bureaucrats are perceived as being unconcerned with personal problems, limiting their attention to narrowly defined circumstances that rules happen to define as significant. Bureaucrats are caught within a double-bind. If they do not administer the rules rigidly in order to avoid appearing to be inflexible and inhuman, they will be accused of abusing their power, exercising too much discretion, and moving outside their circumscribed jurisdiction; if they apply the rules rigorously, they will be accused of being bureaupathological. The bureaucrat treads a difficult path between those two alternatives.

Finally, 'bureaucracy' can also mean a *type of regime*, a category of governmental system along with democracy or aristocracy. It can mean government by officials, rather than government by the people, a single person, or a hereditary caste. This has been widely experienced and is, in many ways, very reminiscent of colonial government, which was also government by appointed officials, both military and civil. In such regimes, exemplified by military oligarchies and dictatorships, the bureaucracy is not merely a powerful political force within the political process. Government is virtually coterminous with the bureaucracy, which may also take on some of the characteristics of a ruling class, as well as a ruling elite.

## The political power of bureaucracy

A major theoretical issue concerns the political power of the bureaucracy and how this may be conceptualized. Ideological and methodological choices have been important here. Functionalists and Marxists have both had distinctive things to say about the bureaucracy in the Third World. What they chose to focus upon and the way they have interpreted the role of the bureaucracy has depended very much upon their wider views and theories of society and the state.

One source of political power is *knowledge*. In the Third World, bureaucracies often monopolize the knowledge and expertise relevant to government. The concentration of technical, professional, and administrative expertise within the bureaucracy is unrivalled. Even when there is strong parliamentary government, and virile political parties and other centres of political power, and when the bureaucrats have a constitutional role which only permits them to advise the political executive, they do so from positions of great authority. In many developing countries, there are no political institutions which can compete with the bureaucracy in terms of a monopoly of technical and professional expertise. In addition, the majority of professionals have, for many years, been employed in the public sector and public services. This, again, limits the availability of countervailing forces that can present political leaders with alternative plans, policy advice, and techniques of implementation to those put forward by government officials.

Development planning has consequently tended to be highly centralized, technocratic, and of the 'top down' variety, where the experts at the top make the decisions about what the masses need in terms of programmes of development, whether in health care, agriculture, education, or other areas of planned development. This feature of bureaucracy reflects the concept of a specially recruited group appointed on the basis of merit to produce rational and efficient methods of working. A system of recruitment that admits only those that can demonstrate the required level of expertise and competence is bound to produce organizations which lay politicians find it difficult to dominate.

Even when the dominant ideology demands a reduction in the role of the state, bureaucratic expertise remains crucial in the search for solutions to the problems which continue to beset Third World countries: 'More than ever before, it should assist the policy-makers in crafting alternatives to contemporary development policy and, particularly, to the ongoing "poverty reduction" schemes' (Balogun, 2002, p. 541).

Bureaucratic power also arises from *dependency*. Insofar as the state has been at the forefront of planning change in economy and society through programmes of investment, education, family planning, nutrition, sanitation, and the like, it has been dependent for the success of those plans upon a powerful and effective administration. Without officialdom, nothing is properly implemented. What the politicians might win through electoral support or force of arms has to be consolidated by administrative proceedings and by the multitude of development programmes formulated by governments in the Third World. Dependence on the bureaucracy applies not only to the implementation of social and economic policy, but also to administrative reforms and political transitions (Balogun, 2002).

A third source of bureaucratic power is the social esteem and *status* enjoyed by senior bureaucrats. This may originate from a number of different sources – the public's acknowledgement of the impartiality of the public service, or of its professional expertise; and the legacy of colonialism when, particularly in the rural areas, officials stood at the apex of the power structure. When post-colonial officials inherited the offices, pay scales, and perks of the colonial expatriates, they also inherited their prestige and standing in the community. When, also, there are few other opportunities for educated people to find employment, posts in the public service become the goal of the technocratic elite. For many years, the private sector could not offer the opportunities which government service could, and still does, in many societies of the Third World.

Employment in the national government also offers the tempting possibility of secondment to an international bureaucracy of a UN agency such as the Food and Agriculture Organization (FAO), United Nations Development Programme (UNDP), or World Health Organization (WHO), with the World Bank, the IMF or even a regional organization such as the Organization of American States (OAS) or the United Nations

Economic Commission for Latin America and the Caribbean (ECLA). The universal values that are disseminated through such movements and contacts further enhance the elite status of bureaucrats in their own countries. This may lead to a bureaucracy that performs a kind of hegemonic role, disseminating an ideology and a particular view of the state and its role in development. In the functionalist literature, this has been especially identified as aimed at national integration through the enunciation of universalistic, Westernized and modern values. Bureaucrats were identified as pulling countries along the path to progress. They not only influence the policy choices of governments, but also the way people outside government perceive the role of the state in development.

A fourth factor was alluded to in the earlier discussion of the post-colonial state. This is the *relative* power of the bureaucracy as a political institution *vis-à-vis* others (Wallis, 1989). This perception is common to both Marxist and functionalist political science. Both schools of thought emphasize that one colonial legacy was the retarded development of political institutions that might have held the bureaucracy accountable. Colonialism developed bureaucracies at the expense of other institutions, being more interested in the power of officials in relation to society than in the power of representative assemblies, political parties, pressure groups, and other organizations representative of different sections of society and expected to evolve into institutions capable of controlling the bureaucratic apparatus of the state.

Post-colonial states inherited bureaucracies that were prestigious, well-organized and with a strong sense of corporate identity, and other political institutions lacking the same power and legitimacy. As party organizations became stronger, this situation changed. As mass parties threw up leaders not dependent upon the bureaucracy but, rather, on mass support at elections, and the longer that parliamentary institutions had to establish themselves, the stronger techniques for controlling the bureaucracy grew. The more that groups outside the state – in business, agriculture, the labour movement, and the professions – developed and produced their own organizations, the more the bureaucracy was further held accountable to other groups of policy-makers.

The political power of the bureaucracy is not necessarily matched by administrative competence. It frequently has to work with inadequate information, particularly statistical. The fact that it monopolizes policy-relevant knowledge does not mean that it will have the quantity of skilled manpower for the tasks allotted to it. It may also be reluctant, for political reasons, to complete projects started under the preceding political leadership. The greater the political power of the bureaucracy, the weaker the incentives for effective administration and the more ineffectual the bureaucracy. Bureaucratic efficiency is further reduced by the imbalance between bureaucracies and other political institutions, and the consequent preoccupation among bureaucrats with furthering their bureaucratic interests, rather than serving political masters (Riggs, 1964).

The bureaucratic capacity of Third World states is of concern to international agencies such as the World Bank which are trying to redefine the role of the state in economic and social development. But the crisis of administrative capacity persists, especially in parts of sub-Saharan Africa, despite huge investment in 30 years of largely ineffective administrative reform. Failure to improve the quality of public services, such as education and health, stems from a lack of commitment on the part of public servants and other obstacles to effective administration (Crook, 2010).

Bureaucratic power can also have adverse consequences for the development of political systems. Bureaucratic centralism and control of local governments weaken the educative effects of political participation. The bureaucratic mobilization of interest groups weakens centres of autonomous political pressure. Parliaments do not thrive on a foundation of weak parties, pressure groups, and popular participation. Bureaucracies, rather than parliaments, control revenue raising, expenditure, and policy initiatives. Bureaucratic 'formalism', whereby laws are enacted but not implemented, further undermines representative institutions. The judicial system can be exploited by the bureaucracy to assist its abuse of power. Consequently, 'too rapid expansion of the bureaucracy when the political system lags behind tends to inhibit the development of effective politics ... separate political institutions have a better chance to grow if bureaucratic institutions are relatively weak' (Riggs, 1963, p. 126).

Thus, a bureaucracy can positively discourage the development of institutions which can ensure accountability and function as alternative policy-making bodies. The development processes of different political institutions such as bureaucracies and parties are not separate and unrelated. In effect, the bureaucracy creates political vacuums for it to fill itself (Heeger, 1973).

The functionalists conceptualized this institutional imbalance as 'multi-functionality', arguing that, in transitional societies, political structures have not become as specialized as they would when society had become fully modern. The functionalist idea of political modernity included a bureaucracy fully specialized in rule application. In advanced societies, power resides with the people, and public servants are there to give advice and obey orders. Transitional society has political structures that have not become fully specialized, but are multifunctional. It becomes logically possible for bureaucratic structures to perform all the input and output functions of the political system, and be as much concerned with the function of rule-*making* as rule-*application* (Almond, 1960). However, it was not always easy to fit the behaviour of Third World bureaucrats into the functionalist taxonomy (Smith, B. C., 1988).

Marxist social theorists have adopted a different approach to bureaucratic overdevelopment. In Mali, a 'crisis of colonialism' brought about independence before any viable political structures other than the bureaucracy had had a chance to develop (Meillasoux, 1970). Alavi's (1972) analysis of Pakistan and Bangladesh also refers to the overdevelopment of the bureaucracy relative to other political institutions. Once freed from direct metropolitan control, this oligarchy was able to extend its dominant power in society, assume a new economic role, proliferate bureaucratic controls and public agencies, manipulate the facade of parliamentary government and, eventually, even seize power from the democratic regime.

Experience elsewhere, however, indicated the need for qualifications to this depiction of the bureaucracy. In Kenya, for example, the bureaucracy was divided into different branches and strata. Civil servants did not always have identical interests to the managers of state-owned enterprises, and the latter were 'especially exposed to the bourgeois values embodied in the technology, management practices, "efficiency" ideology, etc. of the firms they take over'. Career bureaucrats also needed to be distinguished from party officials inserted into the civil administration, particularly in terms of their respective class linkages (Leys, 1976, p. 44). This remains the case. In India, for example, the bureaucracy is divided at both federal and state levels into specialists and generalists, with the former further divided into police, revenue, education, telecommunications, agriculture, and so on (Krishna, 2010).

Other observers have qualified the post-colonial model by seeing it as a passing phase and one that in some Third World societies has been left behind – notably in India, where the colonial administration was overdeveloped and had enormous prestige supported by a complex ideology of racial superiority, paternalism, and tolerance of those indigenous institutions deemed to be compatible with metropolitan interests. But, following independence, an Indian middle class increasingly articulated its interests through the formal institutions of political democracy. Administrative behaviour in post-colonial India has become increasingly bureaucratic and instrumental 'as a response to the emergence of legislatures, political parties, and new forms of class differentiation which together have functioned to undermine the autonomy of the state administrative apparatus' (Wood, G. D., 1977, p. 307). The establishment of democratic institutions meant a loss of authority, power, and status for the bureaucracy. When class interests sought to oppose reforms by undermining administrative authority, the bureaucracy retreated into ideologies of professionalism, instrumentalism and neutrality.

Once democratization tips the balance in favour of other institutions, the bureaucracy moves closer to the instrumental model of administration, where officials are the servants of elected representatives. In India, for example, this means that the bureaucracy is held increasingly accountable by a range of institutional developments: stronger parliaments, more effective mass media, legislation supporting freedom of information, a greater willingness and ability on the part of the public to contest administrative decisions, and stronger political intermediaries between ordinary people and public officials (Krishna, 2010).

Bureaucratic stability, or the *continuity* of the bureaucratic elite compared with other political elites, is a further source of power. Governments come and go; *coups*, revolts, and revolutions bring about changes of regime – but the bureaucracy remains. New elites come to be dependent on it. In the case of Pakistan, it seems that the bureaucracy had been in control from the very inception of 'military' rule (Alavi, 1990). The same applied to Africa: 'In countries like Togo, Nigeria, Ghana, Sierra Leone, Liberia and the former Zaire, it was to the civil service that the military juntas turned when embarking on the difficult challenge of "suspending" the constitution, dissolving parliament, and ruling by decree' (Balogun, 2002, p. 547). Under conditions of political instability, the continuity of the bureaucracy enhances its power. It is impossible to dispense with it as an institution and often extremely difficult to replace its personnel with those who have the ideological commitment needed by the leaders of a new government or regime, especially if administrative expertise is monopolized by the old guard.

## A ruling class

Bureaucracies may become more than just powerful political institutions. They may form a new kind of class – and a ruling class, at that. There has, first, to be a bureaucratic mode of production, when the bureaucracy controls and manages the means of production through state ownership. The bureaucracy provides the necessary organization, and proliferates opportunities for bureaucratic careers by the creation of public bodies needing public managers – marketing boards, development corporations, and other parastatal organizations and their subsidiaries (Hirschmann, 1981). It articulates an ideology of state ownership and planning. It organizes the means of its own reproduction by passing on to the offspring of bureaucrats disproportionately advantageous opportunities to obtain the qualifications needed for entry into bureaucratic occupations – and, therefore, the new class.

For example, the post-independence bureaucracy in Mali used its access to political power to acquire some of the characteristics of a social class. It controlled the infrastructure of the economy and the means of repression, using them to maintain its dominance, particularly in its conflict with weak indigenous social classes, notably the landed aristocracy and the petty-bourgeois class of traders. Above all, it created a nationalized sector of the economy which, under the label of socialism, enabled the economy to be brought under bureaucratic control. Tanzania provides a further example.

The expertise of the bureaucracy is another factor of production, in addition to land, labour, and capital. The bureaucracy supplies the organizations necessary and the managerial, scientific, and technical knowledge required. It takes over that legacy of colonialism in which the bureaucracy dominated embryonic indigenous classes. The bureaucracy monopolizes organization and all its attributes necessary for the management of the economy. It articulates an ideology in support of this, since any mode of production requires a set of ideas to justify control of the surplus by the ruling element in society.

There are, then, bureaucratic features which have been taken to be signs of the emergence of a new kind of ruling class. The fact that ownership resides with society and not the bureaucracy becomes a legalistic fiction. Control is what matters – as, indeed, has been said about capitalism: that the managers not the owners of corporate assets are the power-holders. The accumulation of personal wealth is made possible by a career in the bureaucracy. The salaries enjoyed by the upper ranks in many African states; their easy access to credit; and their control over permits, licences, and tenders have enabled them to acquire urban and rural real estate, and business ventures (Hirschmann, 1981).

However, the class interests of the state bureaucracy do not necessarily describe the class character of the state. For example, the dominant class in African society in the 1970s was the *foreign* bourgeoisie. Any class interests which the personnel of the state might have had were only reflected in state policy in a secondary way (Leys, 1976). Senior members of the bureaucracy might be able to embourgeoise themselves through the opportunities to acquire property made available by their official positions, siphoning off 'a large part of the economic surplus that is generated in society to accumulate wealth for themselves' (Alavi, 1990, p. 23) and even enjoy substantial social mobility for themselves and their families as a result, but this alone does not amount to evidence of the emergence of a new class structure.

**Bureaucracy and access**

Bureaucratic power is also related to the administrative allocation of scarce state resources to meet politically defined needs among different sections of the population – for income support, employment, land, agricultural inputs, food, health care, education, credit, shelter, and other public provision that has to be bureaucratically administered.

If we recall the different meanings attached to bureaucracy – and, in particular, bureaucracy as a certain kind of rationality – we find that, in the context of the bureaucratic allocation of scarce resources, rationality takes on a special political significance. High levels of need – particularly among the poorer sections of society, but also among other sections, such as private capital – mean that the bureaucracy has to allocate scarce resources according to politically determined categories of need. The market is not left to make such allocations; it is done through official action.

For example, if the poor are deemed to be in need because they lack the resources to obtain from the market what is required to maintain life at a certain officially designated standard, bureaucratic allocations have to be made. In the case of income, steps may be taken to create jobs such as a public works programme into which will be recruited labour from a target group whose need has been officially identified and which the public intervention has been set up to meet. Or the need may be identified as land, so that people can support themselves. The policy might then be a land reform programme which allocates land to the landless. The need might be for shelter which cannot be demanded in the private housing sector. Similarly, the private market for education may be beyond the reach of certain categories of people who are politically defined as 'needing' educational provision. Health care is in a similar category.

Such allocations affect other client groups. Particular categories of agricultural or industrial producers might be identified as having a need for inputs such as fertilizer, seeds, or equipment which should increase levels of productivity. A potentially productive group may be unable to obtain credit in the financial markets because of the lack of secure collateral or ability to repay at the market rate of interest, so the state provides loans at a subsidized rate.

A wide range of state interventions aimed at particular groups of beneficiaries is virtually synonymous with development planning in many parts of the Third World. Those state interventions should be managed bureaucratically by officials acting according to the Weberian model of public service. Rules and regulations will be applied to specific cases. Entitlements to public benefits are created for specified groups. In theory, the intended beneficiaries will be able to identify themselves as such, will be informed of their newly defined rights, and will be able to comprehend the way bureaucratic organizations arrive at final decisions in individual cases. Officials correspondingly behave according to norms which structure the decision-making process, seeking relevant information to test whether specified conditions have been met. The conditions may be numerous and complex. Nevertheless, a claim can still be systematically examined to see whether a claimant falls into the eligible category.

Many have no problem in understanding the way public organizations plan such expenditure and interventions, and the way they make decisions about its allocation. There may be political interference with the process of administrative allocation, leading to deviation from the bureaucratic norm. Allocations may not then be made impartially and according to the rules. It is a highly politicized process but, for the more Westernized and educated sections of society, the processes of decision-making are comprehensible. However, for other sections of society in poor, agricultural economies that are in the process of change, adjustment to bureaucratic methods of decision-making is difficult.

In a peasant community, such bureaucratization may appear very alien: this is not because people lack intelligence, are irrational, or are backward; it is because bureaucratic rationality does not coincide with their own. The behaviour of the bureaucrat, who can only deal with information that is relevant to the case that falls within his jurisdiction, may appear very strange in the context of rural society in many parts of the world. To dismiss information about a person's current situation as irrelevant is difficult for a person to accept when they are part of a community in which aspects of different lives interact. People do not see themselves as standing in a single-stranded relationship with others, but in multi-stranded relationships (Wood, G. D., 1977). A money-lender rather than an agriculture extension officer may be approached for credit, but the relationship with the money-lender will be very different from that with a government official. The multi-stranded relationships of peasant communities combine debt, kinship, tenancy, employment, reciprocity, political factionalism, and patronage. A bureaucrat treating like cases alike and focusing exclusively on officially selected aspects of an individual's circumstances is using a peculiarly Westernized form of rationality that rich and educated farmers in the community may be able to appreciate and with which they will cooperate. But poor, illiterate, uneducated and *dependent* members of the community, at whom the programmes of public expenditure may have been specifically and deliberately targeted, may find it difficult to adapt to the process. A bureaucrat cannot be approached in a multi-stranded way. Other aspects of an individual's economic and family circumstances which are currently all-pervading will be defined as irrelevant to the bureaucrat. Needs will have been defined in terms of officially selected attributes of a person's existence. The claimant, on the other hand, will not want to present a case. He will want to present a story about the integrated parts of his whole existence.

Bureaucrats then discover that their programmes do not have the impact which the policy-makers hoped for. Resources provided by officialdom are used to satisfy what the beneficiaries regard as more pressing needs (Wood, G. D., 1977). Or the intended beneficiaries do not come forward and claim their rights. Entering a government programme may be risky, if it involves disengaging from the traditional obligations of the community. If the bureaucratic allocation fails to work as intended, and if one has withdrawn from community structures, no longer seeking the protection, assistance and reciprocity of local relationships, the consequences could be disastrous. A position of dependency, and even exploitation, may be preferred to the position of recipient of a state programme.

The bureaupathologies referred to earlier create other problems for those who cannot avoid contact with administrative agencies. A bureaucratic culture can be so infected with formalism, delays (despite overstaffing), corruption, and arbitrary discretion that relations between officials and their publics have to be negotiated by agents employed to pursue cases through the bureaucracy by claimants wishing to avoid face-to-face contact with officials. Clearly, such a system puts the poor at a further disadvantage when seeking access.

Pressures on officials, including corruption, may mean that the resources to be allocated are not received by the target group but, instead, find their way to other destinations. Administrative officials may to a certain extent be at the mercy of political pressures to benefit local elites at the expense of target groups identified by government programmes. Bureaucrats need to be able to demonstrate success. They can use their discretion to allocate resources to those who can produce results – say, in terms of agricultural output – that can be translated into the levels of administrative performance that will satisfy superiors: for example, farmers who have experience of modern agricultural techniques and commercial transactions. Since it is the capitalistic, rationally economic, literate, and market-oriented *farmer* who corresponds to the model of behaviour on which bureaucratically administered programmes are predicated, such programmes will inevitably favour him, rather than the survival-oriented, indebted, dependent, marginal, and vulnerable poor peasant. In this way, bias is introduced into much development planning that directs state interventions at particular groups of beneficiaries (Wood, 1977, 1984).

## Reducing bureaucracy

In the last 20 years, the role of bureaucracies in the politics of developing countries has been heavily influenced by the principles of economic liberalization and new public management (NPM). Under conditionalities imposed by multilateral agencies such as the World Bank, the IMF, UNDP and the Asian Development Bank, and with the support of powerful bilateral donors such as the USA's Agency for International Development, some Third World governments have been obliged to undergo structural adjustment programmes. Others, such as China and Thailand, have embraced such reforms autonomously (Worthley and Tsao, 1999; Bowornwathana, 2000).

Reforms have included reducing the size of the public sector through the privatization of state-owned enterprises. The same international agencies have also required and supported administrative reforms according to the principles of NPM. The results of these policies for the role of bureaucracies in the politics of Third World states have been mixed, and by no means all in the direction of securing greater democratic control over public officials (Turner and Hulme, 1997; Hughes, 1998; Brett, 2009).

On the face of it, a programme of privatization would seem inevitably to reduce the power of bureaucrats simply by taking the production of goods and services out of their hands and selling them off to the private sector. There is, then, much less for bureaucrats to manage. However, no sooner had Third World states been instructed to privatize than they were advised to regulate. As part of its discovery that the state must, after all, play a central role in developing a country, the World Bank revealed that 'governments are learning that market reforms and fast-changing technology pose their own regulatory challenges. States cannot abandon regulation' (World Bank, 1997, p. 61).

Depending on local administrative capabilities, states need officials to enforce rules that support competitive markets, protect the environment, foster industrial innovation, prevent the abuse of monopoly powers, enlighten consumers and workers (e.g. about health and safety risks in production or consumption), safeguard the health of the financial system (e.g. by regulating banking), and protect savers and borrowers from 'information asymmetry'. Regulation has to be performed by public administrators, and regulators need discretionary power to respond flexibly to changing circumstances. Once again, the public interest and welfare are heavily dependent upon the competence and integrity of public officials.

The importance of public services to vulnerable people has also been rediscovered. Services giving the poor access to health care, education, clean water, sanitation, and other vital resources have become part of a new 'poverty agenda' advocated by aid donors and some progressive governments (Smith, 2007).

Nevertheless, the NPM approach to administrative reform also has among its aims a reduction in the size of the bureaucracy. A central requirement of NPM is to make greater use of the private sector by contracting out to private firms activities that were once performed 'in-house', in the expectation that competition will ensure reduced costs and, therefore, greater efficiency. Governments then become more concerned with 'enabling' the supply of services than with their direct production.

Governments have also been urged to de-bureaucratize by delegating to the 'Third Sector' of non-governmental organizations (NGOs), consisting of non-commercial entities such as business associations, youth groups, women's organizations, voluntary bodies, community associations, religious foundations, professional bodies, and autonomous organizations providing economic and social services such as agricultural extension, vocational training, social welfare, irrigation, and credit. 'Third Sector' organizations often fill gaps left by inadequate state provision.

NGOs may be preferred to bureaucratic provision because they are presumed to offer better access to services, and to respond more flexibly to the needs of individual clients. Their altruism may motivate them to work in areas which civil servants and other professionals try to avoid, such as remote rural localities. Democratization in parts of the Third World, especially Latin America, has created political space for NGOs to develop. In some new democracies, NGOs have been set up by the state.

Relationships between the state and NGOs include contracts, service agreements, grants, subsidies, tax exemptions, and the provision of accommodation. Contractual arrangements with NGOs have been recorded in the policy areas of agricultural extension (Uganda and Mozambique), rural water supply and sanitation (Bolivia and Chile), tube well installation for landless irrigation groups (in Bangladesh), training home visitors in child health for the Ministry of Health in Brazil, forest conservation in Nepal, the distribution of government-subsidized food in Mexico, child health and family planning in Haiti, and therapy under India's national tuberculosis programme.

State–NGO relations depend on the level of pluralism in the political system, the state's capacity to provide services itself, and how NGOs see their own political roles. NGOs usually engage in advocacy and pressure group activity. The more radical the NGO, the less favourably will it be viewed by governments. Relationships range from equal partners at one extreme to virtual absorption into the bureaucracy at the other.

The potential political advantages for governments of contracts with Third Sector organizations, in addition to reducing bureaucracy, include demonstrating a commitment to accountability and participation, and reducing political patronage. A further attraction is that NGOs can easily be discarded when politically necessary.

The benefits to the non-governmental sector include access to funds (especially from aid donors), a heightened profile, and opportunities to influence public policy. But there are also potential costs. Civic organizations risk becoming professionalized, bureaucratized, and dependent, rather than voluntary, creative, and autonomous. Cooperation with governments may strike at the independence of voluntary bodies, espe-cially the freedom to campaign politically as pressure groups. Government agencies may force NGOs into a 'responsible' mode by defining politically acceptable behaviour, leading to a loss of credibility among client groups. Contracts may require conformity to government objectives, rather than objectives defined by NGOs. Governments are likely to be interested in NGOs as service providers, rather than as sources of new ideas about public policies. Indeed, states often impose a restric-tive environment of laws, taxes, controls, bureaucratic resistance, and even political repression on civic organizations and other parts of the Third Sector. Conflicts are particularly likely when state officials are closely allied socially and politically to local economic elites, but then have to collaborate with NGOs attempting to extend the economic and political opportunities of the poor and other disadvantaged groups.

Some NPM principles point to an increase in the autonomy, and there-fore power, of public officials in both their enabling and service-provid-ing roles. New public managers are given greater discretion to use the resources at their disposal. While they are judged against performance standards that have been made more explicit and quantifiable than in the past, their accountability to political leaders is weakened. Furthermore, the constraints of the public service ethic are abandoned in favour of private sector management techniques and practices, particularly in rela-tion to personnel management. NPM also discards the unrealistic distinc-tion between politics and administration, acknowledging that public managers will inevitably decide on policy issues of political significance.

While there are obvious public benefits to be derived from any greater efficiency and effectiveness in the provision of public services and func-tions achieved by the employment of better managers, an emphasis on achievements rather than budgetary inputs, the use of effective incentives, and greater concern for the economical use of public resources, it is far less obvious that such reforms weaken the power of officials *vis-à-vis* political leaders. Public officials become more like the equals of politicians than their servants. The requirement under NPM that officials be responsive to the needs of their clients actually increases their political power by acknowl-edging their right to decide what needs to meet and how to meet them.

Under NPM the actions of public officials may become more transpar-ent, making it easier for the public to judge the wisdom of government policies. But the politicians' control of their bureaucrats is weakened. It is by no means clear that administrative reforms inspired by NPM will ensure as much accountability of public officials to elected representatives as more traditional methods of public administration, especially under Third World conditions where legislatures are weak and client groups poorly organized, as in Tanzania (see Box 6.1).

## Box 6.1   *Public sector reform in Tanzania*

Like many changes to African public sectors, the reforms being introduced into Tanzania are significantly different from earlier ones. Most are inspired by the new public management (NPM) paradigm. Among their aims are: to reduce the core functions of the state, redraw the boundaries between political and administrative responsibilities, emphasize efficiency, redefine relations between public and private sectors, strengthen accountability, reduce corruption, change values and attitudes, and exploit new technologies. Initially, there was fragile domestic political support for reform, external pressure, fragmented domestic policy-making, weak links between policy-making and implementation, and questionable assumptions about some of the key NPM-inspired reform measures. In the past decade or so, government capacity to design and implement reforms, such as the Public Service Reform Programme, has grown stronger. However, Tanzanian experience questions whether the NPM model is universally applicable.

The post-colonial Tanzanian administration was originally part of a bureaucratic mode of production. The ideology of African Socialism justified public ownership and bureaucratic management, and direction of, at the very least, the commanding heights of the economy. The inefficiencies, corruption, and poor quality of public services associated with this form of bureaucracy eventually led to a spate of reforms affecting personnel and administrative structures, commencing in the early 1990s. Economic liberalization undermined the bureaucratic mode of production, and political liberalization in the form of multi-party politics allowed administrative reform to become more salient politically. However, reform programmes have, in the absence of adequate domestic finance and effective high-level decision-making, been heavily dependent on donor funding and heavily influenced by donor objectives. Political support for reform remains weak, increasingly so as improvements in public services fail to materialize. Reforms are seen as a matter for political and administrative elites, and are little affected by pressures from civil society.

The power of bureaucrats – especially the Permanent Secretaries of ministries, and the Chief Executives of executive agencies such as the Tanzanian Revenue Authority, the Business Registration and Licensing Authority, the National Roads Agency and the Civil Aviation Authority – has increased under reforms which delegate administrative and regulatory powers to officials who monopolize information and management skills and who, in the absence of effective audit and political accountability, exercise unusual levels of autonomy. Public sector reforms designed to improve efficiency, strengthen motivation, and reduce corruption, have increasingly shielded decision-makers from public scrutiny and parliamentary control. And, instead of reducing the size of the bureaucracy, reforms have actually been accompanied by an increase in the numbers of government agencies and personnel. So, the economic context in which bureaucratic power is exercised may have been fundamentally altered, but its strength in relation to the new functions of the Tanzanian state remains formidable (Shivji, 1976; Therkildsen, 2000; Caulfield, 2002; Mamuya, 2008).

The practice of the new dogma in public management also affects the balance of power within civil society. Redefining the citizen as 'customer' or 'client' – an approach adopted by many countries in Asia, Africa and Latin America – implies a monetary transaction and exchange rather than a public duty to provide a service to those entitled to receive it. Charging for services makes essential services such as education and health care less affordable to low-income groups. Divestment and 'downsizing' of public services and social expenditure reduces the capacity of the state to serve the basic needs of citizens for health, education, and shelter – services which are critical to the living standards of the poor (Haque, 1999).

Partnerships with the private sector give corporate elites a privileged relationship to bureaucrats compared with those sections of society dependent on public services financed through taxation. The loss of a 'democratic tradition of ethical standards' requiring accountability, the representation of minorities and women, impartiality, and responsiveness, in favour of market values, productivity, competition, and profitability, means that 'the normative criteria or rationales for public policies and administrative decisions are likely to be based on market driven criteria rather than the opinions and expectations of citizens'. The role of bureaucracy as the facilitator, regulator and coordinator of private sector contractors makes it more difficult to create a culture of public service in the public interest (Haque, 1999). Attempts to create an entrepreneurial culture in the public service turn public accountability into 'formalistic irritants'. Managerial autonomy weakens 'important institutional and legal safeguards in areas of vital concern to vulnerable segments of the population', especially the rule of law, and encourages 'the abuse of power, corruption and arbitrariness' (Argyriades, 2007, pp. xxvi, 16).

Despite the strength of the advocacy in its favour, public management reform may encounter contextual and cultural obstacles that are difficult to overcome. In Ghana, for example, reform has been impeded by poor communications, low levels of literacy, ethnic diversity, regional imbalances, and politicization of the civil service. Changing the practice of public management has proved incompatible with cultural values, including trust in traditional indigenous political institutions, gender biases, ethnic obligations, and distinctive approaches to community life and collective action. In Southeast Asia, the introduction of NPM has encountered obstacles in the form of state structures inherited from authoritarianism, whether military (Thailand) or communist (Vietnam); the persistence of patronage and patron–client relations (Philippines); the weakness of the private sector; politicized civil services (Laos), and ethnic discrimination (Malaysia). There is also fear that NPM has an adverse effect on the poor and weakens the state's capacity to manage financial crises. The precepts of New Public Management also conflict with the fatalism, paternalism, and nepotism found in many Third World bureaucracies (Haruna, 2003; Soeters and Tessema, 2004; Haque, 2007).

## Conclusion

Bureaucracy as a form of government stands in stark contrast to the concept of a neutral administrative instrument of democratically chosen political leaders. The former rests on a perception of bureaucracy as being able to exercise power in its own right, either relative to other political institutions of parliamentary democracy or party government, or as a consequence of having usurped them in alliance with the military, or as having emerged as a new kind of politically *and* economically dominant class. The latter civil service model must form part of the democratization process that is under way in many Third World countries. To secure bureaucracy's place in a democratic regime requires institutions capable of ensuring recruitment on the basis of merit rather than patronage, nepotism, or corruption; transparency in the administration of public policy; and accountability for maladministration and incompetence. Most developing countries are still a long way from enjoying effective scrutiny of bureaucracy by legislatures, courts, and civil society, and are under pressure from the international development community to reform in ways which are unlikely to redress the imbalance in political power.

# 7
# Military Intervention in Politics

## Understanding military intervention

Direct military intervention in the politics of Third World countries has been a depressingly regular occurrence since the high-water mark of post-war independence. Between 1960 and 1980, three quarters of Latin American states experienced *coups*, as did half of the Third World Asian states and over half of the African states (Clapham, 1985; Woddis, 1977). The 1980s saw the trend continue strongly. Not a year passed without there being a *coup*, or an attempted *coup*, in some part of the Third World (World Bank, 1991). Despite the wave of democratization in the 1990s, there were *coups*, or attempted *coups*, in Chad (1990), Togo (1991), Peru, Sierra Leone, Venezuela, and Haiti (1992), Guatemala and Nigeria (1993), Gambia (1994), Pakistan (1999), and Venezuela (2002). Between 1990 and 2003, 11 African states attempting to democratize experienced no fewer than 26 instances of military intervention, including successful *coups*, failed *coup* attempts, and military rebellions (Clark, 2007). The military intervened in Mauritania, Guinea-Bissau, and Guinea in 2008, Honduras in 2009, Niger in 2010, and Mali and Guinea-Bissau in 2012.

The question as to why the military became the political force that it did in so many newly independent African and Latin American countries, and remained a dominant force in Latin America, despite longer histories of independence and higher levels of economic development, is of more than just academic interest. With fragile democracies being created in all regions of the Third World, sometimes following prolonged periods of military rule, it becomes of paramount importance to understand the conditions which relate to military intervention and, therefore, threaten the consolidation of democracy. Attention has focused in particular on the *coup d'état* and how, often with apparent ease, the military is able to supplant civilian regimes. This is the problem with which this chapter is concerned, in order to establish when a threat to a new democracy might emerge, and what conditions are necessary to increase the likelihood that the armed forces will remain loyal to civilian political leadership and amenable to its direction.

No single explanation has achieved total acceptance, as might be expected with such a complex phenomenon occurring in such widely differing societies. Many of the explanations produced of military intervention have dwelt more on why the preceding civilian regimes were so fragile and unstable – almost taking it for granted that, if a civilian regime collapses in less developed societies, the military will inevitably be the successor. In the context of underdevelopment, this is not an altogether unwarranted assumption. In some circumstances of political instability, the military is the only alternative. Other explanations, however, have looked at the political advantages which the military enjoy under such conditions.

### Explaining military intervention

Much of the research that has been done on the military in Third World politics has been from a macro and quantitative standpoint. Here, the literature is based on statistical analysis of a large number of countries which are ranked by variables that measure levels of instability or military intervention. These are then correlated with socio-economic factors that seem likely to have explanatory value. A good example is a study of 31 countries in sub-Saharan Africa in 1970 which related, through multivariate analysis, social and economic variables to military *coups* in order to explain why some African countries had experienced them and others had not. Population size and growth rate, urbanization, literacy, mass-media availability, GNP per capita, economic growth rate, and measures of 'centrality' (the geographical concentration of political and economic life) were taken as relevant indicators of social and economic conditions that might be thought, *a priori*, to be related to the likelihood of military intervention. Indicators of the size of the military and police force, and of defence expenditure, were used to establish the significance of organizational characteristics in military intervention. The level of loans from the USA was taken as indicative of external influence on vulnerability to the *coup d'état*. The results were disappointingly inconclusive. Even combining all the independent variables only explained 56 per cent of the variation in *coup* activity. The final explanatory model produced owed more to case studies than statistical analysis (Wells, 1974).

This is fairly typical of the problems that are encountered when making quantitative statistical analyses to explain and predict military *coups* (Jackman, 1986; Johnson *et al.*, 1984; O'Kane, 1986). First, there is the question of which states should be included in the analysis. Were colonies 'states'? Should they be included in the populations at risk? Statistical explanations require the rule of *ceteris paribus* to be satisfied, so the cases compared have to have things other than military intervention equal. With nation-states 'other things' are hardly ever 'equal'. Grouping together 'Black African states', for example, could be said to produce heterogeneity, rather than homogeneity. Aggregating a meaningfully comparable collection of countries produces problems, the solutions to which do not repay the effort put into finding them.

Second, the specific measurable variables chosen to represent factors such as social mobilization, characteristics of the military itself, degrees of political development, international economic dependence, and so on are not always satisfactory. For example, how well do 'voter turnout' or 'degree of multi-partyism' represent 'political development' as an independent variable? How satisfactory is the total of US loans and credit in a single year as an indicator of the external influences that might encourage a military takeover? The weak conceptual foundation of much multivariate analysis can result in unjustifiable conclusions being drawn from the statistical results.

Third, measures used as dependent and independent variables should cover the same time periods, otherwise temporal variation introduces problems of 'simultaneity bias'. How, for example, can it reasonably be claimed that 'party fractionalization' in 1975 caused *coups* starting 15 years earlier, especially when the military commonly banish political parties and therefore themselves determine the level of pluralism (or 'fractionalization') in the political system?

Finally, there are tautological pitfalls that await the quantitative analyst, when some part of what is to be explained is contained within the definition of the *explicandum* (the explanatory or independent variable). An example is when 'increased military expenditure' is used as an independent variable but has resulted from military domination of the state, the dependent variable that is to be explained by expenditure on the military. The same problem is found in the attempt discussed later (pp. 158–9) to explain military *coups* by reference to the level of the political culture in a society, when political culture is defined by reference to a lack of consensus, evidence for which is found in the failure of the civilian system to withstand military supplantment.

The use of doubtful indicators of the variables under consideration and the unwillingness of researchers to replicate each others' methods in different regions undoubtedly account, along with the problems of correlational analysis already mentioned, for the widespread dissatisfaction with this mode of analysis. However, it would be wrong to be too dismissive, either on the grounds that there are no identifiable patterns of military intervention – that it is totally random, or that statistical comparisons and correlations force the use of indicators of political, social, and economic development that are of doubtful validity. Quantitative analysis generates interesting hypotheses. The fact that so far they have produced nothing more conclusive and leave us still needing a convincing theory – and are probably incapable of meeting these needs – possibly explains some of the disappointment which they engender.

## Forms of intervention

The main focus of academic interest has been supplantment – the act of taking political control by force and replacing civilian institutions with military leadership forming a self-appointed junta with absolute power unconstrained by any civilian political institutions. Government is then by decree. Constitutional niceties such as parliamentary procedures, popular consent, or political representation are ignored, because elected assemblies are dissolved, elections are suspended, and political parties are abolished. Some constitutional principles might be observed, if it is judged necessary to obtain a modicum of legitimacy, such as leaving the judiciary intact and with the power to declare on the legality of some administrative decisions. But supplantment may be defined as the substitution of a civilian regime by a military one by means of armed coercion. An example is Burma (see Box 7.1).

Supplantment is by no means the only role which the military can perform. It is an important organized interest or pressure group in all states. It is one of the best-endowed organizations in terms of access to the state apparatus. The military leadership is always incorporated into the machinery of government through various consultative and executive arrangements such as defence and security councils, advisory committees, and the close working relationships between top political, bureaucratic, and military personnel. In no system of government should the political importance of the military be underestimated. A key question about the military in politics is whether it has values that extend beyond decisions about how best to defend a country and wage war, to those which express not only a corporate interest in good pay, good conditions, and the highest level of weapons technology, but also a sense of how society and the state should be organized.

Furthermore, in its normal constitutional role the military is very difficult to subject to democratic control and accountability because it is so easy for it to surround itself with secrecy, and so avoid parliamentary and other forms of scrutiny. This secrecy commonly extends far beyond what is necessary to keep from potential or actual foreign aggressors, to include detailed financing of expensive projects for which the taxpayer has to pay.

**Box 7.1    *The military in Burma***

The first Burmese *coup* in 1962 has many of the hallmarks of a guardian *coup*, following the promotion of Buddhism by the government as a state religion, separatist tensions, and civil war. This was followed in 1990 by an anticipatory veto *coup*, when, having placed leaders of the democratic opposition in detention or under house arrest, the junta held parliamentary elections following protests against economic mismanagement. However, the National League for Democracy (NLD) still won 392 of the 485 seats. The junta annulled the results of the poll and retained legislative, executive, and judicial powers.

The junta consolidated its hold on politics in readiness for any return to civilian rule by building up its political base, as well as by measures to limit opposition. A youth movement and militia were created, with special privileges to intimidate opposition groups. The junta doubled the size of the armed forces between 1990 and 2003, all of whom enjoy subsidized housing, food, and transportation. A quarter of a million poor urbanites were dispersed from the centre of Rangoon to make political protest more difficult to mobilize. Opportunities for student protests was minimized by splitting the University of Rangoon into three campuses miles from the centre, with access routes easily controlled by the army. The military integrated themselves more strongly into the economy, especially with the formation in 1990 of the Union of Myanmar Economic Holdings, a company backed by the armed forces (and reputedly using forced labour on construction sites).

In 2005, the Burmese junta convened a National Convention to write a new constitution. Representatives of the major pro-democracy organizations were excluded, enabling a constitution to be drafted which prevented the leader of the democratic opposition National League for Democracy, Aung San Suu Kyi, from electoral politics (a ban lifted in 2011), reserved one quarter of the seats in both houses of parliament for the military, and required three quarters of parliamentarians to support any amendment, enabling the military to veto any change it does not like, including any proposal to reduce the power of the armed forces. The commander-in-chief appoints the ministers of defence, home affairs, and border affairs. The Constitutional Tribunal cannot review the actions of the military. In a state of emergency, the commander-in-chief can take over legislative, executive, and judicial powers, and suspend civilian government. The Constitution recognizes the right of the military to safeguard the Union and 'national solidarity' (Smith, M., 2002; Williams, 2011).

Another form of intervention is when the military displaces one civilian regime and replaces it with another. A refusal to act as the instrument of the government against its opponents is one way in which the military can bring about a change of regime (Woddis, 1977). Whether a new regime has control of the army and can use military power against remnants of the *ancien régime* is a critical factor determining the outcome of a period of revolutionary upheaval. This was clearly the case in Iran in 1979 and Egypt in 2011.

Changes of government resulting from the military switching its allegiance from one group of political leaders to another has occurred frequently in Latin America. The military is often the power behind the throne. For example, in Ecuador the military ruled from 1972 to 1978, but has intervened on several occasions since to change the civilian government, most recently in 2000 when the military responded to economic crisis, corruption, and instability by replacing the elected president with someone of their choosing. In 2009, the Honduran military replaced a president supported by trade unions, peasant groups, and leftist popular organizations with one backed by private business, the security forces, most of the media, the Church, and most of the middle class. Further examples are found in Indonesia and Thailand where the military has long been the final arbiter in political conflict (Danapoulos and Zirker, 2006; Ruhl, 2010).

When military regimes hand back power to civilian politicians, it is often to people of their own choosing in a constitution of their own design. The constitutions of many new democracies protect the privileges of the military, especially exemption from prosecution for human rights violations, quotas of legislative seats, and control of the state security apparatus. In Egypt, following the success of radical Islamist parties in parliamentary elections in 2011, the traditionally secular military expressed its intention to limit the influence of religious extremists on the drafting of a new constitution for the post-military regime. In addition, military leaders sometimes turn themselves into politicians, creating new political parties, and competing for political office. Venezuela's President Chavaz, a ringleader of a *coup* in 1992, is a case in point. Civilian politics in developing countries is often a veneer behind which lies military power that is ready to take full control (Baburkin *et al.*, 1999; Croissant *et al.*, 2010).

### The *coup d'état*

Most military *coups* fall into one of four categories (Huntington, 1968). First, there is the governmental or *guardian coup* – for example, Pakistan in 1999. The military's role is one of guardianship in the sense that the new regime leaves the prevailing economic system intact, brings about little fundamental change in government policy, and bases its right to rule on the claim that its task is to provide a period of stability before handing power back to civilians. The leadership of the government is changed, but not the social or political structure. An 'arbitrator army' accepts the existing social order, creates no independent political organization, and expresses an intention to return to barracks once the civilian disputes are settled, or an alternative and acceptable regime is established (Perlmutter, 1971).

For example, the Sudanese Islamic *coup* of 1989 was designed to prevent the signing of a peace treaty with the southern secessionists which would have allowed the Dinka and Nuer Christians and animists to be governed by secular rather than Sharia laws. The *coup* in Thailand in 2006 also falls into this category, with the military deposing the prime minister, suspending the Constitution, and dissolving parliament while accusing the government of corruption, electoral irregularities, and human rights abuses (which the military junta proceeded to emulate). In 2011, the Egyptian armed forces took on a guardianship role when President Mubarak relinquished power to the military following protests against his regime. A Supreme Council of the Armed Forces dissolved parliament, suspended the Constitution, and ruled by decree while overseeing a return to civilian rule.

The *veto coup* occurs when the military supplants a civilian government that is committed to radical social and economic reform that will be to the cost of the wealthier classes in society. Examples are Chile in 1973, and Haiti in 1991 when the army ousted President Aristide, Haiti's first democratically elected president who, because of his liberationist theology and reformist programme, was idolized by the poor, and hated by the rich and their military allies.

A sub-set of the 'veto' *coup* is the *anticipatory veto*, when the military intervene to pre-empt power passing to a revolutionary or radical government as distinct from the overthrow of an existing progressive and reformist government. Ajub Khan's *coup* in Pakistan in 1958 may be seen as one to pre-empt the electoral success of a left-wing party (Woddis, 1977). Similarly, in Algeria in 1991, when the Islamic Salvation Front, with a programme of social change, won twice as many votes as its nearest rival in the first of two ballots and the military cancelled the second round, appointed a 'High State Council', and embarked on repression of the fundamentalist movement.

An anticipatory *coup* may even be encouraged by the incumbent civilian government, if it fears it is about to lose power through the ballot box. In Zimbabwe, the government party Zanu-PF indicated it would welcome military intervention, if it lost the 2002 general election. In 2008, senior police and military officers warned the presidential electorate that they would not allow Robert Mugabe to be beaten. Opposition candidates were told that any victory on their part would not be recognized, amounting to what the Movement for Democratic Change (MDC) saw as a *coup* threat.

The military's intrusion into the electoral process was mainly motivated by fear that an MDC government would not secure them immunity from prosecution for criminal acts and human rights abuses.

Finally, in a *reforming coup* the military seeks to change the social order, and place state and society on a new ideological foundation. Three sub-types can be distinguished within the category of intervention which rejects the existing order, challenges its legitimacy, and creates its own political organization to legitimize and maximize military control over the state: the anti-traditionalist, radical reformer (for example, Argentina, 1945–55); the anti-traditionalist, anti-radical reformer (for example, Nasser's Egypt); and the anti-traditional, republican reformer (for example, Turkey under Ataturk) (Perlmutter, 1971).

The political motives of a country's armed forces do not necessary fall into a single category. In the 1980s, the Venezuelan military contained adherents of the Bolivarian Revolutionary Movement, with radical ideological leaning and which staged a failed *coup* in 1992. It also contained a more moderate faction concerned with the corruption and incompetence of politicians, but without a radical or ideological agenda, which also attempted to lead a *coup* later in the same year (Baburkin *et al.*, 1999). In 1999, the coup in Pakistan was prompted by economic and political crises at home, conflict with India abroad, and governmental corruption within the civilian regime, giving the military an excuse to intervene in the name of national stability, unity, integrity, and sovereignty. But there was also an element of self-preservation in the military's motives, after the government attempted to alter the command structure of the armed forces in response to failures in the disputed area of Kashmir.

## Social mobility and military intervention

One explanation of military intervention focuses on the destabilizing effects of social mobility. As societies become more open and fluid, people can use the opportunities provided by new economic activities and institutions to change their status in society. Wealth, education and skills confer status on groups that, in traditional society, had lacked such opportunities. Social mobilization is followed by political mobilization as the new socio-economic interests brought into existence as a result of modernization, particularly in the economy, seek effective means of expression within the political system. Such political mobilization will be encouraged by the democratic milieu and participative ethos of post-colonial society.

Higher rates of political participation and mobilization place intolerable burdens of conflict management on civilian regimes. The division of society into more complex groups and structures has to be politically articulated through unions, voluntary associations, political parties, professional bodies, trade associations, industrial organizations, and chambers of commerce. These are rarely sufficiently developed for the task. Political resources become spread over a larger number of actors than in traditional societies, where a privileged minority has command of political decision-making. In modern society, power becomes more dispersed – at least in principle and expectation, if not in practice. Such participation needs institutions through which it can operate in a structured and ordered way.

The propensity for military intervention will be reduced, the more such institutionalization occurs (Huntington, 1968; Perlmutter, 1971). Where there are organizations through which political participation can be channelled, the population will develop a commitment to their civilian institutions and regime. They will see them as effective means of obtaining access to power and the resources that follow from it. The military will not find themselves in an environment conducive to their intervention, over and above that of a technical and professional elite in whose hands a major function of the state rests: that of national defence.

There is a related technological argument. Social mobility results from changes in the level of economic development. This not only increases the wealth and political significance of a wide range of groups with an interest in preserving civilian forms of government. It also increases the technological complexity of government and puts it beyond the grasp of the military.

One problem with this theory is that it is of too high a level of generality, trying to provide a framework that can encompass all instances of military intervention. As soon as one tries to apply it to specific countries, all sorts of exceptions and variations begin to appear (Philip, 1984). The other is that social mobility might explain political instability, but not why the military is the only solution.

The hypothesis that rapid social change will lead to political violence and military intervention has received support from some comparative studies but not others. For example, negligible correlations were found between military intervention in Latin America and political participation and the strength of parties and pressure groups, leading to the conclusion that stable civilian rule does not depend on strong political institutions. Countries sharing the same level of economic development were less prone to military intervention, if more socially mobilized. If two countries are equal in their levels of social mobility and one has had more economic development, it will be more likely to experience a *coup* (Putnam, 1967).

African data from 1960 to 1975 suggested different conclusions: that social mobilization did have a destabilizing effect and that political participation, when measure by electoral turnout, decreases the probability of *coups*: 'political mobilization in the form of higher levels of mass electoral participation may reflect a higher degree of acceptance of conventional non-violent processes of élite succession' (Jackman, 1978, p. 1274). Party competition, especially between mass parties with nationwide rather than ethnic or regional support, can give strong protection against military intervention (Johnson *et al.*, 1984).

## The military and the middle class

Social explanations of military intervention can be given a class dimension. The more developed the indigenous middle class, the stronger the political foundation of civilian democracy. The middle class is seen by modernization theorists as a stabilizing force but one which, in the early stages of development, is 'small, weak, ineffective, divided and therefore politically impotent'. The economic and political interests of a fragmented middle class diverge, thereby encouraging 'praetorianism' or a potential for the military to dominate the political system (Perlmutter, 1971, p. 309).

The lack of alternatives to the military when social cohesion breaks down may be explained by reference to divisions within all sectors of society, including the middle class. Praetorianism occurs when the middle class is too weak to defend democratic civilian institutions. But it can equally happen when it is large, growing, and more cohesive, as in Latin America, where 'military intervention assures the middle class of power if and when they fail to come to power by electoral means' (Perlmutter, 1971, p. 309). This is consistent with the view that, in societies that are too underdeveloped to have produced a middle class, the military will be a radical force (trying to abolish feudalism), but that when a middle class has developed, the military will side with it as a conservative force (Huntington, 1968; Jackman, 1986). Unfortunately, attempts to prove this quantitatively have failed, throwing serious doubt on the proposition that the effects of military government change systematically as countries become wealthier.

It might be assumed that a new middle class will have a vested interest in civilian government which represents their interests, rather than those of the classes of the pre-industrial era. The development of a middle class should produce obstacles to military intervention. The middle class might not feel that its interests are best served by military dictatorship. The military may deny political power to newly emerging factions of the bourgeoisie. The repression of workers may disrupt production and reduce the profits derived from mass consumption. The state under the military may encroach upon the private sector. The intellectual element of the bourgeoisie may have a different ideological position from that of a military dictatorship. Bourgeois politicians resent being ousted from power, and foreign aid and investment may be dependent on showing a democratic face to the world (Therborn, 1979).

An alternative interpretation of the significance of class development is to see it as a source of fragility in civilian institutions. The key development is not that there is a new middle class, but that there can be conflict between factions within the middle class, particularly under conditions of dependency and underdevelopment. Such conflict has often preceded the *coups* that have been staged in the Third World. The very category of a 'guardian' *coup* reflects awareness of this possibility. This may be accounted for by the centrality of political power to the needs and interests of the middle class in less developed societies, when capital comes largely from state sources. If sections of the middle class feel disadvantaged by the operation of the political system, they may support its overthrow by a military that is allied to their interests.

If the political consensus and ideological foundation of the system are weak, support for modern democratic, civilian institutions can be fragile. The rules of politics are not firmly established in such a context. If one middle-class faction attempts to secure a permanent monopoly of power, and therefore of the limited resources available for the generation of wealth, there is a strong temptation for other factions to resort to extra-constitutional means to gain power. This is the classic Bonapartist scenario where the pure form of bourgeois rule through liberal democratic institutions is impossible to sustain during crisis, and where other classes become increasingly difficult to manage and incorporate into the social order – again, because of a weak ideological base.

The 'crisis of hegemony' in post-colonial societies to which a form of Bonapartism responds includes conflicts between tribes and regions as well as interests founded on pre-capitalist, capitalist, and comprador class structures. Military intervention often represents a way of managing such conflict, rather than a way of profoundly changing the power structure of society. In many instances, *coups* just 'speed the circulation of élites and the realignment of factions of the ruling classes more often than they bring about fundamental change in the organization of state power and its allocation between (rather than within) social classes' (Luckham, 1991, p. 368).

Military intervention is further related to class interests by the opportunities it gives for military embourgoisement. Take, for example, the 1971 *coup* in Uganda. One interpretation was that the *coup* reflected the interests of the army as a marginalized group subordinate to a post-independence elite based on Westernized educational attainment and the use of English as a *lingua franca*. This excluded the armed forces from elite status because army personnel operated in the vernacular Swahili. The *coup* therefore provided an opportunity for social mobility for an uneducated *lumpen militariat*. Thus, without altering the class basis of political power, the *coup* produced a realignment of ruling groups and an opportunity for upward mobility for groups not prominent under the previous civilian regime because they were drawn from underprivileged sections of society or regions of the country that had not been a major source of political recruitment for leadership positions. Other examples from Africa would include the 'middle belt' tribes of Nigeria, and the northerners of Togo. Political and economic power for a minority group, especially one with an ethnic identity, has often 'flowed from the barrel of a gun' (First, 1972, p. 435; Lloyd, 1973).

Embourgeoisement may take an even more literal form when the senior ranks of the military use their political power after a successful *coup* to enrich themselves with wealth and property. Members of the armed forces can rise from petty-bourgeois status, with social origins among rich peasants, technocrats, intellectuals, state bureaucracy, industrial management, and small-scale private capitalists, into the new bourgeoisie through the accumulation of wealth from commissions, corruption, land acquisition and speculation, trade, and rents (Woddis, 1977).

## Economic development and military intervention

The economic explanation of military intervention argues that it is encouraged by a lack of economic development, low per capita incomes, and slow economic growth. When civilian governments are perceived as having failed to modernize the economy, they run the risk of being ousted by frustrated sections of the modernizing elite that are out of office. A study of military intervention in sub-Saharan Africa between 1956 and 1984 found that the lower the economic growth and level of industrial employment, the higher the incidence of military intervention in politics. However, causation is unlikely to run in one direction: the political instability caused by *coups* hinders economic development. 'We are left with the image of a vicious circle in which economic stagnation and decline lead to military interventions, which themselves in turn usually produce more economic uncertainty and stagnation' (McGowan and Johnson, 1984, p. 659; Collier and Hoeffler, 2007).

Economic underdevelopment can work in other ways to encourage *coups*. Dependence on primary export products, the world prices of which can fluctuate wildly, produces economic instability because a lack of a diversified economy means there are no alternative goods and services to offset those fluctuations. This is conducive to *coups*, because it produces problems which can be blamed on governments. When a very high proportion of tax revenues comes from the export of a single commodity, the terms of trade have an immediate impact on the ability of a government to develop the economy and provide for the welfare of society. Government inevitably is the focus of attention when the value of the country's commodities falls in world markets. So, in a country which has a high level of specialization because of the nature of its exports and a high level of dependence of its economy on those export revenues, the probability of a successful *coup* is increased (O'Kane, 1981).

There will always, however, be factors which will reduce the likelihood of a *coup*. First, there is the proximity of independence. *Coups* are more likely the longer a country is independent, giving governments time to demonstrate an inability to cope. Second, there is the experience of military intervention – what might be called 'internal contagion'. Once a *coup* has occurred, there is likely to be another. A country with no experience of the *coup d'état* is less likely to have one than a country where one has already taken place. Here, the military gain skills in domestic coercion, popular support for government is discouraged by experience under the military, and subsequent periods of civilian rule become increasing difficult to sustain. Third, the presence of foreign troops is an obstacle. They would not be present with the approval of the domestic government in the first place if there was any chance of them being sympathetic to military takeover. Even though there is evidence of foreign powers encouraging rather than hindering *coups*, the presence of foreign troops invited in by the civilian government will deter interventions by the local military. The absence of these three conditions removes the obstacles to military supplantment and increases the probability of a *coup* (O'Kane, 1981).

## The political culture

Military intervention has also been related to the level of the political culture – mature, developed, low or minimal in a descending scale of modernity. Each level is related to the propensity of the military to intervene, and to different kinds of military intervention. A mature political culture is one in which the military is an important force in defence policy-making, but has no wider role ascribed to it by social values, attitudes, and expectations. A sense of legitimacy supporting the civilian regime is widespread. At the other end of the scale are found countries with 'minimal' political cultures, where the legitimacy of civilian government is almost totally lacking. Such countries are likely to experience the most extreme form of military intervention: the *coup d'état*.

Low levels of political culture and a weak sense of political obligation are found predominantly in the Third World. Here, there is a lack of confidence that political demands will be heard, and a lack of trust in other groups which might gain power. If political values and beliefs do not coincide with the presuppositions upon which the regime is built, there may well be widespread popular support for direct military intervention. The destruction of democracy and the rise of authoritarianism may be tolerable in societies that do not feel that the form of civilian government which they have is the best that could have been devised (Finer, 1962).

There is risk of tautology here. A low level of political culture is defined as a lack of consensus and so defined by reference to what it is supposed to explain. Rather than offering an explanation of a lack of political consensus, the concept of political culture offers a statement that is true by definition. There is further circularity in the argument, in that military intervention is taken to be evidence of a low political culture because it is evidence of the breakdown of consensus. Military intervention is explained by reference to conditions which are represented by that intervention itself. Insofar as there is explanatory value in the theory of political culture, it is more about how civilian governments fail than why the military should be the inevitable successor. Furthermore, the theory does not explain why *coups* occur in some states with minimal political cultures but not others (First, 1972). The only solution to this problem is to make intervention itself an indicator of the level of political culture, but this makes the explanation even more tautologous.

## Organizational factors

Knowledge of why the military have usurped power in so many states may depend more on observations of the military itself than the socio-economic context in which Third World governments find themselves. There has been a long-standing debate between the supporters of an 'environmental' approach to military intervention, emphasizing the influence of social and economic factors, and the 'organizationalists' (Charlton, 1981). The organizational characteristics of the military may be crucial to understanding military intervention, especially when the socio-economic conditions of different countries, such as India and Pakistan, look similar, yet their experience of military intervention has been so markedly different.

The military appears to have many political advantages over other organizations involved in politics. It has a clear chain of command, with a well-understood and rigorously observed set of superior–subordinate relationships. Decisions are obeyed, not debated until some consensus is reached. The military is well-organized for striking at civilian institutions. When the military intervenes, the leadership of the *coup* is often drawn not from the top-ranking officers but from the middle echelons of younger officers – perhaps because their senior officers are too closely associated with the civilian regime, or because that particular stratum of the officer corps is drawn from an ethnic group that feels disadvantaged by the way political power is being used. Even if the decision to stage a *coup* is not taken by the most senior ranking officers, those who do lead the over-throw have at their disposal an organization that is likely to respond to their commands.

However, the organizational unity of the military in the Third World should not be exaggerated. The armed forces are riven with factions based on age, education, rank, religion, or tribe, reflecting divisions within the wider political community (Charlton, 1981). For example, in October 2001 Pakistan's military ruler, General Musharraf, felt it necessary to dismiss two of his most senior generals, regarded as hard line Islamists and leaders of a faction opposed to the President's pro-American policies. The military thus needs to be viewed as thoroughly integrated into society in this respect and not as a self-contained entity. It is also worth noting that when the importance of variations in organizational characteristics to the propensity for intervention was measured using Latin American data – a difficult feat given the availability of 'only a few gross characteristics of the armed forces' – the size of the military establishment was nega-tively correlated with the extent of military intervention. Of course, as with all such quantitative analysis, it is easy to reject the indicator used on the grounds that it is an unreliable proxy for the variable under investiga-tion (Putnam, 1967, pp. 110–11). And a study of politics in 35 African states between 1960 and 1982 found that military 'cohesion' (a large and ethnically homogeneous armed forces) and political 'centrality' (its role in repression against the government's opponents and its share of public expenditure) to be positively related to military intervention, showing that 'variables specific to African military establishments must be considered in any search for the structural determinants of military intervention in African politics' (Johnson *et al.*, 1984, p. 634).

The military also have a symbolic status which can endow them with legitimacy should they intervene in the world of civilian politics. Without articulating this as part of a corporate philosophy or belief system, the military may symbolize something valuable to the rest of society. They may represent modernity because of their technological expertise, struc-tures of authority, and training. Symbolic status can also derive from successful performance. Shortly before the first military *coup* in Nigeria in 1966, the army had been involved in a UN peacekeeping force in the Congo in which it acquitted itself well, gained an international reputation for being well-disciplined and effective, and so brought credit to the coun-try internationally.

The apparent modernity of the military seems an obvious reason why it should be an alternative to a civilian government that has failed to function effectively. Its rational structures, capable of relating means to ends and associated with rapid technological development and specialist skills, enable the military to be viewed as 'possible saviours' where there is 'a sense of failure in the country' (Pye, 1971, pp. 278–83). However, though the military may be a modern organization in structural terms, in Africa, where soldiers are frequently recruited from the rural and less Westernized areas, 'the attitudes of the soldiers to the wider society is probably more deeply conditioned by traditionalist sympathies than by the modern characteristics of a particular profession ... the military as an organisation might in part be a carrier of scientificity, while the soldiers remain carriers of more primordial habits' (Mazrui, 1976, pp. 251–2). Consequently the military, in Africa at least, may play a traditionalizing role.

The availability of modern weapons is clearly an organizational asset to the military, providing it with a near-monopoly of physical force. If the civilian regime lacks military support, but the idea of a military government lacks legitimacy, then the deciding factor will be the deployment of coercion. Communications, too, are vital in this kind of political intervention, particularly in a large country with many administrative centres. The military's communications system enables them to strike at different centres of government simultaneously and to coordinate their activities in the immediate disorderly aftermath of the *coup*. Such organizational advantages offset the political weaknesses of the military, such as its lack of legitimacy and administrative expertise.

The professional culture of the military may also be related to intervention in politics. Professionalism can mean that the code of conduct within the military, into which recruits are trained and socialized, supports the supremacy of the civilian government. Here, the professional soldier's duty is to obey the directives of the properly constituted civil authorities. Professionalism is made up from expertise, social responsibility, and corporate loyalty. The more professional in this sense the military is, the more politically neutral it will be.

However, military professionalism in some cultures can mean something quite different: that the army sees itself as having a duty to defend the state against forces that would undermine its integrity, even though such forces might be the civilian politicians. If the politicians appear to be weakening the nation and making it vulnerable to external forces, economic as well as military, the army might give priority to the defence of society's basic values. The military is then not a neutral instrument of the government of the day but, rather, an instrument of the nation, whose interest is capable of interpretation by the military itself. If the military contains within its corporate culture such a set of attitudes, it might

provide sufficient justification for direct intervention in politics, especially since there will almost certainly be sections within civil society that
will approve of the military taking such responsibility. Military involvement in politics may have a powerful ideological foundation such as
nationalism, *dirigism*, a moral code, or 'a deep distrust of organized civilian politics' (Janowitz, 1970, p. 145).

Two myths underpin the military's acceptance of responsibility for the
nation's core values: the integrity of the state, and political order. One is
that, without the military, the nation would not have been formed or
survived. The other is the belief that the military are more competent at
managing affairs than civilian politicians (Koonings and Kruijt, 2002).
Neither claim is supportable as a general proposition, though there have
been occasions when the military has played a major role in creating a
new state, such as in the struggle against colonialism. But the latter claim
is rarely defensible. Many military regimes have proved as corrupt and
incompetent as their predecessors. For instance, by 1987 Burma was
transformed by the military junta from a prosperous economy to one of
the world's poorest, such that the government had to apply to the UN for
the status of a Least Developed Nation.

### Foreign influence

Finally, external involvement by a foreign power has sometimes been
crucial in the decision of the military to stage a *coup d'état*. For example,
the USA supported the Chilean military in overthrowing the Allende
regime. The USA also played a role in the failed *coup* against President
Chavez of Venezuela in April 2002.

Continuity of links with developed countries through military aid,
training, and equipment have also strengthened national armies in the
Third World relative to the civilian authorities. The influence of foreign
support, through clandestine military, security, and intelligence agencies,
such as the USA's CIA, has been critical in a number of Third World
*coups*. Foreign influence has penetrated deeply into Third World societies
through covert operations, subsidies to political organizations and individuals, propaganda, training, economic interventions, paramilitary support
to domestic groups, and the infiltration and co-option of local agents and
allies in trade unions, corporations, political parties, the media, and the
military itself (Woddis, 1977).

In recent years, with most Western governments supporting democratization in the Third World (and Eastern Europe), foreign influence has
tended to be exerted to stave off the *coup d'état*, and leading Western
powers have made it clear they will not recognize or deal with a military

regime. This may have been responsible for reducing the incidence and effect of military intervention (Danapoulos and Zirker, 2006). *Coup* attempts in Guatemala, Paraguay and Ecuador were foiled in this way. France helped to prevent military intervention in Cameroon, Côte d'Ivoire, Gabon, and Senegal. In 2008, the American government warned the Thai military to respect civilian rule and refrain from intervening in politics during a period of anti-government protests. However, it is always possible that the USA will feel that security concerns make authoritarianism acceptable, as in the case of America's support for the recent military regime in Pakistan which was committed to restraining Islamic terrorism.

International organizations also attempt to restrain the military. In 2008, the African Union imposed sanctions on civilian and military involved in the *coup* in Mauritania. The Economic Commission of West Africa suspended Guinea's membership following the *coup* of 2008. The South African Development Community suspended Madagascar following the illegal removal of the democratically elected government in 2009. The European Union and World Bank suspended aid to Honduras in 2009 (Frazer, 1995; UN 2009; Ruhl, 2010).

Foreign influence may also be felt through 'contagion'. There have been times when it appeared as though some states experienced *coups* because neighbouring states had shown how easily it could be done, and what advantages accrued to the armed forces as a result. There is some evidence from West Africa that military commanders did 'learn' from the experience of their counterparts in other countries as to how to take power, and about the financial attractions of it – lessons which entered into their calculations about whether and when to intervene. However, this argument cannot be taken too far in general explanatory terms, since the logic of it would be that there would be no end to military intervention as it spread like wildfire from one state to another. Neither Latin America nor Africa offers empirical evidence to confirm the contagion hypothesis (Putnam, 1967; Wells, 1974). There are clearly effective barriers to contagion.

External influences also include the international context in which domestic conflict and insecurity occur. When Third World countries were at the periphery of the Cold War or the centre of regional conflicts, the strength and significance of the armed forces, concerned with both national security and national pride, were enhanced and their motivation to intervene strengthened (Luckham, 1991).

## The military and democratization

A major concern during democratization, especially after a period of military rule, is how to ensure that the military remain loyal to civilian political leadership. Inadequate civilian control of the military puts the democratic principles of representation, political rights, civil liberties, and accountability at risk (Croissant *et al.*, 2010). Experience of democratic transitions suggest a number of hypotheses about the conditions necessary to restrict the power of the military during the consolidation of democracy in order to establish civil–military relations consistent with democratic government.

First, it is necessary to demobilize the military and reintegrate into society those not needed by a professional army. This is particularly important when armed insurgency has been part of the transition to democracy, as in Zimbabwe, South Africa, and Mozambique (Griffiths, 1996). The challenge here is starkly revealed by the case of Afghanistan, where some 700,000 people are estimated to be armed, when a standing army needs about 200,000 and when most militias owe allegiance to tribal warlords, rather than the state. Integrating rebel militias into the country's armed forces is one way to bring them under government control, as well as providing employment to a potentially volatile group. A combination of integration into the military and alternative opportunities for civil employment was tried without lasting success in Mali, where demobilization in 1996 following civil war with Taureg separatists was assisted by a United Nations trust fund enabling 7,000 rebels to be incorporated into the regular army and other government bodies.

Second, civilian political control over the military must be institutionalized by organizational changes. Professionalism in the armed forces has to be strengthened by improvements to the management of military establishments, and changes in senior military personnel. Privileges which are not appropriate for a military which is subordinate to civilian control may need to be removed, such as special banks, welfare systems, and economic enterprises.

Political mechanisms which hold the military accountable to civil control and establish civilian control of defence policy need to be made more effective, such as by strengthening parliamentary supervision, ensuring civilian political control of defence ministries, and giving legislatures authority to control defence spending and endorse senior appointments in all the security services. The military has also to be brought under the Rule of Law. An imbalance between civilian and military institutions, which in Latin America 'contributes to military perceptions that they are better organized, better trained, more cohesive and more patriotic than civilian political leaders' has to be corrected (Fitch, 1998, p. 159). The right incentives to induce the military to accept subordination to civilian leadership have to be chosen. Military attitudes have to be reoriented away from a guardian role and towards loyalty to civilian political leaders. Any duplication of roles between the military and civilian politicians must be minimized – for example, by ending the military's role in internal security, environmental protection, development projects, and the war against narcotics trafficking (though the earthquake in the Sichuan province of China in 2008 showed how indispensable the military can be in relief work following a disaster). The military leadership must be restricted to an advisory role in defence policy. Equally, political leaders have to agree not to draw the armed forces into conflict resolution and to recognize that military leaders have a legitimate role in defence policy-making. Politicians need to be able to communicate on equal terms with the military on defence matters and demands for military expenditure, a capacity that has been conspicuously lacking among legislators in developing countries (Frazer, 1995; Huntington, 1995; Bland, 1999; de Kadt, 2002).

Third, keeping the military under civilian control requires extensive public support for democracy and hostility to military rule, perhaps fuelled by recollections of past authoritarianism, as in Venezuela in 1992 (Baburkin *et al.*, 1999). Unfortunately, not all sections of society are hostile to military intervention. Many sections of the middle class in Chile supported the 1973 *coup*, feeling that their privileges were threatened by the Allende regime. There is no guarantee that during the consolidation of democracy such support for the military will not resurface. In Honduras, weak support for democracy, which in 25 years failed to reduce poverty, inequality, human rights abuses, patronage, corruption, and crime, paved the way for military intervention in 2009 and a repoliticization of the armed forces. Support for the military may also come from technocrats in the bureaucracy, who have been closely associated with military governments in Latin America; and political parties which originated as offshoots of the army, as in Eritrea and Ethiopia (de Kadt, 2002; Koonings and Kruijt, 2002; Ruhl, 2010).

Comparison of different levels of military intervention in liberalizing African states since 1990 suggests strongly that intervention is less likely, the stronger the democratic legitimacy of the civilian regime in the minds of the public. Economic or political crises may prompt military intervention even when successful elections and peaceful transitions from one government to another cause it to appear as though democracy is being consolidated. But, in general, 'liberalizing states which enjoy relatively high levels of public legitimacy do not experience military interventions' (Clark, 2007, p. 149). The Brazilian case also supports the theory that removing social support from a politicized military is necessary for the consolidation of democracy. In Brazil 'the military never made any political move without the support of important social groups' (Castron, 2002, p. 108), so a broadening of support for democratic politics, and a decline in civilian social support for military involvement, reduce the risk of intervention.

The timing of reforms to civil–military relations is also important. Movement towards reform should start in the transition to democracy when negotiations are being conducted between officials and political leaders who are committed to change. This will go some way towards guarding against the new regime acquiring an inheritance of disloyal and disaffected military personnel (Frazer, 1995).

The extent to which the conditions for reform are achievable is affected by a number of factors. Past patterns of civil–military relations (e.g. the extent to which the armed forces have been politicized or a lively civil society allowed to exist), and threats posed by democratization to the sectional interests of the military (e.g. the scale of cuts to the military budget proposed by the new civilian government) will be important. Popular support for democracy may be fragile and disillusioned. There may need to be 'ethnic balance' in the social composition of the armed forces, though there may be costs if ethnic representation means foregoing the benefits of recruitment solely on merit: there are risks in turning the military into an equal opportunities institution (Fayemi, 2002). The effect of military reorganization during democratization on the policy goals of the new government, such as whether the military is assisting in the control of drug trafficking, may also be important for the establishment of democratic civil–military relations (Griffiths, 1996). It is not easy to find new missions for the military that do not undermine their professionalism and exclusion from politics, such as UN peacekeeping rather than combating crime.

The new civilian regime may have to compromise on demands for military leaders to be brought to justice for their crimes (Rouquie, 1986). The military will continue to have much political influence, especially if during the transition it has been able to negotiate immunity from prosecution for human rights violations (Fitch, 1998). Equally, removing immunity may prompt an adverse reaction from the military. Hence the anxiety in Argentina in 2001 when the courts struck down as unconstitutional the immunity laws which had protected military officers from prosecution for human rights abuses during the military regime of 1976 to 1983.

Political developments confronting the new civilian government will also be significant. Of particular importance are factors which distract governments from the reform of civil–military relations, such as hyperinflation and other economic crises which undermine public confidence in the civilian authorities. Excluding the military from civilian governmental roles may be made difficult by confrontations with revolutionary movements and/or organized crime (as in Colombia) that make it difficult to avoid using the military in policing activities.

Despite the scale of the challenge, there has nevertheless been some success in newly democratizing countries in reforming civil–military relations. Norms of military professionalism and civilian control have become more widely diffused and accepted. Military leaders have learned that attempts to govern have been destructive for the armed forces. Civilian politicians recognize that their interests lie in a professionalized, a-political military. Popular support for an end to excessive military budgets, abuse of human rights, and military involvement in economic enterprises has grown. *Coup* attempts might occur, but are less likely to be successful in newly democratized countries with a reasonable level of economic development. Huntington was even prepared to specify the cut-off points: 'Countries with per capita GNPs of $1,000 or more do not have successful coups; countries with per capita GNPs of $3,000 or more do not have *coup* attempts' (1995, p. 15).

## Conclusion

Many of the factors associated with military intervention, particularly social and economic variables, have also figured in attempts to understand the context of political instability within which military *coups* may occur. Military intervention is by no means the only form or outcome of political instability. Communal violence, separatist movements, and ethnic conflicts can escalate into civil war and create prolonged instability. This more general and widespread picture of instability is the subject of Chapter 9. The present chapter has identified the circumstances surrounding military interventions in Third World politics in order to explore how successful explanations of the phenomenon have been. An understanding of military intervention is particularly important when it undermines democracy, either by the *coup d'état* or by refusing to reinstate democratic politics in response to widespread popular demand. There are implications for public policies and governmental strategies if it can be shown that the propensity for military intervention is related to political institutionalization, economic development, political participation, economic specialization, the development of mass political parties, the centrality of the state in the process of capital accumulation, and the development of a middle class, or the professional culture of the military itself.

# 8
# Nationalism and the Politics of Secession

## Political self-determination

In most regions of the Third World, there are political movements campaigning, in most cases through armed struggle, for political self-determination on behalf of minority groups. In the Western Sahara, Polisario fights for liberation from Morocco. In Western Somalia, the Liberation Front aims to restore the Ethiopian Ogaden to Somalia. The Kurds of Turkey, Iran, Iraq, and Syria seek an independent and united Kurdistan. The National Resistance Council in Iran aims to establish an autonomous Baluchistan. In India, there are movements for autonomy among the Sikhs, Nagas, Mizos, and Tripuras, as well as in Kashmir. The Shanti Bahini of Bangladesh seek autonomy for the Chittagong tribes. In Burma, the programme of the Federal National Democratic Front includes a federal union based on self-determination for the Shan, Karen, Mon, Arakan, and Kachin peoples. The Karen National Union has been fighting for independence since 1948. The Tamil minority in Sri Lanka engaged in an unsuccessful civil war from 1983 to 2009 with the objective of forming a separate state in the north-east of the island. Indonesia has movements struggling for independence in West Papua and Acheh. In the Philippines, the Moro National Liberation Front seeks independence of the Muslim Moros in the south. There has been a strong ethnic revival since 1960 and a corresponding growth of interest among social scientists (Brown, 1989).

Such organizations should be distinguished from revolutionary movements seeking to overthrow the incumbent regime. Secessionist movements do not want to overthrow national governments; they want to withdraw from their jurisdiction. This, from the perspective of the centre, may appear very revolutionary; and the movement itself may have a revolutionary agenda in addition to independence, though this is not inevitable. Only in Latin America are revolutionary movements almost exclusively concerned with a different kind of freedom – that of a whole country from repression by an authoritarian regime. Separatism in Latin America is largely an aspect of nineteenth-century history (Anderson *et al.*, 1974).

Few secessionist movements are likely to be successful in achieving full independence for the people they represent, but it is unlikely that they will give up the struggle and disband. They may, however, be crushed by the superior military might of the national government – as in Nigeria, Zaire, and Sri Lanka. Occasionally, however, a separatist movement succeeds, as in the case of the violent separation of East Pakistan to form the state of Bangladesh, the secession of Somaliland from Somalia in 1991, the secession of Eritrea from Ethiopia in 1993, East Timor's independence from Indonesia in 2002, and the creation of the Republic of South Sudan in 2011 (see Box 8.1). Military conflict usually marks the passage from integration to autonomy.

This chapter examines the demand for independence on the part of ethnic or national minorities. Three theories of separatism are examined: political integration, internal colonialism, and 'balance of advantage'. It is suggested that explanations of nationalism and secession need a class dimension because of the social stratification found within cultural minorities, the petty-bourgeois leadership of ethnic secessionist movements, and the significance for the outcome of nationalism of the reaction of the dominant class in the 'core' community to nationalist political mobilization.

The political movements fighting for separation often do so in the name of nationalism. Their aim is secession, though other organizations and factions may be prepared to negotiate for less than full separation. Before examining the causes of ethnic separatism, the main aim of this chapter, it is necessary to clarify two of the terms that are central to the analysis: secession and nationalism.

## Secession

'Secession' may be defined as the formal separation of a region from a nation-state of which it formerly constituted an integral part. The region may already have experienced considerable decentralization of power. Secession, however, is not further decentralization but complete separation so that the breakaway region becomes a state in its own right, with its own constitution and recognized as such in international law. Normally secessionist movements aim at autonomy, rather than integration with a neighbouring country. Such autonomy does not necessarily mean that all political and economic links with the 'parent' state will be severed. Economic relationships are particularly likely to persist, especially in the form of trade.

170

**Box 8.1**   *Secession in Sudan*

The main factors explaining secession are represented in the case of Southern Sudan, where a referendum in January 2011 resulted in 98 per cent voting in favour of independence following 22 years of civil war, which ended in 2005 with the signing of a peace accord.

The Sudanese state's response to secessionist demands included the usual military repression, including a declaration of *jihad* on the South and a scorched-earth policy in the Nuba Mountains and South Kordofan. Over two million Southerners, mostly civilians, were killed before a ceasefire could be brokered. Attempts were also made to enforce assimilation and suppress language and culture, mainly through a policy of Arabizing and Islamizing Africans. The government also unconstitutionally divided the South into three provinces, seen by Southerners as a policy of divide and rule. In 2008, census figures were falsified in order to reduce the numbers of those eligible to vote in the referendum on independence. Such policies led to a crisis of political integration in the Sudan.

The nationalism of the Southern Sudanese has its origins in artificial colonial boundaries which brought different ethnic and religious groups together into a single state. Sunni Muslims are the majority in the north of Sudan, where the regime has enforced strict Islamic law since 1983, while the South is mostly Christian and animist. However, Sudan is a multi-ethnic nation containing 600 different ethnic groups, and neither North nor South is ethnically homogenous, a factor ominous for the future of democracy in the new Republic of South Sudan. And there has already been armed conflict over the oil-rich border region of Abyei.

Internal colonialism is represented by the central government's longstanding neglect of Sudan's periphery and the excessive concentration of jobs, wealth, and public services in the Arab region, and its exploitation of the South's resources, particularly oil, to provide government revenues and developments that favoured the North. Successive national governments have deepened regional disparities by favouring the North with development projects and public investment. For example, the oil fields in the Southern region were exploited to pay an accumulated debt of US$8 billion, incurred to finance development projects in Northern Sudan. Consequently, South Sudan has a severe infrastructure deficit. The balance of advantage swung towards secession when oil was discovered in the South and Khartoum claimed ownership of the oil fields, brokering terms of trade favourable to the North. At the same time, an independent South became economically viable (Raftopoulos and Alexander, 2006; Medani, 2011).

The central authorities of the parent state may attempt to contain secessionist tendencies by offering various concessions, such as constitutional autonomy which stops well short of separation (Brass, 1991). There is some evidence that a measure of devolution or federalism, rather than encouraging secession by increasing the resources and identity of regional minorities, actually reduces separatist demands by increasing the power of moderate nationalist leaders. The case of Bougainville in Papua, New Guinea supports the view that democratic provincial devolution, based on effective and accountable provincial government, strengthens relations with the state and resolves grievances, preventing rather than promoting secession (Ghai, 2000). In the Tamil area of India, Tamil nationalism abandoned separatist demands after Tamil nationalist political parties gained representation in the federal parliament. Tamil nationalism now only seeks 'adequate representation in power-sharing and maintenance of cultural identity' (Oommen, 2006, p. 445). By making concessions to ethnic minorities, Thailand has been able to de-radicalize Malay–Muslim separatism (Brown, 2006). Acehnese independence was averted when Indonesia, having learnt how counter-productive military repression can be, granted Aceh Special Autonomy Status in 2001, which entitled the province to 70 per cent of oil and gas revenues, control over educational and judicial policies, and, in 2006, to organize elections in which regional parties could compete (Smith, A.L., 2010).

National governments may be assisted in their negotiation of a compromise by nationalist factions that are prepared to accept less than complete political independence. Surveys of political attitudes – mainly, it has to be admitted, in developed countries – have revealed that significant numbers, and often majorities within the ethnic groups concerned, are prepared to accept a degree of constitutional autonomy, rather than separation for their country – a finding that almost certainly applies to developing countries. However, surveys also show that, even among those who do not favour separation and who reject violence as a means to that end, there are many who sympathize with those engaged in violent resistance – explaining 'how guerrilla struggles have been maintained for years in the face of overwhelming odds' (Connor, 1988, p. 216).

The demands of separatist movements may be significantly modified over a period of time, so that national independence is displaced by lesser objectives, such as the creation of a new territorial unit within a federation, official recognition of a language, and symbolic distinctions. Equally, modest demands can escalate under pressure of events, such as East Pakistan's progression from linguistic equality to autonomy in a loose federation, and from there to secession (Wright, 1976). Ethnic groups vary in their demands. In South Asia, for example, some have demanded reforms within existing state structures, such as affirmative action policies. Others have called for the restructuring of the regime, including devolution and provincial autonomy. Still others agitate for the restructuring of the state through secession and irredentist change (Phadnis and Ganguly, 2001). In Palestine, the nationalist movement is divided between those who support the creation of a sovereign state consisting of the occupied territories, and those wishing to transform Israel from a Jewish state to a democracy for all its citizens, regardless of religion and ethnicity (Farsoun and Aruri, 2006). But the ultimate goal of secessionists is the creation of a new nation-state. Decentralization is unlikely to provide a lasting solution, if there is widespread support within the affected region for the secessionist cause; and there is likely to be widespread support, if the secessionist movement is founded on a sense of nationalism within the aspirant state.

## Responses to secession

Ethnic demands are partly a function of the state's orientation to them, such as the imposition of 'nationality' under the Ethiopian constitution (Ghai, 2000). Though the Bengalis of East Pakistan had long been conscious of their cultural distinctiveness, and had found it necessary to assert this from time to time in the face of assimilationist policies (notably the one-language issue of 1950–52), it was not until their gains through the democratic process had been vetoed by the central authorities that they were driven towards secession. Until then, their programme had been for reforms within the state of Pakistan (such as the Six Point Programme which called for a confederal constitution, fiscal devolution, and separate trading and commercial relations with foreign countries). Secessionist demands were precipitated more by the intransigence of the central authorities than by spontaneous articulation. In the Philippines, secession-ist demands by the Moslem community in Mindaneo were preceded by communal conflict over land. The community was not in conflict with the state. When the state intervened punitively on the side of Christian communities, and martial law was declared in 1972, the Muslim Moros began an armed insurrection organized by the Moro National Liberation Front with the aim of creating a separate Moro state (Brown, G. K., 2008).

State response to nationalism and separatism have ranged from geno-cide to expulsion, assimilation, language policies, quotas in political and bureaucratic elites, revenue allocation formulae, positive discrimina-tion, cultural autonomy, and political decentralization (Coakley, 1993). In South Asia, responses to secessionist movements have included mili-tary action, police restrictions, constitutional obstacles, electoral manip-ulation, economic subsidies, policy concessions (such as job quotas, the co-option of separatist leaders and language rights), constitutional accommodation and, in principle only, the granting of autonomy (Wright, 1976; Phadnis and Ganguly, 2001).

Repression is always part of the state's response to separatism – often accompanied by attempts at forced assimilation, and the suppression of language and culture, as in Sudan's attempt to Arabize and Islamize the Africans of southern Sudan and Darfur (Neuberger, 2006). An alternative strategy is to dilute the dominant ethnic group, as in Tibet, where the Chinese government has encouraged the mass immigration of Han Chinese while dispersing ethnic Tibetans to other parts of China.

It is extremely rare for a national government to approve the breaking away of a distinctive region, especially if part of that region's distinctiveness is its endowment with valuable natural or other economic resources. Thus, the fact that Boluchistan, Pakistan's poorest province, has 68 per cent of the country's reserves of natural gas, the economy's main source of energy, means that Pakistan's response to Baloch nationalism will have to be either complete suppression or a political bargain (Wirsing, 2010). Demands for independence are revolutionary from the perspective of the centre (Clay, 1989), and history teaches us that 'attempts at secession are generally seen by governmental leaders as a threat to the authority of their regime which is so intolerable that it is worth spilling blood to prevent it' (Birch, 1978, p. 340; Ahrari, 2010).

In Southeast Asia, for instance, responses to separatism prove conclusively that 'the nation-state clings above all to territory' (McVey, 1984, p. 13). The Sri Lankan state's successful war against Tamil separatists cost over 70,000 lives and required military expenditure of almost 17 per cent of GDP in its final year alone (Akhtar, 2010). Until 2006, the Thai government's response to secession consisted almost entirely of repressive military and police action (Storey, 2010). In 1994, Morocco's King Hassan threatened a return to war, if the people of the western Sahara voted for independence in any referendum which the UN might organize. The people of East Timor suffered hugely at the hands of the Indonesian military and local militias allied to it when they attempted (ultimately, successfully) to secede. Since 2003, the Sudanese government has used its own armed forces, security, and intelligence services, and an unofficial militia known as 'Janjaweed' – mobilized by members of the ruling party, former military officers, and leaders of nomadic tribes – to commit 'crimes against humanity and war crimes on a massive scale' against insurgents in Darfur. The 'ethnic cleansing' of Sudan's western region has entailed air strikes against civilians, summary executions, rape, torture, and the destruction of property, bringing about a collapsed economy and the loss of over 3 million livelihoods (HRW, 2005, p. 1). Ethiopia's response to the rebellion by ethnic Somalis in the Ogaden included extra-judicial killings, rape, torture, forced migration, the destruction of villages, public executions, and the slaughter of livestock (HRW, 2008). The Burmese army takes the view that, if Karen fighters are in a locality, then local civilians can be killed and their villages burnt. Hostility to secession is particularly strong among African governments, where state boundaries imposed by imperialism have fuelled disaffection on the part of minority groups.


## Nationalism

Nationalism has become increasingly widespread in recent decades. It has been argued that it, rather than ideology built on class, was 'the dominant political passion' of the second half of the twentieth century (Payne, 1975, p. 249), though it may now have been overtaken by religion.

Nationalism presupposes some cultural distinctiveness on the part of the inhabitants of a particular region. Nationalism in the context of colonialism is a relatively straightforward concept, but nationalism among minorities indicates cultural identity and uniqueness, often strengthened by linguistic distinctiveness, that unites a particular population and which may inspire a nationalist movement. Crucial to this sense of identity and the demand for autonomy to which it can lead is a belief that the group once enjoyed self-government. Tibet is a case in point. Although the Chinese government claims Tibet is an integral part of China, and just one of its Autonomous Regions, Tibetans claim that they have always been an independent nation, despite periods of Chinese intervention, until China's invasion in 1950 which reduced them to the status of a colony (Smith, P. J., 2010). A history of sovereignty also sustained Acehnese ethno-nationalism which was independent until 1873 and provided the region's strongest resistance to Dutch colonialism (Smith, A.L., 2010).

What constitutes a 'nation', which may seek the status of a nation-state, is a question that has occupied the minds of political theorists for many decades. One view is that ethnic groups simply become nations when they develop ideas about obtaining political self-determination (Phadnis and Ganguly, 2001). But, generally, it is thought that a sense of nationhood will be based on some combination of religion, language, customs, institutions, mythology, folklore, culture, history, and race, though it should not be assumed that each type of identity will have the same effect on political behaviour (Connor, 1988; Clay, 1989; Kellas, 1991). None, however, is sufficient in itself to define a nation, not even language (Smith, A.D., 1971). Economic and political features may also be considered necessary conditions of nationhood, in addition to cultural factors and group sentiment. A homeland territory and sense of collective history are also bases for national solidarity (Hechter, 2000). Smith (A.D., 1971) lists the following seven features of a nation, and distinguishes 'tribes' and ethnic groups as having some but not all of these: cultural differentiae; territorial contiguity with internal mobility; a relatively large population; external political relations; considerable group sentiment and loyalty; direct membership with equal citizenship rights; and vertical economic integration around a common system of labour.

Tribes have only the first and second characteristics. 'Ethnie' have the first five. Nations have all seven. Some post-colonial societies are collections of tribes and/or ethnie, and therefore lack at least two of the seven features – cultural differentiae and group sentiment – because of the arbitrary nature of colonial boundaries (Smith, A. D., 1971, 2001). Groups supporting secessionist movements, though usually having a sense of cultural identity, are not universally distinct ethnically. Secessionist groups may be ethnically heterogeneous. Nationhood may be claimed, but whether this is justified raises many problems of subjective and objective definition (Symmons-Symonolewicz, 1965; Rustow, 1967; Snyder, 1976; Wood, 1981). So, a subjective belief that people constitute a nation that deserves political recognition is more important than the objective definitions of historians and social scientists (Eriksen, 1993).

Secessionist alienation arises from a perception of special bonds between people which distinguish them from other communities within the nation-state (Enloe, 1973). In South Asia, 'the sociological characteristics of the various provincial populations are at the heart of their demands for autonomy or secession. All of the movements have asserted the primacy of particular criteria of identification which render the populations minorities in the country as a whole even if majorities locally' (Wright, 1976, p. 8). In Kashmir and Nagaland, the principal factor is religion; in Tamil Nadu, East Bengal, and Baluchistan, it is language. South Asian societies and cultures lend support to the belief that territory and language are key to a sense of nationhood, whereas in Xinjiang, a predominantly Moslem region in north-west China, religion is the basis of separatist agitation (Mackerass, 2001). Similarly, in southern Thailand, 'Malay Muslims consider their religious, cultural and linguistic identity to be threatened by the overbearing and insensitive hand of the predominantly Buddhist state'. Religion became the dominant consideration following the Thai government's support for the USA's 'war on terror' (Storey, 2010, p. 40).

The ethnic foundation of nationalism is important not only because it provides a criterion for defining a nation, but also because it is central to the debate about what causes separatism, and whether ethnicity is a sufficient or necessary condition for the existence of demands for political autonomy. The *primordialist* theory of nationalism sees nations as organic ethnic communities with distinct languages, cultures, physiognomies, and homelands. Nationalism occurs when such communities demand self-determination from a 'polyethnic' state. This view of nationalism is backed by the fact that 'ethnicity remains a powerful, explosive and often durable force', generating strong feeling of belonging, obligation and dignity. Its persistence in advanced industrial democracies shows it is not eroded by the forces of modernization (Smith, A. D., 1995, pp. 33–47). But it is equally clear that it would be wrong to think of ethnic attachments as unchanging in relation to political action. They are subject to economic and social changes, especially urbanization, industrialization, and the spread of education, which may alter perceptions of the relationships between minority and majority (Ozkirimli, 2000).

In contrast, the *situationalist* theory of nationalism sees claims to nationhood as based on a sense of common interest and self-preservation among people confronted by a threat to their well-being from uneven economic development, 'internal colonialism', and other forms of discrimination. Ethnic characteristics become important in defining group identity when the circumstances (or situation) make it rational to act defensively. Activists are then needed to mobilize ethnic consciousness as a basis for interest articulation.

*Constructivist* theory sees nationalism as an ideology wielded by political elites to legitimize their demands for power. Nationalist ideology consists of myths about community ancestry, history, culture, and homeland to provide people with a sense of identity, an understanding of contemporary problems, and prescriptions for their solution (Brown, 2000).

These interpretations underpin some of the explanations that have been offered for political secession as a destabilizing force in Third World states. Unfortunately, any attempt to find a simple causal explanation of nationalism and separatism is probably doomed to failure by the sheer diversity of the phenomenon. The history of nationalism reveals wide differences in the size, cohesiveness, and mobilization of ethnic communities; in the goals of nationalist movements; in the threats that they pose to existing states; in the economic contexts in which ethno-nationalism is found; and in the political methods chosen by nationalist movements (Kellas, 1991). An exhaustive review of the literature on nationalism in the Third World is well beyond the scope of this chapter. All that can be attempted is a critical look at the theoretical perspectives which seem to be of greatest value for understanding why part of a country might seek to break away.

## Political integration

The theory of political integration attaches great weight to ethnicity in explaining separatism. In the Third World context, this emphasizes the fact that new states were frequently the arbitrary creations of colonialism. They consisted of a multiplicity of ethnic groups bound together under colonial domination and a common administrative and economic system, after the European powers had divided their tropical dependencies among themselves with scant regard to existing social and political boundaries. Differences of caste, region, and ethnicity were further exacerbated by the representation of these incorporated societies in racial and tribal categories, and by the unequal impact of colonial educational, economic, and political experiments (Nafziger and Richter, 1976). The nationalism which subsequently drew such communities together was based solely on opposition to subjugation by an alien power. They were united (and, often, far from completely) only in their desire to throw off colonial domination. The state created by the achievement of independence thus 'preceded' nationalism, in that there was no other common identity than anti-colonialism. The nation-state was not built on a basis of common religious, cultural, linguistic, or racial factors as it is when nationalism precedes the state (Kohn, 1945; Coleman, 1954).

If cultural pluralism and sub-national loyalties are not eroded by a diffusion of cultural values during the process of modernization, separatist tendencies will develop. A 'crisis of integration' is therefore likely to occur after independence unless a sense of territorial nationality can be created by unifying independent social, cultural, and political entities. National integration is at risk not only when a minority is threatened by a single numerically and politically dominant group (as in Sri Lanka); self-determination may also be demanded where there is a more 'balanced' pluralism of ethnic groups, as in India and Nigeria (Weiner, 1965). Cultural diffusion should ensure that when countries modernize, sub-cultures lose their significance. Ethnic loyalties become superseded by loyalties to the wider state. There are four factors involved in this process: bureaucratic penetration, social mobilization, industrialization, and mass communication. In conjunction, these developments produce cultural diffusion that may even extend beyond the boundaries of the nation-state.

Demands for self-determination by minority groups are viewed from this perspective as deviations from the path to modernity. The 'problem' for the post-colonial state is one of 'nation-building' – creating loyalties and attachments to the new nation-state which supersede the parochial loyalties evoked by traditional values. Secession may then reflect a failure to integrate at all (for example, during colonialism) or a process of disintegration after a relatively stable period of unity (Wood, J. R., 1981).

In common with the theories of modernization and development from which this concept of integration springs, it mystifies, rather than illuminates, the sources of political conflict which may lead to attempts at secession. Integration theory presents the 'crisis' of integration as a deviation from the functional process of political change. Political 'disintegration', of which secession is one form, is portrayed as the consequence of an incompatibility between traditional and modern values, rules, and modes of behaviour (Phadnis and Ganguly, 2001). Failure to incorporate regions successfully into the state system is regarded as evidence of persistent parochial loyalties, often founded on tribal communality, which elevate the legitimacy of traditional community above that of the modern form of political association – the nation-state. The 'primordial' attachment to tradition is thus seen as an obstacle to political development.

The 'integration' approach to understanding secession suffers from the teleological and ethnocentric defects of modernization theory generally (see Chapter 2). Although it is true that political hostility to the inequalities of contemporary states may be reflected in an appeal to a sense of common identity and historical continuity, such 'parochialism' is itself the consequence of other factors, rather than the prime mobilizer of political action. These other factors have to be understood. It is inadequate to dismiss them as failures on the part of disaffected sections of society to understand how to articulate political demands through an (essentially imaginary) egalitarian and pluralistic political system. It is unhelpful to talk about national integration as if it were simply a question of minorities becoming aware that new nation-states are the modern form through which politics must be carried on. It is necessary to analyse what lies behind ethnic unrest. Ethnicity cannot be regarded as a primordial 'given'. It is subject to a range of economic and political forces, such as economic competition between regions, the manipulation of ethnic identity by ruling elites to divert attention from other forms of socio-economic conflict, and the attraction of communalism in the absence of other effective forms of political participation (Nafziger and Richter, 1976). One reason for turning to ethnically defined activism is despair at ever protecting one's interests through other political associations.

Furthermore, there is also evidence ethnicity can be supportive of national integration. In West Africa, for example, ethnicity assists national integration in at least four ways. First, it provides the social support needed during periods of social upheaval that cannot be provided by either the state or the extended family. Second, ethnic groups aid the process of re-socialization during periods of rapid social change by providing opportunities for a range of social and political contacts to be made. Third, by offering opportunities for social mobility, ethnic groups help to prevent the formation of castes, and so assist in the maintenance of a fluid stratification system.

Finally, they are an important 'outlet for political tensions'. Such potentialities have to be recognized and set against the inevitably particularistic and separatist potential of ethnic sentiment (Wallerstein, 1960).

## Internal colonialism

The concepts of uneven development and internal colonialism were largely developed with reference to the UK, and used to explain Celtic nationalism. But it is a theory that owes its origins to interpretations of Third World colonialism and dependency. It would seem to have considerable resonance as an approach to territorial economic and political differentiation in the post-colonial states of the Third World and the consequent demands for autonomy on the part of the groups experiencing discrimination and exploitation.

This thesis finds some plural societies divided into a 'core' community and one or more peripheral communities, exploited by the core from a position of primarily economic advantage. The economy of the periphery is usually highly specialized, and thus more vulnerable to fluctuations in world markets than the economy of the core community. This core-periphery distinction is a function of capitalism which entails territorial as well as class inequalities and conflicts through a process of uneven development (Orridge, 1981). A cultural division of labour is created in the course of such development. Nationalism feeds on this cultural division of labour, a stratification system which links a person's life chances to cultural distinctions, thereby giving culture a political salience. People see a shared material interest in cultural terms. This is a necessary but not sufficient condition of group solidarity and collective action. Other conditions are necessary to encourage solidarity with a nationalist organization – namely, a high level of dependence on a nationalist movement as a source of benefits, and control of the movement's members (Hechter, 1975, 1985).

The politics of the peripheral regions are controlled by the core. Influential positions in the state are disproportionately occupied by people from the core community. This applies to the central state apparatus, as well as to its local arms in the minority areas. Political organizations seeking to represent the interests of minority cultures may be restricted or banned. The repressive instruments of the state may be used selectively to counter expressions of dissent by a nationalist group. Such repression has often been justified by means of a racist ideology.

In addition to economic discrimination, the marginalization and exclusion of an ethnic or regional minority may take the form of cultural discrimination, by stereotyping the cultural group as backward, uncivilized, unreliable, inferior, or dangerous. Such claims can easily become self-fulfilling prophecies when, because of economic and social discrimination, a disproportionately large number of people from the minority group are found to be suffering from unemployment, low incomes, poor health, bad housing, illiteracy, low life-expectancy, high crime rates, high rates of suicide, and other indicators of social disadvantage. Discrimination may be more overt, as when minorities are denied the use of their own language in education, the media, and local administration. Indirect measures include requiring that education, information, and social advancement generally are only available to those using the official language. Discrimination may even involve attempts by the core group to deny any ethnic distinctiveness, as in the case of the Iranian government's claim that the Kurds are 'pure Iranians' (Bulloch and Morris, 1993). Discrimination may well escalate as regimes retaliate against the agitation of nationalist groups, including forced migration and even attempted genocide.

The internal colonialism thesis would seem to fit some cases of secession, such as Bangladesh which, as East Pakistan, was economically exploited and politically marginalized by West Pakistan, especially following the abolition of representative government after the military *coup* in 1958, and the consequent dominance of a predominantly West Pakistani bureaucratic-military oligarchy (Jahan, 1973). The liberation movement was strengthened by the existence of a political movement, the Awami League, which had a powerful presence in national politics because of East Pakistan's large population and, therefore, strong representation in the national legislature. This power was resisted by Western Pakistani political factions. The national cause, on the other hand, was weakened by the costly logistical problems of controlling an area separated by one thousand miles of Indian territory, and by eventual Indian military support to the Bengalis.

In Southeast Asia, too, separatism has been a minority response to domination by an 'ethnic core' of Thai, Burman, Lao, and Malay communities, for example, as well as Javanese in Indonesia, Khmer in Cambodia, and Kinh in Vietnam. Discrimination against minorities has, then, been partly structural – arising from geographical, social, and economic marginalization, and partly an object of government policy – involving the imposition of alien officials, fiscal regimes, education systems, and economic planning (as in Malaysia's New Economic Policy which disadvantaged the Indian and Chinese minorities: Brown, 2006). In the Middle East, the struggle to form an independent state of Palestine is in response to a unique form of settler colonialism that produced internal colonialism within the state of Israel (Farsoun and Aruri, 2006).

The internal colonialism thesis clearly provides a framework for explaining secession in some contexts. However, there are some problems with it as a general theory of nationalism and secession. The main difficulty is that there have been prosperous regions that have demanded political autonomy from the state, and many poor ones that have not (Orridge, 1981; Ozkirimli, 2000). It is arguable that Katanga (now Shaba) in the Congo, Bougainville in Papua, New Guinea, and Biafra in Nigeria attempted to secede because of their relative wealth, based on their natural mineral resources, rather than their backwardness. The internal colonialism thesis is further weakened by the phenomenon of ethnic nationalism and separatism in regions yet to be extensively penetrated by capitalist development – the Kurds, Naga, and Eritreans, for example (Smith, A. D., 1979).

Thus, 'uneven development', producing overdeveloped peripheral regions within poor countries, is awkward to fit into the internal colonialism model. A 'power disparity' can develop, when an economically better off region with *de facto* power demands *de jure* equality within the state. The attempt by Nigeria's Ibo-dominated Eastern Region to secede as Biafra in 1967 is an example of a relatively well-endowed area seeking to break away.

Consequently, it may be theorized that, if a region combines 'ethnic potential' with an improved economic position (or a faltering core economy), it may become politically assertive (Wood, J. R., 1981). Part of the 'faltering core' may be a failure to develop effective political bargaining, notably through national political parties. The development of powerful regional parties in Nigeria and Pakistan increased secessionist instability by focusing political conflict on regional rivalries. Competition for economic and political power after independence became increasingly regional in character. The regional orientation of political elites intensified regional identities, conflict, and the subordination of national class differences to tribalism.

This still leaves a need for an explanation of nationalism in the context of 'even' development, such as the nationalism in East Africa, French Saharan Africa, and the West Indies which prevented workable federal amalgamations between more or less evenly developed territories. There is also the problem of why uneven development can exist without nationalist and secessionist movements, though this may be a puzzle more for the developed than the developing regions of the world.

Explaining ethnic secession may require a distinction between spatial and population disparities. This, then, gives three scenarios. First, 'backward' populations (i.e. with below average educational attainments, per capita incomes, and non-agricultural employment opportunities) from 'backward' areas (i.e. with low regional incomes per capita) attempt secession soon after independence from a colonial power because of their inability to compete. The southern Sudanese are an example, while the

Hausa of northern Nigeria might have been had it not been for their numerical size, which endowed them with political power. Southern Thailand falls into this category, with low educational levels, low incomes, high unemployment, and economic dependence on two declining sectors: agriculture and fishing (Storey, 2010). Second, an 'advanced' group in a 'backward' region is only likely to attempt secession as a last resort, and as a result of discrimination and violence. The Tamils in Sri Lanka are such a case. Third, an 'advanced' group in an 'advanced' region may attempt secession when it feels it is subsidizing the rest of the country, unless there are economic and political advantages of remaining part of the state (Horowitz, 1985). Such distinctions point to the significance of internal social divisions within minority groups, and their political and economic calculations, necessitating analysis it terms of elite and class interests (see p. 186).

A possible answer to the question of why inter-ethnic inequality is not sufficient to produce nationalism, and why dominant groups sometimes become nationalistic, is relative deprivation, in the sense of aspirations to standards of living which have yet to be reached but to which the 'deprived' group feels it has a right (Hah and Martin, 1975). This idea has been criticized because it is not possible to specify and measure the level of relative deprivation needed to turn an ethnic group towards nationalism. The theory also accepts as evidence of relative deprivation the claims made by the nationalists themselves. And 'deprivation theory cannot explain the nationalism of privileged groups, such as that of Afrikaners in South Africa' (Brass, 1991). However, it is not clear why objective measures of relative deprivation should not be constructed to compare two ethnic groups in conflict about political autonomy; nor why the theory cannot be applied to the examples of relative privilege for which it was designed. So, the theory of relative deprivation would appear to retain some heuristic value.

A further problem with the theory of internal colonialism is that it does not explain why *nationalism* should be the response to uneven development and internal, colonial-style exploitation – rather than, say, a return to pre-modern politics or revolutionary class consciousness. Why should a deprived community aspire to become a nation-state? The theory of uneven development also requires a clearer definition of what constitutes unevenness than has so far been provided (Orridge, 1981). Unless it is known how to identify the significant spatial variations between regions, it is impossible to test whether or not the theory applies to a particular country.

The lack of consistent correlation between peripheral economic status and nationalistic mobilization draws us back to the significance of ethnic identity, which some would argue is the main cause of nationalism. Cultural differences are perceived by the groups they define, while spatial economic differences may or may not be. Ethnicity would seem to be a necessary condition for separatism. But economic exploitation by the core community does not seem to be a necessary, let alone a sufficient, condition of nationalism. The roots of separatism must be sought in other than economic factors. People must see themselves as a distinct nation before they will contemplate independence (Polese, 1985). Yet, ethnicity seems not to rank as a sufficient condition either. The history of nationalism clearly shows that:

> the objective existence or subjective perception of inequality is indispensible to justify nationalism, but it is not in itself an explanation for it. The only certainty is that every nationalist movement has always justified itself in terms of existing oppression or anticipated oppression by a rival group. (Brass, 1991, p. 43)

Not all 'objective' cultural groups are nationalistic. Group identity becomes important under external threat, especially from the state, through assimilationist policies, discrimination, environmental damage, and the expropriation of natural resources, for example (Brown, 1989; Clay, 1989). The claims of both Eritrea and Somaliland to self-determination were based on a 'consciousness of oppression' (Adam, 1994, p. 35). Hence the appeal of political integration theory, which concentrates on interpretations of ethnicity and the conflicting cultural values – particularly those relating to politics – of different ethnic groups.

## The balance of advantage

This theory builds on the idea that communities weigh up the costs and benefits of integration and separation. It entails a cost-benefit perspective on nationalism, seeing ethnicity as an independent variable, producing identities and loyalties which persist over long periods, largely regardless of other factors (Birch, 1978). Therefore, ethnicity should be treated as given and not explained in terms of political discrimination, economic exploitation, or relative deprivation. Nationalism will be supported or opposed depending on whether people anticipate greater wealth, power, and prestige from independence, or feel that their welfare depends on ties with the larger political unit (Hechter, 2000). Thus, in the case of Biafra, 'the benefits of regional autonomy for the East increased relative to the benefits of continued membership of the federation as a result of the discovery and commercial exploitation of crude oil centred in the region in the late 1950s' (Nafziger, 1972, p. 185). Unfavourable decisions on revenue allocations, the federal structure in the Eastern Region of Nigeria, and employment policies meant that the benefits of secession were therefore perceived to be greater than the benefits of integration.

There will be a changing balance of advantage from time to time in being incorporated into a wider community, and the incorporation is unlikely to be total, contrary to the basic premise of the diffusionist school that ethnic loyalties will eventually be superseded by loyalties to the wider political unit because of bureaucratic penetration, social mobilization, industrialization, and mass communication. Ethnic groups resist the erosion of their cultural identity, even gaining 'psychic income' from pride and satisfaction with the assertion of an identity which compensates for a sense of inferiority and deprivation engendered by a dominant culture.

Since the Second World War, the balance of advantage between the small community and the large state has swung in favour of the former, first, because 'changes in the international order have removed one of the main benefits to be derived from membership of a sizeable state' – namely, diplomatic and military security (Birch, 1978, p. 335). Free trade and regional defence alliances also reduce the benefits of integration in a large domestic market and a state with an expensive defence capability. A weakening economy in the larger unit may also increase the cost of remaining integrated (Hechter, 2000; Phadnis and Ganguly, 2001).

Second, the development of global and regional international organizations for aid and trade give small states access to markets, loans, employment, and investment that make their small economies more viable than they would be otherwise. Third, the impact of the mass media on minority cultures and languages has heightened consciousness of, and hostility towards, cultural imperialism and homogenization.

Finally, political agitation for minorities is less costly than in the past. Rights are more readily demanded and conceded. Agitation and terrorism are easier and achieve instant worldwide publicity. National energy supplies are more vulnerable to sabotage. Hence a decline in the acceptability to minorities of piecemeal reforms and in the value attached to the benefits of integration in the wider nation-state.

This explanation sounds highly plausible in the context of developing regions of the world. There are problems associated with it, however. First, it concentrates more on the relative ease with which the break can be made, rather than on the factors that prompt disillusionment among some ethnic minorities and not others with the existing territorial jurisdiction of the state. It implies that the demand for separation is constant, only awaiting an easing of the circumstances under which a new, small state can be born and survive. Yet, the demand is clearly not constant, so the factors precipitating nationalist mobilization have to be identified. Separation will only appear a more rational choice than integration, giving the minority the 'maximum net advantage' and worth the high risks involved, when specific conditions exist, such as material inequalities, the exclusion of minority elites, the movement's organizational capacities, and geopolitical support (Mitra, 1995).

Second, as an explanation it pays insufficient attention to the organizational requirements of a successful bid for independence and the variable political context in which it is made. The following organizational factors affect a nationalist movement's chances of political success: command of community resources, identification with the community represented, an ability to shape the identity of the group to be led, continuity in leadership, and exclusive or dominant representation of ethnic demands. The intensity and form of nationalist politics is also affected by contextual factors, especially the realignment of political and social forces (as when an organization based on class proves more attractive to members of an ethnic group than a nationalist body), the willingness of elites from dominant ethnic groups to share political power, and the availability of alternative political arenas – such as federalism (Brass, 1991).

Third, it is important not to underestimate the ideological, governmental, and repressive apparatus which the state can bring to bear on separatist movements. Impressive powers are available to central governments in dealing with separatist regions, in addition to the more obvious and risky strategies of military coercion and the withholding of public funds. Governments have the ability to conduct a census which defines social categories for the purpose of internal comparisons. They have the authority to define the issues and conflicts that are to be politically managed, and an internationally recognized right to negotiate with the separatists. They control taxation (and, therefore, redistribution), define economic strata, collect information, and invest capital. Governments have the right to control internal migration which can 'alter drastically the ethnic composition of certain regions, usually diluting the indigenous populations and thus undermining possibly separatist tendencies' (Enloe, 1976).

Central governments can also call on diplomatic, administrative, and political resources, blocking external sponsorship of separatist dissidents and exploiting divisions within regional communities. Sometimes, they add foreign interference to the list of reasons for not conceding independence, as in the case of India's handling of the Kashmir crisis.

Finally, support from within the international community – in the form of military assistance, economic aid, and international recognition – is essential for success (Wirsing, 2010). It should not be assumed that the international context will always be supportive of aspirant nation-states. External intervention can take the form of moral support – such as publicizing human rights grievances, or material support – such as economic and military aid. Such assistance will be dependent on the supporting state's strategic and other foreign policy objectives, its previous relationships with the 'parent' state, and the presence of ethnic kinsmen within the supporting state's own territory – affecting, for example, India's attitudes towards Tamil separatists in Sri Lanka (Phadnis and Ganguly, 2001). The attitudes of world powers and neighbouring states to Bangladesh and Biafra were important factors in the contrasting outcomes of these two instances of secession (Wood, J. R., 1981). External influences are usually critical to the outcome of independence struggles (Wright, 1976; Tinker, 1981). They were conclusive in the history of the short-lived Kurdish Republic of 1946 (Ghassemlou, 1980). While Eritrea's secession depended much more on the internal political situation than external support, its long-term viability is dependent on international cooperation (Adam, 1994).

But support from outside is a difficult commodity to acquire, even when ethnic groups straddle national frontiers. In Southeast Asia, for instance, there has been surprisingly little support for ethnic separatism from neighbouring states when ethnic minorities are located in frontier regions. Existing boundaries have been regarded as sacrosanct (McVey, 1984). Neighbouring states may be impressed by claims, such as Indonesia's with regard to the province of Aceh, that secession will cause regional instability and insecurity. Securing external support for nationalist movements is dependent on their ability to obtain foreign financial, diplomatic, and political backing, as well as their skill at publicizing their demands among the international community, both governmental and non-governmental (Phadnis and Ganguly, 2001). A fundamental change in the international context can have a profound effect, as when secessionist movements, especially those in Asia, were branded as 'terrorist' following the attacks on the USA on 11 September 2001.

**Elites and class**

It is a mistake to expect all sections of an ethnic minority to arrive at the same conclusion after calculating the costs and benefits of integration. Cultural minorities are not socially homogenous. Like all societies, they are stratified. Different classes in a peripheral community will experience different costs and benefits from incorporation into a wider economy, society, and polity. A major influence on the degree of mobilization of ethnic groups for nationalistic ends is the relationship between elites and classes in the core and peripheral communities. One of the ways in which national governments attempt to manage secessionist tendencies is through alliances and collaboration with elites within national or ethnic minorities. Central elites (which in Third World countries usually means bureaucrats, whether civil or military, partisan or professional) form alliances with local ethnic organizations to manage ethnic conflict, either by opposing or supporting local elites. An economically dominant class within the minority community may be well-integrated into the wider state and economy, so that 'locally powerful economic, religious and political élites find it to their advantage to co-operate with external authorities and adopt the language and culture of the dominant ethnic group in order to maintain or enhance their own power' (Brass, 1991, p. 26).

Nationalism is often a weapon which regional elites use in their competition for national political power. Appeals to ethnic loyalties to build and sustain political support may be a consequence of a struggle for power between ethnic elites, rather than a cause of mobilization on the part of minority groups. For example, Indonesian experience of separatist regionalism in the 1950s was not an assertion of primordial loyalties, but an attempt to consolidate political support. Eventually, the regionalist movements in Sumatra and Sulawesi came to nothing because their ethnic foundations were insufficiently meaningful (McVey, 1984).

Similarly, in India provincial bourgeoisies have, from time to time, espoused nationalism in order to obtain powers which could be used to strengthen their position in relation to national bourgeoisies whose interests lay in an economic market and political state coterminous with the whole of India. In Nigeria, on the other hand, the reinforcement of political mobilization on the basis of ethnicity by politicians exploiting growing inter-ethnic competition was a major factor in the descent into civil war (Melsom and Wolpe, 1970; Oommen, 2006).

Thus, ethnic conflict reflects competition between elites for 'political power, economic benefits and social status'. In modernizing societies, the development of ethnic consciousness is heavily dependent upon industrialization, the spread of literacy, urbanization and the growth of government employment opportunities, and the new social classes which such developments produce. Conflict between elites over the distribution of resources and political power between ethnic groups precipitates nationalism. The potential for nationalism is not realized 'until some members from one ethnic group attempt to move into the economic niches occupied by the rival ethnic group' (Brass, 1991, p. 47). Secession is a strategy likely only to be adopted when minority elites have no chance of acquiring economic and political power within the existing state, and when there is a good chance of foreign support.

Separatism may be seen as a way of gaining access to power for excluded elites, especially when the state in developing countries has boundaries that are recent and artificial, few constitutional outlets for 'minority grievances', few resources for helping poor regions, and a form

188

## Box 8.2 *East Pakistan and Bangladesh*

The secession of East Pakistan as Bangladesh shows how responses to nationalist demands for self-determination depend upon class interests in the rest of the country. The land-owning class in the West felt threatened by the Eastern leadership's proposal to tax hitherto exempt agricultural incomes in order to provide development capital. The Western bourgeoisie had an interest in retaining the East as a market for their manufactured goods and as a source of foreign exchange earnings. At the same time, however, Western agriculture was becoming an increasingly profitable source of investment to them, and they were concerned about revolutionary stirrings in the East. So, it was mainly the bureaucratic-military oligarchy that opposed secession and used armed force in the attempt to prevent it. Bureaucrats in Western Pakistan resented the promotion of Bengalis as a response to pressure from a political movement seeking to redress the regional imbalance within senior ranks. Regional autonomy also threatened their control over resources. The army was even more directly threatened by regional autonomy, which would have deprived the central government, responsible for defence, of funds. In the East, the Awami League was committed to a substantial reduction in expenditure on the military. The army's hostility was further strengthened by its belief that Bengali nationalism had been engineered by India to destabilize Pakistan.

In the 1960s, the central government under President Ayub Khan decided to create an East Pakistani bourgeoisie to provide the President with a political base in the province and restrict the spread of socialist ideas. Educated Bengalis with useful contacts in the bureaucracy and political elite were given permits, licences, construction contracts, loans, official support, and equity. However, this new Bengali bourgeoisie also benefited from the pressures created by Bengali nationalism, and so was inclined to be favourably disposed towards it. Greater economic autonomy for the East increased nationalism's appeal among Bengali industrialists and businessmen when they found themselves unable to compete with the stronger West Pakistan businesses. At the same time, they were uncertain as to whether an independent East Bengal could continue to provide the support and protection that the government of Pakistan could offer.

However, East Bengali separatism existed before the Bengali bourgeoisie was created. The class basis of the movement was mainly petty bourgeois. The urban salaried classes believed economic independence would reduce prices by removing the power of West Pakistan cartels. Bengali bureaucrats looked forward to freedom from the central government's fiscal policies. The radical intelligentsia supported autonomy because they believed it would provide greater opportunity for economic reform in a region with few indigenous capitalists (Alavi, 1971; Jahan, 1973).

of government that is prone to discrimination rather than conciliation (Smith, A. D., 1979). For example, the bureaucracy can be an arena of ethnic conflict when trained, educated, and ambitious professionals from minority groups find themselves excluded from bureaucratic occupations for which they are qualified as the supply of such professionals outstrips the capacity of bureaucracies to absorb them. The state bureaucracy can be particularly discriminatory when the state itself is dominated by a core community. The case of East Pakistan and Bengali nationalism is particularly illuminating to the question of how different classes respond to regional disparities (see Box 8.2).

## Conclusion

Even if investigations are restricted to the Third World, the phenomenon with which this chapter has been concerned is far too complex and diverse for simple generalizations of a causal nature to be reached. Each situation is unique in what prompts nationalism, how central governments respond to nationalist demands, and what further political forces are mobilized as a reaction to such responses. Variations are found in the way states attempt to manage ethnic separatism (Wolff, 2011), the basis on which minority elites are selected for collaboration and accommodation, and the influence of such co-option on the movements involved in the struggle for independence. The socio-economic make-up of the factions within ethnic communities and nationalist movements may generate a willingness to negotiate for less than complete separation. Nationalist movements also vary in terms of organization, objectives, and strategy (including the extent to which they are prepared to resort to violence).

Consequently, the outcomes of ethno-nationalism are affected by the kind of political agenda which a nationalist movement has, whether there is more than one, and what those agenda prescribe for the future governance of the territory should independence be achieved.

# 9

# Instability and Revolution

## The costs of political instability

The number and social cost of military *coups*, civil wars, communal conflicts and other manifestations of political instability in the Third World have been too great not to attract a great deal of attention within political science. Since 1945, both inter-state and intra-state conflict (the latter far more common) moved from the industrialized to the developing countries, a trend only slowed by the outbreak of conflict in the states of the former Soviet bloc following the demise of communist regimes (Singer, 1996).

When political instability is accompanied by violence and armed conflict, as it usually is, the economic and social costs are extremely high. Since 1990, over 4 million people have died as a result of civil conflicts, either directly from military action or indirectly from the destruction of food supplies and health facilities. Civil war causes GDP per capita to decline by some 2.2 per cent per year, the result of a loss of production from the destruction of transport networks, capital stock, physical capital, infrastructure, and natural resources, and the loss of highly skilled workers who are driven to emigrate. Civil wars deter both domestic and foreign investment, and harm trade. Poverty reduction and improvements in infant mortality are adversely affected by civil conflict. The health and education of the young suffer. Displaced populations increase the likelihood of communal violence and further political instability.

Then there is the 'culture of violence' that develops from the breakdown of government, the dislocation of civil society, the violation of human rights, and the growth of corruption. Vigilante and paramilitary groups proliferate, either beyond the control of government or with its tacit support, as in Colombia and Sudan. Military expenditure increases at the expense of government spending on social services and economic development, in turn leading to further hardship, insecurity, and 'crowding out' of social expenditure to finance spending on law and order (Mohammed, 1999; World Bank, 2011c).

This chapter examines the theoretical preconditions for political stability that have been formulated in terms of poverty, the rate of economic

190

growth, the revolution of rising expectations, foreign influences, ethnicity, the political culture, inequality, crises of authority, and political institutionalization. But, first, the theoretical or empirical weaknesses of these conclusions are identified. Problems with the concept of 'political stability' itself are addressed: its normative content, the question of whether the analysis is concerned with stable government whatever the type of regime or just stable democratic government, and the lack of a satisfactory operational definition of 'instability'.

## Conceptual difficulties

The concept of 'stability' in politics is fraught with difficulties which need to be recognized before a proper evaluation of causal explanations can be made. First, it is a highly normative concept. What is instability for one person might well constitute the welcome overthrow of a detestable regime for another. Many in the West welcomed the 'Arab Spring' of 2011 which brought down governments in Tunisia, Libya, and Egypt, and threatened regimes in Syria and Yemen. The USA has a long history of destabilizing regimes that it does not like. One person's stability is another person's repression.

It is not easy to exclude values from the analysis of political stability. Outside the Marxist tradition, instability is seen as deviancy, a slip on the path to progress. It is an aberration that has to be explained. In the Marxist tradition, instability is accepted as inevitable in the progression of history. Class conflict is an unavoidable stage in the movement of society towards its end-state. Crisis is the inevitable consequence of the contradictions of economic development.

Consequently, some would argue that it is not possible to handle the concept in a scientific way at all. An analytical obsession with instability simply indicates a preference for the regime that is under threat. Understanding a particular type of political change – especially one that often entails violence, loss of life, and severe economic dislocation – has to be based on an objective analysis of the conditions leading to such change. This is not easy when there are so many values at stake when political instability is experienced.

Second, there is the question of whether the analysis should be concerned with stable government or stable democratic government. Interest has not concentrated exclusively on the travails of democracy. Whereas the attention of political science focused on the preconditions of stable democracy in the 1950s and early 1960s, interest shifted in the 1960s and 1970s to a concern with political order, whether in democracies or other types of regime. In the 1970s, US political science in particular concentrated more on the prerequisites of order and control, rather than pluralism and democracy, revealing a strong ideological impulse (Leys, 1982). Since 1980, attention has swung back to democratic stability.

Concern for the maintenance of regimes and elites, political order and stability in policy-making arose from changing political realities in the Third World, the pessimism which developed during the first Development Decade, and perceptions of continuing external influence over supposedly independent nation-states and sovereign governments. Attention concentrated on the policy-making capabilities of national elites, their ability to bargain with foreign interests, and the need for strong centralized government. Successful governmental interventions were seen to be obstructed by competition between national and local elites, and passive traditionalism. High rates of growth were seen as requiring authoritarianism, democracies apparently having relatively poor economic records both in terms of growth and distribution (Higgott, 1983; Huntington, 1987). However, cross-national quantitative studies indicate that coercion provokes, rather than deters, political violence, especially if the repression is not total but permits some political mobilization by opposition groups (Muller and Seligson, 1987). So, authoritarianism cannot guarantee stability.

It has also to be recognized that stable democracy might be replaced by stable authoritarianism, or even by a stable regime which may not conform to some definitions of democracy, particularly those entailing multi-partyism, but which would be regarded by few as authoritarian. The failure of democracy should not be equated with the breakdown of stable government. It may simply be that a particular definition of democracy determines the scale of the failure, as in one analysis of the 'failure' of democracy in sub-Saharan Africa where, by the early 1970s, multi-party democracy had disappeared in all but Botswana, Gambia, and Mauritius (Diamond, 1988).

Handling the concept of stability is made additionally difficult by the fact that it is often used in a way which fails to distinguish between countries that have experienced the overthrow of a democratic regime and its replacement with a stable but authoritarian one, and countries where there is constant civil disorder and change of regime. Much of the concern for the health of democracy over the past 30 years has been prompted by tendencies to 'drift away' from democratic standards, rather than a drift into instability, though the two trends are usually closely related.

Third, there is the problem of finding a satisfactory operational definition of 'stability'. Various indicators have been employed, such as the turnover rate among heads of government, deaths from internal group violence per million of population, and the total number of violent incidents (Russett, 1964). Attempts have been made to measure the aggression of groups within the political system, the longevity of govern-ments, and the constitutionality of governmental acts (Hurwitz, 1973; Ake, 1974). None of these completely captures a sense of what is involved in political instability. Even when political structures change, it may not necessarily be destabilizing. A formulation of instability in terms of members of society deviating from 'the behaviour patterns that fall within the limits imposed by political role expectations' has the advantage of extending the types of events that are to be considered beyond the elite interactions, which are conventionally regarded as indicators of political instability – *coups*, electoral violence, political assassinations, and so on – as well as acknowledging that what is destabilizing to one political structure may not be to another. For example, a refusal of leaders to seek an electoral mandate may be destabilizing to a constitutional democracy, but not to a hereditary monarchy (Ake, 1974, 1975; Castles, 1974).

Some indicators of political instability appear unhelpful when their occurrence coincides with the persistence of regimes. There may be frequent and serious political violence, perhaps associated with commu-nal identities as in India, yet the system of government survives. It may be that instability can only be understood in retrospect. But this can only be done if instability is defined as events leading to the collapse of a regime (as distinct from a government or policy). Indicators of political instabil-ity should be taken as important and costly events whose causes and consequences deserve to be understood regardless of whether they lead to the breakdown of a regime. So, the violent transfer from one form of government (e.g. democracy) to another (e.g. military rule) is only one of the consequences of civil war, riots, communal or religious conflicts, and other forms of unconstitutional behaviour.

Finally, there is the time factor. In addition to knowing what it is a coun-try must remain free from, it is necessary to specify some time period during which it must remain free from destabilizing events for it to be designated as stable. It is difficult to know how to decide objectively on the timing of instability, especially when a brief period of conflict can bring down one regime (e.g. the Marcos regime in the Philippines) while years of recurring communal violence are accompanied by stable democracy (e.g. India).

Despite such difficulties, much effort has been made to explain political instability, broadly conceived as the failure of a system of government to persist over a prolonged period. These explanations will now be examined.

## Affluence and poverty

First, increasing affluence is said to improve the chance of stability, espe-cially in countries with democratic regimes. Conversely, absolute poverty has been seen as a major cause of political instability. For example, in Asia 'people who live at the margin of subsistence are either indifferent or hostile to government … it remains true for most of the new Asian states that all-pervasive poverty undermines government of any kind' (Brecher, 1963, p. 623). In one study (which admittedly included some countries from Eastern Europe and the former USSR, as well as two Western countries), per capita income was found to be a strongly significant variable when correlated with vulnerability to civil war, with a drop of US$1,000 raising vulnerability by 41 per cent (Feardon and Laitin, 2003). Poor countries are thus more likely to suffer greater political violence than rich ones. So, as a country becomes richer and per capita incomes increase, political instability should be eased.

However, there have been many poor and underdeveloped countries with stable political systems. What they have had in common is authoritarian, rather than democratic, regimes. In fact, it seems that the poorer the dictatorship, the more stable it is likely to be. It also seems feasible that political stability might cause affluence and economic growth, rather than be the consequence of it. Some politically stable nations achieved stability before they achieved their affluence. Similarly, some totalitarian regimes have also been able to produce stability before economic development. There is certainly empirical evidence that political instability causes macroeconomic decline (Gasiorowski, 1998).

Poverty and political stability can coexist because of the many constraints on effective political action by the poor in defence of their rights and interests. Even with the right to vote, the power of the ballot box is easily emasculated by electoral frauds of one kind or another. Poverty also means that successful appeals to the judiciary against the economically powerful and their allies in the bureaucracy, when they obstruct the implementation of government reforms, are rarely made because of the social and financial costs involved.

Political mobilization of the poor is further limited by their isolation as economic actors, such as peasants working their own land with their own labour in scattered fields. Similar experiences may be felt in some industrial situations, such as mining, where workers are isolated in industrial villages and provided with their needs at the point of employment. They may become unionized, and that may constitute an important basis for political agitation. But union activity can be restricted to concerns in the workplace, rather than extend to political issues. In the informal sector of the urban economy, households and units of production are also isolated. Separate producers act in isolation to acquire minimal levels of capital, confronting antagonistic social classes in isolation – landlords, merchants, money-lenders, bureaucrats, and wholesalers who can exploit and further weaken them because of clientelist relationships. Class, or even group, consciousness is difficult to create as a basis for political organization.

The poor are also in competition with each other, rather than sharing a common experience that forms a basis for a common sense of identity and exploitation (Harris, 1970; Moyo and Yeros, 2005). Poverty, far from acting to unify people, intensifies the competition for scarce resources – land (whether for purchase or rent), jobs, loans, and access to grazing, water, and implements. The members of the informal sector are in competition for cheap items with which to trade. Solidarity is further undermined for those who have exchanged rural for urban poverty by the precariousness of their existence in shanty towns and the constant threat of eviction. Tribal attachments, encouraged by the competitiveness of urban life and employment, have been a major source of conflict among the rural and urban poor in Africa. Competition for jobs has been an especially potent force in exacerbating ethnic rivalries, and ethnic associations have been one way of providing mutual support and protection for immigrants into the urban areas. Such experiences are not conducive to class solidarity.

The daily grind of hard manual labour leaves little opportunity to take part in political activity. The intensity of this problem is especially great for women. Poor women in Third World societies have heavy domestic chores in addition to cultivating, marketing, and engaging in waged labour. This may include carrying large quantities of water long distances to service the home. With energy consumed at such a rate and inadequately replenished by a poor diet, it is not easy to persuade people to spend what little free time they have travelling by foot to and from political meetings. The physical effort and malnourishment experienced by the poor cannot sustain political activism.

There are also great risks for the poor in political participation, especially alienating the people upon whom one is dependent – landlord, employer, money-lender, and kinsmen of higher status (Migdal, 1974). These are all participants in the local political process whose interests may be threatened by successful political agitation by the poor. Relations of dependency support the poor through systems of reciprocal obligations within the traditional framework of the local community. Kinsmen will help in times of need and adversity. Kinship networks consist of rich and poor, making it difficult for poor people to engage in political activism which appears threatening to their own kin. Similarly, political action may be seen as putting other members of the kinship group at risk, even though the objective is the improvement of conditions for people of that class. Kinship ties cut across class lines, further reducing political consciousness (Wolfe, 1968).

Political action also risks severe repression by the state. Awareness of growing inequalities may breed a degree of radicalism, but this is easily contained by state repression, and by clientelist and populist modes of political incorporation 'which facilitate state control and regimentation' (Mouzelis, 1989, p. 20).

The potential for political organization and communication on the part of the poor is further reduced by low levels of literacy and education, extreme parochialism, and respect for traditional authority, religion, and custom. Access to the mass media is limited. It is also difficult to organize and unionize when there are substantial reserve armies of labour available to much better organized employers. Women may feel reluctant to join male-dominated organizations such as trade unions. Another factor inhibiting political organization, whether of workers or peasants, is that leadership needs to be drawn from people with education and experience outside the countryside and from the intelligentsia (Migdal, 1974; Shanin, 1982). In parts of Latin America, the Roman Catholic clergy have provided badly needed leadership, organization, and consciousness-raising. But leaders can be incorporated into 'conformist' roles, including membership of officially approved non-governmental organizations which 'depoliticize and co-opt rural grievances into welfarist projects' (Moyo and Yeros, 2005, p. 41).

Finally, the poor experience cultural subordination, sometimes originating in colonial racialism. Domination is exercised through ideological devices which confer subordinate status on exploited groups such as indigenous Latin Americans, Untouchables and tribals in India, and women in most countries. An important task of such ideology is to instil the belief that subordination is natural and irreversible.

## The rate of growth

An alternative hypothesis is that the rate of economic growth is crucial to political stability. The more rapid the rate of development, the more difficult it is to maintain stability (Huntington, 1968). Rapid economic growth produces social groups that find themselves left behind and excluded from the new economic opportunities. For example, peasant proprietors may be turned into a rural proletariat. Discontent then arises from a loss of status and autonomy. Economic development produces opportunities for social mobility by releasing the bonds that positioned people in a social order. New economic roles create new opportunities for economic independence for individuals who, in a traditional society, would not expect to enjoy them. The unity and bonds of family, kin group, and village community are undermined by these new roles and values.

Rapid economic development also means that mass movements seeking fundamental political change will be made up from people whose bonds to the established order are changing. Rapid economic growth increases the number of such *declasses* by changing methods of production and the distribution of income. The *nouveaux riches* use their economic power to challenge the social and political order. The *nouveaux pauvres* resent their poverty, a particularly significant fact given that economic growth can significantly increase the number of losers. Rapid growth concentrates material gains in relatively few hands as prices increase faster than wages and technological change replaces people with machines. At such times, and especially in the early stages of industrialization, there are unlikely to be welfare arrangements to compensate for economic hardship. There will also be those who, though making some absolute gains from economic growth, find that their relative position has deteriorated, a further source of dissatisfaction and of contradiction between the structure of economic and political power. Furthermore, levels of consumption can decline with rapid economic growth. Standards of living may have to be reduced to produce the required rate of savings. Consequently, 'it is economic stability – the absence of rapid economic growth or rapid economic decline – that should be regarded as conducive to social and political tranquility' (Olson, 1963, p. 550).

Urbanization is another threat to stability. In moving from an economy based on agriculture to an economy based on manufacturing and services, there is a shift of population from rural to urban areas. The expanding cities of the Third World harbour activism and sometimes extremism. Urban people are attracted to volatile forms of political expression. Urban political organizations provide opportunities for power, status, and social mobility to otherwise underprivileged groups, so political activism becomes even more attractive. When cities are full of 'marginalized' people, the opportunity costs of political activism may be very low. With poverty, unemployment, inequalities of income, insecurity, bad working conditions, and poor health, accompanied by a lack of governmental provision for the poor and by disparities in political power that exacerbate disparities in wealth, it is not surprising that the process of urbanization is thought to be a major cause of political instability in the Third World.

Evidence supporting the 'rate of growth' hypothesis was found in Central America where rapid growth in agriculture and industrialization reduced the relative and absolute living standards of the working class, who then revolted against their governments. Only when, as in Costa Rica and Honduras, governments responded with policies to reduce inequalities and increase the real value of wages, did popular protest subside. Where the state responded with repression (Nicaragua, El Salvador, and Guatemala), 'opposition mobilization and unity increased and led to a broad, rebellious challenge to regime sovereignty' (Booth, 1991).

## The revolution of rising expectations

A period of rapid economic growth can be followed by an economic downturn. Then, there may be a 'revolution of rising expectations', meaning that frustration is felt by people whose expectations are rising faster than can be satisfied by the economy. This frustration can be politically destabilizing because of the ways in which it is likely to be expressed. Marx's observation that we measure our desires and pleasures by social comparison and not by the objects that provide the satisfaction, and de Tocqueville's conclusion that 'Evils which are patiently endured when they seem inevitable become intolerable when once the idea of escape from them is suggested', leads to a largely psychological explanation of one particular kind of instability which postulates that: 'Revolutions are most likely to occur when a prolonged period of objective economic and social development is followed by a short period of sharp reversal' (Davies, 1972, pp. 136–7).

Rather than deprivation causing instability, a sudden decline in the opportunities to continue improving one's condition in line with expectations leads to revolution. A 'revolutionary state of mind' requires an expectation of improvements in the satisfaction of needs (for physical, social, and political benefits) to be under 'a persistent, unrelenting threat'. The 'crucial factor' is the fear that 'ground gained over a long period of time will be quickly lost'. The relationship between expectations of needs satisfaction and their actual satisfaction can be demonstrated by a J curve (see Figure 9.1).

This theory explains the Egyptian revolution of 1952, when a series of strikes, peasant uprisings, and urban riots culminated in a *coup d'état* by army officers (Davies, 1972). In 2008, Egypt again experienced riots and strikes in its larger cities following increases in basic food prices, threatening the livelihoods of people already close to the poverty line. The uprising in Tunisia in 2010 was, in part, prompted by a reversal in the well-being experienced by at least one million citizens since 2008 (Schraeder and Redissi, 2011).

Other contemporary factors leading to perceptions of a widening gap between achieved and expected levels of welfare include environmental problems, such as deforestation and land degradation, leading to lower levels of economic output and the displacement of communities (Mohammed, 1999).

**Figure 9.1**    *Needs satisfaction and revolution*

SOURCE:    Davies (1972), p. 137. Reproduced with permission.

## Foreign influences

Some explanations of instability emphasize the importance of foreign influences. International demonstration and diffusion may be important, as in the case of the Cuban revolution within Latin America, military *coups* in neighbouring countries, or the attitude of the USA towards dictators and democracies. Aid is increasingly used as a weapon against political practices, albeit in the direction of democracy. External threats, real or perceived, to a country's security have fostered authoritarianism, militarization, and curbs on civil liberties.

Foreign involvement can take the form of spillovers from crises in neighbouring states, as in the Democratic Republic of Congo where over one million Hutu refugees from Rwanda have imported the ethnic conflict that led to genocide in their own country. Alternatively, intervention may be orchestrated by powerful neighbouring governments, as with Syria's and Israel's incursions into Lebanon, especially if there are domestic political factions supported by foreign governments, such as Lebanon's Shia movement, Hizbullah. Foreign intervention in the name of 'the war on terror' currently fuels the border conflict between Eritrea and Ethiopia, with the USA supporting Ethiopia against Eritrea's Islamic government, which is accused of links with al-Qaeda.

Foreign intervention has often set out to destroy a whole regime – sometimes covertly, as with the USA's involvement in Chile in the early 1970s; sometimes overtly, as with the USA's and Britain's invasion of Iraq in 2003, which destroyed the country's physical and administrative infrastructure and reduced politics to sectarian violence and the prospect of new forms of authoritarianism. Foreign intervention backed by NATO on behalf of one side in the civil war in Libya, though of dubious legality, brought down the Gaddafi regime in 2011.

## Ethnicity

The destabilizing effect of economic and social modernization is related to the problems that many societies have had when loyalty to an ethnic group transcends loyalty to a new state. As we saw in Chapter 8, that problem is sometimes referred to as the crisis of integration or nation-building. Nation-building is sometimes seen as an ethical and psychological activity designed to re-orientate people's loyalties towards a new political entity. But primordial attachments based on tribe, language, religion, or race have been – and still are – enormously powerful in most regions of the Third World. They have been extremely divisive, and frequently lead to armed insurgency. Ethnic demands are currently the most important source of violent political conflict in the Third World, ranging from secession to equal rights, greater political participation, an end to economic and social discrimination, and the protection of cultural traditions (Horowitz, 1994; Gurr and Harff, 1994).

Ethnic conflict has increased greatly since the end of the Cold War, sometimes originating in historic antagonisms (for example, Sinhalese and Tamils in Sri Lanka), competition for scarce resources (especially employment), the disproportionate benefits from modernization enjoyed by some ethnic groups (for example, the Ibo in Nigeria), or exclusive ethnic occupational specialization and 'division of labour'. Colonial discrimination left legacies of ethnic hierarchies and disparities in material well-being (such as in Uganda). Fears of political domination have been exacerbated by the exclusive right to rule claimed by some ethnic groups (such as the Pushtuns of Afghanistan) and by the designation of a single language as 'official' (as with Malay in Malaysia) (Horowitz, 1985). Political discrimination of one ethnic group by another led to civil war in Côte d'Ivoire in 2002. In Burundi, a government dominated by the Tutsi minority and kept in power by military dictatorship led to 12 years of civil war with the majority Hutu population. Ethnicity is, in many respects, a special dimension of inequality (see p. 205).

Ethnicity has become the foundation for the mobilization of indigenous groups, especially in Latin America, where indigenous people make up some 10 per cent of the population. Their grass-roots organizations have become particularly significant in Bolivia, Chile, Colombia, Ecuador, and Mexico. Their demands have mainly focused on land rights, bilingual education, self-determination through the decentralization of political authority to traditional political organizations, and opposition to neo-liberal economic policies and the 'light-skinned' elites who prosper from them.

In parts of India with tribal minorities (or *adivasi*) indigenous movements are engaged in opposition to the loss of tribal rights to water, forests, and land, and the consequent displacement of tribal people, indebtedness, and loss of livelihoods. In Orissa, for example, tribal movements such as Gandhamardan Surakhya Parishad, have put up resistance against hydroelectric projects and minerals extraction. Many such groups are notable for the level of women's involvement and the emergence of indigenous leadership (Padhi and Panigrahi, 2011). In some areas, tribal activism has successfully demanded self-government, leading to the recognition of a new State of the Indian Union, as with the creation of Jharkhand in 2002.

In Latin America, political mobilization has sometimes progressed from the activism of social movements such as the Confederation of Indigenous Nationalities of Ecuador, Bolivia's Kataristas, and Mexico's Zapatistas, to the formation of political parties such as Ecuador's Pachakutik, or participation in coalitions to field candidates for legislative elections.

Indigenous social movements found their opportunity to press for reforms in the freedom of association and waning repression consequent upon political liberalization. However, such political liberalization has frequently been accompanied by economic liberalization and its threats to indigenous land rights, wages, expenditure on programmes of benefit to peasants and small farmers such as social services and agricultural subsidies (including credit), and consequently livelihoods. This has created incentives to mobilize and exert political pressure: 'rural organizations and protest respond to the material uncertainty raised by indebtedness, declining incomes, and the loss of land'. The capacity of indigenous people to mobilize politically has been strengthened by the communication networks provided by unions, churches, non-governmental organizations, and even the state when earlier agrarian reform policies entailed the incorporation of peasant producers in cooperatives and other economic associations (Yashar, 1998, p. 34; Van Cott, 2005).

Whether ethnic diversity threatens political stability depends very much on how it is structured and managed. It does not necessarily lead to conflict, as shown by Ghana and Bolivia; and when it does, the resulting communal violence is not necessarily politically destabilizing, as shown by the case of India since independence. However, even when ethnic groups are not in conflict with the state but, rather, with each other, the state is inevitably drawn in to restore order. If it does so in a way perceived as biased, political order may be threatened.

Cultural diversity, whether primarily ethnic or religious, only leads to conflict when there are socio-economic, political, and cultural inequalities between groups. Political mobilization increases the more an ethnic group experiences multiple forms of inequality and discrimination. The political, cultural, and economic context in which the 'horizontal' inequality occurs then moderates the extent to which inequality leads to inter-ethnic conflict. Politically, the potential for conflict can be reduced by power-sharing arrangements (as in Ghana and Bolivia). Economies with low per capita incomes and low levels of growth are more prone to ethnic conflict. Cultural demography – the geographical location and size of groups – is also relevant to political mobilization (Stewart, 2008).

The type and extent of ethnic conflict is also determined by the level of group cohesion (affected by the strength of grievance and the group's regional concentration), the strategies and tactics of leaders (particularly the use of violence), the type of political system confronted (its level of democracy), and external encouragement (Gurr and Harff, 1994). Ethnicity is reduced in significance when there are cross-cutting identities, rather than a correspondence between ethnic, religious, regional and linguistic cleavages. Combinations of ethnicity and religion have led to insurgencies in Côte d'Ivoire on the part of Moslem Dioulas and Senoufos, and in southern Thailand, where Moslem Malays resist integration into a predominantly Buddhist country. Instability is also more likely where there are a few large ethnic groups whose conflicts dominate politics, and less likely when there is a multiplicity of small ethnic groups – compare Nigeria and Tanzania in this regard.

The proposition that ethnic diversity makes a country more vulnerable to political instability has been tested empirically by quantitative analysis of 127 conflicts in 161 countries between 1945 and 1999. When civil war was taken as the indicator of instability, it was found that neither ethnic pluralism nor state discrimination against minorities, whether religious or linguistic, made instability more likely. Rather, the presence of conditions favouring insurgency, whether inspired by communism, Islamic fundamentalism, or nationalism, increases the risk of civil war. Such conditions are weak and unstable government, topography, a large population, and familiarity with local conditions on the part of rebels (Feardon and Laitin, 2003).

Thus, research into the role of ethnicity in political instability has produced conflicting findings. However, the cultural pluralism which has been cited as almost a hallmark of political underdevelopment has often meant a lack of consensus about political values. There is, then, what is regarded as a crisis of political culture.

## The political culture

'Political culture' is usually defined as the way people evaluate and judge political acts and institutions (Diamond, 1993a). It is a system of beliefs, values, and ideals about the way a system of government should function. Subject to some variations, political culture refers to standards of evaluation about the rules of the political game. Some political scientists have limited the concept to values concerning the procedures of politics, and how political leaders should be selected, how they ought to behave, and how authoritative decisions ought to be made. Others add to this the scope of government action and the legitimacy of government intervention in certain areas of social and economic activity.

Cultural values will include the means for transferring power and the legitimate boundaries of the state. Nationalism and secession are the consequence of values about territorial boundaries and where they ought to be drawn. Ideas about personal political involvement, about who is entitled to participate, and about whether political action is likely to be effective within a given political system also form part of the political culture. Included, too, are attitudes towards other participants and their roles as political actors. A political culture may not endorse the involvement and participation of all sections of society. For example, women may be excluded.

Reservations have been expressed about the concept of political culture and explanations of change in terms of it. First, there is a problem of causality in assuming that certain types of political culture are conducive to the maintenance of certain sorts of political system, and that, if there is no congruence between culture and system, the system will change as a result of being undermined by a lack of consensus and legitimacy. Political culture must not be viewed too deterministically (Diamond, 1993b). There is a presupposition in much of the literature that the line of causality runs in this direction.

A further problem is that a good deal of the political instability which Third World countries have experienced would seem to coincide with widely shared values. The idea that the only way to protect one's own interests is to acquire and hold on to a monopoly of power to the complete exclusion (where possible) of other groups, has characterized the behaviour of many political movements in the post-independence era, as it did the behaviour of some of the fragmented nationalist movements fighting for independence. Because of the significance of the state in social and economic terms it has been the object of attention of political groups seeking to monopolize power, rather than share it in a spirit of trust with other groups. Such widely disseminated attitudes towards power have been very destabilizing.

So, if some shared values are conducive to stability and others are not, the use of the concept of culture implying shared values as an explanation of stability no longer works. At the very least, it becomes a circular argument: stability occurs if members of society share values conducive to stability. It depends what those shared values are. It is not enough to say that a society will be stable when a sufficiently large number of people share common values about how to conduct political affairs.

This is quite apart from the problem as to how many are enough. In any particular society, one is likely to find more than one set of beliefs about the role of government in society, the way it should be conducted, and the proper political roles of different sections of the community. This raises the question of what proportion of society must support one view of government before there can be said to be sufficient consensus to sustain a political system that corresponds to those shared values. How homogeneous does the culture have to be, and how widely shared?

A further difficulty arises if we assume that there is a crisis of legitimacy when some proportion of society feels that the rules of government lack moral authority and so dispute them, not seeing it as immoral to manipulate the constitution for its own ends. It is not easy to predict, simply by knowing that they believe some or all of those rules to lack moral worth, how far people will deviate from the established norms. People might believe that the rules do not deserve their moral approval without being prepared to break them. This is a universal dilemma in politics. A system can lose moral authority if it proves easy to abuse. But acting contrary to some rules because others are being bent and broken may be more damaging than going along with the outcomes of the rules as they are presently being applied.

If it is not possible to know how far people will deviate simply because they lack moral respect for government, it is equally impossible to know whether, when they deviate, it is because of that lack. In the Third World there is frequent flouting of the rules, with electoral malpractices very widespread. Does this signify a crisis of legitimacy? It does not always lead to instability, unless instability is defined as breaking the rules. So, again, it does not seem to be a very useful theoretical explanation to say that, if consensus is lacking, there will be political instability.

Finally, the concept of political culture implies that attitudes and feelings about politics reflect rational choices and high levels of awareness about what a political system means as far as individual interests are concerned. There is no place for the idea of false consciousness or hegemony. Yet, what people believe to be in their interest in terms of structures of government may be ideas and values that are promulgated by socio-economic groups intent on maintaining their own domination. Alternative sets of values would undermine that dominance. Socialization may explain how political values are passed from one generation to another, but this is a generational process rather than a class problem, when one generation passes on to another values that are contrary to their class interests. The idea of political power being, in part, expressed through false consciousness, and an ability to gain acceptance of ways of organizing society, has very wide implications throughout the study of politics. The political consciousness of specific groups in Third World societies is an important issue if we are to understand why so much deprivation, injustice, and inequality is accepted in societies where such features are most severe. The concept of political culture does not really tackle what must be regarded as an important dimension of political power.

## Inequality

A proposition concerning political instability which can be traced back to Aristotle is that equality in society will secure peace and stability. This should be very relevant to the Third World, where there are 'deep, cumulative social inequalities' (Diamond *et al.*, 1990, p. 19; Pinkney, 1993). Inequality within developing countries has increased markedly in the past 30 years, mainly as a result of the spread of neo-liberal economic policies.

One reason why inequality is thought to threaten stability is that, if there are profound inequalities, there will be resentment and discontent with a system of decision-making that is unable to redress the imbalance, or is controlled by those intent on preserving the *status quo*. So maldistribution of income and wealth is likely to be a strong predictor of political violence, not least because it will be felt more strongly among the urban poor who are more able to mobilize collectively. Growing inequality in China led to 87,000 protests and riots in 2006 alone. High levels of inequality encourage the poor to revolt and the ruling class to impose authoritarian rule to avoid the cost of redistribution in favour of the poor (Savoia *et al.*, 2010).

However, analysis of the relationship between inequality and instability has proved inconclusive, and dependent upon the variables chosen to measure inequality. High levels of income inequality in sub-Saharan African states, as measured by household expenditure between 1986 and 1997, did not affect political instability in any statistically significant manner (Nel, 2003). However, there is some evidence supporting a relationship between political instability in poor countries and material inequality as measured by land-holdings (Rueschmeyer *et al.*, 1992). The poorest countries with unequal land distribution are less stable than countries that have inequalities in land, but also have alternative sources of wealth and reasonable levels of income (Russett, 1964; Huntington, 1968). This relates to the economic backwardness argument: that poor countries cannot produce enough wealth to satisfy all needs, whereas richer countries satisfy basic needs and make the standard of living of the poorest tolerable.

Other studies using political violence as an indicator of instability and land ownership as a measure of inequality have shown that, while maldistribution of land ownership – including high levels of landlessness – has preceded revolutionary violence in Nicaragua and El Salvador, other countries in the same region (Cost Rica and Panama) with similar inequalities remained relatively non-violent and stable. Agrarian inequality may not act independently but may simply be part of inequality in the overall distribution of income (Muller and Seligson, 1987). How land inequality is measured is also an important consideration, since landlessness, rather than the distribution of land among the landed population, might be a better predictor of instability, since high levels of landlessness preceded political violence, and even revolution, in Mexico (1911), China (1941), Cuba (1959), and Bolivia (1952). However, extensive cross-national multivariate analysis has revealed the relationship between landlessness and political violence to be statistically insignificant (Muller *et al.*, 1989).

The converse argument is that stable countries have relatively egalitarian distributions of income. But it has to be recognized that the hypothesis would seem to be falsified by inegalitarian societies that have nevertheless experienced considerable stability. India would be a case in point, frequently cited as a stable democracy, at least in Third World terms. It obviously depends on how stability is measured.

Economic inequality was a factor in the protests and revolts that comprised the Arab Spring of 2011. Prior to the protests in Egypt, 40 per cent of citizens lived on under US$2 a day, as did 40 per cent of the population of Yemen, the poorest country in the Middle East. Egypt's absolute poverty rate (the proportion of the population living below a specified amount, in this case US$1 a day) increased from 16.7 per cent in 2000 to 19.6 per cent in 2005, reversing the decline in poverty between 1996 and 2003. Inequality increased by 17 per cent. Almost 2 million (or 11.4 per cent) of the Syrian population lived in extreme poverty. Social and regional inequalities were increasing, as wage increases were cancelled out by inflation. The poverty rate in Tunisia was 24.7 per cent, with 700,000 unemployed, 69 per cent of whom were under 30 years of age. Between 2000 and 2005, growth in per capita consumption was accompanied by a sharp increase in inequality. The top 20 per cent of the people in Tunisia earned 46.3 per cent of the country's total income, while the bottom quintile earned only 5.9 per cent.

In Algeria, some 23 per cent lived below the poverty line, and the wealthiest 20 per cent of Algerians controlled 42.6 per cent of the country's wealth, while the poorest 20 per cent controlled 7 per cent. Protests were triggered by large increases in the prices of basic foods. The poorest 40 per cent of the Bahraini population's share of total annual income dropped from 19.6 per cent to 18.1 per cent between 1995 and 2006, and a considerable portion of Bahraini households fall below the country's relative poverty line (the proportion of the population living on less than a specified percentage of median income, in this case 50 per cent). Bahraini protests were initially aimed at achieving greater equality for the majority Shiite population. Approximately 15 per cent of the Jordanian population lived below the poverty line, two thirds of them in urban areas. Jordan's poorest quintile's share in national income was 7.2 per cent in 2006.

In parts of the Arab world, inequality has also taken the form of discrimination against religious attachments, inciting protests which formed part of the demands for political reforms known collectively as the 'Arab Spring' of 2011. In Bahrain, for example, a majority Shi'a group, which accounts for about 70 per cent of a population, is governed by a Sunni minority. This means that the Shi'a group suffers discrimination in housing, employment, education, the establishment of Shia places of worship, the right to buy land in certain areas of the country. The Shi'ites also experience discrimination in politics, with elections in gerrymandered districts and the strategic naturalizations of Sunnis from neighbouring states combining to prevent opposition parties from winning legislative majorities. Shi'ites hold less than 13 per cent of top ranking positions in ministries and are debarred from senior positions in the military. The religious practices and beliefs of Shi'a Islam are not included in the religious national curriculum. In Syria, the opposition is mainly Sunni Muslims, whereas the government is dominated by Alawis, who are Shi'ites. However, the protests in Syria have been fuelled more by high youth unemployment, a fall in the standard of living, and human rights abuses than by sectarian discrimination.

Gender inequality is a particularly virulent form of inequality in developing countries, but is rarely threatening to the *status quo*. Discrimination against women in politics (and in other walks of life) is the defining characteristic of gender relations in the Third World (as in most other countries). Women's citizenship is limited and their political status is never equal to that of men. A contributory factor is that the management of the family and household falls disproportionately on women at the expense of political participation.

Women are also under-represented in political institutions (such as cabinets) and organizations (especially political parties). Progress has been made in most regions of the Third World since 1990 in the proportion of seats in national legislatures held by women (see Table 9.1). However, the state remains a 'gendered hierarchy' which excludes or marginalizes women by misogynist social and religious conventions which relegate women to the private sphere, especially in Islamic regimes (Whalen, 1996a). In China, levels of women's political participation have actually fallen during the economic and political changes of the past decade or so, with women being disadvantaged by the introduction of multi-candidate elections allowing discrimination in favour of men (Davin, 1996).

Even following periods of democratization in which women had been significant actors, cultures of patriarchy continue to exclude women from politics. The return to 'normality' usually entails restrictions on women's roles, especially in politics and government (Chowdhury and Nelson, 1994). Women in Latin America, for example, have been vulnerable to renewed exclusion after the transition to democracy, as the power of their social movements becomes displaced by male-dominated political parties, and as governments focus on economic objectives, rather than the social objectives for which women campaigned – a 'remasculinization' of politics. Latin American history shows that even revolutionary states 'are as resistant as other states to the participation of women' (Craske, 1999, p. 161). The growing importance of 'identity politics' can also be bad for gender equality when – as, for example, in India – it demands the state

**Table 9.1**  *Proportion of seats held by women in national parliaments, 1990 and 2011*

| Region | 1990 | 2011 |
|---|---|---|
| East Asia and Pacific | 17.1 | 17.7 |
| Latin America and Caribbean | 12.1 | 22.9 |
| Middle East and North Africa | 3.8 | 9.3 |
| South Asia | 6.3 | 20.1 |
| Sub-Saharan Africa | 9.7[a] | 19.9 |
| Low and middle income | 12.5 | 15.4 |

NOTE:    [a] =1997.
SOURCE:    'World data bank gender statistics', www.worldbank.org/ddp/.

endorses conservative cultural traditions, thereby strengthening 'the hands of forces that oppose women's rights' (Hassan, 2010, p. 952).

Women have frequently been involved in campaigns to change politics fundamentally. They have played an important part in the movements for democracy, political reform, and resistance to authoritarianism – especially in Latin America, Taiwan, and the Philippines, forming new social movements to protest, lobby, and articulate political demands (Hensman, 1996). Women's organizations with feminist agendas emerged in the 1980s and 1990s, such as the National Women's Lobby in Zambia and GABRIELA in the Philippines (Whalen, 1996b). Women occupy some top political offices, such as the presidencies of Chile, Argentina, Brazil, Costa Rica, India, and Liberia, and the prime ministerships of Thailand, Mali, Peru, Trinidad, and Bangladesh.

But much of women's political activism and organization – as distinct from self-help projects which sometimes alter the gender imbalance in local power networks (Jaquette, 2001) – has not been directed at gender inequalities, backed perhaps by a feminist philosophy. It has been devoted to economic and social causes which are not gender-specific and from which all would benefit, such as campaigning for human rights, food subsidies, employment protection, and health care. The politics in which women engage has rarely placed equality (for example, through an extension of the suffrage) at the top of the agenda. Even when women have been involved in revolutionary movements which include women's emancipation in their agendas, this has been 'limited and full of contradictions' (Whalen, 1996b, p. 90). Post-revolutionary improvements to women's health, education, and welfare can be accounted for more by improvements to the lives of the poor generally, rather than by women's political activism.

Part of the explanation for this is that women do not constitute a homogenous group, but are as divided as men in terms of class, religion, and ethnicity. In Latin America, for example, 'women stress their class links rather than their gender identities' (Craske, 1999, p. 161).

## Class conflict

From a Marxist perspective, a theoretical explanation of instability would be in terms of class conflict. As classes develop within a capitalist economy and society, their interests become increasingly irreconcilable. The impoverishment of the labouring class is accompanied by its growth until eventually revolution becomes inevitable. But at least one of the problems with this line of thought in the Third World context is that, if class consciousness is developing, it is in a unique way. It is less in terms of the ownership of the means of production, and more in terms of political power. Those who control and manage the means of production, such as bureaucrats earning salaries, often confront a peasant society that has yet to develop class consciousness derived from its material position in society.

Then, there is the problem alluded to earlier, that it is often the privileged members of society who indulge in destabilization. In the Third World, conflict and crisis within the newly emerging middle class have been a source of political instability. In 2006, opposition to Thailand's Thai Rak Thai government was mounted by the urban middle class because of government policies favouring the rural poor, including affordable health care and cheap loans. A military *coup* briefly ended parliamentary government but, following its reintroduction, the middle class again demonstrated against the democratically elected government. Factionalism, perhaps along ethnic lines, among the propertied classes and classes in charge of the state apparatus has often led to military *coups*, or the illegal manipulation of political processes. Rather than peasants rising up against their oppressors, or workers revolting against their exploiters, sections of the middle class compete for control of the state, using methods that fall outside the law and the constitution.

## A crisis of state authority

Third World states have often lacked the power to make their presence felt throughout society. They have experienced legal and administrative incapacity amounting to the collapse of state institutions. Bureaucracies might be overdeveloped in terms of political power, but they are not necessarily effective in terms of administration. The state cannot deliver the services which taxpayers believe they are paying for; it cannot extract the resources from society that it needs to finance its activities; it cannot maintain law and order; it cannot police its territory effectively.

For example, the Thai government does not control its northernmost provinces – they are under the control of drugs barons. In Colombia, there has been virtual civil war between the state and organizations that want to remain outside the scope of the state's authority and the enforcement of its laws. Somalia is an extreme example of state collapse, with 'no internationally recognized polity; no national administration exercising real authority; no formal legal system; no banking and insurance services; no telephone and postal system; no public service; no educational and reliable health system; no police and public security services; no electricity or piped water systems; weak officials serving on a voluntary basis surrounded by disruptive, violent bands of armed youths' (Adam, 1995, pp. 72–8). Parts of southern Yemen are under the control of militias affiliated to al-Qaeda. The Taliban control parts of Nuristan province of Afghanistan. In Mali, the collapse of the state's control of its northern territory led to a military coup in 2012.

The failure of states to extend effective political authority, maintain order, and extract resources for the provision of public goods throughout their territories leads to crises, the erosion of legitimacy and security, and violent civil conflict in 'the already fragile post-colonial state' (Ayoob, 1996, p. 73; Migdal, 1996).

State incapacity springs from a number of sources. Colonialism weakened, fragmented, or destroyed existing means of social control. Politicians have created organizations which compete with and threaten the power of the state's executive leadership. Strong social groups have proved resistant to state domination through the power of chiefs, landlords, bosses, foreign corporations, rich peasants, clan leaders, castes, powerful families, and 'strongmen' (Migdal, 1988).

This view of civil conflict and political instability risks confusing cause and effect. The factors which are presented as the consequences of state failure – such as ethno-nationalism, social conflict, and external military intervention – can equally, and possibly more convincingly, be seen as causes of state incapacity and the collapse of hitherto effective states such as the Lebanon before the mid-1970s. This is not to deny that the collapse of state governance will exacerbate the social and economic forces that have worked to undermine it.

Furthermore, instability often results from the actions of those who control the coercive apparatus of the state, rather than those who control extra-legal means of coercion, whether as criminal organizations, or opposition groups. The military is the most obvious case in point. The crisis of authority arises because the coercive apparatus of the state turns against its civil masters, not because that apparatus is so weak that it cannot resist an external challenge to the state's authority. The strength of the state's coercive apparatus has been increased by Third World expenditure on arms. Such expenditure seems to be driven more by the political pressures which the armed forces in developing countries are able to exert than by defence considerations. It tilts the balance of power and resources towards the military, blocks the development of 'strong and independent social and political institutions', and 'results in state institutions and élite groups being bent to the purposes of the institutions of organized violence' (Krause, 1996, p. 187). Thus, in one sense, the strong, rather than weak, state can be a source of instability.

## Political institutionalization

One consequence of modernization in a pre-industrial society is a rapid increase in political mobilization and participation. If political instability is to be avoided, such participation needs to be matched by a corresponding level of institutional development. By and large, this has not happened in developing countries. Violence and instability have been the consequence of political institutions developing more slowly than the rate at which new socio-economic groups were being politically mobilized. The lack of effective political institutions makes it impossible for demands to be channelled through effective and legitimate procedures (Huntington and Dominguez, 1975).

Unfortunately, this explanation contains an element of tautology (Leys, 1982). 'Institutionalization' refers to a process through which conflict can be managed in a peaceful and structured way. It does not simply mean the creation of organizations. The institutionalization argument seems tantamount to saying that, if individuals and groups are prepared to participate in politics by playing according to the rules and abiding by the outcomes of so doing, there will be stability. An increase in participation leads to instability if political institutions cannot absorb it, but instability is the evidence that institutionalization is insufficiently developed. In other words, there will be stability when there is no instability. We are left needing an explanation as to why people should behave in ways that are not constitutionally sanctioned.

Nevertheless, the view that political participation needs to be matched by institutional development, if instability is to be averted, is supported by comparative research into the 'coherence' or 'consistency' of different types of regime. Statistical analysis of quantitative measures of institutions and stability for a large number of regimes over the nineteenth and twentieth centuries confirms that political instability is a function of institutional consistency. A dictatorship with high levels of political participation is institutionally inconsistent, and consequently unstable. An autocratic regime will be stable, if it prevents the development of institutions capable of challenging the power of the central executive. Similarly, a democracy will be stable if power is diffused, offering opportunities for power to a wide range of interests. Democratic institutions – elections, accountable government, channels of political participation – reinforce one another. Political instability occurs when institutions are inconsistent – for example, when there are elected bodies but restricted political participation. Institutionally inconsistent regimes are unstable not only because they are 'more prone to the expression of grievances, but also because they have weak institutions for addressing challenges to the authority of the regime' (Gates *et al.*, 2006, p. 907).

A cross-national quantitative study of 141 severe political crises – including revolutionary wars, ethnic conflicts, and anti-democratic *coups* between 1955 and 2003 – also found that regime 'coherence' explained instability better than other variables such as ethnic pluralism, poverty, or economic performance. By asking 'what conditions enable a state to remain stable?', it was found that the risk of instability is lowest in full autocracies and full democracies, and highest in hybrid regimes, such as when elections are competitive but not fully free. It was also found that political competition is dominated by particularistic groups (formed on the basis of religious or ethnic identity) which approach politics with a 'winner takes all' mentality. A lack of cross-cutting identities in political competition thus substantially increases the risk of political crisis (Goldstone *et al.*, 2005). An example is the factionalism found in the Lebanon, where exclusive rival communities based mainly on religion, many with their own militias, persistently block the development of stable democracy.

Studies of this kind should only tentatively be applied to the contemporary Third World if they include a large number of countries at different stages of economic development over a very long period. But it is interesting when quantitative analysis confirms what is suggested by contemporary events, as well as being supported by a study of *coups*, riots, and political assassinations in 18 Latin American countries between 1971 and 2000 which found that the more democratic the country, the greater the political stability (Blanco and Grier, 2007).

## Revolution in the Third World

The ultimate manifestation of political instability is revolution. Revolution involves the replacement of a whole social and economic order, and not just a political regime. Ideologies and new forms of organization are required. Solidarity is mobilized, mainly along class lines, but religion may be significant in raising class consciousness, as in the case of Islamic fundamentalism in Iran and Algeria. Existing social and political structures, particularly property relations, are defined as exploitative and oppressive and are challenged as such. The objective is an alternative form of society (Shanin, 1982).

In the first half of the twentieth century, successful revolutions that were not instigated by foreign intervention took place in developing societies, 'peasant revolt being central to all of them' (Shanin, 1982, p. 321). Consequently, the analysis of such events has been largely dominated by a search for the conditions necessary for a peasant-based revolution. Historians and social scientists have asked why these should occur in some societies and not others which seem to be comparable in respect of the social and economic factors which, *a priori*, might be thought likely to lead to revolution (Goodwin and Skocpol, 1989).

Revolution is usually preceded by severe social dislocation, crisis within the political elite, a strengthening of class identity and militancy, and the emergence of an effective revolutionary organization. Crisis is commonly occasioned by fiscal problems, conflict between elites and elite alienation (especially when social mobility is restricted), and widespread grievances leading to popular support for change that can be mobilized against the regime. For example, the *ancien regime* in Iran had built up excessive debts and was unable to control inflation. The exclusion of the middle classes from power, government corruption, and repression alienated the religious elite and the merchant class. Population growth and urbanization outstripped economic opportunities, making society receptive to mobilization by nationalistic Islamic ideology. A coalition of traditional and Westernized elites led to the demise of the Shah's regime (Goldstone *et al.*, 1991; Parsa, 2000).

The significance of crisis is affected by other features of the vulnerable state. 'Exclusive' states which restrict political power to individuals and dynasties, marginalize democratic procedures, exclude other elites from decision-making, and provide no opportunities for change are vulnerable. In times of crisis, such states have to resort to repression and the external support of foreign powers, alienating moderate political opposition and extending the appeal of revolutionary action in the absence of alternative forms of politics. States that are highly interventionist economically (in terms of capital formation, ownership of assets, and economic regulation) are also vulnerable, since they attract criticism for economic, as well as political, failures. All aspects of society become politicized and all social classes are potential victims of state mismanagement (Parsa, 2000). Pre-revolutionary Iran, Nicaragua, and the Philippines were all vulnerable because of the political exclusiveness of their regimes and their unsuccessful interventionism. External support from the USA and reliance on military repression failed to save them. Moderate opposition was weakened or eliminated in Iran and Nicaragua, which radicalized other social elements, especially students and the clergy. In the Philippines, moderate political opponents were tolerated and able to limit the impact of revolutionary change to the political realm (thus not producing a social revolution).

Revolution usually begins with rebellions to redress parochial wrongs. This takes the form of extra-constitutional action, perhaps involving violence, when the rural or urban poor take direct action against the governmental authorities or local power-holders in an attempt to resist the intensification of exploitation through higher workloads, declining real wages, victimization of trade unionists, police harassment, loss of land, or the raising of rents and taxes. Rural movements, such as the Landless Rural Workers' Movement in Brazil, have relied heavily on the occupation of land as a political strategy in conflicts with local and national elites over the expropriation of land by the state, or its private accumulation by powerful landlords. Other forms of direct action include sabotage, as for example in Ghanaian cocoa plantations (Moyo and Yeros, 2005). Such political activism may be in order to redress a wrong. There may be no long-term programme or ideology for fundamental change in social and economic relations.

What, then, turns rebellion into a revolutionary force? First, an *ideology* is needed to redirect and focus political activism, though revolution is not always characterized by a single, coherent ideology – no single ideology united the entire population in Iran, the Philippines, or Nicaragua, for example (Parsa, 2000). Second, outside *leadership* in the form of a coalition between peasants, intellectuals, students, professionals, clerics, and industrial workers is needed to provide a forward-looking revolutionary consciousness. This is confirmed by the cases of Vietnam, Iran, Cuba, and Nicaragua (White, 1974; Goodwin and Skocpol, 1989). Revolutionary leadership generally takes the form of an 'intelligentsia-in-arms', either as a military organization or a paramilitary political party.

Third, revolution needs a *social exchange* between rebellious groups and a revolutionary organization. A rebellious community will seek to solve local problems with the benefits offered by revolutionary leaders as incentives to participate in revolutionary action. Revolutionary organizations, for their part, need to expand their power through recruitment within the community, and by demonstrating that they can deliver what society needs. These needs include substitutes for the socio-economic arrangements that are to be replaced by the revolution – such as markets, land reforms, cooperatives, harvest labour; public utilities such as roads, communications, and irrigation ditches; social services such as health care and education; and, most importantly, destruction of the power of corrupt officials, monopolistic merchants, and landlords. Revolutionary organizations, such as parties and armies, also offer opportunities for social mobility. They must offer more than other political organizations because of the risks involved, not least that of severe retaliation by the state. The Revolutionary Armed Forces of Colombia provide an interesting case of how such an exchange can work (see Box 9.1).

Fourth, in the case of revolution in agrarian societies, the *class structure* is significant for revolutionary potential. The poorest are likely to be the least revolutionary in the initial stages of class conflict because of extreme economic dependency. Those with a measure of independence and security, such as smallholders owning their own land and producing

216

**Box 9.1**  *Colombia and FARC*

The military wing of the Colombian Communist Party was established in 1964 as the Revolutionary Armed Forces of Colombia (FARC). It is a revolutionary body based on a peasant land reform movement which had faced extreme political repression in the early 1960s. FARC had its origins in political crisis, especially the violent conflicts between liberal and conservative militias. It recruits from among subsistence farmers, displaced peasants, landless rural labourers, and occasionally urban workers. Women play an active part in providing communication, education, and health care.

FARC developed its own 'Bolivarian' ideology to direct and focus its political and military activism. Its broad aims are social protection for the lower classes, agrarian reform (including property titles for tenant farmers), greater equality, the protection of human rights, and competent government – none of which could be achieved without revolutionary change of Colombia's economic and political structures.

FARC's leadership is typical of peasant-based revolutionary movements, having its origins in a coalition of students, Catholic radicals, and left-wing intellectuals hoping to emulate Fidel Castro's communist revolution in Cuba, and bringing together communist militants and peasant self-defence groups. In 1985, FARC formed a new political party, the Patriotic Union, which won many seats in municipal and Congressional elections in 1986, only to see over 3,000 of its supporters killed between 1986 and 1992, including many elected representatives, by paramilitary groups acting for the landed oligarchy.

Revolution needs a social exchange between rebellious groups and a revolutionary organization. FARC provides health, education, and public order functions in areas under its control, forming an alternative government, or even a parallel state. It has set up agricultural credit systems, carried out vaccination campaigns, and built roads and irrigation systems. Being an 'alternative public manager' gave it wide appeal among a peasantry used to harsh working conditions, insecurity, state repression, violations of human rights, violence from right-wing paramilitary death squads, and under-investment by the state in social and economic development.

However, the maintenance of public order and protection against government forces also benefits the peasant coca growers and the criminals involved in the narcotics trade, on whom FARC levies taxes covering every stage of the business, estimated to be worth US$300 million a year. Connections with drug traffickers also provide FARC with access to the international black market in arms, but also reduce its legitimacy in the eyes of the international community, as well as within Colombia. In 1998, a large area was ceded to FARC as a ceasefire zone, prompting the USA to provide Colombia with US$6 billion in aid to be spent mainly on military actions against the insurgents (Ortiz, 2002; Ampuero and Brittain, 2005; Rochlin, 2011).

enough to be self-sufficient, are more likely to be revolutionary when aggrieved by injustice. They are vulnerable to the changes brought about by commercialization – population growth, competition, the loss of rights to grazing land and water, falling prices, higher interest payments, and foreclosures – while remaining locked into traditional social structures of mutual aid between kin and neighbours.

Finally, revolution in agrarian societies is dependent on the *threat to the peasantry* from the upper classes and their response to the challenge of commercial agriculture. Explanations of revolution should not concentrate exclusively on the actions of the peasantry. Revolution is most likely when the landed aristocracy damages the interests of the peasantry as a class by exacting a larger surplus from it, but leaves it intact by failing to develop a sufficiently powerful commercial impulse in the countryside. When the commercial interest in rural life is sufficiently strong to destroy the peasantry as a class, peasant-based revolution is less likely. Revolutions in predominantly agrarian societies have occurred when the landed classes, by and large, did not make a successful transition to the world of commerce and industry, and did not destroy the prevailing social organization among the peasantry (Moore, 1973).

## Conclusion

Many factors have been related to political instability, though the direction of causality is not always clear. None is sufficient in itself to explain the complexity of the phenomenon. The significance of each factor will vary according to the circumstances of region, history, level of economic development, and place within the international system. It thus becomes important to know under what circumstances a factor such as economic inequality, rapid economic growth, or social differentiation is likely to lead to political instability.

The recurring theme running through all explanations of political instability is inequality in one form or another. The poor become politically volatile when economic discrimination is in conjunction with developments in society which are conducive to political mobilization. Economic growth displaces existing social and economic hierarchies with new ones which threaten the interests of formerly dominant strata with new types of inequality. Economic downturns then disadvantage those whose newfound prosperity made economic inequalities at least tolerable. Diverse cultural identities become destabilizing the more there are 'horizontal' inequalities among ethnic or religious groups.

Attitudes about the legitimacy of regimes are particularly sensitive to whether the rules of the political game are perceived as fair or permanently discriminatory. So, if extreme inequalities in developing societies are found to be associated with political stability, contrary to the expectations of analysts, this might be because egalitarianism is not part of the dominant image of society. When that image is changed as a result of mass mobilization, inequality becomes less acceptable and political instability can result (Castles, 1974). Stressing the importance of the response to changes in society and economy by the dominant protagonists of current images helps to explain why a group or class that might be expected, *a priori*, to be violently dissatisfied with their lot expresses no political dissent likely to undermine political stability.

# 10

# Democratization in the Third World

## The 'third wave' and the Third World

Recent reforms in the direction of pluralist democracy and away from authoritarianism in the form of military rule, one-party systems, personal dictatorships, and racial oligarchy have revived interest in how to identify the prerequisites of stable democracy. The survival of democratic regimes has long been a preoccupation of political science, but is particularly relevant today when attempts are being made to establish or restore liberal democracy in so many parts of the world. Developing countries have been caught up in the so-called 'third wave' of democratization, starting in Portugal in 1974 and sweeping across southern and eastern Europe and, to varying degrees, most regions of the Third World (Huntington, 1991; Pinkney, 1993).

The latest wave of democratization – which increased the proportion of countries in the world with some form of democratic government from 28 per cent in 1974 to 60 per cent in 2011 – has included remarkable changes in the Third World (see Table 10.1). However, since 1980 the strength of democratization has varied, with the strongest felt in Latin America. Asia, too, has experienced significant democratization. Sub-Saharan Africa has seen both positive and negative trends (Lynch and Crawford, 2011). The Middle East saw very little effort to democratize until the 'Arab Spring' of 2011, and it is debatable how far the affected regimes will change to full democracies, given that there are no true democracies or free societies in the Arab region, and few free or democratic countries among states with a Muslim majority (Keratnyky, 2002).

The process of democratization has not been one of smooth progression. When new countries enter the ranks of newly democratizing states (for example, Mexico and Ghana in 2000), others suffer reversals in the form of *coups* (Ecuador and Fiji), or ethnic violence leading to the collapse of government (the Solomon Islands). While some developing countries register improvements in political rights and civil liberties –

**Table 10.1**   *Freedom: regional variations, 2011*

|  | *States rated:* | | | | | |
|---|---|---|---|---|---|---|
|  | *Free* | | *Partly free* | | *Not free* | |
|  | *Number* | *%* | *Number* | *%* | *Number* | *%* |
| Africa | 9 | 18 | 21 | 43 | 19 | 39 |
| Asia and Pacific | 16 | 41 | 15 | 38 | 8 | 21 |
| The Americas | 24 | 69 | 10 | 28 | 1 | 3 |
| Middle East and North Africa | 1 | 6 | 4 | 22 | 13 | 72 |

NOTE:   Freedom House divides countries into three broad categories on the basis of indicators of political rights (such as the right of all adults to vote in free and fair elections) and civil liberties (such as freedom of assembly, demonstration, and religion): 'free', 'partly free' and 'not free'.
SOURCE:   Freedom House (2012), p. 10.

such as media freedoms in Peru, free and fair elections in Taiwan, and greater economic opportunities for women in Oman, others experience setbacks. There were 26 such reversals in 2011, including restrictions on freedom of speech and association in the United Arab Emirates, the persecution of opposition politicians in Bangladesh, rigged elections in the Gambia, and the unconstitutional restructuring of the judiciary in Ecuador.

This chapter examines theories of democratic transition and consolidation, and the contribution of economic and political factors to stable democracy: national affluence, with its implications for equality and class development; the political culture and the problem of the direction of causality; civil society as a counter-balance to the power of the state; the balance of power within democracies; and the importance of institutional development to democratic consolidation.

To account for the process of democratization and its set-backs, political science has drawn a broad distinction between the *transition* to democracy, or a particular kind of change and its historical antecedents and causes; and *consolidation*, or the conditions necessary for newly established democratic regimes to survive. Before examining attempts to generalize and theorize about these phases of democratization, a cautionary reference to the concept of democracy must be made.

## Concepts of 'democracy'

In the study of Third World democratization, 'democracy' is usually defined in Western liberal terms. It requires a system of government to provide meaningful and extensive competition between individuals and groups, highly inclusive levels of political participation in the selection of leaders and policies, civil and political liberties sufficient to ensure such competition and participation, representative parliaments, the responsibility of government to parliament, regular free and fair elections, freedom of expression and association, and an extensive suffrage. Countries satisfy such criteria to differing degrees, and rules and principles may be contaminated by practice (Diamond *et al.*, 1990; Rueschmeyer *et al.*, 1992).

One of the reasons why understanding democratization is so difficult is the variability of regimes that are labelled democratic, and the nature of the democratic deficit found in so many. Regimes may be classified as 'new' or 'restored' democracies despite the circumvention by parliaments of presidential decrees (for example, Argentina), disregard of constitutional boundaries by the executive branch (for example, Taiwan), the award of veto powers to non-elected bodies such as the military (Chile and Thailand), and other deviations from the democratic ideal. Such variations make it problematic to relate democratization as a dependent variable to factors believed, hypothetically, to explain the process, especially consolidation (O'Donnell, 1998; Merkel, 1999).

The analysis of democratization is further complicated by the contested nature of the concept of democracy. Definitions often refer to the presence of different phenomena: procedures (such as the holding of free and fair elections), recognized human rights (such as freedom of association and speech), extensive participation, and material equality (because economic deprivation leads to political disempowerment). There are both formal and substantive conceptions of democracy. For some, democracy means 'meaningful political citizenship' (Grugel, 2002, p. 5). Analysis of democratization is affected by whatever view of democracy is held by the investigator.

**The transition to democracy**

Transitions from authoritarianism to democracy have been extremely varied, making it difficult to discern patterns that aid explanation. This complexity is sometimes compounded by confusion between the causes of authoritarian breakdown and the processes by which democratic replacements are introduced, as with a classification of the three 'routes' to democracy as: 'modernization', which stresses the economic prerequisites of democracy; 'structural', which focuses on the effects on authoritarianism of changes in class and power; and 'transition', which focuses on the bargaining between elites which negotiate the transition to democracy (Potter *et al.*, 1997). Such confusions make it difficult to distinguish between the definition of a phase such as transition, and its causes. Furthermore, transition and consolidation are not always kept conceptually distinct, as when explanations of transition are used to test whether a democracy has become consolidated (see, for example, Chadda, 2000). It has also proved difficult to distinguish between the causes of authoritarian breakdown and the form taken by the negotiation of change.

It helps to consider, first, what 'triggers' the end of authoritarianism and a movement towards a democratic alternative – though 'trigger' is perhaps not the best term when the causes of democratization may be long-term (such as a programme of industrialization), medium-term (an economic liberalization programme), or short-term (the calculations of political elites or popular struggles) (Luckham and White, 1996). The main causes of authoritarian breakdown are elite conflict, domestic crisis, and international pressure.

*Elite conflict* within authoritarian regimes has characterized all breakdowns, as coalitions begin to disintegrate under pressure from differences over aims, policies, and survival strategies in circumstances which provide no means for consensual conflict resolution: 'the danger for authoritarian regimes is that the weakness of institutional procedures for resolving disputes creates significant potential for instability' (Gill, 2000, p. 32). The disunity preceding many transitions to democracy alerts opposition movements to the possibility of reform.

*Internal crisis* is another factor that often triggers the transition to democracy, such as economic recession, or military failure (for example, Argentina's defeat in the Falklands/Malvinas war in 1983). The breakdown of authoritarian regimes has often followed economic crises brought about by poor economic management and international pressures (such as a steep rise in oil prices, or a reduction in the availability of foreign loans). Policy adjustments, such as devaluation, to deal with the crisis then have adverse consequences for groups supporting the regime that have already been disadvantaged by the crisis itself. Declining domestic legitimacy then increases the cost of authoritarian power. Alternatively, the costs of democracy, or the threat of revolution, may be perceived by authoritarian governments to have receded (Gill, 2000).

In Egypt, the mass protests in the spring of 2011 were a response to a crisis of legitimacy culminating in the grooming of one of President Mubarak's sons as his successor. This was denounced by a range of political groups, and followed more than a decade of strikes and protests, most notably in 2000 in solidarity with the Palestinian *intifada*, riots in early 2003 protesting against the invasion of Iraq, and the creation of the Kefaya movement in 2004 – a coalition of grassroots organizations from across the political spectrum opposed to a transfer of presidential power to Mubarak's son. A successful strike of workers at the country's largest textile mill in

December 2006 was followed by a wave of strikes throughout the whole sector. The price of bread prompted revolts in Mahalla and el-Borollos in 2008. In 2010, workers occupied an area around parliament.

*External pressures* may begin the demise of an authoritarian regime, such as the need to acquire international legitimacy, or satisfy international expectations of political reform which may be made a condition of further development assistance from multilateral and bilateral aid agencies. Alternatively, a foreign power may enforce democratization. International pressures can act in support of domestic factors to cause the breakdown of an authoritarian regime – economic sanctions, trade embargoes, international ideological pressures, global recessions, 'contagion' (as in Latin America) and, rarely, military force. However, how such international factors affect democratizing regimes has depended on how domestic economic and political actors, institutions, and structures were linked to global geopolitical forces (Gill, 2000).

The most recent foreign enforcement of 'democratization' occurred in 2011, when protests in a number of Libyan cities were met with extreme military repression and the conflict rapidly escalated into civil war. The intensity of the repression led the United Nations Security Council to impose an arms embargo on Libya, freeze the assets of the Gaddafi family, and ban members of the government from foreign travel. Since the use of military force against civilians continued, and following a request to the UN from the League of Arab States, the Council next adopted Resolution 1973 of 2011, authorizing member states to enforce a no-fly zone over Libya and take measures to protect civilians and civilian populated areas. Since Article 2(7) of the UN Charter prohibits foreign interventions in domestic conflicts unless they constitute a threat to international peace and security, the action against the Libyan regime was represented as a 'responsibility to protect' the population of a country when its own government is unwilling to do so. Such an understanding of international responsibilities makes it impossible for the UN to remain impartial towards the conflict. If intervention can be justified to *prevent* a humanitarian disaster which the international community thinks might happen, and if the risk of such a disaster arises from government policies, then 'the Council's protection mandate, if taken seriously, might even force UN peacekeepers or UN-authorized "coalitions of the willing" to assist local non-state actors in the removal of the respective regime' (Pippan, 2011, p. 169). The Libyan regime, unable to withstand allied air strikes, was eventually overthrown by the anti-Gaddafi movement in October 2011. It remains to be seen how far this constitutes the start of a transition to democracy.

Transitions have been highly variable processes, in terms of the sources of tension within authoritarian regimes, responses to pressures for political change by authoritarian leaders, the speed of transition, and the behaviour of elites, parties, and civil society bodies. The structural conditions inherited by the transitional government also vary, providing the process of consolidation with 'structured contingencies' in the form of political institutions, informal interest groups, social polarization, and relations between states and classes (Haynes, 2001). This complexity has given rise to a controversy over the process of transition, or how the new regime is planned and designed.

## Elite negotiations

On the one hand, there are those who see transition as predominantly initiated from above. Rather than being overthrown, authoritarian regimes disintegrate. Authoritarianism has been ended by popular protest or revolutionary action in only a minority of cases. Reform efforts launched by mass movements usually encounter anti-democratic resistance from established elites. It has even been argued that mass participation and popular mobilization can harm the democratization process (Huntington, 1984; Weiner, 1987). In Latin America, at least, democratization means the creation of 'pacts' between representatives of regime and opposition which guarantee some measure of protection for the interests involved, such as the military on the government side and trade unions among the opposition. Conversely, Burma's military authoritarianism survived because of the absence of conflict within the military elite (Dukalskis, 2009).

So, while the dissolution of authoritarian regimes is commonly marked by liberalization, the easing of repression, the resurrection of civil society, and the re-emergence of political parties, transition is dominated by negotiations between representatives of the current regime and opposition forces to design the new system of government. Following anti-government protests in February 2011, part of the 'Arab Spring', Morocco's minimal shift towards constitutional monarchy was tightly managed by the regime, with a new Constitution drawn up by a commission appointed and directed by the king, rather than by an elected constituent assembly. A consultative body liaised between the commission and political parties, unions, business associations, human rights groups, and other parts of civil society, but consultation and participation were limited (Ottaway, 2011).

Dominant elites may judge that a move towards democracy will be in their own interest, as in Mexico, leading them to concede to democratic reform. Alternatively, they might have to retreat in the face of opposition pressure, a factor in Argentina's end to military rule. Opposition groups then take the lead in negotiating the end of authoritarianism. Latin American experience shows that successful transitions were usually negotiated by moderates on both sides who were willing to compromise in accommodating each other's interests (Huntington, 1991; Mainwaring, 1992; Little, 1997; Peeler, 1998).

Negotiations and pacts have implications for the quality of the democracy created. For example, when transition requires pacts that protect the interests of groups and classes represented by authoritarian elites, the interests of those supporting greater participation, accountability, and equity are unlikely to be dominant in the transition phase (Karl, 1996). In Indonesia, President Suharto's authoritarian regime (1967–68) allowed a 'semi-opposition' of co-opted interests whose leaders were drawn into the transition, creating a new regime which absorbed and accommodated powerful elites from the Suharto era, compromising the regime's democratic quality but enabling it to neutralize anti-democratic forces in the military, ethnic minorities, and militant Islam (Aspinall, 2010).

By distinguishing between different types of regime and different types of political society, it is possible to develop a theory of transition which combines information about regime and non-regime elites, the latter owing their power to their position in civil society. Regimes are either 'unitary' in the face of challenges, or 'segmentary', with different interests supporting the regime in conflict. Society is either 'atomized' (without independent groups and movements), or 'civil' (with independent organizations enabling interests to be articulated and a degree of popular control to be exercised). A political system's position in relation to these two dimensions determines its prospects for transition to democracy and the path that will be taken. A combination of unitary regime and atomized society makes democratization less likely, because the regime is better placed to deal with challenges to its power and society is unable to produce effective opposition. Conversely, a combination of a segmentary regime and civil society offers better prospects for democratization. If a unitary regime confronts a strong civil society, there is a likelihood of violence. Finally, the prospects for democracy are poor when a segmentary regime exists within an atomized society. Here, authoritarian collapse is likely to be followed by further authoritarianism (Gill, 2000).

Negotiating the end of authoritarianism means attending to three main issues: the construction of a constitutional settlement, the dismantling of authoritarian government agencies, and the abolition of laws unsuitable for democratic politics. The possibility of successful negotiation on these institutional reforms depends on five sets of factors (Pinkney, 1993). First, there is the type of authoritarian regime to be dismantled. For example, a caretaker military regime will be easier to remove than a radical or reforming one. One-party regimes present obstacles according to the level of integration of party, state, and civil society. Second, negotiations will be affected by the ability of opposition groups to plan for democracy, rather than just oppose authoritarianism. A third set of factors is the configuration of institutions and political structures under authoritarianism, and the extent to which parties, legislatures, constitutions, and traditional political authority have survived during authoritarian rule.

Fourth, transition depends on the changing orientations towards reform by key elites – cabinets, juntas, bureaucrats, military officers, and opposition leaders – and organizations representing sections within civil society (church leaders, trade unions, social movements). Such orientations determine whether democratization will be government elite-led, or driven by pressures from below and originating at grass-roots level or within the middle class.

Finally, there is the process of conflict resolution. Patterns have been found in the relationships between process and outcomes. The viability of new democratic regimes has been found to be strengthened by a process of transition characterized by gradual rather than rapid change, moderation rather than radicalism on the part of protagonists, consensus rather than conflict over the objectives of democratization, and a balance of power between negotiating groups. Such patterns, however, are far from fixed, and only tentative conclusions have been generated by observations of their detailed operation in specific cases.

Negotiations eventually lead to some form of provisional government while the institutional basis of democracy is put in place (especially a new constitution), and elites adjust their political behaviour to liberal democratic practices. Uncertainty inevitably surrounds the location of the boundary between the end of transition and the start of consolidation, not least because different analysts have different conceptions of democracy's key characteristics, and change is not always marked by some 'focal event' (Schedler, 2001).

## Transition from below

An alternative explanation of transition emphasizes the role of pressure from below or among opponents to authoritarianism. Stressing the role of negotiating elites may lead to the role of mass movements being overlooked. Authoritarian regimes can be destabilized by public protest, and by industrial and political action by trade unions, even if the subsequent negotiations which design the new democratic regimes are dominated by members of different political and economic elites. Peru, Argentina, the Philippines, and South Korea are cases in point, where transitions have been predominantly brought about by mass protest in which church leaders, trade unionists, professional groups, human rights campaigners, student and youth organizations, and old guard politicians have been involved. Transitions in Africa have also originated in popular uprisings and demands for competitive elections and other democratic institutions, rather than pacts between elites (Diamond, 1997a; Haynes, 2003).

The 'Arab Spring' of 2011 also supports the view that transitions can be initiated by spontaneous uprisings. In Tunisia's 'Jasmine Revolution', demonstrations following self-immolation by a victim of official harass-ment spread throughout the country as young people and members of trade unions and women's organizations used social media to mobilize and coordinate protest against unemployment, rising food prices, corrup-tion, and authoritarianism. In Egypt, the overthrow of the Mubarak regime was the culmination of political protests by judges, tax collectors, indus-trial workers, and eventually men and women from a wide variety of socio-economic and religious backgrounds, which exposed the inability of what was thought to be a 'durable' authoritarianism to manage conflict within the political elite (Masoud, 2011; Schraeder and Redissi, 2011).

Authoritarian regimes, single party more than military, mobilize the public through closely controlled activities – in trade unions, youth groups, business associations, cultural bodies, and political parties. Political mobilization becomes a threat to the regime when it is organized by groups with a degree of autonomy. Such popular mobilization is usually stimulated by economic development or economic crisis (Gill, 2000). Popular participation through social movements such as women's groups (e.g. the Mothers of the Plaza de Mayo in Argentina), labour unions (e.g. the copper miners in Chile), community organizations and indigenous associations (such as the Zapatista movement in southern Mexico) were all important in struggles against authoritarianism (Grugel, 2002). The case of South Korea and some of the other 'Asian Tigers' also show how economic success can generate new elites and lead to social groups demanding more access to power and resources (Haggard, 1990).

Popular mobilization has, then, accompanied some successful transi-tions. So, it should not be inferred from elite domination of negotiations during transition that the causes of authoritarian breakdown had nothing to do with popular pressure or civil society. Popular resistance to authori-tarian regimes is common. And while elites may dominate the process of bargaining and pact-making, they represent non-elites – for example, peasants, workers, campaigners, professionals – whose interests cannot be ignored and whose political activity is the subject of the bargaining process.

Explanations of democratic transition in terms of power struggles within the ruling bloc or alliance may also be insufficiently dynamic to explain the shifting alliances between bureaucrats, the military, representatives of the property-owning classes, labour, and other social entities. Such shifts arise from the inevitable uncertainty about the implications of the retreat from authoritarianism for different socio-economic interests (Przeworski, 1986).

When the capacity for mass involvement in transition is understood, it becomes evident that many of the political leaders involved in negotiating transition to democracy have popular power bases, and that their role cannot be understood in isolation from the sections of the populace they represent and to which they owe their position. However, the precise contribution which social forces and their leaders make towards the transition to democracy depends on the nature of the authoritarian regime to be changed, and the nature of the society within which it is located.

## The consolidation of democracy

The process of consolidating democracy entails strengthening democratic institutions (especially the rule of law and protection of civil rights), extending democratic processes, and preventing authoritarian reversals. Political institutions and civil society need to be infused with democratic practices – for example, by the empowerment of associations in civil society which increase popular participation and make it more difficult for elites to manipulate democratic institutions. Authoritarian political discourses need to be rejected, and authoritarian political actors need to be neutralized. 'Perverse institutions' should be abolished, such as tutelage by non-democratic elites (especially the military), restrictions on the scope of policy-making powers (for example, exclusion of the Chilean parliament from the defence budget), and forms of political recruitment which give some minority interest a disproportionate presence on law-making bodies (O'Donnell, 1992; Valenzuela, 1992; Luckham and White, 1996). Latin America's experience of democratization reveals how persistent authoritarian legacies can be, especially weak and biased judiciaries, clientelism in public services, public toleration of illegal executive action (such as President Fujimori's closure of the national congress in 1992), and the survival of authoritarian organizations (such as Peronism in Argentina) (Philip, 2003).

Consolidation means that democracy has become routinized and internalized in political behaviour. No significant groups pursue unconstitutional, illegal, or undemocratic means to achieve their aims. Elites and the wider public accept democracy as the preferred means of governing and deciding on political succession. A democratic political culture has emerged in which trust, tolerance and compromise are the dominant political norms (Leftwich, 2000; Haynes, 2003).

What, then, are the prerequisites of such beliefs and behaviour? Explanations have variously stressed socio-economic variables, or political factors, including foreign intervention. The remaining sections of this chapter deal with explanations of consolidation in terms of these different sets of factors, recognizing that there are difficulties in applying predictions about consolidation derived from one region, such as Latin America, to another, such as Africa (Wiseman, 1996).

## The economic preconditions of democratic consolidation

There is much evidence to support the conclusion that economic affluence and related social changes are needed to improve the chance of democratic consolidation (Somit and Peterson, 2005). Early studies found the stability of democratic government to be positively correlated with measures of affluence and economic modernization, such as per capita income, the proportion of the population employed in industry, literacy rates, educational enrolments, and levels of urbanization (Lipset, 1959, 1960).

The correlations were taken to show that affluence reduces lower-class discontent. Economic development led to greater economic security and better education, both of which allowed 'longer time perspectives and more complex and gradualist views of politics'. Increased wealth and education also contribute to pluralism 'by increasing the extent to which the lower strata are exposed to cross pressures which will reduce the intensity of their commitment to given ideologies and make them less receptive to supporting extremist ones' (Lipset, 1959, p. 71).

Economic development also enlarges the middle class, whose interest is in moderating conflict – which it is able to do by rewarding moderate political parties and penalizing extremist ones. Economic development affects other classes, too. The greater the wealth of the lower class, the less opportunity there is for the upper class to deny them their political rights. The wealthier a country, the less important it becomes if some redistribution takes place; losing political office becomes less significant and, therefore, non-democratic means of holding on to power become redundant. Growing national wealth creates countervailing sources of power and opportunities for political participation, communication, and recruitment – all of which are supportive of democracy.

Correlations such as these do not necessarily indicate the direction of causality. Nevertheless, a large number of quantitative studies using multivariate analysis, as well as cross-tabulations, find a positive relationship between stable democracy and various indicators of socio-economic development. Considering the different quantitative methods, time-spans, and indicators used, 'this must rank as one of the most powerful and robust relationships in the study of comparative national development' (Diamond, 1992, p. 108). There are, inevitably, some exceptions to the rule, but extensive reviews of the literature make it safe to theorize that 'the more well-to-do the people of a country, on average, the more likely they will favour, achieve and maintain a democratic system' (Diamond, 1992, pp. 109–10).

Democracy is also stable in more egalitarian societies. Democracies become more unstable as inequality in household incomes increases (Przeworski *et al.*, 2000). Other comparative evidence also confirms the relationship between equality and stable democracy. Less-developed countries with democratic regimes and relatively low income inequality tend to experience regime stability. Continuing high inequality following the inauguration of democracy is likely to lead to a loss of legitimacy and breakdown of the regime. Inequalities in land distribution are also less conducive to democracy than a more egalitarian social structure (Muller, 1988; Diamond and Linz, 1989).

There are some problems with this type of analysis, however. First, there is the role in supporting democracy ascribed to the new class structure of a developed economy. The middle classes might be expected to support democracy, but mainly because it legitimizes private property, and because they can 'manage' the democratic process to protect themselves against radicalism and redistribution through ideological control, state apparatuses, financial power, and the threat of capital 'flight'. The managerial middle class also supports democracy because, through it, it can protect its interests and become 'included' in politics (Moore, 1996).

In developing countries, class analysis can also exaggerate the interest which the lower classes will have in democracy. As well as weakening the power of the landed classes and giving rise to a new middle class, capitalist development also increases the power of the working class by creating the capacity for self-organization through urbanization, factory production, transportation, and new forms of communication (Huber *et al.*, 1993). But for democracy to be compatible with capitalism, it has to be limited and not founded on economic equality, social autonomy, and citizenship. It has to be designed to protect the rights of property-owning classes, not the rights of those with conflicting economic interests. Demands for the economic betterment of the working class are a threat to industrial and finance capital. Procedural democracy is the most that can be expected under a capitalist economic system, not political reforms that would protect the social and economic interests of workers. The consolidation of democracy actually requires low levels of political participation, restricted rights of citizenship, a docile working class, and an absence of many of the rights on which full democracy operates. This is why democracy in the Third World is tainted by clientelism, state repression, and electoral manipulation (Cammack, 1997).

Second, quantitative studies of development and democracy actually tell little about the reasons why democracy breaks down, other than that there is likely to have been a drop in the level of some statistically significant socio-economic indicators. Such a mode of analysis cannot explain why a fall in, say, per capita income is likely to reduce the chances of democratic survival. For this, a more qualitative and historical approach to individual countries needs to be taken (Potter, 1992).

However, case studies, most notably by theorists of Latin American dependency, have often challenged the relationships which quantitative analysis purports to establish. Latin America shows no simple correlation between socio-economic development and democracy, with some relatively rich countries losing democracy (Argentina in 1930) and some relatively poor countries developing democratic institutions (for example, Chile in the first half of the nineteenth century). Often, it has seemed that economic performance (i.e. broadly distributed growth) has been more important for democracy than high levels of socio-economic development (per capita income, or structure of production). Other case studies have, however, confirmed many of the hypotheses generated by quantitative analysis: that education strengthens commitment to democracy, that political violence is greatest in poor countries, and that the growth of a middle class is conducive to democracy (Diamond, 1992).

Asia also reveals that the relationship between development and democracy is by no means straight forward. The post-colonial history of India shows that democracy is not necessarily incompatible with a low level of development. A high level of development might increase the demands and supports for democracy through increases in income, education, participation, the political consciousness of the middle class, pluralism, or foreign contacts. Alternatively, it might be destabilizing by loosening traditional forms of authority, generating political demands from newly created political interests, and deepening ideological cleavages. Such developments can push authoritarian regimes in the direction of democracy, or present democracies with unmanageable problems. The consequences of development for democracy are very ambivalent (Diamond, 1989).

**Political mediation**

Despite the evidence suggesting democracy will only be sustained when the economic conditions and their associated structural changes in society are right, it would be wrong to think that socio-economic structures are all that matter. The 'autonomy of political factors' has to be recognized. How else can India's remarkable democratic history be explained, or authoritarianism in countries such as Argentina and Uruguay in the 1960s despite having the highest levels of GNP per capita and literacy in Latin America (Mainwaring, 1992)? It is thus possible for a state to be poor and free (e.g. Benin and Bolivia) or prosperous and repressive (e.g. Brunei and Libya). Politics are important to consolidation in many ways.

The process of socio-economic development may be supportive of democracy, but dependent on how elites respond to the new political demands generated by increased urbanization, industrialization, education, and communications. After all, the middle class has not always opposed authoritarianism. Whether new groups are included in the political process through institutional developments, especially political parties and organized interests, and given access to economic opportunities and rewards (such as land, jobs, health care and consumer goods) are also relevant mediating factors. So, democracy has fared better in countries such as Venezuela and Costa Rica – where the new social forces unleashed by development are accommodated within the political system, than in Brazil and Peru – where, too often, they have been excluded. The centrality of politics to economic opportunity can be a fundamental cause of democratic breakdown (Diamond and Linz, 1989).

Other intervening political variables include the speed at which democracy has been introduced. Thus, in Latin America the abrupt and violent seizure of independence followed by civil and foreign wars produced political turmoil in the nineteenth century that made progress towards any kind of stable government very difficult to achieve. A long history of elite competition is another political factor, significant in some Latin American countries, and supporting the thesis that democracy is most likely to be successful when political competition becomes institutionalized before the expansion of the suffrage and other forms of political participation (Dahl, 1971). Democracy is likely to be more stable if based on a historical sequence that establishes national identity first, followed by the creation of legitimate state structures, followed by the extension of rights to political participation to all members of society (Diamond and Linz, 1989).

## The political culture

It has also been posited that there is a pattern of political attitudes that supports democracy – a 'civic' or balanced culture 'in which political activity, involvement and rationality exist but are balanced by passivity, traditionality, and commitment to parochial values' (Almond and Verba, 1963, p. 30). Democratic consolidation also requires attitudes which recognize the legitimacy of territorial and constitutional arrangements, and a willingness to accept the outcomes when the rules of political life (especially electoral rules) have been adhered to (Leftwich, 2000).

The values and orientations found to be associated with the stability of democracy are moderation, cooperation, bargaining, and accommodation. 'Moderation' and 'accommodation' imply toleration, pragmatism, willingness to compromise, and civility in political discourse. Time is often seen as a critical variable here, producing (for example) a contrast between the time available for India to acquire democratic values and have them disseminated from elites to the masses, and the limited opportunity to develop democratic values in Africa before independence (Diamond *et al.*, 1990; Diamond, 1993b).

There is much convincing evidence that the level of political culture is crucial to democracy. A lack of commitment to democratic principles, procedures, and beliefs on the part of African political elites, for example, has made it difficult to sustain democracy – even though some traditional values support consensus, moderation, consultation, the rule of law, and controlled political authority. Similarly, in Latin America democratic cultures have helped to maintain democracy, and make it more difficult to consolidate and perpetuate authoritarian government – as in Uruguay in 1980 and Chile in 1988, where 'both the fact of the plebiscites and the ultimate popular rejections of the military at the polls reflected the continuing vitality of democratic culture' (Diamond, 1988, pp. 14–15).

However, there is no simple, deterministic link between political culture and democratic stability because experience of democracy is itself a powerful socializing influence. In Latin America, democratic political cultures have been strengthened by the successful performance of democratic government in accommodating new interests, expanding the economy, developing education, and securing the welfare of the lower classes. The legitimacy created by governmental success helps explain the strong correlation between the economic performance of democratic regimes in Latin America and their stability. Since the start of the global financial crisis in 2008, bad governance (corruption, abuse of power, and violations of the rule of law) has been worse for the survival of democracy than changes in the rate of economic growth (Diamond, 2011).

The values which constitute the 'civic' political culture could thus be a consequence of the experience of democratic government. When attitude surveys are carried out to determine what the predominant political culture is, all that may be revealed are the expectations that people have as the result of their experience of a political system. If there is the possibility that the political culture is not cause but consequence, it ceases to have theoretical significance for understanding change, or the loss of critical levels of support for democracy.

The secret is knowing what creates the critical level of consensus. Democratic values are more likely to be preserved during great social change (such as when democracy is first introduced), if all major social groups are given some access to the political system early on, and the status of major pre-democratic institutions (e.g. monarchy) is not threatened during the transition period. Legitimacy is also preserved by governmental effectiveness: efficient political and administrative decision-making which enable governments to meet the needs of the population. In many African states, the squandering of resources by mismanagement, corruption, waste, and greed has alienated support for democratically constituted regimes. It is no coincidence that Botswana is the most stable African democracy, and moved from being one of the poorest African countries to one of the richest in a decade and a half. A problem for many Third World countries is that they are locked into a vicious circle of low legitimacy and ineffective performance (Diamond *et al.*, 1990).

The economic performance of democratic governments may be less important in deepening democratic values than political performance, or the level and quality of the democracy practised. Feelings about corruption, political freedoms, and the trustworthiness of leaders all have an impact on attitudes about the way democracy works, and the greater the level of satisfaction with this, the stronger the democracy (Diamond, 1998). Public responses to the economic crisis of 1997–98 in Thailand, South Korea, Indonesia, and Malaysia show that people were inclined to blame authoritarian tendencies, rather than democratic politics, for economic mismanagement. While not necessarily *deepening* democratization where it had occurred, the crisis did not undermine it. Although there is a long way to go before democracy is consolidated in these countries, the dominant public response to the crisis was a demand for social welfare policies that required a change of government, rather than a change of regime (Freedman, 2006).

Research has also revealed strong statistical relationships between per capita GNP and personal beliefs and values supportive of democracy, suggesting that the political culture may be an important intervening variable in the relationship between development and democracy. As countries become richer, and improvements in education and communications are felt, people have been observed to become politically more aware, effective, and defensive of their political and civil liberties. Evidence from Taiwan, Thailand, and Brazil has been adduced to support this hypothesis (Diamond, 1993a).

Again, the causal relationship is not necessarily in a single direction. The political culture influences behaviour and the operation of institutions, but is itself influenced by the development of new social forces, modes of socialization, leadership, and international influences. Hence, the political culture can sustain democracy despite relatively low levels of economic development. For example, both India and Costa Rica show 'surprising democratic persistence despite low or moderate economic development' because 'political culture at both the élite and mass levels clearly plays a strong supporting role' (Diamond, 1993a, p. 25).

## Civil society and democratization

While stable and effective democracy is, in part, a function of the institutions negotiated and supported by political elites, it is also dependent on the way civil society is organized to influence policy-makers, mobilize public opinion, hold governments at all levels to account, and make governments responsive to the expression of demands and needs (Diamond, 1996; 1997a). Such responsiveness and accountability require a civil society consisting of organizations that are autonomous, voluntary, and protected by the rule of law. A civic community of neighbourhood associations, political parties, non-governmental organizations, private voluntary bodies, grass-roots support organizations, and social movements complement state and market, and form 'the informal sector of the polity' (Reilly, 1995, p. 7). Such bodies often proliferate in transitions to democracy, having, as in Brazil and the Philippines, originally been formed during the authoritarian regime when more overt forms of political participation were banned.

Civil society promotes the consolidation of democracy by monitoring the exercise of state power, stimulating political participation, educating people in democracy, articulating interests, and providing an alternative to clientelism. It creates cross-cutting allegiances, throws up political leaders, and disseminates political information. Associational autonomy entails a move away from clientelism, allowing people – especially the poor – to articulate their interests and so move from being clients to being citizens (Fox, 1994; Diamond, 1997a).

Parts of civil society are undoubtedly supportive of democracy and of the interests of groups hitherto excluded from political power – such as women, different categories of the urban and rural poor, and ethnic minorities. The development of civil society thus provides opportunities for the poor and disadvantaged to redress injustices, as well as to practice democracy within their own associations (Diamond, 1992). Sustainable democracy requires 'democratic deepening', or the infusion of institutions with democratic practices. This requires the empowerment of associations in civil society to increase popular participation, making it more difficult for elites to manipulate democratic institutions (Luckham and White,

1996). A civil society supportive of democracy has to be embedded in a 'civic community' in which relations between civic associations are founded on trust, cooperation and reciprocity. A civic community increases the effectiveness of democratic government which, in turn, increases support for democracy.

However, some elements of civil society are distinctly uncivil, reactionary, authoritarian, and in other ways uninterested in or opposed to democracy (White, 1996). Civil society may reflect the inequalities of resources, knowledge, and mobilization that typically distinguish class and other interests in capitalist society (Grugel, 2002). The strength of civil society differs greatly between different regions of the Third World. In Africa, for example, civil society is 'male dominated and gerontocratic', and includes ethnic and fundamentalist religious associations unlikely to sponsor democratization (Kasfir, 1998, p. 136). Northern Nigeria is a case in point. In newly democratizing countries, civil society may also include groups that openly and freely cooperated with the previous authoritarian regime, as well as criminal elements, drug mafias, and paramilitary groups. Resistance to democratization may also come from a leadership of a non-governmental organization that has been incorporated into political clientelism. In Latin America, while there has been collective empowerment through credit unions, self-help housing, and other community initiatives, new social movements have sometimes been subject to 'capture' by government and clientelist politics (Little, 1997).

Even when elements in civil society are pro-democratic, it may not be easy for them to move from protest and political confrontation to constructive dialogue with governments (Hernandez and Fox, 1995). A contribution to democracy may be difficult when authoritarianism is deeply rooted, political representation a novel phenomenon, and political organizations traditionally monopolized by parties (Reilly, 1995). For example, in Vietnam new social organizations are emerging but their participation is still limited because 'the constraints of the old centralized planning system still exist; the elements of civil society are still underdeveloped; and ways to attract and operationalize people's participation are as yet unreliable and ineffective' (Luan, 1996, p. 1890).

## The balance of power

Theorizing about the conditions necessary for the survival of democracy includes using the methodology of comparative history to develop a 'balance of power' approach (Rueschmeyer *et al.*, 1992). A balance of power between classes (and coalitions of classes), between the state and civil society, and between international and national pressures, is seen as the crucial determinant of whether democracies survive, even under adverse conditions. The stability of democracy has been found to vary according to different historical contexts, depending on the overall balance of power.

In South and Central America, the relative *power of social classes* was found to be dependent upon the reaction of the new middle class, emerging with the development of capitalist economies, to the rising power of the working class. The working class had supported democracy and the landed upper class had consistently opposed it, especially when controlling a large supply of cheap labour and forming a significant part of the economic elite, as was the case in South and Central America throughout the first half of the twentieth century. The relative weakness of the working class in Latin America has always been a contributory factor in the instability of democracy in the region.

The middle class has supported representative government, but opposed the inclusion of the working class. Middle-class support for democracy was apt to disappear when its interests were threatened by lower-class pressures, the middle class often supporting military intervention which curtailed civil rights and parliamentary government, even though it found its own access to the state restricted. Political parties were found to be crucial in consolidating a balance of power between classes, in mobilizing the working class, and in protecting the interests of economically dominant classes so that they had no need to resort to authoritarianism.

As we have already seen, a balance between *state power* and *civil society* is also necessary for the stability of democracy and the avoidance of authoritarianism. In developing countries, the state's autonomy at the time of the emergence of mass pressure for democratization was greater than in the history of European democracy, tilting the balance in favour of the state. Autonomous social organizations, perhaps supported by religion, act as a counterbalance to the state, but their social composition is important for democratic outcomes, as they have sometimes served as the repositories of authoritarian ideologies.

The importance of a countervailing power to that of the state is confirmed by post-colonial African history. Here, the state has been 'the primary arena of class formation' and the 'primary means for the accumulation of personal wealth', leading to corruption, the concentration of power, the emergence of a parasitic bureaucratic bourgeoisie, and the absence of a middle class to demand 'the expansion of democratic rights and limitation of state power'. With a few exceptions, the state has not been balanced by a plurality of autonomous associations – intellectuals, traditional leaders, professionals, trade unions, business associations, religious groups, students, journalists, and so on – that are necessary for stable, responsive, and accountable government. In Asia, similarly, wherever bureaucratic and military dominance has restricted the autonomy of interest groups, voluntary bodies, and political parties, a foundation of democracy has been removed with authoritarian consequences (Diamond, 1988, pp. 21–7; Diamond *et al.*, 1990).

In the Middle East, where authoritarian states have been sustained by a powerful coercive apparatus funded by rentier income from oil resources, and electoral manipulation (including fraud and gerrymandering), opposition is undermined by weak political parties, sectarian divisions, and an underdeveloped civil society. Low levels of political mobilization assist repression by lowering its political costs (Posusney, 2005, p. 16).

A *balance between international and national power* refers to the varying impact which foreign influences can have on the internal balance of power. For example, foreign-owned mineral extraction for export, and import-substituting industrialization, weaken landowners, and strengthen urban classes, both the working class and the domestic bourgeoisie. When the repressive apparatus of the state is reinforced by foreign powers concerned about their strategic and economic interests, the balance between state and civil society is further altered (Rueschmeyer *et al.*, 1992).

**Institutional development**

Political institutions and leadership also have implications for democratic stability. Institutions are seen as crucial to the key attributes of democracy – the rule of law, freedom, accountability, representation, and administrative capacity. Institutions are also needed that can cope with ethnic demands for special treatment, including consociational democracy. State institutions are required to guarantee the effective exercise of citizenship.

Institutions have taken on renewed significance in comparative politics with theoretical developments known as the 'New Institutionalism'. Institutions are the rules of the game, or humanly devised constraints on social interaction, and should be distinguished from organizations such as political parties. There are, in fact, different varieties of new institutionalism (Peters, 2005). Two have been applied to politics in developing countries: rational choice institutionalism and empirical institutionalism.

According to the rational choice version, the answer to fundamental questions about political and economic development in low-income countries lies in the political institutions which influence decision-making, and the economic institutions (especially property rights and contracts) that are so important in the interaction between government and civil society.

Particular attention is paid to the administrative capacity of governments, especially in shaping the institutional environment of the economy. It applies economic reasoning to the rules of the game, to the decisions of individuals whether to obey existing rules, and to collective action to change the existing set of rules, assuming the individual's incentives depend on the behaviour patterns and cultural norms of the rest of society. Institutions are important for investment and economic innovation because property rights and contract enforcement mechanisms, supported by efficient, honest public administration, and the rule of law, provide incentives by lowering the costs of exchange. The supreme importance of the rule of law is a recurring theme in the New Institutionalism. Institutions are important in the alleviation of poverty and educational provision. They are regarded as a form of social capital.

This type of institutional analysis can be applied to public policy, reform of the legal system, tax administration, and the kind of bureaucracy needed to make it rational for citizens and clients to comply voluntarily with policy rules and participate in the policy-making process, thereby strengthening democracy.

Empirical institutionalism is concerned with the institutional weaknesses that have impeded attempts to sustain democracy in most regions of the Third World. Democracy in Asia has been threatened by the willingness of rulers to abuse their constitutional powers to strengthen their position. Military intervention in the region has often been preceded by the severe erosion of democratic constitutionalism by civil politicians seeking to perpetuate their power. A willingness to accept the consequences of democratic practices has been exceptional among Asian political leaders. In Latin America, democratic instability has followed 'shifts in political leadership strategies and styles from consensus to confrontation, from accommodation to polarization'. In Africa, the values and skills of political leaders have been crucial in undermining or sustaining democracy. Democracy in all regions of the Third World requires commitment to democratic values and an accommodating, compromising, and consensual style on the part of political leaders (Diamond, 1989; Diamond and Linz, 1989; Diamond *et al.*, 1990).

Nevertheless, a growing institutionalizing of politics has been observed in Africa since 1990. There have been some notable exceptions, particularly Zimbabwe, but the general pattern that has emerged is that formal constitutional rules have come to matter more than the raw power of 'Big Men' who could only be removed from office by violence. More intensely contested elections have become more important in determining leadership successions. Political executives increasingly 'work *within*, rather than around, institutionalized channels' (Posner and Young, 2007, p. 134), though this does not necessarily mean that they have less power or that the executive branch is not dominant (Lynch and Crawford, 2011). Kenya's new constitution of 2010, which reduced the power of the president, devolved more authority to county governments, strengthened accountability, and enshrined a range of social rights, is an example of how the institutionalization of political power in Africa is displacing personalistic government (Kramon and Posner, 2011).

Institutional weaknesses have been reflected in political parties that are internally divided, unable to articulate interests clearly, or mobilize a significant mass base (see Chapter 5). In Latin America, stable democracy has been associated with parties that are coherent (in policy), complex (organizationally), autonomous (from the state) and adaptable (to social change). But, in Africa, weak 'input' institutions – and, especially, political parties – have excluded the mass of the population from constitutional politics, encouraging elitism and clientelism, and forcing people into 'non-formal' modes of participation (Diamond, 1988).

There is also evidence that a party system with only a small number of parties is most conducive to democratic stability. One reason why the military and bureaucracy have dominated politics in Thailand is because:

> with 143 parties crossing the Thai political stage between 1946 and 1981, political élites have been unable to build strong bases of popular support, to articulate, aggregate and mobilize political interests, to incorporate emerging interests into the political process, and to cooperate with one another in achieving policy innovations. (Diamond *et al.*, 1990, p. 27)

Other institutional prerequisites of democracy that have been proposed include executive accountability to the legislature, a proportional electoral system, a bicameral legislature, and judicial review. Vigorous legislative and judicial institutions capable of controlling an excessively zealous executive are clearly important: 'the strength and autonomy of the judiciary is roughly proportional to the condition of democracy' (Diamond, 1988, p. 31).

Considerable attention has also been paid to the form of executive – that is, whether democracy is best served by presidential or parliamentary government. A strong case has been made in favour of an executive recruited from among parliamentarians. Presidential executives, especially when combined with the personalistic and autocratic political traditions found in Latin America, allow directly elected presidents to claim mandates from the people entitling them to bypass elected representatives, organized interests, and other mechanisms of accountability. The parliamentary system avoids conflicting executive and legislative mandates, gives greater flexibility of response when the executive loses the confidence of the legislature, and provides a stronger opposition and incentives for dialogue between government and opposition. When the head of state is not fused with the chief executive, it is more difficult for the incumbent to claim to represent the national interest, rather than just a partisan position. It is also more compatible with a multi-party system, compared with the tendency for presidential systems to produce deadlock in executive–legislative relations, ideological polarization, and difficulties in coalition building (Mainwaring, 1993; Linz, 1994; Haufman, 1997). So, a parliamentary system might have helped Brazil and Peru in the late 1980s 'where presidents whose programmes had failed catastrophically and whose political support had evaporated were forced to limp through their remaining terms with virtually no capacity to respond effectively to the deepening economic and political crises' (Diamond *et al.*, 1990, p. 28).

However, comparative evidence is inconclusive. While one study found that 'the expected life of democracy under presidentialism is approximately 21 years, whereas under parliamentarianism it is 73 years' (Przeworski *et al.*, 2000, p. 129), another involving a comparison of 56 transitions to democracy in the Third World between 1930 and 1995 found no evidence that constitutional type 'had any significant bearing on the success of Third World experiments in democracy' (Power and Gasiorowski, 1997, p. 144). Neither did they find that a multi-party system gave presidential executives particular problems. They were forced to conclude that this variable might be less important for democratic consolidation than had been thought.

Institutions can help with the consolidation of democracy by embedding appropriate sets of values that become routines of political life. However, the extent of deviation from democratic behaviour despite the institutions created as part of the process of democratization (such as competitive elections and constitutionally enshrined civil rights) strongly suggests that politics is only partially constrained by institutions. Whether norms of trust, accountability, toleration, and other democratic values become institutionalized depends on the distribution of power within society: 'because institutions and the state are the outcomes of society-rooted politics, institutions can shape social outcomes only secondarily. Society-rooted politics is the primary determinant of outcomes' (Sangmpan, 2007, p. 220).

## Foreign influence

Finally, interventions from abroad are clearly relevant to the consolidation of democracy. Such influence is currently supportive in the main, with regional and global trends towards democracy, and with powerful external actors making the promotion of democracy and human rights explicit foreign policy goals. Since 1980, the quality of governance in recipient countries has been an explicit aid objective. Democracy, human rights, and good government, rather than economic reforms, have taken centre stage as aid conditionalities. This was prompted by a number of political developments. The collapse of the Soviet bloc made it unnecessary for the West to support anti-communist authoritarian regimes, and encouraged the view that political liberalization was necessary for economic progress. Indigenous pro-democracy movements in countries in which democratization was already under way (in Latin America and parts of East and Southeast Asia such as Taiwan, South Korea, and the Philippines) legitimized pro-democracy aid policies. Domestic political pressures in donor countries also demanded that democracy be a condition of development assistance, and bad governance be punished by cuts in overseas aid. The poor quality of governance was also blamed for the failure of structural adjustment and economic liberalization to achieve social and economic progress. Development, it is now believed within the aid community, needs the right political context.

However, foreign powers can also work to undermine democracy (Haynes, 2001). For example, in 2001 US politicians and officials sought to influence the election in Nicaragua with money, propaganda, and food aid, and in 2002 instigated an unsuccessful *coup* in Venezuela. While the foreign policy of the USA is officially in favour of democratization, it has 'correlated poorly' with its other actions in international relations. It has fostered 'low intensity' democracy designed to prevent forces opposed to neo-liberal economic restructuring from acceding to power (Whitehead, 1986; Robinson, 1996). Furthermore, the billions of dollars spent by the USA and other Western countries, and the thousands of lives lost, in attempts to establish viable democracy, notably in Iraq and Afghanistan, 'have been largely unsuccessful' (Somit and Peterson, 2005, p. 2).

The consolidation of democracy has also been impeded by the 'war on terror'. Under pressure from the USA, UN and the Commonwealth, at least 33 countries have enacted anti-terrorism legislation, with adverse consequences for the quality of democracy. However, before this is presented as foreign interference, it should be noted that the 'pressure' has been largely symbolic and rhetorical, as there is no correlation between the adoption of anti-terror measures and the receipt of foreign investment or aid. Furthermore, in a number of countries – including India, Indonesia, and Uganda – governments have been quick to use limits on civil liberties and expanded law enforcement powers to silence dissidents and punish political opponents. Elsewhere – including China, Egypt, Eritrea, Malaysia, and Syria, where democracy is either absent or partial – existing authoritarian powers have also been used against political opposition in the name of national security and the 'war on terror' (Whitaker, 2007).

## The democratic deficit

Despite the global approval bestowed upon the concept of democracy, experience has been very mixed. The majority of 'third wave' countries have not established properly functioning democracy, and suffer from severe democratic deficits. In many cases, democratization has been attempted in states which are weak and where state-building has not been compatible with democratization. The extent to which civil and political rights are protected varies greatly. Voting has rarely deepened participation or strengthened accountability. The rule of law is frequently undermined. The scale of poverty is such that it must be doubted whether large sections of the population in newly democratizing states enjoy full citizenship. In Africa, elections have had little impact on the political order, pro-democracy movements are weak, and economic and political crises block change (see Box 10.1). In Latin America and Africa, participative democracy and political equality have been negated by persistent poverty, marginalization, and exclusion of large sections of society. In Asia, authoritarianism has become 'softened', rather than displaced, by democracy. These defects should not be forced into the 'transition' model by the addition of adjectives like semi, formal, facade, pseudo, weak, partial, illiberal, and virtual, because politics in these countries calls the whole paradigm into question. Defective democracies should not necessarily be thought of as in transition or unconsolidated but, rather, as new types of regime which, though rarely regressing into full authoritarianism, will not inevitably become pure democracies (Anglade, 1994; Carothers, 2002; Grugel, 2002; Bogaards, 2009).

While *electoral* democracy might be widely established (with the possibility of alternating governments based on electoral choices), it has not always been accompanied by *liberal* democracy and the protection of individual and group freedoms, pluralism, civilian control of the military, accountability, the rule of law, and judicial independence. In fact, while the number of electoral democracies has grown, levels of political and civil freedom have declined, leaving democracy that is 'shallow, illiberal and poorly institutionalized' (Diamond, 1997b, p. xv). For example, while Ghana's Fourth Republic has made great progress, especially in the development of a democratic political culture and a vibrant civil society, democratic consolidation remains limited by excessive presidential power, class and gender inequalities, and bureaucratic corruption (Abdulai and Crawford, 2010).

**Box 10.1**   *Democratic consolidation in Nigeria*

Nigeria is currently trying to consolidate democratic government after a post-colonial experience of failed democracy and military intervention. The latest transition to democracy was organized by the military in 1999, following authoritarian breakdown caused by a combination of elite conflict, domestic crisis, and international pressure. However, consolidation has been impeded by severe social and political problems.

The first is escalating sectarian violence. Nigeria's population of 140 million contains over 375 ethnic groups, evenly divided between Muslims and Christians. Democracy has intensified the friction between them and is driven by competition for land, employment, and political influence. Since the transition to democracy, over 3000 lives have been lost from sectarian violence, especially between Moslems and Christians. Islamic law has been enforced in several northern states, displacing thousands of Christians. In the oil-rich parts of south-eastern Nigeria, oil companies have sometimes pitted ethnic factions against one another.

Sectarian violence is driven by poverty and inequality. Although oil generates billions of dollars in revenue annually, the majority of Nigerians subsist on less than US$2 per day. Unemployment stands at 21.1 per cent, rising to almost half of 15–24-year-olds in urban areas. Social conditions are bad. The infant mortality rate is 85.8 per 1000 live births, under-fives mortality is 137.9 per thousand, malnutrition affects 41 per cent of the population, and life expectancy is 48 years. Public services, especially health care and education, are of poor quality. Over 8 million school-age children do not attend school. Wealth is unequally distributed, with the population's poorest quintile taking only 5.1 per cent of national income.

Social polarization is a consequence of a rentier state in which elite conflict is over control of oil revenues, rather than alternative public policies, leading to electoral violence and fraud, most recently in 2007. The power structure is dominated by 'godfatherism' and neo-patrimonialism. Electoral choices are between personalities, ethnic or regional identities, or sources of patronage. The 'winner takes all' nature of politics fuels political violence, electoral fraud, and human rights violations. Corruption, embezzlement, and mismanagement are endemic, undermining basic rights and access to justice for ordinary Nigerians.

The rentier state also impedes institutional development, especially effective political parties. Only 4 or 5 of some 50 parties are viable. Only 6 have representatives in the National Assembly. Party weakness stems from a lack of internal democracy, coherent programmes, distinct ideologies, and internal loyalty which depends mainly on whether the party offers access to state patronage. The 'one party dominant' system, in which the People's Democratic Party has governed since 1999 (fraudulently obtaining over 70 per cent of the vote in 2007) lacks legitimacy. Politicians have limited political skills, and the National Assembly is a weak counterbalance to the executive branch (Omotola, 2009; Salawu, 2010).

## Conclusion

With the dominant ideology in the world prescribing a free-market economy, there are very powerful pressures being applied to Third World countries to liberalize their economies and transform their polities in the direction of pluralism. Hence the current interest in what is needed to restore democracy, as well as how to make it function effectively so that its legitimacy becomes firmly established. The significance of economic development to democracy shows how important it is to recognize that political reform cannot sensibly be pursued in isolation from measures designed to strengthen the performance of Third World economies. It is right to assert the importance of political prerequisites of democracy and the status of economic factors as necessary, but not sufficient conditions for consolidation. But it is important that political preconditions should not be part of one's definition of democracy, lest theorizing becomes merely tautological.

It is also important to remember that democracy is a contested concept. The choice of a particular definition – electoral competition, decision-making procedures, civil and political rights, or the distribution of power within society – reflects an ideological or normative position on the part of the user that should be acknowledged. So should the fact that large-$n$ statistical analyses of 'third wave' democratization often include countries outside the Third World, making the application of empirical results to developing countries problematic.

# 11
# Conclusion: Democracy and Development

## States and development

The apparent globalization of political values and institutions represented by the dissolution of the communist regimes in the Second World has lent credence to the view that there is an inevitable trend towards a universal form of government on which all societies will eventually converge. Such interpretations of world history since 1990 gain encouragement from the extent to which pluralist democracy has replaced military regimes or single-party states in Latin America and Africa. History appears to end with political pluralism and free market economies. The ideas about 'good governance' which increasingly inform Western aid policy prescribe the separation of powers, the accountability and efficiency of public bureaucracy, the development of civil society as a counterbalance to the power of the state, and the rule of law. They revive the significance attached by modernization theory to 'organic solidarities', structural differentiation, and specialized political structures which strengthen the extractive, regulative, distributive, symbolic and responsive capabilities of governments. In addition, they preserve the independence of different parts of the state, thus inhibiting the concentration of power in a small and personalized executive élite which is so often the hallmark of Third World politics.

However, economic and social development has often been associated with authoritarianism in post-colonial societies, raising the question of whether the benefits of democracy might be outweighed by the capability of authoritarian regimes to promote development.

In this chapter, the concept of a 'developmental' state is considered in order to understand what qualities appear to be needed if any kind of state is to preside over economic growth and human development. The relationship between type of regime and development will be explored to see whether authoritarianism's developmental record is better than democracy's. The features of the developmental state are identified before asking whether democracies can be developmental, and so provide both political and economic benefits. Is democracy compatible with the type of state that socio-economic development appears to need, or does political underdevelopment mean that the benefits of political pluralism can only be enjoyed at the expense of social and economic progress?

## Regimes and development

There have been different perspectives on whether democracy or authoritarianism is required to lift a poor country out of economic and social underdevelopment. The *conflict* perspective argues that economic development needs an authoritarian regime to push through policies to facilitate rapid growth in the face of resistance. Democracy is regarded as inherently unstable, and permits the expression of powerful pressures to redistribute and consume resources, rather than accumulate and invest them. Both tendencies hamper development. The *compatibility* argument claims democracies are as capable as authoritarian regimes of combining growth with redistribution, leading to expanded markets and economic growth. Democracy is also a precondition for a functioning market economy which promotes growth, human development, and social equality. The *sceptical* view doubts whether there is any systematic relationship between democracy and development (Rock, 2009).

Different perspectives such as these can be attributed to the different time periods, countries, and political and economic indicators used by the researchers. Other methodological problems encountered when relating development to different types of regime include separating out the political from the multitude of factors affecting an economy, the absence of a single definition of democracy, and the fact that development has social, as well as economic, dimensions (Helliwell, 1994; Ersson and Lane, 1996; Blank, 2005).

Since most developmental states have been authoritarian rather than democratic during the decades of rapid economic growth and social development, it has sometimes been assumed that authoritarianism is a necessary condition of development. For example, in Taiwan the Kuomintang monopolized political power from 1949 to 1986 – when the first free, multi-party elections were held – ruling by martial law. In Singapore, the ruling People's Action Party has controlled all parts of the political process, including the media, and much of the economy. Human rights and political opposition have been restricted, as have other parts of civil society (see Box 11.1). In the developmental state, labour markets have been distinctly un-free when capitalist development has needed the repression of trade unions, or state intervention in setting wage levels. The state's relations with civil society have been free from the pressures of

---

**Box 11.1**    *Authoritarianism in Singapore*

Singapore's economic success is usually seen as the result of 'soft authoritarianism'. Between independence in 1965 and 2000, the economy recorded the world's highest rate of growth in national income, and, after slow growth in 2008 and 2009, bounced back with 14.5 per cent growth in 2010, when per capita GDP reached US$33,101. The country has benefited from low levels of inflation, unemployment, and poverty, and high levels of savings, investment, literacy, and life expectancy.

The political system which has overseen these economic and social achievements is *de facto* a single-party state in which the People's Action Party (PAP) has held nearly every parliamentary seat since independence. The candidates and supporters of other parties, and other critics of the government, face punitive deterrents in the form of imprisonment, bankruptingly expensive law suits, gerrymandering, the starving of opposition constituencies of state funding, and media controls.

The other key features of Singapore's developmental state are:

- priority given by the political leadership to economic development;
- an efficient, technocratic, accountable, and honest bureaucracy, closely integrated with the government through the civil service backgrounds of key PAP leaders;
- the introduction of new public management ideas and autonomous agencies since 1990;
- the rigorous enforcement of anti-corruption measures;
- developmental organizations such as the Economic Development Board to assist foreign firms to locate and invest;
- commercially run state enterprises within a system of state capitalism, many of which have been privatized since 1987;
- obligatory savings in the Central Provident Fund, which provides public housing and health care;
- the incorporation of all trade unions into the state-controlled National Trade Union Congress from which hostile unions are excluded, rendering members ineligible to work in Singapore.

Economic and social problems – extreme inequality, low levels of private consumption, over-dependence on MNCs, a lack of domestic entrepreneurship, and even a brain drain – might have been averted, if greater political freedom had allowed appropriate policies on the political agenda (Yeung, 2005; Verweij and Pelizzo, 2009).

---

organized labour and the peasantry, and supportive of emerging domestic capital. Developmental states have not necessarily lacked legitimacy, mainly because the benefits of economic growth have been spread by investment in education, health care, housing, and other social benefits. Some even performed better than average in respect for human rights. Political opposition was often tolerated (White, 1984; Pempel, 1999; Leftwich, 2000).

In the Newly Industrializing Countries (NICs), political authoritarianism achieved remarkable economic results. These countries were transformed into industrial manufacturers and exporters with high growth rates. During the 1960s and 1970s, real GDP in Taiwan grew about 10 per cent (7 per cent per capita) each year. Singapore's average annual growth rate in GNP per capita throughout the 1970s was 7.4 per cent, higher than many southern European countries, such as Greece and Yugoslavia, and with a higher GNP per capita in 1980 than either of them. South Korea similarly had a growth rate in GNP per capita of 6.9 per cent on average throughout the 1970s and 1980s. By the end of the 1980s, the 'Asian Tigers' exported a greater value of manufactured goods than the rest of the Third World together, including other NICs in Asia and Latin America. Whereas between 1965 and 1989 most of the Third World experienced declining terms of trade as prices of primary commodities fell, the four East Asian NICs increased their share of total world trade and manufactured exports by over eight times (World Bank, 1991, pp. 105–6).

However, authoritarianism in the Third World generally has not produced development and has been distinguished more by corruption, rent-seeking, the over-concentration of economic and social power, the impoverishment of the masses, and economic insecurity. In sub-Saharan Africa particularly, authoritarianism, whether civil or military, left a legacy of poverty, illiteracy, debt, displaced populations, corruption, political instability, human rights violations, and the private accumulation of wealth (Agbese and Kieh, 2007). If confirmation were required that authoritarianism is no guarantee of development, one need look no further than Zimbabwe and North Korea.

Such failures were initially attributed to state-led development generally. This had enabled the state to be captured by groups more interested in extracting rents from natural resources, aid, corruption, and inefficient state-owned enterprises than in securing economic growth and human development. Because markets were often controlled to secure political support, through subsidies both to producers and to consumers, the assumption that development could be promoted by the state was abandoned in the 1980s and replaced by neo-liberal approaches to the state and economy which were designed, largely through aid conditionalities, to limit the role of the state and leave economic resources to be allocated by free market mechanisms. The *laissez-faire* state's role was limited to supporting free enterprise by eliminating barriers to competition, and investing in education and the physical infrastructure. Even the exceptional economic achievements of some East Asian countries initially prompted the claim that success had been due to restrictions on state interventions, leaving as much economic activity as possible to be determined by market forces.

Unsurprisingly, these strategies led to the creation of private monopolies and reduced social support for those in need, with harmful consequences for the welfare of the poor in particular. Theorizing about development strategies changed again, partly as a result of an improved understanding of state-led development by the 'Asian Tigers'. The state was rediscovered, not just as an economic agent, but also as essential to meeting basic needs; delivering social services such as public health, education, and basic health care; and reducing poverty (Fritz and Menocal, 2006).

## The developmental state

The remarkable economic – and, to a lesser extent, social – achievements of 'developmental states' make it important to identify their key features. If, rather than economic and political *laissez-faire*, development requires a particular type of interventionist state, what institutions, political forces, and socio-economic structures are required?

The first requirement is a form of state autonomy. The economic success of East Asian countries such as South Korea, Taiwan, Singapore, and Malaysia is due to the state having sufficient autonomy to guide private investment and intervene strongly in other areas of economic management. The approaches to public policy of these developmental states demanded independence from social forces such as landowners, private capital, and labour. Relations between the developmental state and society have entailed an 'embedded autonomy' in which states and entrepreneurial interests have 'shared projects', with the state providing incentives such as protection and subsidies, and firms responding according to prescribed standards of production and investment. Embedded autonomy requires cooperation with the state on the part of those sections of civil society with an interest in industrialization, especially the business community. It refers to a state that is not self-serving and insulated from society but, rather, organized so that negotiations with affected groups over public policy are institutionalized (Evans, 1995).

The developmental state also subordinates powerful pre-industrial groups and classes such as rural elites, and then 'coaxes' into existence economic groups such as industrialists and commercial farmers who share the state's objectives, whether they be industrial transformation, land reform, export-oriented manufacturing, or absorption of foreign investment. Incentives and compulsion enable the state to engineer public–private cooperation, not only to secure economic objectives, but also to curtail the power of organized labour.

Such relationships between state and key economic interests could lead to a form of authoritarian corporatism, as in South Korea and Taiwan, providing restricted access to the state for selected economic interests, and the repression of others. The state has consciously promoted the development of a capitalist class by providing the infrastructure needed by private enterprise, constraining working-class power, mediating between different capitalist interests (industrial, financial, and ethnic), and legislating in support of capital accumulation (Evans, 1995).

Embedded state autonomy leads to a 'governed interdependence' between state and economy, though the state has had the power to choose with which socio-economic interests to cooperate. Linkages and collaboration between state agencies and leading private manufacturing firms, conglomerates, banks, and trading companies are established, and members of the political elite 'circulate' between the bureaucracy, political executive, and business. The integration of state and private sector (including foreign investors and multinational corporations (MNCs)) is facilitated by joint ventures, state-owned enterprises, and networks of government personnel and business interests, sometimes bound by a common ethnicity, as in Malaysia. 'Governed interdependence' and partnership with private industry, rather than its domination, appear essential for effective state intervention. Policy formulation is, thus, not monopolized by the state. Routine negotiations with organized interests to mobilize resources are more important than economic controls and political repression (Hawes and Liu, 1993; Weiss and Hobson, 1995; Polidano, 2001).

So the developmental state is highly interventionist, controlling markets in favour of internationally competitive sectors selected by state technocrats. The state determines the scale and direction of economic growth to a greater extent than free markets, engaging in rational planning through incentives (e.g. credit and price controls), legislation (e.g. on investment, imports, and taxation), and expenditure (e.g. on research and development) to ensure the development of manufacturing, high-technology production, and selected industrial sectors. The policies of the developmental state mix free markets and state planning. Development requires not less, but better, state intervention and structures (Henderson and Appelbaum, 1992; Leftwich, 2000).

Arguably, the most important structure is a unified and competent bureaucracy, recruited on merit, and offering stable and rewarding careers relatively free from political interference by sectional interests, such as traditional agrarian oligarchies, that might compromise the pursuit of economic growth. In developmental states, bureaucratic cultures are oriented towards development, rather than embourgeoisement from corruption, fraud, and nepotism, as in so many Third World states. However, an efficient, well-trained, and technocratic administration can coexist with corruption, as the case of South Korea shows. Meritocratic recruitment provides the state with professional, technical, and managerial talent, enabling economic planning to be placed in the hands of capable personnel with a sense of common purpose oriented towards national policy objectives and attracting the cooperation of business elites. Relatively small-scale bureaucracies have allowed control and accountability, and restricted their interventions to strategic sectors of the economy (Onis, 1991; Evans, 1995; Weiss and Hobson, 1995; Leftwich, 2000).

The developmental state is not a single monolithic entity, but internally divided as different state agencies respond to an increasingly diversified economy. The power relationships between government agencies is another dimension of bureaucracy relevant to the developmental state. A comparison of industrialization policy in South Korea and India between 1950 and 1980 revealed that the greater level of success in South Korea was attributed, in part, to inter-agency coordination and its absence in India. Internal cohesion within the state bureaucracy is secured not only by ensuring that bureaucrats pursue the public interest, rather than their own, but also by the creation of a coordinating agency with powers to ensure compliance with government policy. In India, the Planning Commission had only advisory powers, whereas the Korean Economic Planning Board was empowered to compel ministries to implement government policy, making Korean planning 'one of the most successful endeavours of its kind in the annals of development policy' (Chibber, 2002, p. 983).

Developmental states are also characterized by a 'determined' set of nationalistic political and bureaucratic elites, relating to each other in shifting coalitions but all committed to developmental objectives. They have been motivated by a range of factors varying from country to country and including external threats to national security (e.g. Taiwan), shortages of raw materials (e.g. Singapore), relative material equality in the post-1945 period (resulting from land reforms), and financial and technical assistance from the USA (e.g. Taiwan and South Korea). State elites impose nationalistic aims on civil society, partly through repression, but also by improving living standards, reducing inequality, and raising levels of educational achievement and health. Political elites enjoy credibility in their commitments to development, convincing the private sector, foreign and domestic, that it could risk investment. For example, South Korea's successful shift in policy in the 1960s towards exports demonstrated its credibility in world markets. In Singapore, MNCs knew they could trust the government to live up to commitments because of its proven capacity to produce and implement sound economic policies (Onis, 1991; Castells, 1992; Huff *et al.*, 2001).

## Democratic developmental states

The features of developmental states have been identified through observations of their authoritarian versions. A *democratic* developmental state requires political conditions that are scarce in the Third World and not always compatible with capitalist development.

First, if the form of democracy is to be 'pervasive' and participatory, rather than purely procedural, all interests – particularly disadvantaged groups – will have to be able effectively to voice demands for social welfare, poverty reduction, greater equality, and an end to discrimination. Development would have to be redistributive, 'inclusive', and not just about economic growth. It would also have to include political development, with strong institutions of representation and accountability, as well as empowering, through different forms of participation, a wide range of social groups. State autonomy would have to be based on consensus and inclusion, and 'embeddedness' would have to be in society in its broadest sense, and not just economic elites (White, 1998).

Such a democratic developmental state would require a number of contradictions to be resolved: between autonomous and accountable political leadership; between growth and redistribution; between political consensus and social inclusion; and between the concentration of power in state and business elites, and public participation. These are 'fundamental contradictions which are difficult to resolve in the real world of politics' (White, 1998, p. 44). The institutional context would also have to be receptive – accountable bureaucracy, legal stability, a strong knowledge base, and public–private cooperation – most of which are long-term projects and underline the importance of institution-building and the development of administrative capacity (Onis, 1991).

A developmental democracy also needs institutions to enforce property rights and contracts, providing incentives for investment in machinery, equipment, education, and the financial sector ('keys to development'). Such enforcement requires effective judicial and administrative institutions, which are generally in short supply in the Third World.

Despite such challenges, and the fact that developmental states have tended towards authoritarianism, it has been shown that development can be achieved under a democratic regime, with the added bonus of political freedoms and civil liberties. Comparative analysis of data for 125 countries between 1976 and 1985 found no significant causal influence of variable levels of democracy on economic growth, though there was evidence that democracy stimulates education and investment – both needed for economic development (Helliwell, 1994). Ersson and Lane (1996) similarly found that investment in physical capital and the availability of human capital had more impact on growth than level of democracy, but that democracy is positively correlated with human development generally. It should also be noted that the conditions that were crucial to economic success among the Asian Tigers – including a high rate of domestic savings, and a large number of small and medium-sized enterprises – do not appear to be dependent on an authoritarian political regime (Sandschneider, 1991).

Democratic regimes also preside over economies generally paying higher wages, using labour more effectively, and benefiting more from technological progress than autocracies. Per capita incomes also grow faster in democracies. While some authoritarian regimes, notably the Asian Tigers, produced remarkable economic achievements, many others have not – notably in Africa. A comparison of 135 countries over a 40-year period showed that spectacular development is as likely under democracy as dictatorship, and produced not 'a shred of evidence that democracy need be sacrificed on the altar of development' (Przewroski *et al.*, 2000, p. 271).

Democracy also contributes to development by providing a context for effective policy reforms. For example, political participation was necessary for educational reform in Burkina Faso. The rule of law enabled community-based resource management to go ahead in Tanzania. In Africa, the quality of economic policy-making is central to an economy's overall performance, and democracies have developed better policy-making processes. While both authoritarian and democratic regimes have been capable of protecting property rights, there has been a 'substantial connection' between the institutions of representative government, and individual rights of property and contract (Clague *et al.*, 1997, p. 97). Long-lasting democracies provide better property rights than autocracies. Democratic governance gives 'stakeholders' incentives and opportunities to improve public services. Democracy strengthens political accountability (through elections, legislative scrutiny and audit of the executive, and judicial review), making it difficult for political elites to engage in rent-seeking and other forms of predatory policy-making. There is a reciprocal relationship here – sectoral reforms support democracy when they provide opportunities for participation, accountability, and transparency, so generating social capital, and providing experience of government mechanisms and processes.

South Asia's variable experience of democracy also suggests that context is important. In this region, democracy provides a foundation of popular support for government that is necessary for economic, and especially social, development to occur (Brinkerhoff, 2000; Blank, 2005; Lewis, 2010; Savoia *et al.*, 2010). It is significant that India, the region's (and possibly the whole of the Third World's) most stable democracy recorded an average economic growth rate of more than 7 per cent in the decade between 1997 and 2007. In the mid-2000s, India became one of the fastest-growing economies in the world. The country's GDP is predicted to overtake France and Italy by 2020; Germany, the UK, and Russia by 2025; and Japan by 2035, making it the world's third largest economy after the USA and China. Economic growth has been accompanied by reductions in poverty, and improvements in life expectancy, literacy rates, and food security.

Though the experience of some East Asian developmental states suggests that authoritarian regimes are capable of protecting the interests of the poor, there is also evidence that democracy has a positive effect on a range of social indicators, including public health, infant mortality, and education. African democracies have been shown to produce greater improvements in human development than autocracies, though still leaving much to be done in terms of popular welfare. Significantly, what constrains governmental performance are the residues of authoritarianism: neo-patrimonialism, clientelism, patronage, an under-developed civil society, and governmental incapacity (Carbone, 2009; Lewis, 2010).

Democracy also provides more stable growth. A statistical comparison of 149 states between 1961 and 1998 showed that democracy leads to stable and consistent economic growth, compared with the volatility and crises associated with autocracies. This is because the accountability provided by extensive participation in electoral competition produces policies derived from compromise and response to voters, who have the most to lose from economic volatility. Consequently, 'democratic countries have fewer and/or shorter crises than do autocracies' (Armijo and Gervasoni, 2010, p. 165).

Democracies even compare well with developmental autocracies. Comparisons of Asian economies show that Asian democracies do no worse than the region's authoritarian developmental states; and that, while democracies need good bureaucracies and the rule of law to achieve economic growth, so do autocracies. Thus, democracy offers political as well as economic benefits, while developmental autocracies offer only economic ones, and predatory autocracies offer neither (Rock, 2009).

**Conclusion: fragile democracy**

As was shown in earlier chapters, democracy inhabits a hostile environment in the Third World. It is encouraging that political legitimacy is increasingly seen to reside with democratic forms of government as pro-democracy movements gather momentum in all regions of the Third World. Yet the most pronounced feature of democratic regimes is their fragility.

The concentration of political power in the executive (as in Ecuador and Malawi) remains a threat to the accountability of the executive to the legislature, an indispensable part of democratic government. It makes it easier for political elites to misappropriate state resources for their own benefit, to finance patronage, and to buy political support. The right to vote is too often negated by electoral fraud, and the suppression of opposition, media, and civil society during election campaigns (as in the Gambia). Democratic consolidation is also vulnerable to incumbent elites refusing to accept electoral defeat (as in Côte d'Ivoire). Freedom of speech is vulnerable when governments impose limitations in the interest of national defence, public safety, public order, and public morals (as in Zambia). Freedom of association can be compromised by regulations governing the registration and funding of civil society organizations (as in Bangladesh).

Political equality remains undermined by multiple forms of discrimination. Even when women are not excluded from political life by law, their political participation is constrained by discrimination in the workplace, gender-based violence, patriarchal traditions, unawareness of rights, and inadequate access to judicial remedies (throughout the Third World). Ethnic and sectarian conflict threatens democratic stability in areas prone to competition for scarce land and other resources (as in Nigeria).

Poverty and material inequality constrain effective political mobilization and political equality in all parts of the Third World. Even if poverty does not threaten political stability, the poor suffer disproportionately from a lack of effective leadership and organization, barriers to freedom of association, low levels of education on human rights, and illegalities encountered when attempts are made to exert political influence or enforce rights: arbitrary arrest, police harassment, violence from thugs hired by economic elites, and bureaucratic discrimination. Their rights as citizens are thereby fatally diminished. Economic equality further undermines democracy by encouraging populism, personalism, authoritarianism, extremism, and the erosion of human rights and the rule of law (Bermeo, 2009).

The development of programmatic political parties, needed if civil society is to act as an effective counterbalance to the power of the state, is often blocked by the prevalence of patronage, clientelism, and traditional affiliations. The political culture in a new democracy may include anti-democratic values which endorse authoritarian modes of government, especially among classes that believe their privileges to be threatened by the wider distribution of political power which democracy entails. The military is a ubiquitous political force and should never be underestimated politically, especially in Guatemala, Egypt, Thailand, and most West African states.

Political interference and corruption undermine the rule of law – for example, in the Philippines, and negate two fundamental democratic principles: that all are equal before the law; and all are subject to the law, including the law-makers and their officials.

Democracy can also be threatened by economic change, though this is often the result of government policies, leading to a 'revolution' of rising expectations as the withdrawal of subsidies and other neo-liberal economic 'reforms' cause reversals in the welfare of groups experiencing growing prosperity (as in Malawi in 2012). Dependency constitutes another threat to democracy when foreign investment renders a Third World economy vulnerable to the extraction of valuable surplus, growing disparities of income between the new industrial and business classes and the rural poor, and increasing debt. The political liberalization which is supposed to accompany the economic liberalization required by global capitalism has often been of much less concern to private foreign investors. Aid dependency has adverse consequences for democracy when it creates incentives for governments to be accountable to donors rather than to their own voters, introduces disincentives to raise revenues domestically and so create strong demand for accountability, and generally marginalizes parliamentary audit and scrutiny by civil society.

The trend away from the observation of democratic rules since 2005 is thus perhaps not surprising, and should warn against assuming that democracy will be the inevitable outcome of the latest agitation against authoritarianism in the Arab world. However, much of the backsliding is accounted for by the post-communist states of Eastern Europe and central Asia, and by reversals in countries still under authoritarianism. The long-term trend in the Third World is encouraging. Since democracy seems capable of not only providing freedom, but also economic progress, the reversals which occur in countries in which a transition from authoritarianism has taken place, but in which democracy needs to be consolidated, are particularly frustrating, threatening as they do to delay the economic and social progress so eagerly awaited by millions of Third World citizens.

# Bibliography

Abdulai, A.-G. and G. Crawford (2010) 'Consolidating democracy in Ghana: progress and prospects', *Democratization*, vol. 17, no. 1.

Abrahamson, M. (1978) *Functionalism*. Englewood Cliffs, NJ: Prentice-Hall.

Adam, H. M. (1994) 'Formation and recognition of new states: Somaliland in contrast to Eritrea', *Review of African Political Economy*, no. 59.

Adam, H. M. (1995) 'Somalia: a terrible beauty being born?', in I. W. Zartman (ed.), *Collapsed States. The Disintegration of Legitimate Authority*. London: Lynne Rienner Publishers.

Adamolekun, L. (2002) 'Africa's evolving career civil service systems: three challenges – state continuity, efficient service delivery and accountability', *International Review of Administrative Sciences*, vol. 68, no. 3.

Agbese, P. O. and G. K. Kieh (eds) (2007, *Reconstituting the State in Africa*, Basingstoke: Palgrave Macmillan.

Ahrari, E. M. (2010) 'Ethnic separatism in geopolitical perspective', in R. G. Wirsing and E. Ahrari (eds), *Fixing Fractured Nations. The Challenge of Ethnic Separatism in the Asia-Pacific*. Basingstoke: Palgrave Macmillan.

Ake, C. (1974) 'Modernisation and political instability: a theoretical explanation', *World Politics*, vol. 26, no. 4.

Ake, C. (1975) 'A definition of political stability', *Comparative Politics*, vol. 7, no. 2.

Akhtar, S. (2010) 'Managing ethnic conflict in Sri Lanka: going beyond the LTTE', in R. G. Wirsing and E. Ahrari (eds), *Fixing Fractured Nations. The Challenge of Ethnic Separatism in the Asia-Pacific*, Basingstoke: Palgrave Macmillan.

Alavi, H. (1972) 'The state in post-colonial societies: Pakistan and Bangladesh', *New Left Review*, no. 74.

Alavi, H. (1990) 'Authoritarianism and legitimation of state power in Pakistan', in S. K. Mitra (ed.), *The Post-Colonial State in Asia: Dialectics of Politics and Culture*. London: Harvester Wheatsheaf.

Almond, G. A. (1960) 'Introduction', in G. A. Almond and J. Coleman (eds), *The Politics of the Developing Areas*. Princeton, NJ: Princeton University Press.

Almond, G. A. (1965) 'A developmental approach to political systems', *World Politics,* vol. 17, no. 1.

Almond, G. A. (1987) 'The development of political development', in M. Weiner and S. P. Huntington (eds), *Understanding Political Development*. Boston: Little, Brown.

Almond, G. A. and J. Coleman (eds) (1960) *The Politics of the Developing Areas*. Princeton, NJ: Princeton University Press.

Almond, G. A. and S. Verba (1963) *The Civic Culture: Political Attitudes and Democracy in Five Nations*. Princeton, NJ: Princeton University Press.

Amin, S. (1982) 'The disarticulation of economy within "developing societies"', in H. Alavi and T. Shanin (eds), *Introduction to the Sociology of 'Developing Societies'*. London: Macmillan.

Ampuero, I. and J. J. Brittain (2005) 'The agrarian question and armed struggle in Colombia', in S. Moyo and P. Yeros (eds), *Reclaiming the Land. The Resurgence of Rural Movements in Africa, Asia and Latin America*. London: Zed Books.

Anderson, C. W., F. R. von der Mehden and C. Young (1974) *Issues of Political Development*, 2nd edn. Englewood Cliffs, NJ: Prentice-Hall.

Anglade, C. (1994) 'Democracy and the rule of law in Latin America', in I. Budge and D. McKay (eds), *Developing Democracy*. London: Sage.

Antunes, R. (2003) 'Trade unions and struggles', in R. H. Chilcote (ed.), *Development in Theory and Practice: Latin American Perspectives*. Lanham, MD: Rowan & Littlefield.

Apter, D. and C. G. Rosberg (1994) 'Changing African perspectives', in D. Apter and C. G. Rosberg (eds), *Political Development and the New Realism in Sub-Saharan Africa*. Charlottesville, VA: University Press of Virginia.

Arce, M. (2010) 'Parties and social protest in Latin America's neoliberal era', *Party Politics*, vol. 16, no. 5.

Argyriades, D. (2007) '"Resisting change": some critical remarks on contemporary narratives about reform', in D. Argyriades, O. P. Dwivedi and J. G. Jabbra (eds), *Public Administration in Transition. A Fifty-Year Trajectory Worldwide*. London: Vallentine Mitchell.

Armijo, L. E. and C. Gervasoni (2010) 'Two dimensions of democracy and the economy', *Democratization*, vol. 17, no. 1.

Aspinall, A. (2010) 'The irony of success', *Journal of Democracy*, vol. 21, no. 2.

Ayoob, M. (1996) 'State-making, state breaking and state failure: explaining the roots of "Third World" insecurity', in L. van de Goor, K. Rupesinghe and P. Sciarone (eds), *Between Development and Destruction: An Enquiry into the Causes of Conflict in Post-Colonial States*. London: Macmillan.

Baburkin, S., A. C. Danopoulos, R. Giacalone and E. Moreno (1999) 'The 1992 coups attempts in Venezuela: causes and failure', *Journal of Political and Military Sociology*, vol. 27, no. 1.

Balogun, M. J. (2002) 'The democratization and development agenda and the African civil service: issues resolved or matters arising?', *International Review of Administrative Sciences*, vol. 68, no. 4.

Banuazizi, A. (1987) 'Socio-psychological approach to political development', in M. Weiner and S. Huntington (eds), *Understanding Political Development*. Boston: Little, Brown.

Baran, P. A. (1957) *The Political Economy of Growth*. New York: Monthly Review Press.

Barratt Brown, M. (1963) *After Imperialism*. London: Heinemann.

Batley, R. (2002) 'The changing role of the state in development', in V. Desai and R. B. Potter (eds), *The Companion to Development Studies*. London: Arnold.

Bauer, P. (1971) *Dissent on Development*. London: Weidenfeld & Nicolson.

Bauer, P. (1981) *Equality: The Third World and Economic Delusion*. London: Weidenfeld & Nicolson.

Becker, D. G. and R. L. Sklar (1987) 'Why post-imperialism?', in D. G. Becker, J. Frieden, S. P. Schatz and R. L. Sklar (eds), *Post-Imperialism. International Capitalism and Development in the Late Twentieth Century*. London: Lynne Rienner Publishers.

Berger, M. (1994) 'The end of the "Third World"?', *Third World Quarterly,* vol. 15, no. 2.

Berger, M. (2004) 'After the Third World? History, destiny and the fate of Third Worldism', *Third World Quarterly*, vol. 25, no. 1: 9–39.

Berger, M. and H. Weber (2009) 'War, peace and progress: conflict, development, (in)security and violence in the 21st century', *Third World Quarterly*, vol. 30, no. 1: 1–16.

Berman, B. (1974) 'Clientelism and neocolonialism: centre–periphery relations and political development in African states', *Studies in Comparative International Development,* vol. 9, no. 1.

Berman, B. (1984) 'Structure and process in the bureaucratic states of colonial Africa', *Development and Change,* vol. 15, no. 2.

Bermeo, N. (2009) 'Does electoral democracy boost economic equality?', *Journal of Democracy*, vol. 20, no. 4.

Bernstein, H. (1979) 'Sociology of underdevelopment vs. sociology of development', in D. Lehmann (ed.), *Development Theory: Four Critical Studies*. London: Frank Cass.

Bhatt, C. (2004) 'Democracy and Hindu nationalism', *Democratization*, vol. 11, no. 4: 133–54.

Birch, A. H. (1978) 'Minority nationalist movements and theories of political integration', *World Politics,* vol. 30, no. 2.

Bisley, N. (2007) *Rethinking Globalization*. Basingstoke: Palgrave Macmillan.

Bjorkman, J. W. and K. Mathur (1996) 'India', in J. Blondel and M. Cotta (eds), *Party and Government: An Inquiry into the Relationship between Governments and Supporting Parties in Liberal Democracies*. London: Macmillan.

Blanco, L. and R. Grier (2007) 'Long live democracy: the determinants of political instability in Latin America', Department of Economics Working Paper, University of Oklahoma.

Bland, D. L. (1999) 'A unified theory of civil–military relations', *Armed Forces and Society,* vol. 26, no. 1.

Blank, J. (2005) 'Democratization and development', in D. T. Hagerty (ed.), *South Asia in World Politics*. Lanham, MD: Rowan & Littlefield.

Bodenheimer, S. (1971) 'Dependency and imperialism: the roots of Latin American underdevelopment', in K. Fann and D. Hodges (eds), *Readings in United States Imperialism*. Boston: Porter Sargent.

Bogaards, M. (2009) 'How to classify hybrid regimes? Defective democracy and electoral authoritariansim', *Democratization*, vol. 16, no. 2.

Bogaards, M., M. Basedau and C. Hartmann (2010) 'Ethnic party bans in Africa: an introduction', *Democratization*, vol. 17, no. 4.

Booth, J. A. (1991) 'Inequality and rebellion in Central America', *Latin American Research Review*, vol. 26, no. 1.

Bowornwathana, B. (2000) 'Governance reform in Thailand: questionable assumptions, uncertain outcomes', *Governance: An International Journal of Policy and Administration*, vol. 13, no. 3.

Brass, P. R. (1991) *Ethnicity and Nationalism: Theory and Comparison*. London: Sage Publications.

Brecher, M. (1963) 'Political instability in the new states of Asia', in H. Eckstein and D. E. Apter (eds), *Comparative Politics: A Reader*. New York: Free Press.

Brett, E. A. (2009) *Reconstructing Development Theory*. Basingstoke: Palgrave Macmillan.

Bretton, H. L. (1973) *Power and Politics in Africa*. London: Longman.

Brewer, A. (1980) *Marxist Theories of Imperialism: A Critical Survey*. London: Routledge & Kegan Paul.

Brinkerhoff, D. W. (2000) 'Democratic governance and sectoral policy reform: tracing linkages and exploring synergies', *World Development*, vol. 28, no. 4.

Brinkerhoff, D. W. and A. A. Goldsmith (2002) *Clientelism, Patrimonialism and Democratic Governance*. Cambridge, MA: Abt Associates Inc.

Brown, D. (1989) 'Ethnic revival: perspectives on state and society', *Third World Quarterly*, vol. 11, no. 4.

Brown, D. (2000) *Contemporary Nationalism: Civic, Ethnocultural and Multicultural Politics*. London: Routledge.

Brown, D. (2006) 'Contending nationalisms in South-East Asia', in G. Delanty and K. Kumar (eds), *The SAGE Handbook of Nations and Nationalism*. London: Sage Publications.

Brown, G. K. (2008) 'Horizontal inequalities and separatism in Southeast Asia: a comparative perspective', in F. Stewart (ed.), *Horizontal Inequalities and Conflict*. Basingstoke: Palgrave Macmillan.

Bulloch, J. and H. Morris (1993) *No Friends but the Mountains: The Tragic History of the Kurds*. Harmondsworth: Penguin.

Cameron, R. (2010) 'Redefining political-administrative relations in South Africa', *International Review of Administrative Sciences*, vol. 76, no. 4.

Cammack, P. (1997) *Capitalism and Democracy in the Third World: The Doctrine for Political Development*. London: Leicester University Press.

Cammack, P., D. Pool and W. Tordoff (1993) *Third World Politics: A Comparative Introduction*, 2nd edn. London: Macmillan.

Carbone, G. (2003) 'Political parties in a "no-party democracy". Hegemony and opposition under "Movement democracy" in Uganda', *Party Politics*, vol. 9, no. 4: 485–501.

Carbone, G. (2009) 'The consequences of democratization', *Journal of Democracy*, vol. 20, no. 2.

Cardoso, F. H. (1973) 'Associated-dependent development: theoretical and practical implications', in A. Stepan (ed.), *Authoritarian Brazil: Origins, Policies and Future*. New Haven, CT: Yale University Press.

Carey, S. C. (2002) 'A comparative analysis of political parties in Kenya, Zambia and the Democratic Republic of Congo', *Democratization*, vol. 9, no. 3.

Carnoy, M. (1984) *The State and Political Theory*. Princeton, NJ: Princeton University Press.

Carothers, T. (2002) 'The end of the transition paradigm', *Journal of Democracy*, vol. 13, no. 1.

Castells, M. (1992) 'Four Asian Tigers with a dragon head: a comparative analysis of the state, economy and society in the Asian Pacific rim', in R. Appelbaum and J. Henderson (eds), *States and Development in the Asian Pacific Rim*. Newbury Park, CA: Sage.

Castles, F. G. (1974) 'Political stability and the dominant image of society', *Political Studies,* vol. 22, no. 3.

Castron, C. (2002) 'The military and politics in Brazil, 1964–2000', in K. Koonings and D. Kruijt (eds), *Political Armies. The Military and Nation Building in the Age of Democracy*. London: Zed Books.

Caulfield, J. (2002) 'Executive agencies in Tanzania: liberalization and Third World debt', *Public Administration and Development*, vol. 22, no. 3: 209–20.

Chadda, M. (2000) *Building Democracy in South Asia. India, Nepal, Pakistan*. London: Lynne Rienner.

Chandra, K. (2011) 'What is an ethnic party?', *Party Politics*, vol. 17, no. 2.

Charlton, R. (1981) 'Plus ça change … a review of two decades of theoretical analysis of African *coups d'état*', *Culture et Developpement*, vol. 13, no. 2.

Chibber, V. (2002) 'Bureaucratic rationality and the developmental state', *American Journal of Sociology*, vol. 107, no. 4: 951–89.

Chowdhury, N. and B. J. Nelson (1994) 'Redefining politics: patterns of women's political engagement from a global perspective', in B. J. Nelson and N. Chowdhury (eds), *Women and Politics Worldwide*. New Haven, CT: Yale University Press.

Chu, Y.-H. (2001) 'The legacy of one-party hegemony in Taiwan', in L. Diamond and R. Gunther (eds), *Political Parties and Democracy*. Baltimore: Johns Hopkins University Press.

Clague, C., P. Keefer, S. Knack and M. Olson (1997) 'Democracy, autocracy and the institutions supportive of economic growth', in C. Clague (ed.), *Institutions and Economic Development: Growth and Governance in Less-Developed and Post Socialist States*. Baltimore: Johns Hopkins University Press.

Clapham, C. (1982) 'Clientelism and the state', in C. Clapham (ed.), *Private Patronage and Public Power: Political Clientelism in the Modern State*. London: Frances Pinter.

Clapham, C. (1985) *Third World Politics: An Introduction*. London: Croom Helm.

Clark, J. F. (2007) 'The decline of the African military coup', *Journal of Democracy*, vol. 18, no. 3.

Clay, J. W. (1989) 'Epilogue: the ethnic future of nations', *Third World Quarterly,* vol. 11, no. 4.

Coakley, J. (1993) 'The territorial management of ethnic conflict', *Regional Politics and Policy,* vol. 3, no. 1.

Cohen, B. J. (1973) *The Question of Imperialism: The Political Economy of Dominance and Dependence*. New York: Basic Books.

Coleman, J. S. (1954) 'Nationalism in Tropical Africa', *American Political Science Review*, vol. 48, no. 2.

Coleman, J. S. (1960) 'Conclusion: the political systems of the developing areas', in G. A. Almond and J. Coleman (eds), *The Politics of the Developing Areas*. Princeton, NJ: Princeton University Press.

Coleman, J. S. and C. G. Rosberg (eds) (1964) *Political Parties and National Integration in Tropical Africa*. Los Angeles: University of California Press.

Collier, D. (1979) 'The BA model: synthesis and priorities for future research', in D. Collier (ed.), *The New Authoritarianism in Latin America*. Princeton, NJ: Princeton University Press.

Collier, P. and A. Hoeffler (2007) 'Military spending and the risks of coups d'etat', Oxford: Centre for the Study of African Economies.

Compton, R. W. (2000) *East Asian Democratization. Impact of Globalization, Culture and Economy*. London: Praeger.

Connor, W. (1988) 'Ethnonationalism', in M. Weiner and S. P. Huntington (eds), *Understanding Political Development*. Boston: Little, Brown.

Coppedge, M. (2001) 'Political Darwinism in Latin America's lost decade', in L. Diamond and R. Gunther (eds), *Political Parties and Democracy*. Baltimore: Johns Hopkins University Press.

Craske, N. (1999) *Women and Politics in Latin America*. New Brunswick, NJ: Rutgers University Press.

Croissant, A., D. Kuehn, P. Chambers and S. O. Wolf (2010) 'Beyond the fallacy of coup-ism: conceptualizing civilian control of the military in emerging democracies', *Democratization*, vol. 17, no. 5.

Crook, R. C. (2010) 'Rethinking civil service reform in Africa: "islands of effectiveness" and organisational commitment', *Commonwealth and Comparative Politics*, vol. 48, no. 4.

Crow, B. (1990) 'The state in Bangladesh: the extension of a weak state', in S. K. Mitra (ed.), *The Post-Colonial State in Asia. Dialectics of Politics and Culture*. London: Harvester Wheatsheaf.

Dahl, R. (1971) *Polyarchy: Participation and Opposition*. New Haven, CT: Yale University Press.

Dalton, R. J. and S. Weldon (2007) 'Partisanship and party system institutionalization', *Party Politics*, vol. 13, no. 2: 179–96.

Danapoulos, C. and D. Zirker (2006) 'Governability and contemporary forms of military intervention: expanding Ecuadorian and Turkish models', *Journal of Security Sector Management*, vol. 4, no. 1.

Davies, J. C. (1972) 'Toward a theory of revolution', in D. H. Wrong and H. L. Gracey (eds), *Readings in Introductory Sociology,* 2nd edn. London: Collier-Macmillan.

Davin, D. (1996) 'Chinese women: media concerns and the politics of reform', in H. Afshar (ed.), *Women and Politics in the Third World*. London: Routledge.

de Kadt, E. (2002) 'The military in politics: old wine in new bottles', in K. Koonings and D. Kruijt (eds), *Political Armies. The Military and Nation Building in the Age of Democracy*. London: Zed Books.

de Zeeuw, J. (2010) '"Sons of War": parties and party systems in post-war El Salvador and Cambodia', *Democratization*, vol. 17, no. 6.

Deneulin, S. and C. Rakodi (2011) 'Revisiting religion: development studies thirty years on', *World Development*, vol. 39, no. 1: 45–54.

Denoeux, G. (2002) 'The forgotten swamp: navigating political Islam', *Middle East Policy*, vol. 9, no. 2.

Diamond, L. (1988) 'Introduction: roots of failure, seeds of hope', in L.

Diamond. J. J. Linz and S. M. Lipset (eds), *Democracy in Developing Countries*, vol. 2. *Africa*. Boulder, CO: Lynne Rienner Publishers.

Diamond, L. (1989) 'Introduction: persistence, erosion, breakdown and renewal', in L. Diamond, J. J. Linz and S. M. Lipset (eds), *Democracy in Developing Countries*, vol. 3, *Asia*. Boulder, CO: Lynne Rienner Publishers.

Diamond, L. (1992) 'Economic development and democracy reconsidered', in G. Marks and L. Diamond (eds), *Re-examining Democracy: Essays in Honor of Seymour Martin Lipset*. London: Sage.

Diamond, L. (1993a) 'Causes and effects', in L. Diamond (ed.), *Political Culture and Democracy in Developing Countries*. Boulder, CO: Lynne Rienner Publishers.

Diamond, L. (1993b) 'Introduction: political culture and democracy', in L. Diamond (ed.), *Political Culture and Democracy in Developing Countries*. Boulder, CO: Lynne Rienner Publishers.

Diamond, L. (1996) 'Is the Third Wave over?', *Journal of Democracy*, vol. 7, no. 3.

Diamond, L. (1997a) *Civil Society and the Development of Democracy*, Working Paper 1997/101. Madrid: Juan March Institute.

Diamond, L. (1997b) 'Introduction: in search of consolidation' in L. Diamond, M. F. Plattner, Y. Chu and H. Tien (eds), *Consolidating the Third Wave Democracies: Themes and Perspectives*. Baltimore: Johns Hopkins University Press.

Diamond, L. (1998) *Political Culture and Democratic Consolidation*, Working Paper 1998/118. Madrid: Juan March Institute.

Diamond, L. (2011) 'Why democracies survive', *Journal of Democracy*, vol. 22, no. 1.

Diamond, L. and J. J. Linz (1989) 'Introduction: politics, society and democracy in Latin America', in L. Diamond, J. J. Linz and S. M. Lipset (eds), *Democracy in Developing Countries*, vol. 4, *Latin America*. Boulder, CO: Lynne Rienner Publishers.

Diamond, L., J. J. Linz and S. M. Lipset (eds) (1990) 'Introduction: comparing experiences with democracy', in L. Diamond, J. J. Linz and S. M. Lipset (eds), *Politics in Developing Countries. Comparing Experiences with Democracy*. London: Lynne Rienner Publishers.

Dirlik, A. (2004) 'Spectres of the Third World: global modernity and the end of the three worlds', *Third World Quarterly*, vol. 25, no. 1.

Dix, R. H. (1992) 'Democratisation and the institutionalisation of Latin American political parties', *Comparative Political Studies*, vol. 24, no. 4, January.

Dos Santos, T. (1973) 'The crisis of development theory and the problem of dependence in Latin America', in H. Bernstein (ed.), *Underdevelopment and Development*. Harmondsworth: Penguin.

Dowse, R. E. (1966) 'A functionalist's logic', *World Politics,* vol. 18, no. 4.

Dukalskis, A. (2009) 'Stateness problems or regime unification? Explaining obstacles to democratization in Burma/Myanmar', *Democratization*, vol. 16, no. 5.

Eckstein, H. (1982) 'The idea of political development: from dignity to efficiency', *World Politics*, vol. 34, no. 4.

ECLAC (2011) *Foreign Direct Investment in Latin America and the Caribbean.* New York: United Nations Economic Commission for Latin America and the Caribbean.

Eisenstadt, S. N. and L. Roniger (1981) 'The study of patron–client relations and recent developments in sociological theory', in S. N. Eisenstadt and R. Lemarchand (eds), *Political Clientelism, Patronage and Development.* London: Sage.

Elliot, C. (2011) 'Moving from clientelist politics towards a welfare regime: evidence from the 2009 assembly election in Andhra Pradesh', *Commonwealth and Comparative Politics*, vol. 49, no. 1.

Emmanuel, A. (1974) 'Myths of development versus myths of underdevelopment', *New Left Review*, no. 85.

Emmanuel, A. (1976) 'The multinational corporations and the inequality of development', *International Social Science Journal*, vol. 28, no. 4.

Enloe, C. H. (1973) *Ethnic Conflict and Political Development.* Boston: Little, Brown.

Enloe, C. H. (1976) 'Central governments' strategies for coping with separatist movements', in W. H. Morris-Jones (ed.), *The Politics of Separatism*, Collected Seminar Papers no. 19. London: University of London Institute of Commonwealth Studies.

Eriksen, T. H. (1993) *Ethnicity and Nationalism. Anthropological Perspectives.* London: Pluto Press.

Ersson, S. and J. E. Lane (1996) 'Democracy and development: a statistical exploration', in A. Leftwich (ed.), *Democracy and Development. Theory and Practice.* Cambridge: Polity Press.

Evans, P. B. (1995) *Embedded Autonomy. States and Industrial Transformation.* Princeton, NJ: Princeton University Press.

Evans, P. B., D. Rueschmeyer and T. Skocpol (eds) (1985) *Bringing the State Back In.* Cambridge: Cambridge University Press.

Farsoun, S. K. and N. H. Aruri (2006) *Palestine and the Palestinians. A Social and Political History.* Boulder, CO: Westview Press.

Fayemi, J. (2002) 'Entrenched militarism and the future of democracy in Nigeria', in K. Koonings and D. Kruijt (eds), *Political Armies. The Military and Nation Building in the Age of Democracy.* London: Zed Books.

Feardon, J. D. and Laitin D. D. (2003) 'Ethnicity, insurgency, and civil war', *American Political Science Review*, vol. 97, no.1.

Filali-Ansary, A. (2003) 'The challenge of secularization', in L. Diamond, M. F. Plattner and D. Brumberg (eds), *Islam and Democracy in the Middle East.* Baltimore: Johns Hopkins University Press.

Finer, S. E. (1962) *The Man on Horseback: The Role of the Military in Politics.* London: Pall Mall Press.

First, R. (1972) *The Barrel of a Gun: Political Power in Africa and the Coup d'État.* Harmondsworth: Penguin.

Fitch, J. S. (1998) *The Armed Forces and Democracy in Latin America.* Baltimore: Johns Hopkins University Press.

Fox, J. (1994) 'The difficult transition from clientelism to citizenship', *World Politics*, vol. 46, no. 2.

Frank, A. G. (1966) 'The development of underdevelopment', *Monthly Review*, vol. 18, no. 4.

Frank, A. G. (1969a) *Capitalism and Underdevelopment in Latin America: Historical Studies of Chile and Brazil*. London: Monthly Review Press.

Frank, A. G. (1969b) *Latin America: Underdevelopment or Revolution*. New York: Monthly Review Press.

Frank, A. G. (1972a) 'Economic dependence, class structure and underdevelopment policy', in J. D. Cockcroft, A. G. Frank and D. L. Johnson (eds), *Dependence and Underdevelopment. Latin America's Political Economy*. New York: Doubleday.

Frank, A. G. (1972b) 'Sociology of development and the underdevelopment of sociology', in J. D. Cockcroft, A. G. Frank and D. L. Johnson (eds), *Dependence and Underdevelopment: Latin America's Political Economy*. New York: Doubleday.

Frazer, J. (1995) 'Conceptualising civil–military relations during democratic transition', *Africa Today*, vol. 42, nos 1–2.

Freedman, A. L. (2006) *Political Change and Consolidation. Democracy's Rocky Road in Thailand, Indonesia, South Korea and Malaysia*. Basingstoke: Palgrave Macmillan.

Freedom House (2011) *Freedom in the World 2011: The Authoritarian Challenge to Democracy*. New York: Freedom House.

Freedom House (2012) *Freedom in the World 2012. The Arab Uprisings and their Global Repercussions*. New York: Freedom House.

Fritz, V. and A. R. Menocal (2006) *(Re)building Developmental States*, ODI Working Paper 274. London: Overseas Development Institute.

Fritzen, S. (2007) 'Discipline and democratize: patterns of bureaucratic accountability in Southeast Asia', *International Journal of Public Administration*, vol. 30, nos. 12–14.

Fukuyama, F. (1992) *The End of History and the Last Man*. New York: Free Press.

Gasiorowski, M. J. (1998) 'Macro-economic conditions and political instability: an empirical analysis', *Studies in Comparative International Development*, vol. 33, no. 3.

Gates, S., H. Hegre, M. P. Jones and H. Strand (2006) 'Institutional inconsistency and political instability: polity duration 1900–2000', *American Journal of Political Science*, vol. 50, no. 4.

Ghai, Y. (2000) 'Ethnicity and autonomy: a framework for analysis', in Y. Ghai (ed.), *Autonomy and Ethnicity: Negotiating Competing Claims in Multi-ethnic States*. Cambridge: Cambridge University Press.

Ghassemlou, A. R. (1980) 'Kurdistan in Iran', in G. Chaliand (ed.), *People Without a Country*. London: Zed Press.

Gill, G. (2000) *The Dynamics of Democratization. Élites, Civil Society and the Transition Process*. Basingstoke: Macmillan.

Goldstone, J. A., R. H. Bates, T. R.Gurr, M. Lustik, M. G. Marshall, J. Ulfelder and M. Woodward (2005), 'A global forecasting model of political instability', Paper presented to the Annual Meeting of the American Political Science Association, Washington, 1–4 September.

Goldstone, J. A., T. R. Gurr and F. Moshiri (eds) (1991) *Revolutions of the Late Twentieth Century*. Boulder, CO: Westview Press.

Goodwin, J. and T. Skocpol (1989) 'Explaining revolutions in the contemporary Third World', *Politics and Society,* vol. 17, no. 4.

Goulbourne, H. (1979) 'Some problems of analysis of the political in backward capitalist social formations', in H. Goulbourne (ed.), *Politics and State in the Third World*. London: Macmillan.

Graham, B. D. (1993) *Representation and Party Politics: A Comparative Perspective*. Oxford: Blackwell Publishers.

Griffiths, R. J. (1996) 'Democratisation and civil military relations in Namibia, South Africa and Mozambique', *Third World Quarterly,* vol. 17, no. 3, September.

Grindle, M. S. (2010) *Constructing, Deconstructing, and Reconstructing Career Civil Service Systems in Latin America*, Faculty Research Working Paper 10-025, John F. Kennedy School of Government, Harvard University.

Grugel, J. (2002) *Democratization. A Critical Introduction*. Basingstoke: Palgrave Macmillan.

Gunther, R. and L. Diamond (2001) 'Types and functions of parties', in L. Diamond and R. Gunther (eds), *Political Parties and Democracy*. Baltimore: Johns Hopkins University Press.

Gurr, T. R. and B. Harff (1994) *Ethnic Conflict in World Politics*. Boulder, CO: Westview Press.

Haggard, S. (1990) *Pathways from the Periphery: The Politics of Growth in the Newly Industrializing Countries*. Ithaca, NY: Cornell University Press.

Hah, C. and J. Martin (1975) 'Towards a synthesis of conflict and integration theories of nationalism', *World Politics*, vol. 27, no. 3.

Hamid, S. (2011) 'Arab Islamist parties: losing on purpose?', *Journal of Democracy*, vol. 22, no. 1.

Haque, M. S. (1999) 'Relationship between citizenship and public administration: a reconfiguration', *International Review of Administrative Sciences*, vol. 65, no. 3.

Haque, M. S. (2007) 'Theory and practice of public administration in Southeast Asia: traditions, directions, and impacts', *International Journal of Public Administration*, vol. 30, nos. 12–14.

Harris, N. (1970) 'The revolutionary role of the peasants', *International Socialism,* no. 41, December–January.

Haruna, P. F. (2003) 'Reforming Ghana's public service: issues and experiences in comparative perspective', *Public Administration Review*, vol. 63, no. 3.

Hassan, Z. (2010) 'Gender, religion and democratic politics in India', *Third World Quarterly*, vol. 31, no. 6.

Haufman, R. (1997) *The Next Challenge for Latin America*, Working Paper 1997/108. Madrid: Juan March Institute.

Hawes, G. and H. Liu (1993) 'Explaining the dynamics of the Southeast Asian political economy', *World Politics*, vol. 45, no. 4.

Haynes, J. (1993) *Religion in Third World Politics*. Buckingham: Open University Press.

Haynes, J. (1999) 'Conclusion', in J. Haynes (ed.), *Religion, Globalization and Political Culture in the Third World*. London: Macmillan.

Haynes, J. (2001) *Democracy in the Developing World*. Cambridge: Polity Press.

Haynes, J. (2003) 'Democratic consolidation in Africa: the problematic case of Ghana', *Commonwealth and Comparative Politics*, vol. 41, no. 1.

Haynes, J. (2009) 'Religion and democratization: an introduction', *Democratization*, vol. 16, no. 6: 1041–57.

Heady, F. (1959) 'Bureaucratic theory and comparative administration', *Administrative Science Quarterly*, vol. 3, no. 4.

Hechter, M. (1975) *Internal Colonialism: The Celtic Fringe in British National Development, 1536–1966*. London: Routledge & Kegan Paul.

Hechter, M. (1985) 'Internal colonialism revisited', in E. A. Tiryakian and R. Rogowski (eds), *New Nationalisms of the Developed West*. London: Allen & Unwin.

Hechter, M. (2000) *Containing Nationalism*. Oxford: Oxford University Press.

Heeger, G. A. (1973) 'Bureaucracy, political parties and political development', *World Politics*, vol. 25, no. 4.

Hein, W. and K. Stenzel (1979) 'The capitalist state and underdevelopment in Latin America: the case of Venezuela', in H. Goulbourne (ed.), *Politics and State in the Third World*. London: Macmillan.

Held, D. and A. McGrew (2000) 'The great globalization debate: an introduction', in D. Held and A. McGrew (eds), *The Global Transformation Reader. An Introduction to the Globalization Debate*. Cambridge: Polity Press.

Held, D., A. McGrew, D. Goldblatt and J. Perraton (1999) *Global Transformations: Politics, Economics and Culture*. Cambridge: Polity Press.

Helliwell, J. F. (1994) 'Empirical linkages between democracy and economic growth', *British Journal of Political Science*, vol. 24, no. 2.

Henderson, J. and R. Appelbaum (1992) 'Situating the state in the East Asian development process' in R. Appelbaum and J. Henderson (eds), *States and Development in the Asian Pacific Rim*. Newbury Park, CA: Sage.

Hensman, R. (1996) 'The role of women in the resistance to political authoritarianism in Latin America and South Asia', in H. Afshar (ed.), *Women and Politics in the Third World*. London: Routledge.

Hernandez, L. and J. Fox (1995) 'Mexico's difficult democracy: grassroots movements, NGOs, and local government', in C. A. Reilly (ed.), *New Paths to Democratic Development in Latin America*. London: Lynne Rienner Publishers.

Higgott, R. A. (1983) *Political Development Theory: The Contemporary Debate*. London: Croom Helm.

Hilary, J. (2004) *Profiting From Poverty. Privatisation, Consultants, DFID, and Public Services*. London: War on Want.

Hilliard, V. G. and Wissink, H. F. (1999) 'Alternative Administration: a southern African perspective', in K. M. Henderson and O. P. Dwivedi (eds), *Bureaucracy and the Alternatives in World Perspective*. Basingstoke: Macmillan.

Hinnebusch, R. (2008) 'Modern Syrian Politics', *History Compass*, vol. 6, no.1: 263–85.

Hirschmann, D. (1981) 'Development or underdevelopment administration?: a further "deadlock"', *Development and Change*, vol. 12, no. 4.

Hirst, P. and G. Thompson (1999) *Globalisation in Question: The International Economy and the Possibilities of Governance*, 2nd edn. Cambridge: Polity Press.

Hoglund, K. and A. Piyarathne (2009) 'Paying the price for patronage: electoral violence in Sri Lanka', *Commonwealth and Comparative Politics*, vol. 47, no. 3.

Holt, R. T. and J. E. Turner (1966) *The Political Basis of Economic Development*. Princeton, NJ: D. Van Nostrand Co.

Hoogvelt, A. M. M. (1982) *The Third World in Global Development*. London: Macmillan.

Horowitz, D. L. (1985) *Ethnic Groups in Conflict*. Berkeley, CA: University of California Press.

Horowitz, D. L. (1994) 'Democracy in divided societies', in L. Diamond and M. F. Plattner (eds), *Nationalism, Ethnic Conflict and Democracy*. Baltimore: Johns Hopkins University Press.

Howell, J., A. Ishkanian, E. Obadare, H. Seckinelgin and M. Glasius (2006) *The Backlash against Civil Society in the Wake of the Long War on Terror*, Civil Society Working Paper no. 26. London: Centre for Civil Society, London School of Economics and Political Science.

HRW (2005) 'Entrenching impunity. Government responsibility for international crimes in Darfur', *Human Rights Watch*, vol. 17, no. 17(A).

HRW (2008) *Collecive Punishment. War Crimes and Crimes against Humanity in the Ogaden Area of Ethiopia's Somali Region*. New York: Human Rights Watch.

Huber, E., D. Rueschemeyer and J. D. Stephens (1993) 'The impact of economic development on democracy', *Journal of Economic Perspectives*, vol. 7, no. 3.

Huff, W. G., G. Dewit and C. Oughton (2001) 'Building the developmental state: achieving economic growth through co-operative solutions: a comment on bringing politics back in', *Journal of Development Studies*, vol. 38, no. 1.

Hughes, O. E. (1998) *Public Management and Administration: An Introduction*, 2nd edn. London: Macmillan.

Hulme, D. and M. Turner (1990) *Sociology and Development: Theories, Policies and Practices*. London: Harvester Wheatsheaf.

Huntington, S. P. (1965) 'Political development and political decay', *World Politics,* vol. 17, no. 2.

Huntington, S. P. (1968) *Political Order in Changing Societies*. New Haven, CT: Yale University Press.

Huntington, S. P. (1971) 'The change to change', *Comparative Politics,* vol. 3, no. 2.

Huntington, S. P. (1984) 'Will more countries become democratic?', *Political Science Quarterly,* vol. 99, no. 2.

Huntington, S. P. (1987) 'The goals of development', in M. Weiner and S. P. Huntington (eds), *Understanding Political Development*. Boston: Little, Brown.

Huntington, S. P. (1991) *The Third Wave: Democratization in the Late Twentieth Century*. Norman: University of Oklahoma Press.

Huntington, S. P. (1995) 'Reforming civil-military relations', *Journal of Democracy,* vol. 6, no. 4.

Huntington, S. P. (1996) *The Clash of Civilizations and the Remaking of World Order*. New York: Simon & Schuster.

Huntington, S. P. and J. I. Dominguez (1975) 'Political development', in F. I. Greenstein and N. W. Polsby (eds), *Micropolitical Theory, Handbook of Political Science*, vol. 3. Reading, MA: Addison-Wesley.

Hurwitz, L. (1973) 'Contemporary approaches to political stability', *Comparative Politics,* vol. 3, no. 3.

Hyden, G. (2006) *African Politics in Comparative Perspective*. Cambridge: Cambridge University Press.

Hymer, S. (1982) 'The multinational corporation and the law of uneven development', in H. Alavi and T. Shanin (eds), *Introduction to the Sociology of 'Developing Societies'*. London: Macmillan.

ILO (2011) *Global Employment Trends 2011. The Challenge of a Jobs Recovery*. Geneva: International Labour Organization.

Inglehart, R. and C. Welzel (2005) *Modernization, Cultural Change and Democracy*. Cambridge: Cambridge University Press.

Jackman, R. W. (1978) 'The predictability of *coups d'état*: a model with African data', *American Political Science Review,* vol. 72, no. 4.

Jackman, R. W. (1986) 'Explaining African *coups d'état',* *American Political Science Review,* vol. 80, no. 1.

Jahan, R. (1973) *Pakistan: Failure in National Integration*. New York: Columbia University Press.

Jain, R. B. (1992) 'Bureaucracy, public policy and socio-economic development', in H. K. Asmerom, R. Hope and R. B. Jain (eds), *Bureaucracy and Development Policies in the Third World*. Amsterdam: VU University Press.

Janowitz, M. (1970) *Political Conflict. Essays in Political Sociology*. Chicago: Quadrangle Books.

Jansen, K. (2001) 'Thailand, the making of a miracle', *Development and Change*, vol. 32, no. 2.

Jaquette, J. S. (2001) 'Regional differences and contrasting views', *Journal of Democracy,* vol. 12, no. 3.

Jessop, R. (1977) 'Recent theories of the capitalist state', *Cambridge Journal of Economics,* vol. 1, no. 4.

Johnson, T. H., R. O. Slater and P. McGowan (1984) 'Explaining African military *coups d'état,* 1960–1982', *American Political Science Review,* vol. 78, no. 3.

Jones, D. M. (1997) *Political Development in Pacific Asia*. Cambridge: Polity Press.

Judy, R. A. T. (1998) 'Islamiyya and the construction of the human being', in A. S. Moussalli (ed.), *Islamic Fundamentalism: Myths and Realities*. Reading: Ithaca Press.

Kamat, S. (2004) 'The privatisation of public interest: theorizing NGO discourse in a neo-liberal era', *Review of International Political Economy*, vol. 11, no. 1.

Kamrava, M. (1995) *Politics and Society in the Third World*. London: Routledge.

Karl, T. L. (1996) 'Dilemmas of democratization in Latin America', in R. A. Camp (ed.), *Democracy in Latin America: Patterns and Cycles*. Willmington: Scholarly Resources Inc.

Kasfir, N. (1983) 'Relating class to state in Africa', *Journal of Commonwealth and Comparative Politics*, vol. 21, no. 3.

Kasfir, N. (1998) 'Civil society, the state and democracy in Africa', *Journal of Commonwealth and Comparative Politics*, vol. 36, no. 2.

Kaufman, R. R., H. I. Chernotsky and D. S. Geller (1974) 'A preliminary test of the theory of dependency', *Comparative Politics*, vol. 7, no. 3.

Kay, G. (1975) *Development and Underdevelopment: A Marxist Analysis*. London: Macmillan.

Kedourie, E. (1992) *Politics in the Middle East*. Oxford: Oxford University Press.

Kellas, J. G. (1991) *The Politics of Nationalism and Ethnicity*. London: Macmillan.

Keratnyky, A. (2002) 'Muslim countries and the democracy gap', *Journal of Democracy*, vol. 13, no. 1.

Kiely, R. (1995) *Sociology and Development: The Impasse and Beyond*. London: UCL Press.

Kiely, R. (2010) *Rethinking Imperialism*. Basingstoke: Palgrave Macmillan.

Kilson, M. L. (1963) 'Authoritarian and single-party tendencies in African politics', *World Politics*, vol. 15, no. 1.

Kitschelt, A., K. A. Hawkins, J. P. Luna, G. Rosas and E. J. Zechmeister (2010) *Latin American Party Systems*. Cambridge: Cambridge University Press.

Kohn, H. (1945) *The Idea of Nationalism: A Study of its Origins and Background*. London: Macmillan.

Koonings, K. and D. Kruijt (2002) 'Military politics and the mission of nation building', in K. Koonings and D. Kruijt (eds), *Political Armies. The Military and Nation Building in the Age of Democracy*. London: Zed Books.

Kostiner, J. (1997) 'State, Islam and opposition in Saudi Arabia: the post-Desert Storm phase', in B. Maddy-Weitzman and E. Inbar (eds), *Religious Radicalism in the Greater Middle East*. London: Frank Cass.

Kothari, R. (1968) 'Tradition and modernity revisited', *Government and Opposition,* vol. 3, no. 2.

Kramon, E. and D. N. Posner (2011) 'Kenya's new constitution', *Journal of Democracy*, vol. 22, no. 2.

Krasner, S. D. (1995) 'Compromising Westphalia', *International Security*, vol. 20, no. 3.

Krause, K. (1996) 'Armaments and conflict: the causes and consequences of military development', in L. van de Goor, K. Rupesinghe and P. Sciarone (eds), *Between Development and Destruction: An Enquiry into the Causes of Conflict in Post-Colonial States*. London: Macmillan.

Krishna, A. (2010) 'Continuity and change: the Indian administrative service 30 years ago and today', *Commonwealth and Comparative Politics*, vol. 48, no. 4.

Kuenzi, M. and G. Lambright (2001) 'Party system institutionalisation in 30 African countries', *Party Politics,* vol. 7, no. 4.

Lall, S. (1975) 'Is "dependence" a useful concept in analysing underdevelopment?', *World Development*, vol. 3, no. 4.

LaPalombara, J. and M. Weiner (eds) (1966) *Political Parties and Political Development*. Princeton, NJ: Princeton University Press.

Larrain, J. (1989) *Theories of Development: Capitalism, Colonialism and Dependency*. Cambridge: Polity Press.

Lawson, L. (2003) 'Globalization and the African state', *Commonwealth and Comparative Politics*, vol. 41, no. 3.

Leftwich, A. (2000) *States of Development*. Cambridge: Polity Press.

Levine, D. (1988) 'Assessing the impacts of liberation theology in Latin America', *Review of Politics*, vol. 50, no. 2.

Lewis, P. (2010) 'Growth without prosperity in Africa', in L. Diamond and M. F. Plattner (eds), *Democratization in Africa. Progress and Retreat*. Baltimore: Johns Hopkins University Press.

Leys, C. (1975) *Underdevelopment in Kenya: The Political Economy of Neocolonialism*. London: Heinemann.

Leys, C. (1976) 'The "overdeveloped" post-colonial state: a re-evaluation', *Review of African Political Economy*, vol. 5, no. 1.

Leys, C. (1977) 'Underdevelopment and dependency: critical notes', *Journal of Contemporary Asia*, vol. 7, no. 1.

Leys, C. (1978) 'Capital accumulation, class formation and dependency – the significance of the Kenyan case', in R. Miliband and J. Saville (eds), *The Socialist Register, 1978*. London: Merlin Press.

Leys, C. (1982) 'Samuel Huntington and the end of classical modernisation theory', in H. Alavi and T. Shanin (eds), *Introduction to the Sociology of 'Developing Societies'*. London: Macmillan.

Leys, C. (1996) *The Rise and Fall of Development Theory*. London: James Curry.

Lijphart, A. (1984) *Democracies: Patterns of Majoritarian and Consensus Government in Twenty-One Countries*. New Haven, CT: Yale University Press.

Linz, J. J. (1994) 'Presidential or parliamentary democracy: does it make a difference?', in J. J. Linz and A. Valenzuela (eds), *The Failure of Presidential Democracy*. Baltimore: Johns Hopkins University Press.

Lipset, S. M. (1959) 'Some social requisites of democracy: economic development and political legitimacy', *American Political Science Review*, vol. 53, no. 1.

Lipset, S. M. (1960) *Political Man*. New York: Doubleday.

Lipton, M. (1977) *Why People Stay Poor: Urban Bias in World Development*. London: Temple Smith.

Little, W. (1997) 'Democratisation in Latin America, 1980–95', in D. Potter, D. Goldblatt, M. Kiloh and P. Lewis (eds), *Democratisation*. Cambridge: Polity Press.

Lloyd, P. C. (1973) *Classes, Crises and Coups: Themes in the Sociology of Developing Countries*. London: Paladin.

Long, N. (1977) *An Introduction to the Sociology of Rural Development*. London: Tavistock.

Luan, T. D. (1996) 'Vietnam', in P. McCarney (ed.), *The Changing Nature of Local Government in Developing Countries*. Toronto: University of Toronto Centre for Urban and Community Studies and Federation of Canadian Municipalities.

Luckham, R. (1991) 'Militarism: force, class and international conflict', in R. Little and M. Smith (eds), *Perspectives on World Politics*, 2nd edn. London: Routledge.

Luckham, R. and G. White (1996) 'Introduction: democratizing the South', in R. Luckham and G. White (eds), *Democratization in the South: The Jagged Wave*. Manchester: Manchester University Press.

Lust, E. (2009) 'Competitive clientelism in the Middle East', *Journal of Democracy*, vol. 20, no. 3.

Luton, H. (1976) 'The satellite metropolis model: a critique', *Theory and Society,* vol. 3, no. 4.

Lynch, G. and Crawford, G. (2011) 'Democratization in Africa 1990–2010: an assessment', *Democratization*, vol. 18, no. 2.

Mack, A. and R. Leaver (1979) 'Radical theories of underdevelopment: an assessment', in A. Mack, D. Plant and V. Doyle (eds), *Imperialism, Intervention and Development*. London: Croom Helm.

Mackerass, C. (2001) 'Xinjiang at the turn of the century: the causes of separatism', *Central Asian Survey*, vol. 20, no. 3.

Macpherson, C. B. (1966) *The Real World of Democracy*. Oxford: Clarendon Press.

Mainwaring, S. (1992) 'Transitions to democracy and democratic consolidation: theoretical and comparative issues', in S. Mainwaring, G. O'Donnell and J. S. Valenzuela (eds), *Issues in Democratic Consolidation: The New South American Democracies in Comparative Perspective*. Notre Dame, IN: University of Notre Dame Press.

Mainwaring, S. (1993) 'Presidentialism, multipartism and democracy: the difficult combination', *Comparative Political Studies*, vol. 26, no. 2.

Mainwaring, S. (1998) 'Party systems in the Third Wave', *Journal of Democracy,* vol. 9, no. 3, July.

Mainwaring, S. and T. R. Scully (1995) 'Introduction: party systems in Latin America', in S.Mainwaring and T. R. Scully (eds), *Building Democratic Institutions: Party Systems in Latin America*. Stanford: Stanford University Press.

Mainwaring, S. and Zoco, E. (2007) 'Political sequences and the stabilization of inter-party competition', *Party Politics*, vol. 13, no. 2.

Mamuya, I. (2008) 'What has gone wrong?', *Development and Cooperation*, vol. 35, nos. 7–8.

Manning, C. (2005) 'Assessing African party systems after the Third Wave', *Party Politics*, vol. 11, no. 6.

Manning, C. (2010) 'Mozambique's slide into one-party rule', *Journal of Democracy*, vol. 21, no. 2.

Masoud, T. (2011) 'The road to (and from) Liberation square', *Journal of Democracy*, vol. 22, no. 3.

Mazrui, A. A. (1976) 'Soldiers as traditionalisers: military rule and the re-Africanisation of Africa', *World Politics*, vol. 28, no. 2.

McGowan, P. J. (1976) 'Economic dependence and economic performance in Black Africa', *Journal of Modern African Studies*, vol. 14, no. 1.

McGowan, P. J. and T. H. Johnson (1984) 'African military *coups d'état* and under-development: a quantitative historical analysis', *Journal of Modern African Studies*, vol. 22, no. 4.

McGowan, P. J. and D. L. Smith (1978) 'Economic dependency in Black Africa: an analysis of competing theories', *International Organisation*, vol. 32, no. 1.

McMichael, P., J. Petras and R. Rhodes (1974) 'Imperialism and the contradictions of development', *New Left Review*, no. 85.

McMillan, A (2008) 'Deviant democracy in India', *Democratization*, vol. 15, no. 4: 733–49.

McVey, R. (1984) 'Separatism and the paradoxes of the nation-state in perspective', in L. Joo-Jock and S. Vani (eds), *Armed Separatism in Southeast Asia*. Singapore: Institute of Southeast Asian Studies.

Meacham, C. E. (1999) 'Development administration and its alternatives in Latin America and the Caribbean: reforms and redirections', in K. M. Henderson and O. P. Dwivedi (eds), *Bureaucracy and the Alternatives in World Perspective*. Basingstoke: Macmillan.

Medani, K. M. (2011) 'Strife and secession in Sudan', *Journal of Democracy*, vol. 22, no. 3.

Meillasoux, C. (1970) 'A class analysis of the bureaucratic process in Malawi', *Journal of Development Studies*, vol. 6, no. 2.

Melsom, R. and H. Wolpe (1970) 'Modernisation and the politics of communalism', *American Political Science Review*, vol. 64, no. 4.

Merkel, W. (1999) *Defective Democracies*, Working Paper 1999/132. Madrid: Juan March Institute.

Merton, R. (1952) 'Bureaucratic structure and personality', in R. Merton *et al.* (eds), *Reader in Bureaucracy*. Glencoe, IL: Free Press.

Migdal, J. S. (1974) *Peasants, Politics and Revolution: Pressures toward Political and Social Change in the Third World*. Princeton, NJ: Princeton University Press.

Migdal, J. S. (1988) *Strong Societies and Weak States: State–Society Relations and State Capabilities in the Third World*. Princeton, NJ: Princeton University Press.

Migdal, J. S. (1996) 'Integration and disintegration: an approach to society formation', in L. van de Goor, K. Rupesinghe and P. Sciarone (eds), *Between Development and Destruction: An Enquiry into the Causes of Conflict in Post-Colonial States*. London: Macmillan.

Migdal, J. S., A. Kohli and V. Shue (eds) (1994) *State Power and Social Forces: Domination and Transformation in the Third World*. Cambridge: Cambridge University Press.

Mitra, S. K. (1995) 'The rational politics of cultural nationalism: subnational movements of South Asia in comparative perspective', *British Journal of Political Science*, vol. 25, no. 1.

Mohammed, N. A. L. (1999) 'Civil wars and military expenditures: a note', Paper to Conference of World Bank's Development Economics Research Group, Washington, DC.

Moore, B. (1973) *Social Origins of Dictatorship and Democracy: Lord and Peasant in the Making of the Modern World*. Harmondsworth: Penguin.

Moore, M. (1996) 'Is democracy rooted in material prosperity?', in R. Luckham and G. White (eds), *Democratization in the South: The Jagged Wave*. Manchester: Manchester University Press.

Moore, M. and J. Putzel (1999) *Politics and Poverty*, Background Paper for the World Development Report 2000/1. Washington, DC: World Bank.

Morgenthau, R. S. (1964) *Political Parties in French-Speaking West Africa*. Oxford: Clarendon Press.

Mouzelis, N. (1989) 'State and politics in the parliamentary semi-periphery', in C. Thomas and P. Saravanamuttu (eds), *The State and Instability in the South*. London: Macmillan.

Moyo, S. and Yeros, P. (2005) 'The resurgence of rural movements under neo-liberalism', in S. Moyo and P. Yeros (eds), *Reclaiming the Land. The Resurgence of Rural Movements in Africa, Asia and Latin America*. London: Zed Books.

Muller, E. N. (1988) 'Democracy, economic development and income inequality', *American Sociological Review*, vol. 53, no. 1.

Muller, E. N. and M. A. Seligson (1987) 'Inequality and insurgency', *American Political Science Review*, vol. 81, no. 2.

Muller, E. N., M. A. Seligson and H. Fu (1989) 'Land inequality and political violence', *American Political Science Review*, vol. 83, no. 2.

Munck, R. (2003) *Contemporary Latin America*. Basingstoke: Palgrave.

Muni, S. D. (1979) 'The Third World: concept and controversy', *Third World Quarterly*, vol. 1, no. 3.

Nafziger, E. W. (1972) 'Economic aspects of the Nigerian civil war', in R. Higham (ed.), *Civil Wars in the Twentieth Century*. Lexington: University of Kentucky Press.

Nafziger, E. W. and W. L. Richter (1976) 'Biafra and Bangladesh: the political economy of secessionist conflict', *Journal of Peace Research*, vol. 13, no. 2.

Naidu, S. and Jansson, J. (2011) 'Africa's engagement with China: perpetuating the class project?', in J. N. Pieterse and B. Rehbein (eds), *Globalization and Emerging Societies. Development and Inequality*. Basingstoke: Palgrave Macmillan.

Nel, P. (2003) 'Income inequality, economic growth, and political instability in sub-Saharan Africa', *Journal of Modern African Studies*, vol. 41, no. 4: 611–39.

Neuberger, B. (2006) 'African nationalism', in G. Delanty and K. Kumar (eds), *The SAGE Handbook of Nations and Nationalism*. London: Sage Publications.

Niles, K. J. (1999) *Economic adjustment and targeted social spending: the role of political institutions*, Background Paper for the World Development Report 2000/2001. Washington, DC: World Bank.

Nkrumah, K. (1965) *Neo-Colonialism: The Last Stage of Imperialism*. London: Nelson.

Nordlinger, E. (1987) 'Taking the state seriously', in M. Weiner and S. P. Huntington (eds), *Understanding Political Development*. Boston: Little, Brown.

Norris, P. and R. Inglehart (2004) *Sacred and Secular. Religion and Politics Worldwide*. Cambridge: Cambridge University Press.

Nove, A. (1974) 'On reading Andre Gunder Frank', *Journal of Development Studies*, vol. 10, nos 3–4.

O'Brien, D. C. (1972) 'Modernisation, order and the erosion of a democratic ideal: American political science 1960–70, *Journal of Development Studies*, vol. 8, no. 4.

O'Brien, P. J. (1975) 'A critique of Latin American theories of dependency', in I. Oxaal, T. Barnett and D. Booth (eds), *Beyond the Sociology of Development*.

*Economy and Society in Latin America and Africa*. London: Routledge & Kegan Paul.

O'Connor, J. (1970) 'The meaning of economic imperialism', in R. I. Rhodes (ed.), *Imperialism and Underdevelopment*. New York: Monthly Review Press.

O'Donnell, G. (1992) 'Transitions, continuities and paradoxes', in S. Mainwaring, G. O'Donnell and J. S. Valenzuela (eds), *Issues in Democratic Consolidation: The New South American Democracies in Comparative Perspective*. Notre Dame, IN: University of Notre Dame Press.

O'Donnell, G. (1998) *Polyarchies and the (Un)rule of Law in Latin America*, Working Paper 1998/125. Madrid: Juan March Institute.

O'Kane, R. H. T. (1981) 'A probabalistic approach to the causes of *coups d'état*', *British Journal of Political Science*, vol. 11, no. 3.

O'Kane, R. H. T. (1986) 'Explaining African *coups d'état*', *American Political Science Review*, vol. 80, no. 1.

Olson, M. (1963) 'Rapid growth as a destabilising force', *Journal of Economic History*, vol. 23, no. 4.

Omid, H. (1992) 'Theocracy or democracy?: the critics of "westoxification" and the politics of fundamentalism in Iran', *Third World Quarterly*, vol. 13, no. 4.

Omotola, J. S. (2009) '"Garrison" democracy in Nigeria: the 2007 General Elections and the Prospects of Democratic Consolidation', *Commonwealth and Comparative Politics*, vol. 47, no. 2

Onis, Z. (1991) 'The logic of the developmental state', *Comparative Politics*, vol. 24, no. 1.

Oommen, T. K. (2006) 'Nation and nationalism in South Asia', in G. Delanty and K. Kumar (eds), *The SAGE Handbook of Nations and Nationalism*. London: Sage Publications.

Orridge, A. W. (1981) 'Uneven development and nationalism', *Political Studies,* vol. 29, nos 1 and 2, March and June.

Ortiz, R. D. (2002) 'Insurgent strategies in the post-cold war: the case of the Revolutionary Armed Forces of Colombia', *Studies in Conflict and Terrorism*, vol. 25, no. 2: 127–43.

Ottaway, M. (2011) 'The new Moroccan constitution: real change or more of the same?', *Commentary*, Carnegie Endowment for International Peace, June 20.

Ozkirimli, U. (2000) *Theories of Nationalism. A Critical Introduction*. Basingstoke: Palgrave.

Padhi, S. and Panigrahi, N. (2011) *Tribal Movements and Livelihoods: Recent Developments in Orissa*, CPRC-IIPA Working Paper No. 51. New Delhi: Indian Institute of Public Administration and Chronic Poverty Research Centre.

Parsa, M. (2000) *States, Ideologies and Social Revolutions*. Cambridge: Cambridge University Press.

Parsons, T. (1966) *Societies: Evolutionary and Comparative Perspectives*. Englewood Cliffs, NJ: Prentice-Hall.

Payne, S. (1975) *Basque Nationalism*. Reno: University of Nevada Press.

Peeler, J. (1998) *Building Democracy in Latin America*. London: Lynne Rienner.

Pempel, T. J. (1999) 'The developmental regime in a changing world economy', in M. Woo-Cumings (ed.), *The Developmental State*. Ithaca, NY: Cornell University Press.

Perlmutter, A. (1971) 'The praetorian state and the praetorian army: toward a taxonomy of civil–military relations in developing polities', in J. L. Finkle and R. W. Gable (eds), *Political Development and Social Change*, 2nd edn. London: John Wiley.

Peters, B. G. (2005) *Institutional Theory in Political Science*. London: Continuum.

Petras, J. (1975) 'New perspectives on imperialism and social classes in the periphery', *Journal of Contemporary Asia*, vol. 5, no. 3.

Petras, J. (1981) *Class, State and Power in the Third World*. London: Zed Press.

Petras, J. (2006) '"Centre-left" regimes in Latin America: history repeating itself as farce?', *Journal of Peasant Studies*, vol. 33, no. 2.

Phadnis, U. and R. Ganguly (2001) *Ethnicity and Nation-Building in South Asia*. London: Sage.

Philip, G. (1984) 'Military-authoritarianism in South America: Brazil, Chile. Uruguay and Argentina', *Political Studies*, vol. 32, no. 1.

Philip, G. (1990) 'The political economy of development', *Political Studies*, vol. 38, no. 3.

Philip, G. (2003) *Democracy in Latin America. Surviving Conflict and Crisis?*. Cambridge: Polity Press.

Pinkney, R. (1993) *Democracy in the Third World*. Buckingham: Open University Press.

Pippan, C. (2011) 'The 2011 Libyan uprising, foreign military intervention, and international law', *Juridikum,* no.2.

Poku, N. K. and J. Whitman (2011) 'The Millennium Development Goals and development after 2015', *Third World Quarterly*, vol. 32, no. 1.

Polese, M. (1985) 'Economic integration, national policies and the rationality of regional separatism', in E. A. Tiryakian and R. Rogowski (eds), *New Regionalisms of the Developed West*. London: Allen & Unwin.

Polidano, C. (2001) 'Don't discard state autonomy: revisiting the East Asian experience of development', *Political Studies*, vol. 49, no. 3.

Posner, D. N. and Young, D. J. (2007) 'The institutionalization of political power in Africa', *Journal of Democracy*, vol. 18, no. 3.

Posusney, M. P. (2005) 'The Middle East's democracy deficit in comparative perspective', in M. P. Posusney and M. P. Angrist (eds), *Authoritarianism in the Middle East. Regimes and Resistance*. London: Lynne Rienner.

Potter, D. (1992) 'Democratization in Asia', in D. Held (ed.), *Prospects for Democracy: North, South, East, West*. Cambridge: Polity Press.

Potter, D., D. Goldblatt, M. Kiloh and P. Lewis (eds) (1997) *Democratization*. Cambridge: Polity Press.

Power, T. J. and M. J. Gasiorowski (1997) 'Institutional design and democratic consolidation in the Third World', *Comparative Political Studies*, vol. 30, no. 2.

Pratt, R. P. (1973) 'The underdeveloped political science of development', *Studies in Comparative International Development*, vol. 8, no. 1.

Przeworski, A. (1986) 'Some problems in the study of the transition to democracy', in G. O'Donnell, P. Schmitter and L. Whitehead (eds) (1986) *Transitions from Authoritarian Rule: Tentative Conclusions about Uncertain Democracies*. Baltimore: Johns Hopkins University Press.

Przeworski, A., M. E. Alvarez, J. A. Cheibub and F. Limongi (2000) *Democracy and Development: Political Institutions and Well-Being in the World, 1950–1990*. Cambridge: Cambridge University Press.

Putnam, R. D. (1967) 'Toward explaining military intervention in Latin American polities', *World Politics*, vol. 20, no. 1.

Pye, L. W. (1971) 'Armies in the process of political modernisation', in J. L. Finkle and R. W. Gable (eds), *Political Development and Social Change*, 2nd edn. London: John Wiley.

Raftopoulos, B. and Alexander, K. (eds) (2006) *Peace in the Balance: The Crisis in Sudan*. Cape Town: Institute for Justice and Reconciliation.

Ram, H. (1997) 'Exporting Iran's Islamic revolution: steering a path between Pan-Islam and nationalism', in B. Maddy-Weitzman and E. Inbar (eds), *Religious Radicalism in the Greater Middle East*. London: Frank Cass.

Randall, V. (1988) *Political Parties in the Third World*. London: Sage.

Randall, V. (2004) 'Using and abusing the concept of the Third World: geopolitics and the comparative study of political development', *Third World Quarterly*, vol. 25, no. 1.

Randall, V. (2008) 'Party regulation in conflict-prone societies: more dangers than opportunities?', in B. Reilly and P. Nordlund (eds), *Political Party Regulation in Conflict-Prone Societies*. Tokyo: United Nations University Press.

Ray, D. (1973) 'The dependency model of Latin American underdevelopment: three basic fallacies', *Journal of Interamerican Studies and World Affairs*, vol. 15, no. 1.

Razavi, S. and A. Jenichen (2010) 'The unhappy marriage of religion and politics: problems and pitfalls for gender equality', *Third World Quarterly*, vol. 31, no. 6: 833–50.

Reilly, C. A. (ed.) (1995) *New Paths to Democratic Development in Latin America: The Rise of NGO–Municipal Collaboration*. London: Lynne Rienner.

Renwick, N. (2011) 'Millennium Development Goal 1: poverty, hunger and decent work in Southeast Asia', *Third World Quarterly*, vol. 32, no. 1: 65–89.

Rice, R. (2011) 'From the ground up: the challenge of indigenous party consolidation in Latin America', *Party Politics*, vol. 17, no. 2.

Riggs, F. W. (1963) 'Bureaucrats and political development', in J. LaPalombara (ed.), *Bureaucracy and Political Development*. Princeton, NJ: Princeton University Press.

Riggs, F. W. (1964) *Administration in Developing Countries: The Theory of Prismatic Society*. Boston: Houghton Mifflin.

Riley, S. P. (1991) *The Democratic Transition in Africa: An End to the One-Party State?*, Conflict Studies 245. London: Research Institute for the Study of Conflict and Terrorism.

Robinson, W. I. (1996) *Promoting Polyarchy. Globalization, US Intervention and Hegemony*. Cambridge: Cambridge University Press.

Robinson, W. I. (1998) '(Mal)Development in Central America: globalisation and social change', *Development and Change*, vol. 29, no. 3.

Robinson, W. I. (1999) 'Latin America in the age of inequality: confronting the new "Utopia"', *International Studies Review*, vol. 1, no. 3: 41–67.

Robinson, W. I. (2001) 'Social theory and globalisation: the rise of a transnational state', *Theory and Society*, vol. 30, no. 2: 157–200.

Robinson, W. I. (2010) *Latin America and Global Capitalism. A Critical Globalization Perspective.* Baltimore: Johns Hopkins University Press.

Robles, A. C. (2008) 'Whose service?', *Development and Cooperation*, vol. 35, nos. 7–8: 285–9.

Rochlin, J. (2011) 'Plan Colombia and the revolution in military affairs: the demise of FARC', *Review of International Studies*, vol. 37, no. 2: 715–40.

Rock, M. T. (2009) 'Has democracy slowed growth in Asia?', *World Development*, vol. 37, no. 5.

Roniger, L. (1994) 'The comparative study of clientelism and the changing nature of civil society in the contemporary world', in L. Roniger and A. Gunes-Ayata (eds), *Democracy, Clientelism and Civil Society*. London: Lynne Rienner Publishers.

Rosen, G. and W. Jones (1979) 'The radical theory of development', in A. Mack, D. Plant and U. Doyle (eds), *Imperialism, Intervention and Development*. London: Croom Helm.

Rouquie, A. (1986) 'Demilitarization and the institutionalisation of military-dominated politics in Latin America', in G. O'Donnell, P. C. Schmitter and L. Whitehead (eds), *Transitions from Authoritarian Rule*. Baltimore: Johns Hopkins University Press.

Roxborough, I. (1979) *Theories of Underdevelopment*. London: Macmillan.

Rueschmeyer, D., E. H. Stephens and J. D. Stephens (1992) *Capitalist Development and Democracy*. London: Polity Press.

Ruhl, J. M. (2010) 'Honduras unravels', *Journal of Democracy*, vol. 21, no. 2.

Ruparelia, S. (2008) 'How the politics of recognition enabled India's democratic exceptionalism', *International Journal of Politics, Culture and Society*, vol. 21: 39–56.

Russett, B. M. (1964) 'Inequality and instability: the relation of land tenure to polities', *World Politics,* vol. 16, no. 3.

Rustow, D. A. (1967) *A World of Nations: Problems of Political Modernisation.* Washington, DC: Brookings Institution.

Salawu, B. (2010) 'Ethno-religious conflicts in Nigeria: causal analysis and proposals for new management strategies', *European Journal of Social Sciences*, vol. 13, no. 3.

Sanchez, O. (2009) 'Party non-systems: a conceptual innovation', *Party Politics*, vol. 15, no. 4.

Sandbrook, R. (1976) 'The crisis in political development theory', *Journal of Development Studies*, vol. 12, no. 2.

Sandschneider, E. (1991) 'Successful economic development and political change in Taiwan and South Korea', in J. Manor (ed.), *Rethinking Third World Politics*. London: Longman.

Sangmpan, S. N. (2007) 'Politics rules: the false primacy of institutions in developing countries', *Political Studies*, vol. 55, no. 1.

Sartori, G. (1970) 'Concept misinformation in comparative polities', *American Political Science Review*, vol. 64, no. 4.

Saul, J. (1974) 'The state in post-colonial societies: Tanzania', in R. Miliband and J. Saville (eds), *The Socialist Register, 1974*. London: Merlin Press.

Savoia, A., J. Easaw and A. McKay (2010) 'Inequality, democracy and institutions: a critical review of recent research', *World Development*, vol. 38, no. 2.

Schedler, A. (2001) 'Taking uncertainty seriously: the blurred boundaries of democratic transition and consolidation', *Democratization*, vol. 8, no. 4.

Schraeder, P. J. and H. Redissi (2011) 'Ben Ali's fall', *Journal of Democracy*, vol. 22, no. 3.

Schuurman, F. J. (1993) 'Introduction: development theory in the 1990s', in F. J. Schuurman (ed.), *Beyond the Impasse: New Directions in Development Theory*. London: Zed Books.

Scott, J. and Wilkinson, R. (2011) 'The poverty of the Doha Round and the least developed countries', *Third World Quarterly*, vol. 32, no. 4.

Seers, D. (1981) 'Development options: the strengths and weaknesses of dependency theories in explaining a government's room to manoeuvre', in D. Seers (ed.), *Dependency Theory: A Critical Reassessment*. London: Francis Pinter.

Shanin, T. (1982) 'Class, state and revolution: substitutes and realities', in H. Alavi and T. Shanin (eds), *Introduction to the Sociology of Developing Societies*. London: Macmillan.

Shivji, I. G. (1973) 'Tanzania: the silent class struggle', in L. Cliffe and J. S. Saul (eds), *Socialism in Tanzania*. Nairobi: East African Publishing House.

Shivji, I. G. (1976) *Class Struggles in Tanzania*. London: Heinemann.

Singer, J. D. (1996) 'Armed conflict in the former colonial regions: from classification to explanation', in L. van de Goor, K. Rupesinghe and P. Sciarone (eds), *Between Development and Destruction: An Enquiry into the Causes of Conflict in Post-Colonial States*. London: Macmillan.

Sirowy, L. and A. Inkeles (1991) "The effect of democracy on economic growth and inequality', in A. Inkeles (ed.), *On Measuring Democracy: Its Consequences and Concomitants*. New Brunswick: Transaction Books.

Six, C. (2009) 'The rise of postcolonial states as donors: a challenge to the development paradigm?', *Third World Quarterly*, vol. 30, no. 6, 1103–21.

Smith, A. D. (1971) *Theories of Nationalism*. London: Duckworth.

Smith, A. D. (1979) 'Towards a theory of ethnic separatism', *Ethnic and Racial Studies*, vol. 2, no. 1.

Smith, A. D. (1995) *Nations and Nationalism in a Global Era*. Cambridge: Polity Press.

Smith, A. L. (2010) 'Indonesia: letting go to hold on', in R. G. Wirsing and E. Ahrari (eds), *Fixing Fractured Nations. The Challenge of Ethnic Separatism in the Asia-Pacific*. Basingstoke: Palgrave Macmillan.

Smith, B. C. (1988) *Bureaucracy and Political Power*. Brighton: Wheatsheaf.

Smith, B. C. (2007) *Good Governance and Development*. Basingstoke: Palgrave Macmillan.

Smith, M. (2002) 'Army politics as an historical legacy: the experience of Burma', in K. Koonings and D. Kruijt (eds), *Political Armies. The Military and Nation Building in the Age of Democracy*. London: Zed Books.

Smith, P. J. (2010) 'Tibet: at the crossroads of ethnic nationalism and geopolitical rivalry', in R. G. Wirsing and E. Ahrari (eds), *Fixing Fractured Nations. The Challenge of Ethnic Separatism in the Asia-Pacific*. Basingstoke: Palgrave Macmillan.

Snyder, L. L. (1976) *Varieties of Nationalism: A Comparative Study*. Hinsdale: Dryden Press.

Soage, A. B. and J. F. Franganillo (2010) 'The Muslim Brothers in Egypt', in B. Rubin (ed.), *The Muslim Brotherhood. The Organization and Policies of a Global Islamist Movement*. Basingstoke: Palgrave Macmillan.

Soeters, J. L. and Tessema, M. T. (2004) 'Public management in developing countries', *International Review of Administrative Sciences*, vol. 70, no. 4.

Somit, A. and Peterson, S. A. (2005) *The Failure of Democratic Nation Building*. Basingstoke: Palgrave Macmillan.

Sridharan, E. and Varshney, A. (2001) 'Toward moderate pluralism: political parties in India', in L. Diamond and R. Gunther (eds), *Political Parties and Democracy*. Baltimore: Johns Hopkins University Press.

Stewart, F. (ed.) (2008) *Horizontal Inequalities and Conflict. Understanding Group Violence in Multiethnic Societies*. Basingstoke: Palgrave Macmillan.

Stockton, H. (2001) 'Political parties, party systems and democracy in East Asia', *Comparative Political Studies*, vol. 34, no. 1.

Storey, I. (2010) 'Southern discomfort: separatists conflict in the Kingdom of Thailand', in R. G. Wirsing and E. Ahrari (eds), *Fixing Fractured Nations. The Challenge of Ethnic Separatism in the Asia-Pacific*. Basingstoke: Palgrave Macmillan.

Strange, S. (1996) *The Diffusion of Power in the World Economy*. Cambridge: Cambridge University Press.

Symmons-Symonolewicz, K. (1965) 'Nationalist movements: an attempt at a comparative typology', *Comparative Studies in Society and History*, vol. 7, no. 2.

Taylor, D. (2005) 'Religion and politics', in D. T. Hagerty (ed.), *South Asia in World Politics*. Lanham, MD: Rowan & Littlefield.

Therborn, G. (1979) 'The travail of Latin American democracy', *New Left Review*, nos 113–14, January–April.

Thérien, J.-P. (1999) 'Beyond the North-South Divide: The Two Tales of World Poverty', *Third World Quarterly*, vol. 20, no. 4: 723–42.

Therkildsen, O. (2000) 'Public sector reform in a poor, aid-dependent country, Tanzania', *Public Administration and Development*, vol. 20, no. 1: 61–71.

Tinker, H. (1981) 'The nation-state in Asia', in L. Tivey (ed.), *The Nation-State: The Formation of Modern Politics*. Oxford: Martin Robertson.

Tipps, D. (1973) 'Modernization theory and the comparative study of societies: a critical perspective', *Comparative Studies in Society and History*, vol. 15, no. 2.

Toye, J. (1987) *Dilemmas of Development: Reflections on the Counter-Revolution in Development Theory and Policy*. Oxford: Blackwell.

Trager, E. (2011) 'The unbreakable Muslim Brotherhood', *Foreign Affairs*, vol. 90, no. 5, September/October.

Transparency International (2010) *Global Corruption Barometer 2010*, www.transparency.org

Turner, M. and J. Halligan (1999) 'Bureaucracy and the alternatives in East and Southeast Asia', in K. M. Henderson and O. P. Dwivedi (eds), *Bureaucracy and the Alternatives in World Perspective*. Basingstoke: Macmillan.

Turner, M. and D. Hulme (1997) *Governance, Administration and Development: Making the State Work*. London: Macmillan.

Ufen, A. (2009) 'Mobilizing political Islam: Indonesia and Malaysia compared', *Commonwealth and Comparative Politics*, vol. 47, no. 3.

UN (2009) *Update Report No. 3: The Resurgence of Coups d'Etat in Africa*. New York: United Nations

UN (2011) *Millennium Development Goals Report*. New York: United Nations.

UNCTAD (2011) *Foreign Direct Investment in LDCs: Lessons Learned from the Decade 2001–2010 and the Way Forward*. Geneva: UN Conference on Trade and Development.

UNDP (1999) *Debt and Sustainable Human Development,* Technical Advisory Paper No. 4. New York: United Nations Development Programme.

UNDP (2001) *Human Development Report 2001: Making New Technologies Work for Human Development*. New York: United Nations Development Programme.

UNDP (2010a) *An Overview of Trends and Developments in Public Administration and Local Governance*. New York: United Nations Development Programme.

UNDP (2010b) *The Human Development Report 2010: The Real Wealth of Nations*. New York: United Nations Development Programme.

UNDP (2011) *The Millennium Development Goals Report 2011*. New York: United Nations Development Programme.

Valenzuela, J. S. (1992) 'Democratic consolidation in post-transitional settings: notion, process and facilitating conditions', in S. Mainwaring, G. O'Donnell and J. S. Valenzuela (eds), *Issues in Democratic Consolidation: The New South American Democracies in Comparative Perspective*. Notre Dame, IN: University of Notre Dame Press.

Van Cott, D. L. (2005) 'Building inclusive democracies: indigenous peoples and ethnic minorities in Latin America', *Democratization*, vol. 12, no. 5.

Vandermoortele, J. (2011) 'If not the MDGs, then what?', *Third World Quarterly*, vol. 32, no. 1.

Vanley, I. S. (1980) 'Kurdistan in Iraq', in G. Chaliand (ed.), *People Without a Country*. London: Zed Press.

Varma, B. N. (1980) *The Sociology and Politics of Development: A Theoretical Study*. London: Routledge & Kegan Paul.

Vengroff, R. (1977) 'Dependency and underdevelopment in Black Africa: an empirical test', *Journal of Modern African Studies*, vol. 15, no. 4.

Verweij, M. and Pelizzo, R. (2009) 'Singapore: does authoritarianism pay?', *Journal of Democracy*, vol. 20, no. 2.

Wallerstein, I. (1960) 'Ethnicity and national integration in West Africa', *Cahiers d'Etudes Africaines,* no. 3, October.

Wallis, M. (1989) *Bureaucracy: Its Role in Third World Development*. London: Macmillan.

Ware, A. (1996) *Political Parties and Party Systems*. Oxford: Oxford University Press.

Warren, B. (1973) 'Imperialism and capitalist industrialization', *New Left Review*, no. 81.

Warren, B. (1980) *Imperialism: Pioneer of Capitalism*. London: New Left Books.

Webber, M. (1993) 'The Third World and the dissolution of the USSR', *Third World Quarterly*, vol. 13, no. 4.

Weber, M. (1919) 'Politics as a vocation' in H. H. Gerth and C. Wright Mills (eds), *From Max Weber: Essays in Sociology*, London: Routledge.

Weber, H. (2004) 'The "new economy" and social risk: banking on the poor?', *Review of International Political Economy*, vol. 11, no. 2.

Weiner, M. (1965) 'Political integration and political development', *The Annals of the American Academy of Political and Social Science*, no. 358, March.

Weiner, M. (1987) 'Empirical democratic theory', in M. Weiner and E. Ozbundun (eds), *Competitive Elections in Developing Countries*. Durham, NC: Duke University Press.

Weiss, L. (1998) *The Myth of the Powerless State: Governing the Economy in a Global Era*. Cambridge: Polity Press.

Weiss, L. and J. M. Hobson (1995) *States and Economic Development: A Comparative Historical Analysis*. Cambridge: Polity Press.

Wells, A. (1974) 'The *coup d'état* in theory and practice: independent Black Africa in the 1960s', *American Journal of Sociology*, vol. 79, no. 4.

Westlake, M. (1991) 'The Third World (1950–1990) RIP', *Marxism Today*, August.

Whalen, G. (1996a) 'Analysing women in the politics of the Third World', in H. Afshar (ed.), *Women and Politics in the Third World*. London: Routledge.

Whalen, G. (1996b) *Gender in Third World Politics*. Boulder, CO: Lynne Rienner Publishers.

Whitaker, B. E. (2007) 'Exporting the Patriot Act? Democracy and the "war on terror" in the Third World, *Third World Quarterly*, vol. 28, no. 5.

White, C. P. (1974) 'The Vietnamese revolutionary alliance: intellectuals, workers and peasants', in J. W. Lewis (ed.), *Recent Rebellion and Communist Revolution in Asia*. Stanford: Stanford University Press.

White, G. (1984) 'Developmental states and socialist industrialization in the Third World', *Journal of Development Studies*, vol. 21, no. 1.

White, G. (1996) 'Civil society, democratisation and development', in R. Luckham and G. White (eds), *Democratization in the South: The Jagged Wave*. Manchester: Manchester University Press.

White, G. (1998) 'Constructing a democratic developmental state', *Democratization,* vol. 5, no. 3.

Whitehead, L. (1986) 'International aspects of democratization', in G. O'Donnell, P. Schmitter and L. Whitehead (eds), *Transitions from Authoritarian Rule: Tentative Conclusions about Uncertain Democracies*. Baltimore: Johns Hopkins University Press.

WHO/UNICEF (2010) *Progress on Sanitation and Drinking Water*, Geneva/New York: World Health Organization/United Nations Children's Fund.

Williams, D. C. (2011) 'Cracks in the firmament of Burma's military government: from unity through coercion to buying support', *Third World Quarterly*, vol. 32, no. 7.

Williams, D. C. and T. Young (1994) 'Governance, the World Bank and liberal theory', *Political Studies,* vol. 42, no. 1.

Wirsing, R. G. (2010) 'Ethnic separatism: an introduction', in R. G. Wirsing and E. Ahrari (eds), *Fixing Fractured Nations. The Challenge of Ethnic Separatism in the Asia-Pacific.* Basingstoke: Palgrave Macmillan.

Wiseman, J. A. (1996) *The New Struggle for Democracy in Africa.* Aldershot: Avebury Press.

Woddis, J. (1977) *Armies and Politics.* London: Lawrence & Wishart.

Wolfe, E. R. (1968) *Peasant Wars of the Twentieth Century*, New York: Harper & Row.

Wolff, S. (2011) 'Managing ethno-national conflict: towards an analytical framework', *Commonwealth and Comparative Politics*, vol. 49, no. 2.

Wolf-Phillips, L. (1987) 'Why Third World?', *Third World Quarterly*, vol. 1. no. 1.

Wong, C-H., J. Chin and N. Othman (2010) 'Malaysia – towards a typology of an electoral one-party state', *Democratization*, vol. 17, no. 5.

Wood, G. D. (1977) 'Rural development and the post-colonial state: administration and the peasantry in the Kosi region of North-East Bihar, India', *Development and Change*, vol. 8, no. 3.

Wood, G. D. (2000) 'Prisoners and escapees: improving the institutional responsibility square in Bangladesh', Institute for International Policy Analysis, University of Bath.

Wood, J. R. (1981) 'Secession: a comparative analytical framework', *Canadian Journal of Political Science*, vol. 14, no. 1.

World Bank (1990) *World Development Report 1990: Poverty.* Oxford: Oxford University Press.

World Bank (1991) *World Development Report 1991: The Challenge of Development.* Oxford: Oxford University Press.

World Bank (1993) *World Development Report 1993: Investing in Health.* Oxford: Oxford University Press.

World Bank (1997) *World Development Report 1997: The State in a Changing World.* Washington, DC: World Bank.

World Bank (2001) *World Development Indicators 2001.* Washington, DC: World Bank.

World Bank (2006) *World Development Report 2006: Equity and Development.* Oxford: Oxford University Press.

World Bank (2007) *World Development Report 2007. Development and the Next Generation.* Washington, DC: World Bank,

World Bank (2010) *World Development Report 2010: Development and Climate Change.* Washington, DC: World Bank.

World Bank (2011a) *Global Economic Prospects, Maintaining Progress Amid Turmoil.* Washington, DC: World Bank.

World Bank (2011b) *World Development Indicators 2011.* Washington, DC: World Bank.

World Bank (2011c) *World Development Report 2011. Conflict, Security and Development.* Washington, DC: World Bank.

Worsley, P. (1984) *The Three Worlds: Culture and World Development.* London: Weidenfeld & Nicolson.

Worthley, J. A. and K. K. Tsao (1999) 'Reinventing government in China: a comparative analysis', *Administration and Society*, vol. 31, no. 5.

Wright, R. (1996) 'Islam and liberal democracy: two visions of Reformation', *Journal of Democracy*, vol. 7, no. 2.

Wright, T. P. (1976) 'South Asian Separatist Movements', in W. H. Morris-Jones (ed.), *The Politics of Separatism*, Collected Seminar Papers no. 19. London: University of London Institute of Commonwealth Studies.

Yanai, N. (1999) 'Why do political parties survive?: an analytical discussion', *Party Politics,* vol. 5, no. 1.

Yashar, D. J. (1998) 'Contesting citizenship: indigenous movements and democracy in Latin America', *Comparative Politics*, vol. 31, no. 1.

Yeung, H. W.-C. (2005) 'Institutional capacity and Singapore's developmental state', in H. E. S. Nesadurai (ed.), *Globalization and Economic Security in East Asia: Governance and Institutions*. London: Routledge.

Ziemann, W. and M. Lanzendorfer (1977) 'The state in peripheral societies', in R. Miliband and J. Saville (eds), *The Socialist Register 1977*. London: Merlin Press.

# Index

access, 126, 135, 136–9, 140, 141
  and claimants, 129, 139
accountability, 35, 97, 110, 116, 127,
    133, 141–5, 149, 164, 225, 235,
    238, 240, 241, 243, 246, 252–7
age groups, 14
agriculture, 3, 11, 14, 18, 20, 57, 60,
    63, 66–9, 87, 89, 90, 131, 132,
    134, 137–8, 141, 181, 182, 188,
    197, 201, 216–17
aid, 5, 7, 26, 54, 55, 60, 62, 64, 69,
    72, 75, 76, 85, 89, 105, 114,
    140, 141, 156, 163, 178, 184,
    185, 216, 217, 221, 223, 242,
    246, 249
  military, 47, 63, 162, 186
  and technical assistance, 252
authoritarianism, 26, 48, 51, 53, 65,
    90–2, 101, 108, 109, 117, 124,
    144, 159, 163, 165, 192, 199,
    200, 209, 219, 221, 222, 224,
    225, 226, 227, 228, 231, 232,
    236, 237, 243, 246–9, 253,
    255–7

Bonapartism, 85, 156
bonded labour, 58
bourgeoisie, 61, 62, 67, 68, 69, 70, 71,
    72, 83, 85, 86, 87, 92, 100, 111,
    155, 156, 157, 188, 238
  bureaucratic, 88–90, 135–6, 237
  comprador, 9
  metropolitan, 86–8
bureaucracy, 33, 37, 40, 43, 60, 62,
    63, 70, 79, 88, 89, 90, 91, 94,
    100, 120, 121, 122, 125, 157,
    165, 188, 189, 194, 239, 240
  concepts of, 126–30
  and developmental states, 246,
    248, 251–3

and New Public Management,
    140–5
  power of, 131–5
  and state allocations, 136–9,
bureaucratic-military oligarchy, 86,
    180, 188

capitalism, 5, 6, 9, 42, 57, 59, 75, 79,
    87, 89, 97, 99, 106, 110, 122,
    136, 179, 230
  and dependency, 65–6, 68–73
  and the post-colonial state, 82–4,
    248, 257
caste, 12, 40, 43, 82, 107, 123, 124,
    129, 130, 177
civil liberties, 11, 26, 44, 164, 199,
    219, 234, 242, 253
civil society, 26, 28, 32, 34, 64, 82,
    84, 85, 89, 90, 100, 101, 119,
    123, 143, 144, 145, 162, 166,
    190, 220, , 237, 238, 243, 246,
    247, 250, 252,
  and democratization, 235, 236
  and state–society dialectics, 93–4
  and democratic transition, 224–8
  and the future of democracy,
    255–7
civil war, 24, 34, 150, 164, 167–8,
    170, 187, 190, 193–4, 200, 202,
    210, 223
class, 9, 35, 41–3, 45, 60, 62, 71, 72,
    74–5, 77, 79, 91, 92, 94, 95, 98,
    100, 114, 123, 126, 128, 130,
    145, 151, 165, 167, 169, 174,
    179, 181, 182, 195, 197, 205,
    209, 210, 220, 221, 226, 243,
    251
  and the balance of power, 236,
    237, 238
  and bureaucracy, 134, 135, 136

287

state (*cont.*)
    161–70, 171–89, 190, 191,
    195–8, 200–4, 208, 210, 211,
    213–16, 220, 223, 226, 230,
    232, 235–8, 240–4, 246–53, 256
  Bonapartist, 85–8
  and bureaucracy, 126–44
  bureaucratic-authoritarian, 90–2
  and globalization, 96–100
  and political parties, 108–13
  post-colonial, 59, 68, 77, 80, 82–5,
    88, 90, 100, 126, 132, 177, 179,
    211
  and state–society relations, 93–5
status, social, 2, 3, 10, 11, 22, 23, 27,
    29, 34, 38, 40, 46, 48, 54, 55,
    89, 103, 108, 129, 153, 156,
    157, 160, 162, 174, 182, 187,
    195–7, 205, 207–8, 234, 245
  and bureaucracy, 131, 132, 134
structural adjustment, 26, 140, 242

tautology, 50, 159, 212
trade, 27, 57, 59, 61–2, 65–6, 69–70,
    72, 81, 84, 86,105, 111, 116,
    118, 151, 154, 157, 162, 169,

    184, 190, 195, 196, 215, 216,
    223, 224, 226, 227, 237
  and development, 2, 4, 7, 9,
    247–9
  and economic integration, 20–2
  and globalization, 94–9
tradition, 28–9, 36, 45, 111, 144, 178,
    191
  and development, 39–41
  and traditional leaders, 13, 237
  and traditional oligarchy, 79
tribe, 32, 37, 40, 104, 107, 111, 123,
    129, 156, 157, 160, 168, 173,
    175, 200

underdevelopment, 27, 47, 108, 111,
    147, 156, 157, 203, 247
  and dependency theory, 57, 71, 75
urbanization, 43, 121, 147, 176, 187,
    197, 214, 229, 230, 232

women, in politics, 25–6, 42, 44, 96,
    98, 105, 108, 129, 141, 144,
    195–6, 201, 203, 220, 227,
    235–6
  and inequality, 207–9